W. E Manley

Biblical Review

Intended as a New and Improved Commentary on the Bible: Vol. I.

W. E Manley

Biblical Review

Intended as a New and Improved Commentary on the Bible: Vol. I.

ISBN/EAN: 9783337100056

Printed in Europe, USA, Canada, Australia, Japan

Cover: Foto ©Lupo / pixelio.de

More available books at **www.hansebooks.com**

INTENDED AS A NEW AND IMPROVED

COMMENTARY ON THE BIBLE:

WHEREIN THE AUTHOR ATTEMPTS TO GIVE MORE

RATIONAL INTERPRETATIONS OF SUBJECTS AND PASSAGES,

THAN ARE COMMON IN WORKS HAVING THE SAME GENERAL PURPOSE; ON A PLAN THAT RENDERS THE BOOK AS WELL FITTED FOR READING AS FOR REFERENCE.

VOL. I.

BY REV. W. E. MANLEY.

AUBURN:
PUBLISHED BY THE AUTHOR.
1869.

Entered according to Act of Congress, in the year 1859, by
W. E. MANLEY,
in the Clerk's Office of the District Court of Massachusetts.

PREFACE.

The author of this volume, has, for many years, entertained the purpose of preparing a work upon the Bible, that should present more rational views of that venerable book, and of the subjects contained therein, than are commonly put forth in other works, having the same general object; and the present volume is an attempt to carry out that purpose. We have waited for circumstances to be more favorable to the execution of this design, till we have become convinced that waiting for favorable circumstances is not the best way to accomplish any important object. We have not had access to as many valuable books, relating to the subjects treated of, as we could have desired; and hence our interpretations are mostly original; but this circumstance we do not so much regret, when we consider the tendency of writers to *rely* on other authors, where they have them at hand, and can easily consult them, rather than make the requisite effort to search out original facts, in which case, however skilfully the borrowed knowledge may be applied, the aggregate of human ideas has received no accessions. If, therefore, the present work is less highly valued, (or if it be less highly valuable,) on account of its comparative deficiency in references to standard authors or quotations therefrom, we trust that this lack may be compensated, in part, if not wholly, by certain original thoughts (or what seems to the author to be such, though scores of others, whom he has not consulted, may have entertained the same) which we have put forth on various subjects we have had occasion to refer to and discuss.

If our views on some topics (inspiration for example, visions, etc.,) are regarded by any as unsound, we hope they will hold the author alone responsible, who would be understood as speaking only for himself, and not for others, either in his own denomination or out of it, who may and may not hold the same opinions. We feel a sincere respect and reverence for the Bible, both from education and from the views we have of its teachings; but our respect for that book does not require nor permit us to entertain views concerning it, that plainly conflict with the facts of its history in the world, and which can be accepted by none but the ignorant and superstitious, and the truth of which would imply a perpetual miracle, as unnecessary as the facts on which the presumption of its reality rests, are untrue. The Bible must be accepted, at the present day, if accepted at all, on reasonable grounds, (reasonable, not in view of a very limited number of facts, from which men too generally form their conclusions, but in view of all the facts having a bearing on the subject;) and if it cannot be defended on such grounds, it will and ought to be rejected.

We believe it *can* be defended on such grounds, when we regard it with reference to the claims which are put forth in the book itself, and not the claims that men have falsely set up for it. We have been influenced by an ardent desire to give such views of subjects, and such interpretations of texts, as are true and at the same time fitted to restore the confidence of thinking men for the sacred volume, which has been weakened, and in many minds, destroyed, by the false and unreasonable claims that have been set up for the Bible, as well as the interpretations of its contents that are sanctioned neither by reason nor facts.

The *plan* of this work, is believed to be an improvement on the usual plan of Commentaries, as better fitted for reading, and not less for reference. It is well known that Commentaries are owned by but few persons — that, when owned, they are seldom referred to, and almost never read — not that the matters contained therein are unimportant, for their importance is conceded by most persons, not excepting those who never consult them; but because the form in which they are presented is not fitted to make the reading easy or interesting. We expect Dictionaries to be read, as much as we do Commentaries; and they are read perhaps quite as much. Both are useful for reference; and both are referred to — the former frequently, as the occasion requiring such reference is frequent, the latter seldom, since men seldom feel any necessity for so doing. In view of this consideration, we have sought to make our work a *readable* one; and though this may be difficult from the nature of the work, we trust we have done something in this direction, if not as much as is desirable. As we shall issue only a moderate sized volume at once, we feel the more confidence that the work will be read; for it is well known that men will read more, when they have small books to read, than when they have large ones.

As we treat the contents of the Bible by subjects rather than by texts, we do not always follow the order of passages given in the Bible; but an Index of passages, in the regular order, will enable the reader at once to refer to any passage he may wish to consult; and the numbering of the paragraphs will aid those who may desire to study the book.

If some subjects are treated more extensively in this volume than is deemed suitable for such a work, and others are thought not to have received sufficient attention, we would simply say, that, in our judgment, the first class of subjects here referred to, have generally received too little attention in other works, and the other class, too much ; and it has been our intention to obviate this objection, in doing which, we may have gone to the opposite extreme or in that direction. Whether we have or have not, is merely a matter of opinion. We have acted according to our best judgment in the matter.

With these observations, concerning our humble effort, we submit the present volume to the judgment and candor of all who respect the Bible and wish to understand its teachings.

Chicago, 1858.   W. E. M.

INDEX OF SUBJECTS.

ABEL — page 218. ABRAM, Biography of, 240-279. ADAM, Biography of, 211-226. ANIMALS, Domestic, 86; Wild, 87; in the Ark, 185. ANTIQUITY, of Genesis 9; of the Earth, 124; of Man, 124, 152. ARARAT, mountains of, 190, 104. ARCHÆOLOGY, 70-103. ARK, 184. ARTS, 98. ATTRIBUTES of God, 192. AUTHOR of Genesis, 15.

BARA, (create,) 56. BATTLE of the kings, 247. BIRTH and Birthright, 71; birth of Abel, 217; of Isaac, 267; of Esau, and Jacob, 281. BLESSING, of Esau and Jacob by Isaac, 288; of Joseph's sons by Jacob, 365; of Jacob's sons by their father, 367. BURIAL Customs, 78.

CAIN, 218; "Where did he get his wife" 160, 162. CAUSE of the Deluge, Moral, 174; Physical, 175. CHRONOLOGY, 119-121. CITIES and Towns, 106-118. CIRCUMCISION instituted, 254. COMMERCE, 90. COMPOSITION of Genesis, 16-24. CONTRACTS, 90. Contract of Jacob with Laban, 309. CONDITION primitive, of the Earth, 137. CONFUSION of tongues, 236. COVENANT with Noah, 230; with Abimelech, 269, 286. CREATION considered, &c., 137-156; of man 156; of Adam and Eve, 212. CREATOR, necessity of, 135. CRITICISM, 52-70; on Elohim, 53; on Bara, 56; on Rhua and Nephish, 58; on Olim, 64; on Sheol, 65; on Malak, 67. CUP of Joseph, 354.

DATES, 119. DAUGHTERS of Lot, 264, 75. DAYS of Creation, 155. DEATH and Burial Customs, 78; death of Adam, 220; of Noah, 232; of Sarah, 273; of Abraham, 279; of Isaac, 329; of Rachel, 327; of Jacob, 372; of Joseph, 374. DELUGE and Geology, 174 -184; duration of, 187; extent of, 176. DIVISIONS, geographical, 103. DOCTRINES of Theology, 191-210. DOMESTIC utensils, 82; animals, 86. DRESS, 79. DREAMS, of Jacob, 299, 311; of Joseph, 329; of the butler and baker, 339; of Pharaoh, 341.

ELOHIM, (God), 53. ESAU sells his birthright, 282. EVE, creation of, 214. EXISTENCE of God, 123-136.

FAMILY of Adam, 217; of Ishmael, 280; of Esau, 291; of Jacob, 303. FAMINE, 361. FOOD, 85; during Flood, 187.

GARDEN of Eden, 201. GENEALOGY of Cain, 220; of Seth, 221; of Shem, 233; of Ham, 235; of Japhet, 238. GEOGRAPHY, 103 -118. GEOLOGY and the Creation, 137-156. GOVERNMENT, 93. GOD and his Attributes, 192. GROVES, 105. GOMORRAH, destroyed, 260.

HABITATIONS, 81. Hagar given to Abram, 252; rejected, 268. HOSPITALITY, 97.

INDEX OF SUBJECTS.

INSPIRATION, 24. INTERVIEW at Mt. Gilead, 313; of the brethren with Pharaoh, 359; of Israel with Pharaoh, 360. ISHMAEL, 280. ISAAC, 281.

JACOB, 298. JOSEPH sold, 329. JOURNEY of the brethren to Egypt, 346, 350; of Israel 357.

KING of Edom, 295. KINGS, battle of, 247.

LANGUAGE of Genesis, 39. LOT separates from Abram, 245; his daughters, 264.

MALAK, (angel,) 67. MARRIAGE, 74; second, of Abraham, 278; of Jacob, 302. MEASURES and Weights, 100. MORAL cause of Deluge, 174. MOUNTAINS, 104; of Ararat, 190. MEETING of Jacob and Esau, 319.

NAHOR, 272. NAME of Genesis, 9. NATIONAL designations, 118. NATURAL causes of Creation, considered, 131. NATURE and responsibility of Man, 195. NEPHISH, (soul,) 58. NOAH blessed, 228. NUMBER of animals in the Ark, 185. NUPTIALS of Adam and Eve, 214.

OATHS, 90. OCCUPATION, 83. OFFERING of Isaac, 270. OLIM, (forever,) 64. ORIENTAL hospitality, 97. ORNAMENTS, 79.

PATRIARCHAL wealth, 88. PARENTAGE and relations of Abraham, 240. PHYSICAL causes of Deluge, 175. PLAINS, 105. PHARAOH's dreams, 341. POSSIBILITY of Deluge, 176. PROBABILITY of Deluge, 178. PREDICTION of Noah, 231. PROOFS of the Deluge, 180. PURSUIT of Jacob, 313.

READINGS, various, 50. RELATIONS of Abraham, 240. RELIGION of Patriarchs, 102. REMOVAL of Abram to Haran, 241; of Isaac to Beersheba, 285; of Jacob to Egypt, 357. RETURN of Jacob to Isaac, 327. REWARDS and Punishments, 199. RHUA, (spirit,) 58. RIVERS, 105.

SALUTATION, 98. SARAH, death of, 273. SEAS, 106. SEIR, 295. SERVITUDE, 95. SHEOL, (grave,) 65. SILVER Cup, 352. SOJOURN of Abram in Gerar, 265; of Isaac in Gerar, 283; of Jacob in Shalem, 321. STYLE of Genesis, 45.

TEMPTATION, 217. THEOLOGICAL doctrines 191. TRADE and Commerce, 90. TRUTH of Genesis, 31. THEORIES of Creation, 131, 134; of the Races, 165, 171; of Inspiration, 25. TRIUMPH of good, 200.

UNITY of God, 53, 195; of the Races, 160, 163. UTENSILS, 82.

VARIOUS readings, 50. VALLEYS, 105. VISIONS, 214, 246, 250, 254, 258, 260, 317, 358.

WARS, 92. WEALTH, 88. WEIGHTS, 100. WILD animals, 87. WILDERNESS, 105. WIFE for Isaac, 275. WIVES of Esau, 292. WORDS criticised, 52. WORLD not eternal, 129.

PART I.

INTRODUCTION.

CHAPTER I.

CHARACTER OF THE BOOK OF GENESIS.

CONTENTS. — Its Name—Antiquity—Author—Composition—Inspiration—Truth—Language—Style—Various Readings.

SECTION I.—NAME OF THE BOOK.

1. The first book in the Bible is called in Hebrew, *Bereshith*, that being the word with which the book begins. The Hebrews were accustomed to name the books of the Bible in this way. The name "Genesis" is Greek, and has the meaning of generation or origin, and is given to the book on account of the subject of which it first treats.

SECTION II.—ITS ANTIQUITY.

2. How do we know that the book we call the Bible is an ancient book, and made its first appearance in the world at a far distant period in the past? And how do we know the dates of the several books of which it is composed? We propose briefly to answer these questions. There is a regular succession of writers, both Christian and Infidel, from the days of Christ down to the present time — all recognizing the existence of certain sacred books called the "Bible,"

"Scriptures," or by some similar designation. Such references prove the existence of the Bible, back as far as the Christian era. But the New Testament contains many references to sacred writings, still more ancient. It speaks of them as the "Law and the Prophets," or the "Law, Prophets and Psalms," or by some other equivalent name. The Law is usually associated with the name of Moses; and the Prophets are sometimes called by name; and when they are not thus designated, they are still clearly identified by passages quoted from them, corresponding with such as we now find in the prophetical writings. Other writers, who lived near the time of Christ, furnish us with similar references. Philo and Josephus, both Jewish writers of repute, often refer to the Scriptures. Josephus gives us a particular account of the books held sacred by the Jews; and these correspond with the books we now have in the Old Testament collection. Besides, in giving us his History of the Jews, he quotes largely from the sacred writings; and it is certain that the Bible he refers to, and quotes from, is the same book we now designate by that name.

3. Nearly three hundred years farther back than the time of these writers, and soon after the last of the Old Testament books was written, we find a translation of the Jewish Bible into the Greek language, (though some portions of this translation may have a later date,) which was generally adopted and used by that people, in Egypt, Palestine, and other countries.

4. Thus the Bible is proved to have been in existence nearly as far back as the date of the last book of the collection; and this remark applies to the Old Testament, as well as the New. But how do we know that some of these books date still further back? And if this fact can be ascertained, how are we to determine the particular date of each book? To these questions satisfactory answers can be given, from several considerations; for, though the exact date of

each book may not be ascertained, a sufficient approximation to that result can be arrived at.

5. The later books of the Old Testament refer to earlier books, sometimes directly, and sometimes indirectly. The book of Moses (for what are now five books, was originally one book) is referred to by Ezra, one of the latest of the prophets. He speaks of the people gathering themselves, and offering sacrifices, as required in the "Law of Moses, the man of God." He speaks of "the Priests in their divisions, and the Levites in their courses for the service of God, which is at Jerusalem, as it is written in the book of Moses." Nehemiah, cotemporary with Ezra, also speaks of certain things "written in the Law;" and they are things found in the Law of Moses now in our hands. He mentions "God's Law which was given by Moses, the servant of God;" and he designates a number of the laws and institutions of Moses. The earlier Prophets make frequent references to the same book, or Law of Moses; and they thereby confirm the alleged antiquity of that portion of the Bible. We find such references in Ezekiel, Jeremiah, Micah, Isaiah, Hosea, and Amos. There are numerous references of a similar character in the Psalms; also in the Kings, Chronicles, Samuel, Judges, and Ruth. The author of the books of Kings, speaks of the "Law of Moses," and the "Book of the Law of Moses," and of things written therein, corresponding with what we now find there; and the author of Chronicles refers to the "Book of Moses," and to the "Book of the Law of the Lord." In Joshua, too, we read of the "Book of the Law," and the "Book of the Law of Moses;" and it is said to have been a guide to that hero in the conquest of Canaan.

6. The following references, showing the truth of the foregoing statements, may be passed over by the *reader*, if he desires, and consulted by such only as wish to *study* the subject. See Ezra iii. 2; vi. 18;

Neh. x. 34, 36, 29; 1 Kings ii. 3; ix. 9; xii. 28; 2 Kings xiv. 6; xxi. 4–7; 1 Chron. xvi. 14–18; 2 Chron. xvii. 9; xxiii. 18; 1 Sam. iv. 8; x. 18; xii. 8; 2 Sam. vii. 23; Ruth iv. 11, 12; Judges vi. 7–13. Compare Ezek. xx. 10–28 with Ex. xiii. 3; xiv. 11; Lev. x. 10, 11; xviii. 5; Num. xiv. 11. Compare Jer. xi. 1–8, with Deut. iv. 20; xi. 13, 14; xxvii. 26. Compare Micah vi. 4, 5, with Deut. iv. 20; Num. xxii. 1–3. Compare Isa. i. 9, with Gen. xix. 24, 25. Compare Hosea xii. 12, 13, with Gen. xxix. 18; xxvii. 43—45; Hosea xii. 3–5, with Gen. xxv. 26; xxviii. 12; xxxii. 24; Hosea xi. 8, with Gen. xix. 25. Compare Amos ii. 9, with Num. xiii. 33. Consult Psl. lxxviii., and compare with it, Deut. iv. 9; Ex. xxxii. 9; xiv. 21; xiii. 21; xvii. 6. Consult also Psl. lxxxiii. and Psls. cv., cvi., and cxxxvi. See 1 Sam. iv. 8; x. 18; xii. 8; 2 Sam. vii. 23; Ruth iv. 11, 12; Judges vi. 7–13; Josh. i. 8; viii. 31, 34; xi. 12; xxiii. 6, 10. And, aside from direct references in these books, the transactions they record, are based on the truth of the previous records. They have the same localities, customs, institutions, &c., with such variations only as the progress of affairs would necessarily require.

7. Thus, all through the Old Testament Writings, back to the time of Moses, we find references to the books we now have that pass under his name. And we may safely affirm that there is no book of ancient times, in which such references could be expected, where they are not found. And as to Genesis, there can be no doubt as to its being the first of the five books, since its contents are such as to give it that place; and so far as we know, it has always occupied that position.

8. We may add to the above, several other facts, that will tend to confirm our position, as to the antiquity of the books we now call the Pentateuch. One is, that the Jews and the Samaritans, both have these books; and the hostility that has always existed be-

tween these two branches of the family of Israel, makes it obvious that the one did not obtain them from the other, and that, therefore, both must have been in possession of them, at the time the separation took place; (B. C. 975;) and whatever views we may have of the record, as true or false, we must allow considerable time to have elapsed before a book of such claims and of so much importance, could have come into existence, and have gained the universal acceptance of the people; and this allowance being made, we shall be compelled to place the book in the age to which it is generally referred, and to which its records apply.

9. Another fact is important. There are some variations between the copy in the hands of the Jews, and the one possessed by the Samaritans, resulting obviously from the many transcriptions through which they have respectively passed. This circumstance is favorable to the antiquity of the book, for the variations here referred to, could not have arisen, except through the lapse of many centuries. Another circumstance may be mentioned in this connection. It not unfrequently occurs that some later author has added to the earlier records, occasional explanatory remarks, with a view generally to connect the monuments of former days, with his own times. Such remarks, which are themselves very ancient, presuppose a considerable period, during which the book must have been in existence, to require any explanation to be added, or to furnish a reason for such additions.

10. The difference of style between the modern, and more ancient books of the Bible, has been noticed by some writers, and is indeed an important consideration. "It is an undeniable fact that Hebrew ceased to be the language of the Jews, during the Babylonish captivity; and that the Jewish productions after that period, were in general either Chaldee or Greek. . . . It necessarily follows, therefore, that every book that is written in pure Hebrew, was composed, either before or about the time of the Babylonish captivity. This being admitted, we may advance a step farther, and contend that the period which elapsed between the most ancient and most modern book of the Old Testament, was very considerable; or in other words, that the most ancient books of the Old Testament were written a length of ages prior to the Babylonish captivity. No language continues during many centuries in the same state of cultivation; and the Hebrew, like other tongues, passed through the several stages of infancy, youth, manhood, and old age. If, therefore, on comparison, the several parts of the Hebrew Bible are found to differ, not only in regard to style, but also in regard to character and cultivation of language; if the one discovers the golden, another the silver, a third the brazen, a fourth the iron age, we have strong internal marks of their having been composed at different and distant periods. No classical scholar, independent of Grecian history, would believe that the poems ascribed to Homer were written in the age of Demosthenes, or the orations of Demosthenes in the time of Origen. . . . . . For the very same reason, it is certain that the five books ascribed to Moses, were not written in the time of David, the Psalms of David in the age of Isaiah, nor the Prophecies of Isaiah in the time of Malachi. But it appears from what was said above in regard to the extinction of the Hebrew language, that the book of Malachi could not have been written much later than the Babylonish captivity: before that period, therefore, were written the Prophecies of Isaiah, still earlier the Psalms of David, and much earlier than these, the books which are ascribed to Moses."—*Horne's Introduction*, vol. ii. p. 18.

11. This argument is strengthened by the fact that the language of the Hebrews, like their social customs, underwent changes very slowly; and that slight

differences between Malachi and Isaiah, or Isaiah and David, or David and Moses, would indicate much longer intervening periods, than would be expected, aside from this consideration. And a proper allowance being made, we shall find no difficulty in regarding the Pentateuch as belonging to the time of Moses.

SECTION III.—AUTHOR OF THE BOOK.

12. That the Pentateuch was written by Moses, is the uniform testimony of antiquity; and no dissenting opinion was ever expressed until very modern times. This fact ought of itself to be deemed satisfactory in a case of this kind. If the Book had had any other author, the fact would have been known, and would have been stated, or at least implied, in some of the numerous references to this part of the Bible. To this consideration we may add others. That Moses was instructed to write a book, and that he did accordingly write one, is made known in the book itself. See Ex. xvii. 14; xxiv. 4, 7; xxxiv. 27; Num. xxxiii. 2; Deut. xxviii. 61; xxix. 21, 27, &c. Besides this, the minuteness and particularity with which the events of his day are described, indicate clearly that the record was made at the time, and by one who was intimately acquainted with the transactions he describes; and this can be affirmed of no one so well as of Moses.

13. That Moses did not write every word contained in the book, (the account of his own death, for example,) may be conceded with no detriment to our argument. Nor do we insist on his being the author of the book, with a view of maintaining its reliability as a true record on that ground; but simply because the evidence, so far as ascertained and understood, leads to this conclusion. The truth of the record, depends, aside from its author, on certain considerations which we will give in their proper place.

SECTION IV.—COMPOSITION OF THE BOOK.

14. Assuming that Moses is the author of the book of Genesis, we may ask in what way he came by a knowledge of the facts contained in the book, as the latest of these facts occurred several hundred years before his day. We know of but two answers to this question, one of which only can be true. Either the facts were given him by divine inspiration, or he obtained them from pre-existing records. We adopt the latter theory. Moses nowhere tells us how he came by the records he gives us, which he would not have omitted to do if he had received them directly from God. In other instances he says that "the Lord spake" to him; but he never makes this statement in regard to the facts recorded in Genesis. We conclude then, that there were in existence, at that time, some writings in which these things were made known, and that from these Moses made up his book. Of course he did not need to make any direct statement as to the source of his information, since that was a matter well understood by the people.

15. Besides, there is an intrinsic propriety in this view of the subject. The same reasons for making known these things to Moses, may be urged in favor of their having been made known before. It was quite as necessary that Abraham should be informed of what had occurred previous to his time, as that Moses should be. And if Abraham, why not Noah? And if Noah, why not Adam?

Evidently all these, and all the people between Adam and Moses were interested to know the past history of the world, as much as was Moses and those who succeeded him. We can hardly suppose, therefore, that the records of Genesis were unknown till the time of Moses, and then, for the first time, were revealed to him.

16. But if we go back to Adam, it will not be difficult to see that the events of his time could be known to him and transmitted to others without any special aid of inspiration. The same may be said of Noah. What occurred in his day, he could understand and make known, without any special illumination. So could Abraham; so could Isaac, and Jacob, and Joseph. True, the art of writing may not have been known in the days of Adam; but tradition was quite sufficient to have transmitted the few things that are recorded of that early age, and to have preserved them till the art of writing could put them into a more permanent and enduring form.

17. When this art was first known, cannot be determined by any certain and reliable evidences.—Jewish tradition refers it back to a very ancient period, to the days of Enoch, or to Adam. A more reliable opinion places it in the days of Abraham; and it is certain that writing had been known for a considerable period before the time of Moses. Hence, when first referred to in the Bible, it is not spoken of as a new thing. See Ex. xvii. 14. That it did not exist in the days of the Patriarchs, has been argued from the use of monuments and symbols, as mementoes of certain transactions; for it is contended that written memorials would have taken the place of these, if writing had been known. I take this argument not to be wholly conclusive, since such monuments were in use at a later day, when the art of writing is known to have existed. Indeed, in most cases, if not all, where such monuments were employed, there is reason to believe that they answered the purpose had in view better than any writing could have done; and if so, they may have been chosen on that account. Or, if this fact be not admitted, the *scarcity* of the knowledge of this art, rather than its *entire absence*, is all that we ought to infer from the circumstance in question.

18. The theory that makes Moses to have made up the book of Genesis from former records, known and acknowledged by the people, while it is the most natural theory, does, at the same time, allow of all the inspiration that can be justly claimed for the book. Adam, for example, could know the fact of the creation of the world, more especially the order observed in the creative process, only by divine inspiration; but having received such a communication, he could preserve it along with the facts of his own experience, without any special divine aid. Noah could be informed of God's intention to drown the world, and the proper arrangements to be made in view of such a calamity, only by a commuication from God; but the communication once made, it could be preserved with other events, and the record handed down to the next generation. Abraham, too, received divine knowledge in dreams and visions; but he needed no special aid to relate his experience of this kind, and to hand it down with other transactions.

These remarks will show the views we entertain of the manner in which the book was brought into existence, and the extent and mode of its inspiration. But the subject of Inspiration belongs to another place, and need not be treated of now.

19. Again; in the estimation of some theologians of eminence, there are good reasons for believing that the history of the world prior to the time of Abraham, and perhaps still later, was preserved in two separate and distinct documents, which are combined in the record we now have. We confess that the theory has some strong reasons in its favor, though we are not entirely satisfied of its truth. One of these documents is called, by these theologians, the "Elohim Document," because Elohim, in the original, is the name for God used by its author; and the other, for a similar reason, is called the "Jehovah Document."

20. The Elohim Document commences with the first chapter, and continues to chapter second, 4th verse; or, perhaps to the middle of that verse. It is then resumed in chapter fifth, and continues through that chapter. Then vi. 9–22. It next takes up the record at verse 7th, of chapter seventh, and ends with verse 16th, omitting the last clause. Then chapter viii. 1–19. Then ix. 1–29; and finally xi. 10–26, bringing the account down to the time of Abraham. All these passages are found to connect themselves together as a regular narrative, besides the circumstance before named, that they uniformly call the Deity by the name of God. (Elohim, in the original.)

Of course, what is called the Jehovah Document, is found in the places we have omitted, viz: ii. 4 to iv. 26: vi. 1–8; vii. 1–6; vii. 16–24; viii. 20–22; x. 1 to xi. 9. These do not connect themselves together as in the former case, indicating an omission, it is thought, of some words or paragraphs from this document, when the two were combined. The passage in vi. 1–8, has "God" instead of "Lord," (Jehovah) in three instances; but one of these, (verse 5th,) is a mistranslation, while the other two are regarded as spurious readings. Assuming the theory of the two documents to be correct, the differences between them would require an explanation. We do not see in them the contradictions that are claimed for them by the advocates of the theory.

21. In the one document, as we before said, the name of God is Elohim, while in the other, it is Jehovah or Jehovah Elohim, the first being translated *God*, and the last, *Lord*, or *Lord God*.

Both give an account of the creation, not indeed wholly alike, but not necessarily contradictory. It is better to say, that one account, in chapter first, lays down the exact order, and marks each step of the progress by the term "day," while the other account, in chapter second, gives us the main particulars, but with no intention of giving us the order in which the work was done; and with this view the differences need not be regarded as contradictions.

The Jehovah Document gives us an account of the temptation, of Cain and Abel, and the genealogy of Cain; while the other document passes over these things in silence; but this difference, though important, does not involve a contradiction. The omission of the one does not prove the untruth of the other.

The Elohim Document, in chapter 5th, gives us the genealogy of Adam through his son Seth. The other does not give us this genealogy; but it has that of Adam through Cain. Neither is there a contradiction here. Both genealogies may be alike true.

Each document has a sufficiently full account of the Deluge; and both combined give us many apparent repetitions. The main difference of the two documents, in respect to the Deluge, is, that one makes all the clean beasts, as well as the unclean, to have been preserved by pairs; the other makes the clean beasts to have been preserved by sevens, and the unclean, by pairs. And though this looks like a contradiction, I doubt whether we are authorized to call it such. It is certain that seven of every kind of clean animals, includes two of every kind; and the one writer, having the main purpose in his mind, which was to preserve enough to perpetuate the race, mentions only the two; while the other, more accurately, states the full number, seven; all over two, being intended, as we have suggested in another place, as food during the flood.

The Elohim Document contains some specific instructions to Noah, about the shedding of blood, the bow in the clouds, &c.; but the other document does not contradict these, though it does not mention them.

So on the other hand, the Jehovah Document gives us the genealogies of Shem, Ham and Japhet; while the other has only that of Shem; but it is worthy of note that the genealogy of Shem is alike, on both lists, so far as they are intended to run parallel.

22. The above are all the important differences, between what are thought to have been at first two separate accounts of the creation, the deluge and other ancient events; and our remarks upon them have been offered on the presumption that the theory is true. But we are not yet convinced of its truth; and will, therefore, give a few reasons for our dissent.

One is, that those who adopt the theory, are not agreed how far to extend it. Some stop at Abraham, and others find distinct portions of these documents in all the books of Moses; and some find them in the later writings. Again, *God* and *Lord* are frequently interchanged in the various readings; and hence it does not certainly appear but that *God* should be the reading, in some of the instances, where *Lord* is found in the Jehovah Document, and *Lord* in the Elohim Document; and if this be supposed, the main feature, by which the two documents are distinguished, is done away.

Besides, the differences and repetitions may arise from the imperfection of the art of writing, in its infancy, and not from the combination of two documents. With this view, what is regarded as the second account of creation, is, more properly, a supplement, by the same writer, in which some things are added and enlarged upon, and others repeated from the first chapter, to show the connection between them. The creation of man, is mentioned in chapter first; it is repeated in chapter second, with some additions. So the creation of woman. So the creation of animals. The several statements, that make up the history of the deluge, are considerably mixed up, and sundry repetitions occur; but we detect here an unskilful hand, rather than separate and contradictory documents. And were it otherwise, one of the evidences of the antiquity and primitive origin of the book, would be wanting.

The difference between what are called the two documents, in regard to the number of clean beasts, preserved from the flood, admits of an explanation quite as rational without the theory as with it. We have already suggested the explanation; but if that explanation is not accepted, and a contradiction is contended for, it is quite as rational to suppose that one author should contradict himself, through some inadvertence, as that two authors should contradict each other. Noah is represented as going into the ark, no less than four different times, or rather in four different passages; but it will be observed that each additional statement combines some circumstance not mentioned before. The first passage is a *prediction* of the flood and the preservation of Noah and his family. The next *commands* Noah to go into the ark. The next passage relates the *actual entrance* into the ark, of Noah and his family. And the last passage connects this event, with the *precise time* when it occurred. See vi. 18–22; vii. 1–5; vii. 7–12; vii. 13–16. A similar reason may be given for other repetitions.

Another thing may be noticed in this connection. The Hebrew language has but two tenses, the Past and the Future; and the modes that belong to other languages, are but imperfectly represented here. Repetitions sometimes arise from these defects.

23. In connection with the "Composition of the Book of Genesis," we may mention a feature of the book that seems to belong as properly here as elsewhere. I refer to some passages that seem to have been added by a later writer than the original author of the book. They seem intended to explain some circumstance that might not otherwise be understood, or to connect some ancient practice with more modern times.

24. The language concerning the Sabbath, ii 3, is probably one of those passages. It is not necessary in the place where we find it; but is a very natural addition after the Sabbath was instituted, as giving a reason for that institution. As it now stands, and viewed as a part of the original account, it implies that the Sabbath was instituted immediately after the creation of the world, which is hardly consistent with the silence regarding it all through the book of Genesis. Had it existed at first, some allusion to it would have been found among the Patriarchs; and as no such allusion is seen, we conclude that it did not exist; and that hence the passage now under consideration, is an addition as late at least as the time of Moses.

25. *And the Canaanite and the Perizzite dwelt then in the land.* xiii. 7. This is regarded by some as being added after the conquest of Canaan, when the Canaanites and Perizzites had been driven out; as if the author had said, "at that time these people were in the land; but they have since been expelled." But the passage does not require us to take this view. It was well known by the original author, that Canaan was some time to be the possession of the seed of Abraham, as this promise is often referred to; and the presumption was, that when this should be accomplished, the Canaanites would not occupy that country. *As yet*, however, the writer tells us, they were in that land.

26. *All these were joined together in the Vale of Siddim, which is the Salt Sea,* xiv. 3. "Which is the Salt Sea" was added by a later hand, for the purpose of informing the reader that what was now the Salt Sea had once been the Vale of Siddim, where the battle of the kings was fought.

27. *The same is the father of the Moabites, unto this day. . . . . The same is the father of the children of Ammon, unto this day.* xix. 37, 38. These tribes were numerous and powerful, in the time of Moses, and it is he, probably, that here refers to their parentage.

28. *Therefore, the name of the city is Beersheba, unto* *this day.* xxvi. 33. The passage contains no intimation, when it was written, as the place referred to, retained that name for many centuries.

29. *Therefore, the children of Israel eat not the sinew that shrank, which is upon the hollow of the thigh, unto this day,* xxxii. 32. This is an early gloss, as the custom alluded to, does not seem to have existed, even as late as the time of Moses. At least we know of no allusion to it.

30. *And these are the kings that reigned over the land of Edom, before there reigned any king over the children of Israel,* xxxvi. 31. This remark would not be likely to be made till the time when kings reigned over Israel; and it must therefore be referred to the time of the kings.

31. *And Joseph made it a law over the land of Egypt, unto this day,* xlvii. 26. This law probably existed in Egypt for a long period after the time of Joseph; and at any period during its existence, this gloss might have been made.

SECTION V.—INSPIRATION.

32. If the question were here propounded: What reason have we for supposing that any of the recorded statements of the book of Genesis, were dictated, in any special manner, by the Divine Spirit, we should insist, in the first place, upon a strong antecedent probability that such was the case. There was a time when men began to exist in the world. This is a self-evident proposition. That man is the product of a superior Power and Intelligence is scarcely less self-evident.

And the existence conferred on man at first, must have been preserved by some special aid. No other supposition is admissible. The aid we now have from our parents and friends, in the infancy of life, was not furnished, and could not be, from the nature of the case, to our first parents. Something must have been supplied as a substitute. If they needed no such special aid, then it follows that we have more than we need; and if we have no more than we need, and they needed the same, then some special means were necessary to provide it. To make such special aid necessary, we need not suppose that the first human pair were formed babes. Let it be admitted that they were made with full dimensions, and with the strength of manhood; yet they needed instruction as to the use they were to make of their powers. They needed some special communications as to the purpose of their existence, and the modes of securing it. What is now furnished us by natural means, must have been furnished them, by means supernatural or special. Let the needed knowledge be given them in the form of a superior instinct, or by special impressions produced on the brain, or by dreams and visions, or by any other means, the result is the same;—It is a revelation. The necessity of a revelation, at that time, is, therefore, an obvious and well sustained conclusion. How often revelations should be made, and how long continued in the world, can be judged of better by Him who made us, and knows all our needs, than by any other being.

33. Sundry theories have been put forth concerning the inspiration of the Scriptures. The two extreme theories are the following:—One theory regards every word of the book as immediately dictated by the Divine Spirit, so as to exclude all errors from the record; the other finds in the Bible, no inspiration but such as has been common to men in all ages of the world. It is obvious that the truth lies somewhere between these two extremes; but WHERE between them, it may be difficult to determine.

34. The ground we take, is, that inspiration cannot be affirmed of the *language* of the Bible. This is

made evident from the many imperfections of language found in the book. The composition of its several parts is evidently the work of men; and of men, too, in an age of the world when literature and science were far behind the present age. Again, a difference in style is observable in the several writers; and the style is found to vary, not only with the temper and disposition of the writer, but with the habits and prevailing intelligence of the age when he wrote. These circumstances are not consistent with the doctrine of verbal inspiration.

35. Again; if Moses, for example, was inspired to write the five books ascribed to him, in such a way as to secure the work from all mistakes, we ask for a reason for this, that does not apply, with equal force, to other things for which no such claim is put forth. Doubtless if he was so inspired, it was to keep those who should read his writings, from imbibing errors concerning the matters communicated. Not conceiving any other reason possible, we shall take this to be the one adopted. But would such inspiration secure the object? These books were soon to pass into other hands, and the inspired author could not always retain them. Besides, if more than one copy of the inspired book was to exist, the second must be transcribed from the first, and so on, indefinitely; and this work of transcribing would be attended by mistakes, unless the copyists were also inspired, which we believe no one has yet maintained. Farther than this, the inspired original would not always last. If it were not lost or destroyed, it would at length waste away and disappear; and then none but imperfect and uninspired copies would remain.

36. Again; no one at the present day, that acknowledges the truth of revelation, doubts that the Bible was intended for universal use. It must, then, not only be copied from the first written volume, but it must be translated into other languages; and it is just as important and necessary, to guard men from the errors of a bad translation, as those of a faulty copy. If the original intention was to give men an exact knowledge of divine things, and without any alloy of error, the means of protection, one would suppose, should be continued, and the translations and copies both be placed under the guidance of the Divine Spirit; and as such is not the case, and no one assumes that it is, it occurs to us that the design of God has been mistaken as to the first record. We can conceive of no reason why that should be absolutely infallible that does not apply as well to the copies and translations made from it.

37. There is still another consideration that has some weight with us. Men, constituted and circumstanced as they are, would not all read and understand the Bible alike if every copy in use were infallibly correct; and if they understood it differently, some of them must be in error; and thus the original inspiration would fail of its purpose. There is but one conceivable way to secure such a purpose, and that is, by an inspiration that shall not only make the first record correct, but that shall secure the infallible accuracy of all copies and translations; and, indeed, that shall give an infallible understanding to all readers of the record. But were it desirable to secure the purpose here contemplated, an immediate inspiration to every man, without the record, would be a more natural and consistent method. It was then, no part of the Divine plan, to give us a revelation that should be miraculously protected from error.

38. The book has been subjected to the usual accidents to which other books are exposed, with such exceptions only, (important, to be sure,) as would arise from the character of the book, and the circumstances of the people and times through which it has come down to us. The book has always been regarded with feelings of peculiar sacredness; and this has thrown around it an additional protection over other books; and in this, as in many other things, even superstition has had its beneficial tendencies. There have been, also, many sects and parties, all claiming its authority; and this has led to the same result, as no one party could make any alteration in the book without exposure from the rest; and if any alteration occurred, by mistake or design, the great number of copies in the world would aid the work of correction. With these exceptions, and perhaps some others, we say the Bible has been subjected to the common fortune of other books. It was written by human hands as much as any other work. By human hands it has been transcribed and printed. It has been translated by men of fallible understanding. It was written on perishable materials, and like other books, is subject to decay.

39. The inspiration of the Bible relates to its *principles,* (we mean such as are there expressly referred to God as their author,) and not to its verbal records; and while the latter are subject to imperfection and decay, the former have never been impaired by the revolutions of the world, and will remain, though the world should pass away. That the Bible contains many divine communications, no one can doubt who admits its authority or truth in any respect. The error that Christians have too generally fallen into, (now being followed, as we might expect, by the opposite extreme,) is to ascribe to the Bible what it does not claim, and thereby to weaken its evidences in the view of intelligent and inquiring minds.

40. As examples of its divine communications, as coming within the sphere of our present investigations, we place the creation of the world, more especially the order observed in the creative process, so exactly corresponding with the discoveries of modern science; for we cannot see how men could have learned these things in the early days of the world

without divine aid; since, as far back as we can trace the Bible record, the most profound ignorance has prevailed among men in regard to those sciences that throw light upon this subject. The coming deluge, and the means of preservation, must have been announced to Noah in like manner. The moral principles inculcated in the beautiful allegory of Eden, could have been made known at first only by a divine revelation, for they are even now but imperfectly comprehended by the wisest of men. The announcement that the seed of the woman should bruise the serpent's head, the sense of which we cannot well mistake, contains a sentiment that could not have been known without divine aid. The same remark will apply to the promise to Abraham, that in his seed all the families and nations of the earth should be blessed. That Jesus Christ was the seed of Abraham, we all know; and that his religion is destined to bless the world, none can doubt. A promise, therefore, so far-reaching, both in respect to time and space; and one which, for thousands of years, the merest accident might have defeated, can have emanated from no other source than a divine Omniscience, that could take in the whole history of the world at one view, and a divine benevolence to plan its redemption and salvation.

41. Let it be added here, that no age before the present one has furnished such strong proofs of the inspiration of these announcements, though found in the oldest book in existence, as are now presented before us in the condition of the world, so plainly indicating the triumph of good over evil, and the blessing of the race through Jesus Christ. We are, indeed, farther from the time the book was written, but we are nearer to the fulfilment of its announcements, and are, therefore, made more sure of its truth. Hence, we add, that the objection sometimes urged against the Bible, that its records, the more ancient ones especially, are so far back in the past, that we are wholly uncertain in regard to their truth, here meets with a reply that cannot fail to be appreciated. Its most important announcements become more obviously true with the lapse of ages.

42. There are many less important events that are local and circumscribed, of which we cannot be so certain, when viewed by themselves; but connected as they are with more important events, and resting on the same original basis, our belief of one, so well sustained, makes us yield assent to the others.

43. The *mode* by which divine communications were originally made, is a proper subject of inquiry in this connection, for there seems to be considerable confusion in the minds of men in regard to this matter. Divine communications were obviously made to our first parents, as this was a necessity of their condition; but in what manner they were made, is not defined. Several communications were made to Noah; but *how* made, we are not informed. So revelations were made to Abraham; but in general, the method of making them is left to inference. In regard to these, and all other instances, (unless special reasons oppose,) we feel safe in saying, that the mode was the same as in other instances, where it is definitely and explicitly stated.

When it is said, that the word of the Lord came to Abraham in *a vision;* and that Jacob saw the Lord in a *dream;* and that God spake to Israel in the *visions* of the night; we feel safe in concluding that the same mode was adopted in other cases.—xv. 1; xxviii. 12; xlvi. 2.

44. This is rendered the more evident from several considerations. One is, that no other mode is specified. Another, that the same language and phraseology are found in those passages where the mode is not stated, as in those where it is. Add to these circumstances, that the language following some of these revelations, shows them to have been in the night, and the inference is, that they occurred in a dream or a vision. As examples; immediately after the communication to Abraham, recorded in xxi. 12, 13, it is added, "and Abraham *rose up early in the morning*," &c. When Abraham was instructed to take his son Isaac, and offer him upon a certain mountain, it is not said that this instruction was given him in a dream or vision; but when it is added, that "Abraham *rose up early in the morning*," and proceeded to execute the divine mandate, the conclusion seems plain, that the revelation had been made in the night, and by natural inference, that it was made in a dream. xxii. 3.

When, therefore, God spake to Adam, to Cain, or to Noah, we suppose he spake in the manner here indicated, no other mode being obvious; and this view we deem the more reliable, and worthy of acceptation, from the fact that it removes much of the mist in which this matter seems involved in many minds, and so far as it has this effect, it adds beauty and consistency to the record, and brings it more immediately within the reach of human credibility.

SECTION VI.—Truth of the Book.

45. The truth of the recorded statements, found in the book of Genesis, is quite a different thing from its inspiration. An inspired book would be, no doubt, a true book; but a book, not inspired, may be true. I do not suppose that any special inspiration guided the hand of the writer of the book under consideration, and I trust the reasons already given for this opinion may be deemed satisfactory, founded as they are upon facts. Even the divine messages, that were then given to man, had to be entrusted to human hands, and were written down

with other records by the same fallible agency. That the book is substantially true, however, we have no doubt; and we come to this conclusion, from considerations, affecting its veracity, as we would in any other case. We cannot assume its truth on the previous assumption of its inspiration.

46. That the book is true, as to its pretensions of embracing sundry divine communications, is proved by the necessity before shown to have existed at that time, for such special aid.

Its truth is farther indicated by the views it gives us, in some passages, elsewhere noticed, that seem plainly the product of an early age, and the infant condition of our race. We may mention another circumstance, nearly allied to this, that goes to sustain the same thing. Many events that we are accustomed to refer to secondary causes, the Patriarchs refer directly to God. There are two reasons for this. One is, that divine communications, wherein God appeared to them and spake to them, would make them feel a nearness to him that others would not feel who were not thus distinguished. Another is, that the investigations of science and philosophy had not yet disclosed the existence of secondary causes, as they were understood afterwards.

47. That its historical records may be relied upon, may be made out from various considerations. There is no opposing record. The Jews, who had the best means of judging on this subject, all agree in receiving the book as a true account of ancient and primitive times. Another circumstance, which we may regard as providential, if we will, and an illustration that temporary evils are overruled for good, helps to sustain this argument. The children of Israel, at a very early period, were separated into two parts, and have ever since been hostile to each other; and yet, both portions of the people receive the record we now have, and about which we are prosecuting our inquiries, though they are not agreed in regard to some of the later writings. The book existed, therefore, before the separation; and if we make a reasonable allowance for the time requisite to bring it into general repute, upon the claims it sets up, we shall be compelled to refer it to the age of Moses, and concede that there must have been good reasons, at that time, for receiving its statements as substantially correct.

48. The truth of a book is to be judged of in two ways. One is, by means of external evidences in its favor, and the other is by the indications of truth in the book itself. Most books, with which we are acquainted, may be proved or disproved by other cotemporary documents. Other external marks of the truth of a book (if it be true,) may exist in cotemporary monuments and institutions. As to the record now under consideration, it so occurs, that this kind of evidence is mostly denied us. There is no other book so ancient. There is no cotemporary writing that can corroborate its declarations. Uncertain tradition is all that can be urged, as coming the nearest to evidence of this kind. And few monuments can be found, that can be referred back to so early a period. So far as these traditions and monuments bear upon the subject, they favor the record; and in respect to a few things, they are exceedingly important and convincing. It is hardly to be doubted, for example, that the book gives us a true account of the creation of the world; for all the discoveries of modern science, confirm its truth by monuments found in the depths of the earth, that are every year becoming more convincing. The fact of a deluge, is in harmony with all the phenomena of the past and present, that can affect this question; and the traditions of all nations furnish most extraordinary confirmation.

49. The intrinsic probabilities of the truth of the record, and the harmony of its several statements, furnish the best evidence, perhaps, that can be urged in its favor; and indeed, this kind of evidence is generally most convincing, with regard to any book, whether ancient or modern; nor does the distance of time destroy or materially weaken it.

50. Several particulars may be designated as affording internal evidence of the truth of the Mosaic records, in the book now under consideration. One is, that the degree of intelligence, the book shows to have existed at that time, is precisely what might be expected, under the circumstances. The world, like the individual, has its childhood and youth, its maturity and old age. We know from the past, what is the rate of its progress or growth. When we look at its youth, we know what must have been its childhood or infancy. And though this is a subject about which we may not claim to be above mistakes; yet, in our judgment, the record we have in Genesis, of the infancy and childhood of the race, is a very exact statement of what we should suppose it ought to be, in view of what we know of its subsequent condition and progress. The language of social life, the customs that prevailed, the views of God and his operations there set forth, all indicate a primitive condition of the race. And when we look at its condition at a subsequent period, when seen through the light of authentic history, its advancement is only, and precisely, what it ought to be, from such a beginning, and during the space of time that had preceded.

51. Again, many of the objections to the book, drawn from its internal character, are really arguments in its favor. It is said to contain unworthy conceptions of God and his operations. We admit it does, so far as the author's language may be understood as expressing his own views, or employed in accommodation to the prevailing views of the people; but this is what might be expected, and is indeed a clear mark of its antiquity. But this matter is treated more at large, in another place, to which the reader is referred. (See p. 47–49.)

The book is said to contain many things that are *immodest*. We admit that some things in the book would be immodest under other circumstances; but as the case is, this feature is an internal mark in its favor. It shows that the record belongs to a primitive age, when the ideas of propriety and fitness that now prevail, had not been suggested, at least, had not grown into their present shape and form.

52. Again; a combination of circumstances, each in itself unimportant, will sometimes furnish an argument that amounts almost to a demonstration. In view of this fact, let the following circumstances be added to the particulars already noticed. The early inhabitants of the globe lived, in what we would now call a prairie country. We find them at the very first, with their flocks and herds; and we continue to see notices of this kind, all through the book; nor is there any intimation that the ground had to be cleared of its forests before this branch of labor could be pursued. There are many people in the world by whom this circumstance would be understood as an internal mark of its untruth. There was a time, when to *us*, had it attracted our attention, it would have occasioned not a little embarrassment. But now, knowing that prairie lands form a considerable portion of the earth's surface, I can easily believe that the part of the earth, where the Bible places the origin of the race, was of this kind; and I can farther see great propriety in selecting such a location for such a purpose. The references in Genesis to the wilderness and to groves, are such only as apply to a prairie country where portions of timber land do now and then occur.

53. There is another species of internal evidence, to which more or less importance will be attached. It consists of what are called "undesigned coincidences." In all true writings there are more or less circumstances that are "coincident" with each other, without any apparent intention of the author that they should be so; and it is this last circumstance, that gives them their importance. What is here intended will be best understood by a few examples. It is common with us to name persons after others among our acquaintances or relations; and we find the same practice to have prevailed, to some extent, in ancient times. Hence, in the two genealogies of Adam, one through Cain, and the other through Seth, we find some similar names. Enoch and Lamech occur in both; and some of the other names are so nearly alike, that they may have been originally the same; and indeed are regarded as the same in the Septuagint or Greek version. A fictitious writing might have the coincidence here referred to; but it would be quite as likely not to have it.

54. But there are other examples more to the point. In the genealogy of Ham, we find the names of Sheba and Dedan. They were Ham's great-grandchildren. So in the genealogy of Shem, we find a Sheba; and in the family of Abraham by Keturah, we find a Sheba and Dedan. That the writer intended these coincidences, we have no reason for supposing. Notice also that the father of the last Sheba and Dedan was one Jokshan; and the father of Sheba, in the lineage of Shem, was also Jokshan. One would be inclined to think that the latest Jokshan, named his son Sheba, because another Jokshan had done the same: but at length, having another son, he names him Dedan, remembering that the same combination of names (Sheba and Dedan) was found among Ham's descendants. What was more natural than this, allowing the record to be true; though we should not expect to find such a circumstance in a false or fictitious one. Many other similar examples could be produced; and they are the more remarkable as we know that the Hebrews generally named their children on a different principle, forming the name from some circumstance occurring at the birth of the child.

55. Nearly allied to the foregoing, is the practice of naming places from persons. The writer does not tell us how Haran, the first residence of Abraham, after leaving Ur of the Chaldees, came by its name; but as Abraham had recently lost a brother Haran, it was quite natural that the place should be named from him. So Mamre, the residence of Abraham in Canaan, was obviously named from Mamre, one of Abraham's confederates; though the name of the place and of the person, are never mentioned in such connection, as to make the coincidence obvious, except to the careful reader. Sidon was the oldest son of Canaan, and is mentioned in the list of Ham's posterity; and in process of time, with no special reference to his name, we find an important city, bearing the same name, in the north-west corner of Palestine.

Not very unlike this is the next instance to be noticed. In one part of the narrative, we read of the Amalekites, as one of the tribes of Canaan; in another and still *later passage*, we find one Amalek, among the descendants of Esau. Now it hardly admits of doubt, that the *tribe* was named from the *man*, and are indeed his descendants. This is accounted for, from the fact, that in naming the tribes of Canaan, some are spoken of by anticipation. There is an apparent incongruity, which an impostor would have avoided; but there is also a coincidence which is an evidence of truth; and all the more conclusive, as being joined with the apparent incongruity.

Again; one of the grand-sons of Nahor, is Aram. Was not Padan-*Aram*, the residence of Nahor, named after him? This Nahor and his family are called Syrians; but the original is *Arameans*.

56. Again; we read of Abraham going down to Egypt, in consequence of a famine in the land of Canaan; and while there, he received many valuable presents from Pharaoh, among which were servants and *handmaids*. At a subsequent period, and writing about a very different subject, the author tells us that Sarah had an *Egyptian* handmaid whose name was Hagar. Still later, this Hagar was sent away from her home, and was found in the way to Shur; and we learn in another part of the book that Shur lay in the direction of Egypt. What more natural than that Hagar should seek her former home in Egypt, and being a female and a slave, what more natural than that she should lose her way? At a subsequent period, when driven out, a second time, with her child, she is said to have wandered in the wilderness of Beersheba; and this place, too, we know lay in the same direction.

57. Finally; the difference between Palestine and Egypt, is made obvious by scores of allusions and circumstances, entirely incidental, and plainly having no such purpose on the part of the writer. Going to Egypt from Canaan, is habitually spoken of as going *down* to Egypt; and from the latter place to the former, was going *up* to Canaan. In Egypt, too, we find a regular, established government, a king and his officers, a captain of the guard, a chief butler, a baker, a prison and gallows. Here were fine linen and golden chains, chariots and horsemen; and here the choicest productions of the East found a ready market. In Palestine these things are not found; and it is worthy of being added, that money, and gold and silver ornaments, are not alluded to, until after the first journey to Egypt. The productiveness

of the country, even when famine prevailed elsewhere, is often alluded to, and had, as we all know, a natural cause. Such a circumstance, as seven years of plenty, followed by seven years of famine, was, in Egypt, a natural occurrence, though we know of no other country on the globe, of which the same thing could be affirmed. We say, then, in conclusion of this particular, that Genesis has all the internal and external marks of truth, that can be fairly required or expected under the circumstances.

SECTION VII. — LANGUAGE OF THE BOOK.

58. Except a few passages in Chaldee, the Old Testament was written in the Hebrew language, some peculiarities of which, taken from the book of Genesis, may be here noticed.

1. Hebrew idioms: —

59. (*a.*) The name of God is often used for emphasis. Examples: " The earth was corrupt before God." The earth was *very* corrupt, is the meaning. " The men of Sodom were wicked sinners, before the Lord, exceedingly." They were exceedingly corrupt. " The garden of the Lord," may refer to the garden of Eden, and it may not; but the meaning is, a very beautiful garden. " That I may bless thee, before the Lord," has simply this meaning;—that I may invoke upon thee the richest blessings. " With great wrestlings have I wrestled with my sister," is, in the original, with the wrestlings of God, have I wrestled with my sister. " God's host," may, according to the same idiom, mean, only a great company. vi. 11; xiii. 13; xiii. 10; xxvii. 7; xxx. 8; xxxii. 2.

60. There are other instances, but these are sufficient to illustrate the principle. Sometimes there may be a doubt how such instances should be translated. Hence the phrase, " Spirit of God," i. 2, has, by some, been thought to mean *a great wind;* for

the word for " spirit " has sometimes the meaning of *wind;* and " wind of God," would mean a great wind, according to the idiom we are now illustrating Such appears to have been the understanding of Josephus. Again ; the translators have said that the " terror of God " was upon the cities ; while the more rational idea is, that a great terror was upon the cities. The terror was inspired, not so much by God, as by the sons of Jacob. xxxv. 5.

61. (*b.*) The Hebrew verb is often repeated for the sake of emphasis. Examples :—" Thou mayest *freely* eat," is literally to eat, thou mayest eat. The translation doubtless gives the true idea. " Thou shalt surely die," is literally, to die, thou shalt die. Ye shall not surely die, is a similar example. " Abraham shall surely become a great and mighty nation." To become, shall become, is literal. " He will *needs* be a judge." To judge, he will judge. In describing the blessing of Abraham, the translators have, very singularly, preserved, or nearly so, the Hebrew idiom. " In blessing I will bless thee ; and in multiplying I will multiply thy seed as the stars of heaven." A true rendering would be ; I will greatly bless thee, and I will greatly multiply thy seed, &c. ii. 16, 17; iii. 4 ; xviii. 18 ; xix. 9 ; xxii. 17.

Other examples of the same idiom may be found in the following passages that need not be quoted. xxvi. 13, 28 ; xxx. 16 ; xxxi. 15 ; xxxvii. 8 ; xl. 15 ; xliii. 3,7 ; xliv. 5.

62. (*c.*) The Hebrews used the word *son* to express various relations. Examples :—" Noah was six hundred years old ;" literally, Noah was son of six hundred years. " Abraham was seventy years old :" son of seventy years. " Eight days old :" son of eight days. " A calf," son of the herd. " People of the East," sons of the East. There is generally no difficulty in translating or understanding such instances, as the sense is sufficiently obvious. vii. 6 ; xvii. 1, 12 ; xviii. 7 ; xxix. 1.

2. *Hebrew Modes and Tenses.*

63. The Hebrews had but two Tenses to their verbs, the Past and the Future, in place of the six tenses that belong to our language. This can be regarded only as a defect; and it sometimes embarrasses the translator. Of course the connection and circumstances of the passage are the only resort to determine the true rendering. A few examples will illustrate this peculiarity and its difficulties. Gen. i. 14–19 seems to be an account of the first production of the sun, moon and stars; but as there could be no day and night without a sun, we conclude that that luminary must have existed on the first day; and we are led to ask, whether the translation may not be made to harmonize with this view. We think it may, in the following manner:—Verse 16th should be put in brackets and read thus:—[And God *had* made two great lights, the greater light to rule the day, and the lesser light to rule the night—he *had* made the stars also.] All before and after this, may be read as it now is. We are thus taught, that, before the fourth day, God had made the sun, moon and stars; and that, on the fourth day, he set them in the firmament of heaven, to give light upon the earth. The same change may be made in ii. 19. And out of the ground God *had* formed every beast of the field. Then the passage may proceed as it does in the common version; or, more of it, perhaps all to verse 24, may be thrown into the past in the same manner. This would, at least, obviate some difficulties that men see in this, and other similar passages, and save them the necessity of seeking other modes of interpretation, less obvious and rational. In xii. 1, the rendering is correct. Now the Lord *had* said unto Abraham, Get thee out of thy country, &c. The circumstances alluded to, had taken place on a former occasion; though, aside from these circumstances, it would have been equally correct to have used the expression, " the Lord said unto Abraham." The difference is this: — One translation makes God to have spoken to Abraham in Ur of the Chaldees, and to regard that as the country of Abraham, from which he was to depart. The other makes the command to be given in Haran; and the latter to be the country referred to, in the expression, " thy country." There is in Hebrew no difference in the form of the verb for *says, said, has said, had said.* These modifications must be learned from the sense and circumstances of the passage.

64. The modes, too, of verbs, are but imperfectly represented in the Hebrew language. One peculiarity only need be noticed. To some of the modes it is customary to ascribe what is called a " causative " sense. For example; — I will *cause* it to rain upon the earth, vii. 4; more literally, I *will rain* upon the earth. The same tense in the same form, is so rendered in xix. 24. The Lord *rained* upon Sodom and upon Gomorrah. God made a wind to pass over the earth. viii. 1. God passed a wind over the earth. We suspect that such instances of translating are generally suggested by the supposed necessity of making the ancients express themselves after our modes, rather than their own. On the same principle the translators might have rendered some other passages differently from what they have done, and thereby removed difficulties that are important. " I will remember my covenant." ix. 15. I will cause to remember my covenant, or, I will cause my covenant to be remembered, would be equally sustained by this usage. " I will look upon it, that I may remember the everlasting covenant." ix. 16. I will cause to look upon it, and remember, or, I will cause it (the bow) to be looked upon and my covenant to be remembered, may express the true meaning of the passage. Again; would it not be better to say, that God caused Abimelech and his wife to be healed, rather than to say that God healed them. So in the next verse, God caused to be "closed," some natural cause being immediate, as in the other instance. Did God take away Laban's cattle and give them to Jacob? xxxi. 9, or was it done by a device of Jacob himself? and, if the last, which we know to be the fact, then it was only in a very qualified sense, that God even caused it to be done. The Lord slew Er and Onan, sons of Judah. xxxviii. 7, 10. He caused it to be done, would suit our ideas better.*

65. But in reference to all these examples, it must not be forgotten, as before intimated, that the ancients had not our ideas, and must not be expected to express themselves in the same way. They had not learned the existence of intermediate causes between God and the operations of the world, as the moderns have done; and the latter, we suspect, have something to unlearn before they find the true philosophy. There is a more intimate connection between God and his works, than most of our modern philosophers and theologians have allowed us to believe; and if this be so, the ancient usage may, after all, be more strictly accurate than the modern.

3. *Hebrew Vowels and Consonants.*

66. It is generally conceded that the Hebrew language had originally no vowels, and that what are used as vowels, at the present day, in most printed

---

* If the Hebrew scholar should meet me with the reply, that, in the passage last quoted the form of the verb is not Hiphil, to which the causative sense is generally attached; and that hence the causative form of translating is not required here, as in the other instances; we would say in return, that it is not claimed that Hiphil always has this sense, and that whenever this sense is ascribed to it, the nature of the passage is urged in defence of this construction. We urge the same consideration in favor of giving the causative sense to other forms besides Hiphil; and if the argument is good in the one case, we see no reason why it should not be allowed in the other.

editions, (though some are without them,) are an invention since the language ceased to be spoken. That this opinion is correct, scarcely admits of doubt. The language consisted at first, and as long as it was a living language, of consonants alone, the vowel sounds, without which words cannot be pronounced, in any language, being supplied by custom and controlled by popular usage. At first view, this would seem to involve an impossibility; but a little thought will convince any one, that the English language is but little better off. We have vowels, to be sure, but the sounds we are to give to them, are far from uniform; and what sound is required in each individual case, must be determined with us, as with the Hebrews, by popular usage; and this being so, there is no great difference between popular usage with the vowels, and popular usage without them.

67. It is obvious, however, that when a language ceases to be spoken, popular usage ceases to be available; and the pronunciation must be guided by certain marks placed upon the words of the language in the books where it is used. The Hebrew has such marks; and this is the purpose for which they were invented. They serve to indicate the vowel sounds, accents, &c. They came into use by degrees, and the system was completed several centuries after the Christian era. That they are not a perfect guide to a right pronunciation, but only a help, will readily appear; for though each mark is designed to have but one sound, what that one sound is, must be learned from Jewish Rabbis or Hebrew scholars, who are not perfectly agreed. Hence after all, popular usage determines the pronunciation, and that varies in different countries. In some Hebrew Bibles these marks are omitted, and usage only is relied upon; and in those editions where they are employed, if they affect the sense of a passage, as they sometimes do, they are to be regarded as of no more authority, than the opinion of their inventors.

SECTION VIII.—STYLE OF THE BOOK.

68. There is one peculiarity of style in the book that deserves some attention. It relates to its *repetitions*. A number of particulars, recorded in chapter first, are repeated in chapter second; and this is one reason why, as we have shown elsewhere, some have concluded that the original account was made up of separate documents. So, in describing the Deluge, and the arrangements relating to that event, there are several repetitions. But in both these instances the repetitions seem intended to connect the event repeated, with others.

But the reason here given does not apply to the examples about to be introduced.

69. *Let us make man in our image, after our likeness.* i. 26. We are not able to discover any difference in sense, between the clause, "in our image," and the clause, "after our likeness;" and we suspect there is no difference; and that this usage belongs alone to the *style* of the writer. The importance of the thing asserted, may, in some such cases, be assigned as the reason of the repetition. Still this is only conjecture. *So God created man in his own image; in the image of God created he him.* i. 27. One part of the verse evidently repeats the other. *And on the seventh day, God ended his work which he had made; and He rested* (ceased) *on the seventh day from all his work which he had made.* ii. 2. The last half of this verse is precisely like the first. An instance occurs in xi. 31, which would lead us to believe that the author intended to amuse himself or his readers, by a play upon words, if other and similar instances did not occur often enough to remove this impression. The passage reads as follows:—
And Terah took Abram, his son; and Lot, the son of Haran, his son's son; and Sarah, his daughter-in-law, his son Abram's wife; and they went forth with them,

&c. In a former verse (29) we read of "Milcah the daughter of Haran, the father of Milcah, and the father of Iscah." It was not enough to tell us that Milcah was the daughter of Haran, it is added that Haran was father of Milcah. It may be added, that all the relations mentioned in verse 31, had been before described in the connection; and therefore we see no need of the immediate repetition of them. It is most rationally accounted for, perhaps, by referring it to a habit of describing people by their relations, a matter of necessity in those days, when each individual had but one name; and the habit being established, it would lead to a repetition of such relations sometimes when not necessary.

70. Again; "Esau is Edom," is repeated no less than four times in one chapter, xxxvi. 1, 8, 19, 43. *That we may live, and not die,* xliii. 8, is several times found; though one clause implies the other, and would have been sufficient, except that the author must be permitted to express himself in his own way. *The days of the years of my pilgrimage, are a hundred and thirty years; few and evil have the days of the years of my life been, and have not attained unto the days of the years of the life of my fathers, in the days of their pilgrimage.* xlix. 9. *And Jacob set up a pillar in the place where he talked with him, even a pillar of stone; and he poured a drink offering thereon; and he poured oil thereon.* xxxv. 14. I would improve this statement thus:— And Jacob set up a pillar of stone in the place where he talked with him, and poured a drink offering of oil thereon.

71. Several allusions are made to the cave of Machpelah, and in all the instances, the circumstance of its purchase by Abram of Ephron, the Hittite, and its location before Mamre, &c., are distinctly and specifically mentioned; though one would suppose that a single statement would have been sufficient. For some reason we think the writer intended to place great stress upon that transaction.

72. There is another class of passages, that may as well be noticed here as anywhere, as belonging in a certain sense, to the *style* of the book, since they show the author's *mode* of representing the divine operations. Such passages are not to be understood literally; nor indeed are we authorized to say that the writer himself intended them as literal;—they are his mode of bringing before us certain acts of the Creator.

We read in connection with the creation of the world, such expressions as the following:—"God *said*, Let there be light." "God *called* the light day; and the darkness he *called* night." "God *said*, Let there be a firmament." "God *said*, Let us make man." Of course no human being could have listened to the divine voice on that occasion; and no human being could know what the Lord *said*, unless a divine communication were expressly given to convey this information, for which we see no necessity; and hence we propose a different view of these and some other passages. Such language, ascribed to God, is simply to be referred to the author's *mode of representing the divine operations*, and is to be understood rhetorically rather than literally. This is evident from the comparison of two passages in the first chapter. God said to our first parents, "Be fruitful and multiply and replenish the earth." He is represented as saying the same thing to the *beasts*, which can be understood in no other way than the one we have suggested, that is rhetorically. i. 28, 22.

73. Again; "And God saw that the wickedness of man was great in the earth, and that every imagination of the thoughts of his heart, was only evil continually. And it repented the Lord that he made (had made) man upon the earth; and it grieved him at his heart. And the Lord said, I will destroy man whom I have created, from the face of the earth, both man and beast, and the creeping thing, and the fowls of the air; for it repenteth me that I have made them." vi. 5–7. Let the reader compare this passage with a direct communication from God to Noah, and note the differences. The communication is this:—"And God said unto Noah, The end of all flesh is come before me, for the earth is filled with violence through them; and behold I will destroy them with the earth. . . . And behold, I, even I, do bring a flood of waters upon the earth, to destroy all flesh, wherein is the breath of life, from under heaven; and everything that is in the earth shall die." vi. 13, 17. It is true that some of the statements in this passage are the same as in the other; but it is also true that others are very different. Here we find nothing about the total *corruption* of the race, or of the *repentance* and *grief* of the Creator. We infer that the passage that has these expressions belongs to the *style* of the author, and is not to be literally understood.

74. We place the following on the same list. "And the Lord said, Behold the man has become as one of us." iii. 22. It is not stated that the Lord said this *to* anybody, and we conclude that the expression belongs to the author's rhetoric, rather than his theology. "And the Lord smelled a sweet savor, and the Lord said in his heart, I will not again any more, curse the ground for man's sake, for the imagination of man's heart is evil from his youth; neither will I any more smite every living thing as I have done. While the earth remaineth, seed time and harvest, and cold and heat, and summer and winter, and day and night, shall not cease." viii. 21, 22. How did the writer know what the Lord said *in his heart?* Such language is so obviously to be referred to the author's style, that I can hardly suppose Infidelity so obtuse as not to perceive it.

75. The language concerning Babel, ix. 5–8, is another passage of the same kind. "And the Lord came down to see the city and the tower which the children of men builded. And the Lord said, Behold the people is one, and they have all one language, and this they begin to do; and now nothing will be restrained from them, which they have imagined to do. Go to, let us go down and confound their language, that they may not understand one another's speech. So the Lord scattered them abroad from thence, upon the face of all the earth; and they left off to build the city." We accept this, upon the statement of the writer, so far as it relates a historical fact; but the Lord's cogitations and sayings in bringing the thing about, we may accept or substitute others, with equal propriety.

76. We would add, that, though such passages, literally explained, contain unworthy views of the Creator, there is really no evidence that the author himself intended them to be literal. It is impossible to describe the divine operations in language that is not more or less faulty. This is true now, with even the wisest of men; and more than this certainly could not be expected of the man who wrote the first book the world ever saw. A moment's thought, concerning our own modes of expression, will convince any one of the difficulty of properly representing the Deity by human language. Our language not only fails to represent the divine character and doings as they are, but it fails to represent *our ideas* on these subjects. Our ideas of God are far in advance of our language; and if this be so now, more than this ought not to be required in the earliest age of the world. That was an infant state of society, and its views corresponded. Still it is right to presume that what is true *now*, was true then, that their language was not equal to their ideas.

Such passages as we have been considering, are an evidence of the antiquity of the book where they are found; and if any one is disposed to insist on their grossness, he only adds strength to the argument.

SECTION IX. — Various Readings.

77. Many good Christians, on hearing of the "various readings" of the Bible, have become very much alarmed, lest Christianity should be thrown from its foundations by this discovery; and with equal inconsistency, Infidels have sought to make what they seem to regard, as an overwhelming argument from the same consideration. The copies of the Bible show differences in the readings, as might be expected, and would be expected, by all reasonable men; these copies having been, as of necessity they were, written by human hands, and transmitted by fallible agency from generation to generation. Such readings have been carefully collected from all the manuscripts and copies known in the world; and though they are very numerous, amounting to many thousands; yet, but few of them possess any importance, as affecting the sense of the passages. Much the largest proportion of such readings, relate to the spelling of words, the position of words in the sentence without affecting the sense, the use of synonymous words, or even a dot or mark employed to guide the pronunciation.

78. In respect to the book of Genesis, (and indeed all the five books of Moses,) no various readings have been collected and preserved, with one unimportant exception, but such as relate to the vowel points, or marks before described; and as these are no part of the original language, and are only intended to guide the pronunciation, the variations found in them, can have but little bearing on the interpretation of the book. Doubtless, however, there have been various readings in the consonants as well as vowels, not only from the impossibility of avoiding them; but the ancient translations make the fact quite evident.

Still the same translations, from which such various readings are proved to have existed, make us certain that they could not have been such as to materially affect the sense.

79. To illustrate the little importance that should be attached to the various readings of the Bible, as affecting the meaning of passages, we will give the various readings of the first two chapters of the Septuagint. This version of the Bible dates back three hundred years before the Christian era; and of course there has been no lack of time for various readings to accumulate.

Gen. i. 4. In the phrase, "God saw the light," the spelling of the word for "saw" is not alike in all the copies.

i. 7. Some copies subjoin to this verse, "it was so;" while others omit this phrase.

i. 11. The phrase "after its kind," has, in some copies, the additional expression, "after its likeness."

i. 14. "To rule over the day and over the night" is added by some and omitted by others.

i. 22. The word "blessed" is differently spelled.

i. 25. In one part of this verse, "their kind" has, in some copies, "their," and in some not.

i. 28. "Blessed" differently spelled. So in ii. 3.

ii. 5. Some have Lord instead of God. So in ii. 8.

ii. 10. "Garden" is in a different case in some copies from what it is in others.

ii. 11. "Pison" is differently spelled as to a single letter. So the name Havilah.

ii. 13. The spelling of Gihon varies.

ii. 14. The original for "goeth" is slightly varied.

ii. 17. The word for "eat," in the latter part of the verse, slightly varies.

ii. 19. Some have "*their* name," and some have "*its*" name.

ii. 21, 22. Lord for God.

ii. 23. "She was taken from *ner* husband" is the

reading of some; and "she was taken from *man*" is the reading of other manuscripts; but the use or omission of a single letter, makes all the difference.

ii. 24. "His father and mother," or, "his father and his mother;" so "his wife" has a trifling variation in different copies.

80. How these variations originated, is easy to be seen. Different spelling would naturally occur. That Lord should be used for God, might also be expected. The phrase, "it was so," being several times used in the first chapter, it would very easily be inserted where it did not belong. "To rule over the day and over the night" was presumed to be required in i. 14, because it was used in a similar connection elsewhere. Similar reasons can be given for other variations. In all these examples the sense of the passages is scarcely varied in the slightest degree. Most of the various readings are of this character; and though some are more important, they are not such as to affect the general teachings of the book, or to lessen our confidence therein, as a true and reliable record of ancient times, or as a basis of our theological faith.

CHAPTER II.

CRITICISM ON IMPORTANT WORDS.

Contents: Elohim, Bara, Rhua, Nephish, Olim, Sheol, Malak.

There are some words in the book of Genesis, to which more than ordinary importance should be attached, from their relation to important subjects, or from the use that has been made of them to sustain doctrines that are adverse to the general teachings of the book. These we propose to notice in the present chapter.

SECTION I.—Elohim, the Name of God.

81. This name, in Hebrew, is found in the plural number; and a literal rendering of the first sentence of the Bible would be, "In the beginning *Gods* created the heavens and the earth." What shall we say in regard to this word in this form? Shall we say, as some Infidels have said, that the Hebrew Scriptures, like the Mythology of the Pagans, recognize more Gods than one? or shall we conclude, as some Christian theologians have taught, that the reference is to the plurality of *persons* in the Godhead? or can we find an explanation less objectionable in the idiom of the language? The latter is what we propose to make out.

82. The evidence that Elohim, though plural in form, is singular in sense, and denotes but one being, when applied to the Supreme Divinity, is indicated by several circumstances worthy of note. In the first place, though the word God is plural, it is joined with verbs in the singular. The only consistent explanation that can be given of this fact, is, that though the *form* of the word is plural, the *sense* is singular; for in Hebrew, as in other languages, the rule is applicable, that "the verb must agree with its nominative case in number, &c."

Again; other words joined with Elohim, and meaning the same thing, ("in apposition with it," as grammarians say,) are found in the singular number. Examples: "I am God, the God of thy fathers." xlvi. 3. The first word for God, (El) is in the singular, while the last, (Elohim) is plural; and yet that both words are alike in sense, no one can doubt. The same term, (El) in the singular, occurs again in xlvi. 3, xxviii. 3, xvii. 1, and is used to denote the same being as the other word. Again; Elohim has the singular pronoun joined with it. The following examples are a few of the many that might be adduced under this head. Shall *I* hide from Abraham that thing which *I* do. *I* know that thou didst this in the integrity of thy heart. By *myself* have I sworn. *I* am the God of Abraham. *I* am the God of Bethel. *I* will go down with thee into Egypt. xviii. 17; xx. 6; xxii. 16; xxvi. 24; xxxi. 13; xlvi. 4.

In all these instances, the singular pronoun refers to Elohim, showing that the latter, as well as the former, is singular in sense,

83. But what shall we do with a few exceptions to the principles last noticed? They are the following: Let *us* make man in *our* image. i. 26. Behold, the man is become as one of *us*. iii. 22. Let *us* go down and there confound their language. xi. 7. From the general use of the singular pronoun in connection with the word God, we would infer that the three exceptions here given, must have some special reasons to justify their use, aside from the plurality of the subject to which they relate. We are certainly not to take them as indicating the rule, when they are so few, and a multitude of examples belong to the other side. They are evidently the exception. On this usage I would just remark, that *Gods*, and not three *persons* in the Godhead, is the subject of the sentence. There can really be no controversy between us and Trinitarians, for the Trinity is no way implied in the language. The only controversy that can exist, is between us and those who would make Polytheism a doctrine of the Bible. In the next place, all these passages are found on the list of what we have denominated rhetorical passages, and must be explained accordingly. It is not a far-fetched conclusion, we think, that the author intended to bring before us the fact that God has his attendants, often alluded to in other parts of the book, who are ever ready to execute his will, and whose presence is here recognized. The language does by no means imply an equality among those included in the term *"us."* The king with his officers, or the master with his servants, may say, let us do this or that, without implying an equality between him and them.

84. If it be replied that, "Let us make man" can have no reference to the angels, since we cannot suppose them capable of doing such a work, we answer, that they are not said to have done this work; but it is immediately added, that *God* made man in *his* own image. If, again, it be said, that Adam and Eve were encouraged to expect they would become as Gods, knowing good and evil, and that the declaration afterwards, "the man has become as one of us," has the same reference, and applies to the Gods, and not to his messengers, we would respond, by referring to passages where angels, and even men, are called Gods in the Bible. See even in Genesis, xvi. 10, 7, 9, 11, 13; xxi. 17; xxii. 15; xxiv. 7; xxxi. 13; xlviii. 15, 16, l. 19.

85. Another particular ought to be noticed in connection with the word God in the plural form. It is this: How can we know when to give a *plural* sense to the term, since the *form* does not determine this? We answer, that the context and circumstances of the passage must decide this question. Hence, the translators make the serpent to say, "Ye shall be as Gods," iii. 5, either because the statement afterwards, "the man has become as one of us," seemed to require it, or because they thought it more suitable that the serpent should speak as a Pagan, than as a true believer in one God. So in regard to Laban's gods; they are expressly called images; and hence, in this case, it was obvious that Elohim was to be understood in the plural. xxxi. 30; xxxi. 19, 34, 35; xxxv. 2.

86. In these passages the translators have been guided by circumstances, and have given the true rendering. Why they have not been equally consistent in some other instances, I cannot say. Why, for instance, should they in one breath, make Laban to have his *gods*, and in the next, make him speak as if he believed in one Supreme divinity like the Hebrews? See xxx. 27; xxxi. 29, 50, 53; xxiv. 50. Why, too, did they make the Philistine king, and the king of Egypt, use the language of the patriarchs? See xxi. 22, 23; xxvi. 28; xli. 38; xliii. 23. And why make Joseph in Egypt, while personating the ruler of that country, speak like a Hebrew, and not like an Egyptian? xliii. 29. Or are we to believe that the Syrians, the Philistines, and the Egyptians, were true Theists, like the Hebrews, and not Polytheists and idolators? If they were the former, then the translation is right; but if the latter, as we suppose true, then the translation is wrong.

87. We will add one thing more respecting the use of Elohim in the plural. It is, that the same usage prevails, to some extent, with other words. The word "heaven" is in the plural; (or as the vowel points make it, in the dual;) and so is the word "face," and "mountain," and "life." So is "Lord," as applied to Potiphar, and to Pharaoh, and to Joseph. See i. 1; viii. 5; xxiii. 1; xxv. 7, 17; xxxix. 20; xl. 1; xlii. 30, 32, &c., &c. On the other hand, the singular is often used for the plural. That is the case with "day," "year," "man," &c. v. 5; viii. 5; xxxiii. 1. This usage, in either case, seldom occasions any ambiguity, as the connection generally shows the sense intended, with sufficient clearness. We think the same remark will apply to Elohim.

SECTION II. — Bara, Create.

88. The word *create* has occasioned no little discussion among theologians, some claiming that this word means to *produce from nothing*, and others regarding the word as meaning no more than to *make* or *form*. It is very certain that these words (*create, make, form,*) are used interchangeably, and seem to be synonymous. The following examples will make this obvious:

Compare i. 1 with ii. 2. In the one it is said, God *created* the heavens and the earth; and in the other, that on the seventh day God ended the work which he had *made*. Ch. ii. 4, brings both words together as follows: These are the generations of the heavens and the earth, when they were *created*, in the day that the Lord *made* the earth and the heavens. Compare i. 21 with i. 25. The first reads thus: And God *created* great whales, and every living thing that moveth. The last says: God *made* the beasts of the earth, &c. Compare, again, i. 26 with i. 27. And God said, Let us *make* man. So God *created* man. Add to this, ii. 7. And the Lord *formed* man of the dust of the ground.

89. Add to the above usage, the following fact: It is said, God created great whales; and it is then said, the waters brought them forth; a plain indication that the materials of which they were composed, existed in the waters prior to their conversion into living and moving forms. So God made the beasts of the earth; that is, the earth brought forth the living creature. God *made* man; that is, he *formed* him of the dust of the earth. Create, then, does not mean to *produce from nothing*, but to produce from something — to form, or make, from pre-existing materials.

It is said that some of the old Jewish Rabbis found evidence of the production of the earth from nothing, in the use of a little Hebrew word (eth,) that precedes the word "heaven" and the word "earth" in the first verse of the Bible. But as this word is used in thousands of instances when no such idea can be conjectured, the evidence is entirely unreliable. Indeed, no respectable scholar, at the present day, will venture his reputation on such a pretence.

90. There is one passage relating to the creation of the world, from which a much more reasonable argument has been deduced; but we doubt not that a knowledge of the idiom of the language, would place this argument, with the rest, as equally unsatisfactory. It is ii. 3. "And God blessed the seventh day, and sanctified it, because that in it he had rested from all his work, which God *created and made.*" The meaning is thought to be, that God first *created* the world, and then *made* it; that is, he produced the materials from nothing, and then made the world, or formed it from them. A more literal rendering of the passage, is thought to convey this idea still more clearly. "God created, to make" is literal. We reply, that this language is a Hebrew idiom, and means no more than one of these words alone would do. The same thing, precisely, is expressed more than once in the immediate connection, in the use of only one of these words. God ended his work which he had made. God rested from all his work which he had made. Does the next verse express anything more than this, when it is said that God rested from all his work which he created to make? Evidently not. Let it be noticed farther, that the same form is used with reference to other things. The dove sent forth by Noah, to see if the waters were abated, "went forth to go." viii. 7. Abram "went to go." xii. 9. Such is a literal rendering. Can any one suppose that more is meant than that the dove went forth from the ark, and that Abram went from one place to the other? "Created to make," is precisely like these examples, and means simply *created,* or what is the same thing, *made.*

SECTION III.—Rhua, Nephish.

91. The words *soul* and *spirit* deserve some attention, under the head of Criticism. There are two Hebrew words, *Rhua* and *Nephish*, that ought to be noticed in this place. One is rendered *spirit*, and the other *soul*, though other renderings sometimes occur, as will be seen. There is no method of judging the meaning of words, so reliable as to ascertain their usage. Indeed, this the only reliable method. The origin of words is not to be depended upon; for words may have a primitive signification, quite different from their meaning afterwards acquired; and if we interpret their later usage by their earlier and primitive sense, we shall be led into an error. Lexicographers are not reliable; for if they make up their definitions from any other source than usage, they will certainly lead us astray; and if this is to them the only safe resort, it is so to us; and, indeed, this is the only way we can test the accuracy of their definitions.

92. We propose to collate the passages where these two terms occur, and deduce from them their significations. These passages may be classified as follows:

1. Nephish is used with reference to animals. It is rendered "creature" in the following places: i. 20, 21, 24; ii. 19; ix. 10, 12, 15, 16. In i. 30 it is joined with another word, and rendered "life."

2. It is applied to animals and men, and has the sense of natural life, and is translated *life*. The flesh with the life thereof. Your blood of your lives. Will I require the life of man. Escape for thy life. Saving my life. My life is preserved. His life is bound up in the lad's life. ix. 4, 5; xix. 17, 19; xxxii. 30; xliv. 30.

3. It is rendered *soul* in the following places, where *life* would be equally correct. My soul shall live; meaning my life shall be preserved. Her soul was departing. xii. 13; xxxv. 18.

4. It is rendered *soul*, and denotes simply the *person*. Man became a living soul; ii. 7, a living person or being, a living creature; the same as other living

creatures mentioned in the passages given in No. 1. This passage contains no intimation of man's pre-eminence over the beasts, as the same term, precisely, is applied to both. Man's pre-eminence is taught in i. 26, 27, where he is said to be created in the image of God, a thing not affirmed of any other creatures. Again; the souls they had gotten in Haran. xii. 5. That soul shall be cut off from his people. xvii. 14. See also, xlvi. 15, 18, 22, 25, 26, 27.

5. It is rendered *person*, and means the same as the above. All the persons of his house. Give me the persons. xiv. 21; xxxvi. 6.

6. It is rendered *soul*, and means the same as *I*, or some other personal pronoun. That my soul may bless thee. That I may bless thee, is the evident meaning. The following may, perhaps, be ranked under this head. His soul (he) clave unto Dinah. The soul of my son (simply my son,) longeth for your daughter. xxvii. 4; xxxiv. 3. See also, xxvii. 19, 25, 31. The term occurs in xxxvii. 21, and is not translated; but an equivalent is employed in its place. Let us not kill him. Let us not take his *life*. In sense this passage ranks under No. 2.

7. It is once rendered *mind*. If it be your mind, that I should bury my dead. xxiii. 8. It seems to have the same meaning in xlii. 21. When we saw the anguish of his soul; though this may, perhaps, rank under No. 4, and be rendered "when we saw *his* anguish."

93. It is a somewhat remarkable circumstance, that though this word is translated soul several times, it does in no instance, denote precisely what we mean by that term at the present day. The passage where it is rendered *mind*, comes the nearest to this idea; but the most that can be affirmed of this place, is, that a single action of the mind or soul is intended. The soul, as denoting a distinct substance, and constituting a part of man that is separate from his body,

and destined to immortality, is not had in view. So the soul of Shechem longed for Dinah; but the affections only can be had in view, and no one can suppose any reference to our higher nature.

When it is said of Rachel, that her soul departed, it would suit our modern usage quite well to suppose the soul, or spirit, to be referred to, and that its exit from the body is had in view; but to give this construction to the language, would be opposed to all the usage of that age; while the rendering, "her life departed," has abundant usage to support it. When it is said, that the soul of Isaac blessed his sons, we may put upon that expression a construction analagous to modern usage, and say that the soul of the patriarch invoked a blessing on his sons; but this would evidently be a forced construction, and contrary to prevailing usage at that time. Isaac blessed his sons, is all the idea contained in this passage. His soul simply means he or himself.

94. The other word we propose to discuss, is, perhaps, equally unsatisfactory, as denoting what we call the immortal part of our nature. It is used as follows:

1. To denote the spirit of God. The spirit of God moved upon the face of the waters. My spirit shall not always strive with man. In whom the spirit of God is. i. 2; vi. 3; xli. 38. The meaning here cannot be mistaken. The spirit of God denotes God himself.

2. It is rendered "breath" in the following places, and refers to the breath of life that belongs to all living creatures. It would not be improper to translate all such instances the "spirit of life," or "living spirit;" and it is certain the Bible speaks of the spirit of the beast, as well as of man. vi. 17; vii. 15, 22.

3. It occurs in the phrase "*cool* of the day," iii. 8, and is rendered *wind* in viii. 1.

4. The word is used with reference to men, and seems to denote, and perhaps does denote, the human soul. His spirit was troubled. His spirit revived. A grief of mind unto Isaac. xli. 8; xlv. 27; xxvi. 35.

95. That the same term which denotes the human soul, should, at the same time, have the meaning of "breath," or "wind," may be regarded as a somewhat singular circumstance. We suggest, as a reason for this, that the ancients may have supposed some analogy between the two things; and hence, the same word came to denote them both. But if we can see no analogy from which we can trace the different meanings of this word, there is still another fact that will help us to understand this subject. There is, in the Hebrew language, as there is in every other language, and not less in our own than others, this peculiarity, that the same word is used in senses exceedingly diverse from each other. The explanation is this: that two or more things chanced to be called by the same name, though having no necessary relation to each other. A score of instances, from the book of Genesis, could be adduced to illustrate this peculiarity. The word rendered "naked" in ii. 25, is rendered "subtil" in the very next verse; and in both places the translation seems correct, though we can see no relation which the one word has to the other. We think the words are separate and distinct, as much as though composed of different letters.

The word "repent," in vi. 6, is "comfort" in v. 29; and we can see no error in the translation in either passage, and we conclude that what appears to be the same word, is not the same. The words, though alike in form, are unlike in sense; and are, in fact, different and distinct words.

The word "kneel," applied to the kneeling of camels at the well, xxiv. 11, is the same word that is rendered "bless" in many other passages; nor is it necessary to trace any relation between the two words. They are probably not related. As many different persons are called by the same name, so are many different things, not from any real or supposed resemblance, but merely from accident.

96. These examples are sufficient; and they show that the different meanings of the word "spirit" may be accounted for, independent of any analogy between the things denoted by that term. At the same time, they set aside the argument sometimes used, that, as "spirit" has the sense of breath, or wind, and is, indeed, applied to beasts as well as men, therefore there is no evidence that man has a soul more than other animals. We have just shown, that "spirit" in the one case, may have no relation to "spirit" in the other. The words are really not the same, though alike in form; and if this be so, no argument can be drawn from their usage, that shall bring man down to the level of the beast.

97. In conclusion, I would remark, that in some instances, the translators have made the writer to have used the word "ghost," where there is nothing to correspond with it in the original. This is true of all those instances where persons are said, at their death, to give up the ghost. xxv. 8; xxv. 17; xxxv. 29; xlix. 33. These passages speak of the death of Abraham, Ishmael, Isaac, and Jacob. That these persons *expired* is all that is intended; and though they did give up the ghost, as we are accustomed to speak, yet we ought not to make the writer use our phraseology, when he really did no such thing. The translation here is calculated to mislead us.

SECTION IV.—OLIM.

98. The word *Olim* is generally translated *everlasting* and *forever*. It may be classed under the following heads:—

1. It denotes past time. *Of old*, men of renown. vi. 4.
2. Applied to the covenant with Noah. This is the token of the covenant . . . . . . for *perpetual* generations. That I may remember the *everlasting* covenant. ix. 12, 16.
3. Applied to the covenant with Abraham. An *everlasting* covenant. xvii. 7, 13, 19.
4. The possession of Canaan. All the land which thou seest, to thee will I give it, and to thy seed *forever*. An *everlasting* possession. xiii. 15; xvii. 8; xlviii. 4.
5. The striving of God's spirit. My spirit shall not *always* strive with man. vi. 3.
6. Moral life of Adam. And live *forever*. iii. 22.
7. To God. The *everlasting* God. xxi. 33.

99. The term here used was employed to denote time, and generally duration: but it plainly denotes duration of various extent. The covenant with Noah, was doubtless to last as long as the world should stand; for the explanation given at the time, makes this obvious. The covenant with Abraham was to last as long as the Jews remained God's peculiar people. It was to co-exist with the everlasting possession of Canaan, as both are spoken of in the same connection, and are limited by the same term. The everlasting God, is an expression that gives to the word everlasting its strongest significance. Still, if we had no evidence of his perpetual being, but the use of this term, the proof of his eternity would be quite unsatisfactory. The conclusion to which we come in respect to this word, is, that the duration denoted by it, must be determined, not by the word itself, but by other circumstances connected with it; and this conclusion, we suspect, will be rendered still more certain by reference to other parts of the Bible, which, however, does not come within our present purpose.

SECTION V.—Sheol.

100. The word *sheol* is rendered *grave*. I will go down into the grave to my son, mourning. Then shall ye bring down my gray hairs with sorrow to the grave. Thy servants shall bring down the gray hairs of thy servant, our father, with sorrow to the grave. xxxvii. 35; xlii. 38; xliv. 31.

We have the authority of some forty-seven of the wise men of England, in the days of King James, the First, that the word sheol here means the grave. We are disposed to agree with them; for the usage of the word, the only rightful authority, shows this to be a just conclusion.

True, the term occurs in this book but few times, and these few instances do not develop very many circumstances fitted to define the meaning with precision. But all that *is* said, favors this interpretation. It is very natural and proper to associate the gray hairs of the patriarch, with the grave, or resting place of the dead. And it is certain that the last passage quoted, is spoken with the single reference to the patriarch's death. With its preceding connection it reads thus: Now, therefore, when I come to thy servant, my father, and the lad be not with us, (seeing that his life is bound up in the lad's life,) it shall come to pass, when he seeth that the lad is not with us, that he will die; and thy servants shall bring down the gray hairs of thy servant, our father, with sorrow to the grave. Another circumstance, showing that sheol has properly the meaning of grave, is, that it is spoken of as *below* us. Jacob expected to go *down* to the grave. His son Judah speaks in the same way; he would bring *down* the gray hairs of his father to the grave.

101. To this view, two objections have been offered. One is, that Joseph (when Jacob said he would go down to sheol, to his son, mourning,) was supposed to be torn in pieces by wild beasts, and could not be regarded as properly in the grave. Jacob, therefore, could not have expected to go to his son in the grave, as his son was not there. We reply, that the passage does not necessarily imply that Joseph was in the grave. Doubtless the patriarch regarded his son as having been "gathered to his people," or to his fathers, as the phrase then was; but he knew he could go to him only through death; and this last is the idea, and the only idea, he intended to express. The patriarch expected to go down, mourning, to the grave, and *thereby*, to go to his son in the spiritual state.

102. There is another objection against regarding sheol as the grave. It is this: The Hebrews had another word for grave, and did not need sheol for this purpose. This objection has no force. It is very common to have more than one name for the same thing in all languages. The word "sheol," and the word "keber," (the other word referred to,) denote substantially the same thing; though, like synonymous words in other languages, their respective usage may not be precisely alike. The difference between them seems to be mainly, if not entirely, this: that while sheol denotes the grave in general, keber is more commonly applied to some particular burial place. As an illustration: Jacob expresses his expectation to go down to the grave. When he died, he *did* go down to the grave, as he expected. This was sheol. Jacob, however, was buried, by his request, in the cave at Hebron. This was keber. The burial place at

Hebron, is always called keber; but the grave, with a general and indefinite reference, is denoted by sheol.

103. There are two interpretations of sheol, differing from the one given in the common version. One is, that it denotes a place of departed spirits; and another, that it denotes a place of future punishment. Certainly the last will not be insisted on in the instances now under examination; for that would be to consign Joseph to such a place, and to represent the venerable Jacob as expecting the same destiny. That a place of spirits is had in view, has quite as little to sanction it. It is not consistent to associate a place of spirits with gray hairs, nor to locate it beneath us. And it is certain that no such idea is supported by its usage. We read, indeed, of departed spirits, (if angels are such, as is commonly believed,) but their residence is heaven above us, not sheol, beneath. And I would respectfully suggest, that if heaven is now, or ever is to be, a place of spirits, that it may have been such in the days of the patriarchs.

The patriarchs are said to be gathered to their fathers, or to their people, xv. 15; xxv. 8, 17; xxxv. 29; xlix. 29, 33; language which we understand to imply a place of departed spirits, and a re-union in the other world; but as to the *name* of that place, we are left to inference. That it is heaven, as above suggested, seems the best sustained, if, indeed, we may not regard it as a clearly revealed fact. Of course, what is here said, relates only to the teachings of the book of Genesis, and not to what we might gather from other parts of the Bible.

SECTION VI.—MALAK.

104. The term *malak*, generally rendered *angel*, claims our attention. The term refers, first, to spiritual beings, and second, to men.

1. *To spiritual beings.*

The "angel of the Lord," is a phrase that occurs

four different times in a brief passage relating to Hagar in the wilderness. On another occasion, the angel of God called to Hagar out of heaven. So the angel of the Lord called unto Abraham, as he was about to slay his son. Isaac told his servant that God would send his angel before him. Jacob, in his dream, saw the angels of the Lord. The angels of God met Jacob. In his blessing upon the sons of Joseph, he has this language: The angel which redeemed me from all evil, bless the lads. xvi. 7, 9, 10, 11; xxi. 17; xxii. 11, 15; xxiv. 7; (see verse 40,) xxviii. 12; xxxi. 11; xxxii. 1; xlviii. 16.

105. That the angels here referred to were spiritual beings, is certain from what is said of them. They are called angels of the Lord. They speak from heaven. They are invested with great authority. Hence, the angel said to Hagar: I will multiply thy seed exceedingly; and it is added, that she called the name of the *Lord* that spake unto her: Thou *God* seest me. The angel that appeared to her on another occasion, uses a similar expression; "I will make him a great nation." xxi. 18. The language of the angel to Abraham, on Mount Moriah, indicates a similar authority. The dream of Jacob shows the office of the angels, and the work they perform. That dream speaks of a ladder reaching from earth to heaven. It represents God as standing at the top of the ladder, and the angels ascending and descending upon it, thus showing that it is through the mission of angels, that his administration, having in view the interests of man, is carried on. The angel that spake to Jacob on another occasion, assumes to say, I am the God of Bethel, &c., xxxi. 11, 12, 13. So the angel that was to bless the sons of Joseph, was plainly a superhuman being.

106. It has been observed, by some interpreters, that the word "angel" is not so much the name of a class of beings, as it is the name of an office. I understand it to be the name of both. It is the name of an office, and denotes persons sent on a mission; and in this sense, it applies as well to men as to superior beings, and is, indeed, applicable to inanimate objects that are made the agents of the Divine pleasure. But it is the name of a class of beings, as well as the office they fill; (applied to them, it may be, on account of their office,) and hence, they are ordinarily spoken of as angels, as much as God is spoken of as God, or men as men.

2. *Applied to men.*

107. Jacob sent *messengers* before him to Esau. And the *messengers* returned to Jacob. xxxii. 3, 6. That human beings are here meant, no one will doubt. There is an another instance of the same usage, as we understand the passage, about which there will not be a perfect agreement. We refer to the angels that came to Sodom, and were entertained by Lot. xix. 1. Most persons, we suppose, regard these angels as spiritual beings, having put on the form of men for this particular occasion. But the circumstances convince us that the prevailing notion is incorrect. The translators probably believed them spirits, else they would not have rendered the word angels, and in the other case, mentioned above, rendered it messengers. But it should be observed, that these persons are expressly called *men;* xix. 10, 12, 16; that they ate, and talked, and put forth physical strength, like men; and the usual characteristics given to angels, are mostly withheld from them. They did not come from heaven; they did not speak from heaven. They are not called angels of the Lord. They did not *appear* to Lot, as the term is, in many other places. They came to Sodom at the close of the day, and were entertained by the hospitable Lot. If they were invested with miraculous power, and with a foresight of the future, the same is true of the prophets, who are quite distinct from angels.

108. We are no less disposed to dissent from the common opinion, which makes angels of the men that came to Abraham as he sat in his tent door, and announced the birth of Isaac and the overthrow of Sodom. xviii. 1. The persons here spoken of, as in the other passage, are called men; and we are not authorized to depart from the record.

The whole scene presented in that passage, is, without doubt, a vision; and we have treated it as such in another place; but this circumstance does in no way conflict with the view we take. It is quite as fit that men should be seen in a vision, as that angels should be.

In the light of these remarks, we may understand better than is generally done, what is said of the conflict of Jacob with some unknown person, on his return from Padan Aram. It is said that Jacob was left alone; and there wrestled a *man*, with him until the breaking of the day. xxxii. 24. Observe, the person who wrestled with Jacob, is called a *man;* but the circumstances indicate that it was a man seen in a vision or dream.

CHAPTER III.

ARCHÆOLOGY.

Contents:—Birth and Birthright; Marriage, Death and Burial; Dress and Ornaments; Habitations; Domestic Utensils; Occupations; Food; Domestic Animals; Wild Animals; Patriarchal Wealth; Trade and Commerce; Oaths and Contracts; Wars; Government; Servitude; Oriental Hospitality; Salutations; The Arts; Weights and Measures; Religion.

109. Archæology treats of the customs and institutions of the ancients, including their domestic and social habits, occupations, modes of life, government, religion, &c. It is a department of knowledge that is exceedingly interesting as illustrating the difference between men who lived in the early age of the world, when the arts and refinements of life were but little understood, and men of more modern times, when education, and all the arts and institutions of civilized society are carried to a high degree of perfection. And as there are no people with whose customs and institutions we are at all acquainted, in the earliest period of their history, that date so far back in the past as the Hebrews; so there are no people whose primitive customs can excite a greater interest. Add to this, that a Divine Revelation and a Divine Saviour are to be traced back to this people, and our interest in them will be greatly augmented.

Besides, we ought not to overlook the fact, that a true interpretation of the Scriptures is to be arrived at by a knowledge of the customs of the ancient Hebrews, with more certainty, than by any other means, —a consideration that renders this branch of knowledge more important than most any other within the reach of human attainment.

SECTION I.— Birth and Birthright.

110. One thing will have been observed, even by the casual reader of the book of Genesis, as well as many other parts of the Bible, namely: that what we call *modesty*, at the present day, and in our country, was little known among the cotemporaries of the patriarchs. There is very good reason for this, though, unfortunately, all do not understand the reason; for if they did, they would not bring, as an objection to the book, a circumstance that rightly appreciated, is an argument in its favor.

That the ancients were not void of modesty, is indicated by several circumstances, alluded to in the book; but it is certain that the principle did not show itself after the modern style, as we had no right to expect that it would. Whether they, or we, should claim the advantage in this particular, is a question we will not take upon ourself to decide. I doubt not that we are quite as much exposed to their criticism, as they are to ours. This matter is controlled entirely by custom; and what is perfectly modest and proper in one community, is quite otherwise in another; nor can we always account for the difference, or give a reason for it. The same diversity exists, more or less, at the present time, among the different nations of the earth, and to some extent among the different circles in the same community.

The freedom of speech, among the ancient Hebrews, in the matter of which we are now speaking, is one plain indication of the antiquity of that people, and of the books where this peculiarity is shown. The fact indicates a primitive state of society, and is one important proof of the integrity and truthfulness of the record in which this characteristic prevails.

111. The book of Genesis contains many passages which prove that the *love of offspring* was a predominant characteristic of that age. It was one of the strongest feelings cherished in those days, by both sexes. How else can we account for Sarah's giving up to the embrace of her husband, her Egyptian handmaid, that she might raise up children by her, as she could have none of her own? It is added, that when the handmaid became a mother, her mistress was despised in her eyes. With what satisfaction did Leah offset her fruitfulness against the beauty of her sister. And with what unfeigned earnestness did Isaac pray that Rebekah might have a son. And when she left her father's house to become the wife of Isaac, one clause in the benediction then pronounced upon her, was, that she might be the mother of thousands of millions.

Again; it was one of the particulars embraced in the promise to Abraham, Isaac, and Jacob, that their seed should be as the stars of heaven, for multitude, and as the sands upon the sea shore. xvi. 1–4; xxix. 31–35; xxx. 9–13; xxv. 21; xxiv. 60.

If we seek for a natural reason for this feeling, we may find it partly in the condition of society at that time. The more numerous a family or tribe, the greater their personal security; as each family was a community by itself, and had to depend mainly, for its defence, on the strength of its individual members. Besides, there was a divine command relating to this subject, which they may not have felt themselves at liberty to disregard. i. 22. The existence of a class of females called "midwives," places the ancients before us, in respect to some of their social institutions, to which there seems to be at present a tendency to return. Retracing our steps is sometimes the way to advance. xxxviii. 28.

112. Great importance was, then, attached to being the first-born. It was through the first-born that the lineage was traced, unless special circumstances required a departure from this rule. To the first-born, too, special privileges were given. This was the "birthright" which Esau sold for a mess of pottage. "Thus he despised his birthright." The importance attached to this subject, made particular caution necessary at the birth of twins, that the true first-born might not be mistaken. Hence, the scarlet thread put upon the hand of Zarah at his birth, to distinguish him from his twin brother, Phares. xxv. 33, 34; xxxviii. 28.

113. One circumstance that has some relation to the topic we are now upon, and may, accordingly, be named in connection with it, is but once mentioned in the book, and then in a very brief and incidental manner. It is said that Abram and Sarah, when Isaac was *weaned*, made a great feast; but whether it was common to celebrate that event in this way, cannot be safely inferred from this single reference. xxi. 8.

SECTION II.—MARRIAGE.

114. The institution of marriage is divine; nor can any reasonable construction be put upon the passage where this subject is referred to for the first time, but such as makes it prohibit the possession of more than one wife. And it is believed that this was the usual understanding of that subject by the patriarchs. Lamech, one of Cain's posterity, is the first mentioned as having disregarded that salutary regulation; and the importance attached to this fact, making it worthy special notice, shows plainly that it was not a common occurrence. ii. 18. iv. 19. Abraham had but one wife; so had Isaac. And though the former had a concubine, under peculiar circumstances and at the suggestion of his wife, that does not seem to be regarded as a violation of the marriage institution. Jacob had two wives, but that was no fault of his, as one was put upon him by fraud; and if he had concubines, he had the best reasons for this that the nature of the case admitted of; and these seem to have been satisfactory. It may be remarked here, that if we would understand the ancients, we must not try them by our standards. We must not make them to have seen with our eyes, or more properly, to have seen with the same light that is shed upon us. If revealed religion has not elevated us above them, what good has it done us?

115. Another thing will attract attention in relation to the marriage customs of the ancients. They married their near relations; nor did they express, or seem to feel, that there was the least impropriety in so doing. Nahor married his niece. Abraham married his half sister; and if we go back to the days of Adam, we know that some of Adam's sons must have been joined in wedlock with their own sisters, as they could, at first have had no others, nor with the light that then prevailed, could they discover any reason against such a union; and indeed, under the circumstances, and in the absence of any divine prohibition, there was no reason against it. xi. 29. xx. 12.

116. And here we may remark an interesting circumstance, showing a harmony in the recorded statements of the book on which our discussions are employed. At first we know that brothers must have married sisters; at least one or more such instances must have occurred. This being so, we the more readily account for a union between near relations at a later day; and it may throw some light on what would otherwise seem incredible in the conduct of the daughters of Lot, when they supposed all the rest of the world to be destroyed, and the only hope of a future race, depended on themselves. They had no divine command to restrain them. They had the union of very near relations, as a not uncommon practice. Their residence in Sodom had not improved their sensibilities; and the mountain cave shut out their crime from all the rest of the world, even if they did not suppose (as the passage seems to indicate) that all the rest of the world were destroyed. xix. 30, 38.

117. It was not anciently necessary that the parties who were to be united in marriage should be previously acquainted. Hence Abraham sent his servant to procure a wife for Isaac, whom he had never before seen. It will be farther observed that the parties themselves had very little to do in the matter. The principal things were attended to by their parents. The case of Abraham, just alluded to, is to the point. So when Shechem, son of Hamor, became enamored of Dinah, the daughter of Jacob, he immediately applied to his father, saying, "Get me this damsel to wife." Judah took a wife for Er, his first born. In this particular there is a remarkable coincidence with the practice of the Aborigines of our own country. It may be a matter of question whether this arrangement, if it existed now, would not be quite as favorable to domestic happiness, as the one that prevails among us. It seems a little inconsistent, that the most important transaction of life, should be put wholly into youthful and inexperienced hands — that the father should allow his son to select a wife, when he would not trust him to buy a horse or a cow. xxiv. 4; xxxiv. 4; xxxviii. 6.

118. Another interesting circumstance connected with ancient marriages, is, that the wife was, in some sense, purchased. Hence the presents given to Rebekah by Abraham's servant, and the "precious things" given to her mother and brother; and the labor of seven years exacted by Laban from Jacob, in consideration of giving him his daughter. Hence, too, the offer of Shechem to give to Jacob any amount he might exact for his daughter, Dinah. xxiv. 22, 30, 53; xxix. 20, xxxiv. 12.

119. Every wife seems to have been furnished with a maid to go with her and to be her special companion and attendant. Sarah had the maid Hagar. Leah had Zilpah, Rachel had Bilhah, Rebekah, too, had her "damsels," among whom Deborah is especially named. xvi. 1; xxix. 24, 29; xxiv. 61; xxxv. 8. When Jacob was married, it is said that Laban, his father-in-law, "gathered together all the men of the place, and made a feast;" which shows that marriage entertainments are very ancient. xxix. 22.

120. It will be observed that the Hebrew patriarchs were exceedingly desirous of avoiding all marriage relations, outside of the family or tribe to which they belonged. Abraham sent far away to procure one of his relations for Isaac, and exacted an oath of his servant that he would not obtain for him a wife of the daughters of Canaan. And when Esau married among the people of the land, it was a great grief to his parents. The language of Rebekah to Isaac, betrays the feeling that prevailed on this subject: — "I am weary of my life because of the daughters of Heth. If Jacob take a wife of the daughters of Heth, such as these which are the daughters of the land, what good shall my life do me." This feeling was at length expressed in the law of the land. xxix. 3; xxvi. 35; xxviii. 8; xxvii. 46.

121. There must have been something very peculiar in the marriage rights of those days, else we shall find it difficult to understand, why Jacob should not have known, at the time, whether it was Leah or Rachel, that shared his marriage bed, the first night of his wedded life. That such customs did exist, as would involve this uncertainty is not, however, a thing to be disbelieved, so different were their customs from ours.

122. The reason of the fraud practiced by Laban on that occasion, viz., "it must not be so done in our country, to give the younger before the firstborn," may be construed as a mere pretence, or it may be understood as indicating the usual custom. But if the last, we need not extend the custom beyond the immediate vicinity of Laban, who, it is well known, resided far away from Canaan, the land of the Hebrews. xxix. 26.

123. The language of Laban to Jacob:—"Fulfil her week, and we will give thee this also, for the service which thou shalt serve me, yet seven other years," may be understood as denoting the "week" during which the wedding feast was continued. It would not be proper to give him another wife, till all the ceremonies of the first wedding had been observed. xxix. 27.

124. A somewhat singular custom existed at that time, that, when a brother died, leaving a wife with no children, the next brother should marry the surviving widow, and the fruit of this new marriage, should be regarded in the same light, as if they had been the product of the first union. xxxviii. 8, 9.

125. The wearing of a veil, by unmarried women, in the presence of their intended, is shown in the case of Rebekah, as she approached Isaac, when about to become his wife. The maid descended from the back of the camel, and placing her veil over her face, went forward to meet her husband. xxiv. 65.

SECTION III.—DEATH AND BURIAL.

126. It is worthy of remark, that, nowhere in the book of Genesis, is there any reference to ill health, save in one single instance. The references that come the nearest to this, do not imply actual disease. Leah was tender-eyed; but this may have no allusion to disease. The patriarchs became blind in their extreme old age. So the infirmity of barrenness was not uncommon. Men died in those days, sometimes prematurely by violence, as Abel did by the hand of Cain; and as they were slain in the battle field; or swept away by some divine judgment, but we can recall no instance where they are said to have died of disease. The sickness of Israel, just before his death, xlviii. 1, was evidently nothing more than the infirmity of old age, as life gradually faded away, and the lamp was about to become extinct.

127. How the dead body was prepared for burial, in ordinary cases, we are not informed. In Egypt it was customary to embalm the body and place it in a coffin. At least, this was done with persons of distinction. But Egypt had its own usages, which must not be produced as those of Canaan or the patriarchs, l. 26. The place of burial in Canaan was usually a natural cave. Such was the cave of Machpelah which Abraham bought of the sons of Heth. There Abraham was himself buried, and Sarah, his wife. There too were buried Isaac and Rebekah, and there Jacob buried Leah. Rachel was buried near Bethlehem, and a pillar was placed over her grave, which remained there a long time. Deborah, Rebekah's nurse, was buried under an oak near Bethel. xxiii. 16; xlix. 31; xxxv. 19, 20.

128. The Hebrews, like others, had a strong desire to be buried in their own land. Hence Israel exacted an oath of Joseph that he would carry him back to the land of Canaan, and bury him with Abraham, and Isaac, in the sacred cave near Hebron; and this oath was faithfully executed. Joseph, too, was embalmed, and kept in Egypt, till the removal of the children of Israel from that country. xlvii. 29; l. 25, 26.

129. Mourning for the dead is sometimes mentioned. Abraham mourned for Sarah; but what ceremonies were observed we are not informed. The Egyptians mourned "threescore and ten days" for Israel, such being their custom. And when the procession that attended the body of that patriarch from Egypt to Canaan, had passed into that land they mourned seven days, that being, perhaps the patriarchal custom. The language, "they made a mourning," shows that the allusion is not to the exercise of grief, but to certain funeral ceremonies. It appears that widows were accustomed to wear a peculiar dress, to indicate their widowhood. Hence it is said of Tamar, that she "put off her widow's garments." xxiii. 2; l. 3, 10; xxxviii. 14.

SECTION IV.—Dress and Ornaments.

130. The necessity of dress, became obvious even to our first parents; hence they sewed fig leaves together to make themselves aprons; hence, too, they were afterwards supplied with coats of skin. Allusion is made to the garments of Noah; but whether they were made of skin or other material, does not appear. Other allusions are equally indefinite. The coat of many colors, given to Joseph, was evidently unusual; but more than this cannot be ascertained. Sackcloth, worn on occasions of mourning, was, doubtless, something manufactured; but of what material is left wholly to conjecture. It took its name, *sack* cloth from the use commonly made of it. It is reasonable to conclude that they had something finer for ordinary wear. xxxvii. 34.

The form of their clothing is not less uncertain, than the material of which it was made. There must have been something peculiar in the widow's garments before alluded to. That females wore veils, under certain circumstances, we know. That the garment of Joseph, left in the hands of his mistress was a loose robe, easily parted with, is a plain inference from the circumstances of the case. The shoe-lachet, once mentioned, would imply the use of shoes. but the frequent washing of the feet, mentioned in the book, makes it evident that the shoes, worn in those days, were but an imperfect protection. Necessity would suggest the propriety of a change of garments; and hence we read of such in several places. xxxviii. 14; xxiv. 65; xxxviii. 14; xxxix. 12, 15; xiv. 23; xli. 14; xlv. 22.

131. The Hebrews were not insensible to the claims of beauty: and they sought to add the use of ornaments to their natural charms. The signet, staff and bracelet of Judah, are well known as associated with his personal degradation. Ear-rings and bracelets were given to Rebekah; so also were "jewels of silver and jewels of gold." Other "precious things" were given to her mother and brother, which may have been ornaments, or they may have been things of more substantial value. xxxviii. 18, 25; xxiv. 30, 53.

Fine linen, worn in Egypt, was for beauty, as well as for comfort, no doubt. The ring of Pharaoh, given to Joseph as a badge of his authority, was as much an ornament, as a mark of distinction. The gold neck-chain has the same significance. It must be added, however, that the refinements and luxuries of Egypt, must not be referred to the shepherds of Canaan. It is well to mark the difference in the two countries, as we read the sacred narrative. xli. 42.

As the Egyptians and Hebrews, however, had the same period of history, according to the Mosaic account, it may not be easy to account for the difference. It is perhaps to be attributed mainly to the exceeding fruitfulness of Egypt, and the greater permanency of the people. A nomad life is more favorable to simplicity and integrity, than it is to social cultivation and refinement.

SECTION V.—HABITATIONS.

132. Jabal was the father of such as dwell in tents and have cattle. From the earliest time, therefore, the keeping of flocks and herds was a prominent occupation; and this occupation did not admit of permanent dwellings. The shepherds, therefore, dwelt in tents, which they carried from place to place, as occasion required. And even when they remained in the same locality several years, as they sometimes did, they did not, on that account, relinquish their tents to adopt more permanent habitations. In the cities of Canaan, (which were inconsiderable villages) the people lived in houses, which, by the references to them, are plainly distinguished from the tents of the country. The references to Lot's house in Sodom, are a plain illustration of what is here stated. The strife between him and the men of Sodom, at the door of his house, shows that it was comparatively a permanent and substantial structure. The city itself seems to have been surrounded by a wall, as an allusion to the gate of the city plainly shows. iv. 20; xix. 6, 10. It would seem that men and women, not excepting husbands and wives, occupied separate tents. xxiv. 67; xxxi. 33. It is obvious that the structures of Egypt, the prison, the house of Pharaoh, the house of Potiphar and of Joseph, were more spacious and substantial than any alluded to in Palestine.

4*

SECTION VI.—Domestic Utensils.

133. The knife that Abraham took with him, with the wood for a burnt offering, was not originally intended for any such purpose as he then had in view. It would be safe to regard it as one of the domestic utensils of those days. The instrument, with which, on the same occasion, he "clave the wood for a burnt offering," may be reckoned as another; though its existence is learned only by implication. The pitcher that was used to draw water, was another domestic utensil, and probably combined the advantages both of a bucket and a pitcher, and was more like the former than the latter. The bottle and its use, are indicated by the provision that Abraham made for Hagar, as he sent her away from his house. Carrying it on the shoulder would lead us to infer that it was quite different in form from the bottles of our day; and the art required in making our bottles was not known in those ancient times. xxii. 6; xxiv. 14.

134. Out-door utensils, as well as in-door, were no doubt much more numerous than the allusions would lead us to infer; but what they were, except so far as they are mentioned or implied, we do not assume to say. For hunting they made use of the bow and quiver. For carrying their grain they had sacks. They had watering troughs, out of which their cattle could drink. They sheared their sheep, and of course they had some instrument to do it with. Seeing a ladder in a vision, would imply its existence as a reality. They cut their grain, and must have had something to cut it with, and some mode of threshing and cleaning it. The cup of the butler in Egypt, and the basket of the baker, belong to the refinements of that country, and may have no representatives in the grazing districts of Canaan. xxvii. 3; xlii. 25; xxiv. 20; xxxviii. 12; xxviii. 12; xxxvii. 7; xl. 11, 16.

135. We have mentioned some implements that are known to have existed by implication, as well as those expressly named. Many more may be noticed. Having tents and houses, the Hebrews must have had some implements for constructing them. Milking their kine and their goats, they must have had some vessel for containing the milk. Building the gates of cities, would require some mechanical tools to work with.

But here I may correct a popular error. Some writers make Sodom (a city often referred to,) to have been a city of great magnificence, with mighty works of art, and surrounded by imposing walls of stone. Some have pretended that relics of lofty temples, and other magnificent structures, have been found in the vicinity of the Dead Sea, that once belonged to the doomed city, and are now the monuments of the divine wrath that occasioned its overthrow. It is hardly necessary to say that such a representation betrays vast ignorance of the times in which Sodom was destroyed, and is contradicted by all the facts mentioned in Genesis having any bearing on this subject.

SECTION VII.—Occupation.

136. Man was originally intended for cultivating the earth. This was one object of his creation. Hence in all ages past, and in all ages to come, this has been, and must be, his principal dependence for physical support. When Adam was placed in the garden of Eden, he was instructed to keep it and dress it. And when he was sent forth from the garden, he was to gain his bread by tilling the ground. Cain is mentioned as a tiller of the ground. Of Noah it is said, " This same shall comfort us concerning our work, and the toil of our hands, because of the ground which the Lord hath cursed." It is plain, therefore, that, from Adam to Noah, tillage had been, as it must of necessity be, a principal occupation. When the flood was over, a gracious promise was given to the world, that seed time and harvest should not cease till the end of time, a farther evidence that tillage was to be as perpetual as the world. i. 28; ii. 15; iii. 23; iv. 2; v. 29; viii. 22.

137. The first instance of tillage after the flood was that of Noah, who planted a vineyard and drank of the wine thereof. The next is that of Isaac, who sowed the ground in the land of the Philistines, and received an hundred fold that year. The allusion to the "wheat harvest" shows that this was one of the occupations of the patriarchs, in the time of Jacob. Joseph's dream, in which he supposes himself to be binding sheaves in the field, is of the same import. The threshing floor of Atad implies the same occupation and the mode of making it available. The grain produced in Egypt by which the people were supported during seven years of famine, is a proof not only that agriculture was one of the occupations of that people, but that the country was one of uncommon fruitfulness, as it has always been from that day to this. ix. 21; xxvi. 12; xxx. 14; xxxvii. 7; l. 10.

138. The patriarchs not only occupied themselves with the cultivation of the ground, but with the keeping of flocks and herds. Abel was a keeper of sheep. Jabal was the father of such as dwell in tents and have cattle. Tents and cattle are here associated, because they were in fact inseparable. He who had the one dwelt in the other. As water was not abundant in that country, the digging of wells requiring a good deal of labor, became a matter of necessity; and these being a valuable possession, were not unfrequently the occasion of strife among the herdsmen. The herdsmen of Abram and Lot strove. Through envy the Philistines stopped up the wells that were dug in the days of Abram; and when Isaac was in that country, he caused them to be opened, and called them by the names they had borne at first. A strife between Isaac and the herdsmen of Gerar, is mentioned in the same connection; and the wells were named Esek and Sitnah with reference to this circumstance. Another, about which they strove not, he named Rehoboth. It may be added, that the naming of wells shows the importance attached to them at that time. iv. 2, 20; xiii. 7; xxvi. 18, 20, 21, 22.

139. The immediate care of the flocks and herds was frequently, perhaps generally, given into the hands of females. At least, the business of watering them, which was done once or more every day, was attended to by them. xxiv. 11; xxix. 7—10.

140. A man's prosperity, in those days, was estimated mainly by the increase in the number of his cattle, and the man who had large flocks and herds, gained distinction more by this circumstance, than by any other. xxx. 30, 43; xxvi. 14.

SECTION VIII.—Food.

141. The occupation of the patriarchs, will at once suggest their mode of living, and the food they ate. "Every herb bearing seed, and fruit tree bearing fruit," was originally given to man for food. He was furthermore to have dominion over the beasts of the field, and the fowls of the air, and the fishes of the sea, evidently with the intention of his deriving a part of his subsistence from that source. Animal, as well as vegetable food, was directly allowed after the flood, and was allowed by implication before. A few references will bring to view different kinds of both. The food prepared by Abraham for the men that appeared to him in Mamre, consisted of fine meal, made into cakes and baked upon the hearth; also a fatted calf, tender and good; and butter and milk. i. 29; ix. 2; xviii. 6, 7. Unleavened bread was provided by Lot for the messengers that came to him at Sodom. Bread and a bottle of water were given to Hagar, as she left the abode of her mistress. Pottage is mentioned as that for which Esau sold his birthright. Savory meat, made of the flesh of wild animals, was a favorite dish with Isaac in his old age. It was a kind of meat that could be imitated by a skilful hand. " Plenty of corn and wine," are among the blessings invoked upon Jacob by his aged father. " Mandrakes," about which Rachel and Leah had some altercation, were probably not food but medicine; intended perhaps to remove an infirmity of which Rachel was afflicted at that time. The Ishmaelites of Gilead carried into Egypt " spicery, balm and myrrh." These were luxuries not indulged in at home, but were such as found a ready market in Egypt, another evidence that civilization and luxury go hand in hand. Another passage speaks of " a little balm, and a little honey, spices and myrrh, nuts and almonds," being sent as a present to Joseph in Egypt. xix. 3 ; xxi. 14; xxv. 29, 34; xxvii. 4, 9, 28 ; xxx. 22 ; xxxvii. 25 ; xliii. 11.

142. No mention is made of any kind of drink but water and wine. Noah drank wine; so did Lot. And wine was brought forth to Abraham by Melchizedek, as the former returned from the slaughter of the kings. So wine as well as corn were among the blessings invoked upon Jacob by his aged father. ix. 21; xix. 32; xiv. 18.

SECTION IX.—Domestic Animals.

143. The following domestic animals are alluded to in the book of Genesis:—sheep, oxen, asses, camels, goats, doves, pigeons, mules, and horses. Horses are mentioned only in connection with Egypt. Sheep were kept, not only for food, but for the fleece and skin. Oxen was a name that included both sexes, and they were used as food. Asses were beasts of burden; so were camels The people ate the flesh of goats, and drank their milk. The skins of these animals they made into bottles, or water-sacks. The turtle dove and pigeon, as well as the sheep, heifer and goat, were offered as sacrifices. xii. 16; xv. 9; xxxvi. 24; xlvii. 17; xlix. 17; xxiv. 63; xv. 9.

SECTION X.—WILD ANIMALS.

144. Nimrod is called a mighty hunter; and this implies the existence of many wild and dangerous animals at the time he lived. So was Esau a hunter. Ishmael too, is called an archer, which means the same thing. Speaking of a sacrifice, it is added, "And when the fowls came down upon the carcasses, Abram drove them away," a plain intimation that there were wild and voracious birds, as well as the tame ones before mentioned. x. 9; xxv. 27; xxvii. 3; xxi. 20; xv. 9.

145. When Esau went to procure venison for his father's savory meat, his success of course, implies the existence of wild animals fit for food. When Lot left Sodom, as that city was about to be destroyed, he was unwilling to go to the mountains, "lest some evil take him and he die," a reference, it would seem, to the dangerous animals to which he would be exposed. The sad conclusion to which Jacob came in regard to Joseph, "that some evil beast had devoured him," must have the same application. Jacob in his defence to Laban, refers to the beasts that had infested his flocks. Reference may be here made to the wolf, as we find that animal once alluded to, in a highly figurative passage. The serpent is mentioned in the account of the temptation, and still later, the serpent and adder. The raven was one of the birds sent forth from the ark of Noah. The lion is once mentioned; and this is sufficient to establish the fact that such an animal was known in those days. xxvii. 3; xix. 19; xxxvii. 33; xxxi. 39; xlix. 27; iii. 1; xlix. 17; xlix. 9.

SECTION XI.—PATRIARCHAL WEALTH.

146. The wealth of the patriarchs consisted chiefly of their flocks and herds. Abraham had "sheep, and oxen, and he asses, and men servants, and maid servants, and she asses, and camels." He is also said to have been "rich in cattle, and silver and gold." Lot had flocks, and herds, and tents. Abimelech took sheep and oxen, and men servants and women servants, and gave them to Abraham. The present sent to Esau by Jacob, which seems to have been but a small part of his possessions, was still very considerable. It consisted of two hundred she goats, and twenty he goats, two hundred ewes and twenty rams, thirty milch camels, with their colts, forty kine, ten bulls, twenty she asses, and ten foals. xii. 16; xiii. 2, 5; xx. 14; xxiv. 35; xxxii. 14, 15.

147. Mention is made of money: but it does not seem to have been regarded as any part of wealth. Abraham paid money, four hundred shekels of silver, for the cave of Machpelah and the surrounding field. Several allusions are made to the money that was sent down to Egypt for the purchase of corn. In this instance the money is reckoned by weight, while in most cases it is estimated by the number of pieces. The phrase "current money with the merchant," shows that there was some established usage, as to the mode of estimating it, and the value placed upon each piece. It was only, or principally with the merchant, that money was made the medium of exchange. Hence twenty pieces of silver were paid for Joseph, by the Midianites. Had money been in common use, we can hardly account for its being omitted in other transactions, where it would have been a great convenience. Jacob paid for his two wives by labor, and was afterwards paid for his labor by a certain proportion of the flocks and herds. Judah offered Tamar a kid, when the payment of its equivalent in money, would have been much more convenient, and might have saved him a subsequent disgrace. xxiii. 9, 15; xlii. 25, 35; xliii. 21; xxiii. 16; xxxvii. 28; xxxviii. 17.

143. Real estate possessions are recognized. Cities and countries were separated from each other by certain, not very definite boundaries; and the rights of the people, within such limits, were seldom made the occasion of conflict. The boundaries of Canaan, for example, are described thus: — "And the border of the Canaanites was from Sidon, as thou comest to Gerar unto Gaza, as thou goest unto Sodom and Gomorrah, and Admah and Zeboim, even unto Lasha." In the days of Peleg the earth was divided, which may mean (and may not) that there was some arrangement about the particular portion of territory that should belong to each nation. Hence such language as the following, in the same connection, may have reference to such an arrangement. "These are the sons of Shem, after their families, after their tongues, *in their lands*, after their nations." x. 19, 25, 31. "The plain of Mamre" seems to recognize the right of Mamre (who was one of Abram's confederates xiv. 13,) to the ownership of that region of country. The valley of Shevah is called "the king's dale," referring to the king of Sodom, to whom that valley belonged. The offer of Abraham to purchase the cave of Machpelah was an acknowledgment that the property belonged to another whose consent to its occupancy must first be obtained. Farther than this; as one particular individual among the sons of Heth, namely, Ephron, had to be sought for and consulted, it is evident that the field and cave were not held in common by the tribe, but were the possession of that man alone. So Jacob, when he returned from Padan Aram, and pitched his tent near Shalem, bought a parcel of a field where he had spread his tent, at the hand of the children of Hamor, Shechem's father, for a hundred pieces of money. So in Egypt, when the people had paid all their money to Joseph for food, they say to him: " There is not aught left in the sight of our lord, but our bodies and our lands." It is added; Joseph bought all the land of Egypt for Pharaoh; for the Egyptians sold every man his field." The lands of the priests were exempted from this arrangement. xiii. 18; xiv. 17; xxiii. 15; xxxiii. 19; xlvii. 18–22.

SECTION XII.—Trade and Commerce.

149. In the arrangement that was to have been entered into by Shechem and his father Hamor, on the one side, and Jacob and his sons on the other, the latter were to have the privilege of "remaining in the land and trading and getting possessions therein." The trade, here referred to, however, must have been quite limited. There was a class of professional "merchantmen" whose business is sufficiently described in the only passage that speaks of them. They carried down to Egypt the choicest productions of their country, " balm, spicery and myrrh." And the fact that they purchased Joseph; and the thing is not mentioned as unusual, shows us that they were not unaccustomed to the traffic in human chattels. Indeed the frequent allusion to servants, bought with money, makes it evident that this was one article of commerce in those days, not only with the Ishmaelites and Egyptians but with Abraham and the other patriarchs. That real estate was bought and sold we have seen in another place. xxxiv. 8–11; xxxvii. 28; xxxiii.19.

SECTION XIII.—Oaths and Contracts.

150. As a specimen of contracts, or rather the mode of making them, that between Abraham and Abimelech, may be noticed. Abimelech, said to Abraham: " Now, therefore, sware unto me here by God, that thou wilt not deal falsely with me, nor with my son, nor with my son's son; but, according to the kindness I have done unto thee, thou shalt do unto me, and to the land wherein thou hast sojourned." Abraham did swear as requested, and gave Abimelech sheep and oxen, to remind him of the obligations that rested upon the parties. And, moreover, having had some difficulty with Abimelech concerning a well which the latter had at length admitted to be Abraham's, seven ewe lambs are placed by themselves, and given over to Abimelech as a perpetual memento of the proper ownership of the well. The covenant between Jacob and Laban, after being sufficiently explained, was attested by a monument, a heap of stones, that should ever remind the contracting parties of their mutual obligations, and help to perpetuate the understanding to future times. The bargain of Jacob and Esau, by which the latter sold his birthright, was sanctioned by an oath. xxi. 23–32; xxxi. 44–55; xxv. 33.

The form of swearing, with a view to ratify an engagement, was not always the same. It was sometimes by lifting up the hand and swearing by God, and sometimes by placing the hand under the thigh. Swearing was sometimes by God, and sometimes by other forms. Jacob swore by the fear of Isaac, and Joseph, by the life of Pharaoh. xiv. 22; xxiv. 2; xlvii. 29; xxxi. 53; xlii. 15.

151. The most important of all contracts are such as the Deity condescended to make with man. The Covenant with Noah and his sons, and every living creature, that there should no more be a flood upon the earth, was ratified by a perpetual sign, the bow in the clouds. The promise to Abraham that God would make him exceedingly fruitful, and give to him, and to his seed after him, the whole land of Canaan, was to be remembered by the change of the name Abram to Abraham, the latter more clearly expressing the nature of the divine promise. On another occasion, the promise is repeated with some important additions, and confirmed by an oath. The rite of circumcision was instituted, as another memento of the same thing. ix. 9–13; xvii. 2; xxii. 16–18; xvii. 11.

SECTION XIV.—Wars.

152. The most important war recorded in Genesis, is the one spoken of in chapter fourteenth. It seems to be related chiefly to give the experience of Abraham and Lot in relation to it. The latter was taken captive and afterwards restored by the prompt and energetic movements of his uncle, and brought back to his home in Sodom. The narrative brings clearly before us the state of society, in that country, at the time when the circumstances occurred. Each king is spoken of as exercising authority over a single city and its surrounding country; but what are here called " cities" were obviously but inconsiderable villages of a few scores, or at most, a few hundreds of inhabitants, and are not to be estimated by the cities of modern times.

153. The weapons made use of in the wars of those times, may be learned by several brief allusions. The sword is several times mentioned. So is the sword and bow. xxvii. 40; xxxi. 26; xxxiv. 25; xlviii. 22. In describing the descendants of Ishmael, mention is made of their " castles," which might have been, and probably were, places of defence against an invading foe. xxv. 16. The apprehension of Jacob that the Canaanites and Perizzites would gather themselves together and destroy him and his house, on account of the treacherous conduct of his sons. xxxiv. 30; and the reason given why they did not do this, shows clearly that war was not uncommon in those days. The covenant between Abraham and Abimelech, and that between Laban and Jacob were evidently intended to prevent such an occurrence. That the military forces of those times were subject to some system, seems indicated by the mention of Phicol, the chief captain of Abimelech's host. The captain of the guard, was an officer in Egypt. The incidental allusion to the "digging down of walls" and "putting the hand on the neck of enemies," and "instruments of cruelty," seem to have in view warlike operations. xxi. 22; xxxvii. 36; xlix. 5, 6, 8.

SECTION XV.—Government.

154. Some sort of government is essential in any form of society. In the age of which we are writing, the patriarchal seems to have been the prevailing form. The father was the presiding sovereign over his family, including his own children, and, to some extent, his grand children. And even when a son had a family which he was expected to govern, he still felt bound to regard the wishes of his father. The kings that ruled over the cities mentioned in chapter fourteenth, were both civil and military rulers. They are called "kings," while Abraham is not so designated, yet he was doubtless so regarded by others. And the part he took in the war as leader of his "trained servants," shows that he occupied the same position.

155. The government of Egypt shows a more advanced state of society than that of Canaan. Pharaoh was king, and he had his subordinate princes, his harem, his chief butler and baker, his magicians and wise men, his captain of the guard, his state prison and his gallows; and surely the last named appendages have always been regarded as evidences of civilization. xii. 15, 19; xl. 1; xl. 19; xl. 3; xxxix. 20; xl. 19.

That the officers of government in Egypt were distinguished by some badge of authority, is plain from what is said of the ring of Pharaoh, the vestures of fine linen, and the golden chain, that were put upon

Joseph. xli. 42, 43. When such personages were visited by persons from a distance, asking for favors, it was customary to bring to them, as presents, the choicest productions of the country; not so much, it is presumed, on account of the value of the present, as the respect and deference thus shown to the prince. There is an allusion to the "sceptre," which is a requisite accompaniment, of the exercise of kingly power. xliii. 11; xlix. 10.

156. Lot "sat in the gate" of the city of Sodom. Did he not sit there to administer justice? We know that this language has this meaning at a later day. Did not the mob that surrounded his house, on that memorable night, the last in the history of that city, have in view the exercise of authority by Lot, when they said, "this one fellow came in to sojourn, and he will needs be a judge;" and was it not the administration of that good man, by which he sought to restrain their wild and reckless career, that mainly excited their displeasure? Men are seldom so bad as to commit outrages, such as are here described, without some plausible excuse. The one their language would seem to imply, is, that he had assumed to exercise more authority over them than was proper for a stranger. xix. 1-9. The judge sat at the gate of the city to exercise authority, that being a conspicuous place; and there, too, for the same reason, were contracts entered into. xix. 1; xxiii. 10; xxiv. 60; xxxiv. 20.

157. The only specific punishment for any specific crime mentioned in reference to this subject, as connected with Canaan and the patriarchs, is the punishment of death for harlotry. The punishment, however, is only named, not being inflicted, on account of palliating circumstances. xxxviii. 24. The imprisonment of Joseph was in Egypt, and has reference to that country. It was obviously not what it would have been, had there not been suspicions of his innocence.

And though such suspicions are not mentioned, the mildness of the infliction, clearly justifies the impression that there were such. What offence the butler and baker had committed, we are not informed. It is evident that their punishment was subject to modification by subsequent disclosures, as this is necessary to account for the one being released and the other executed, contrary to their expectations. That being reduced to servitude, was one of the punishments of crime, may be inferred from the proposition to retain Benjamin as a servant, for having stolen (as was supposed) the silver cup. I infer that the punishment of the chief baker was first decapitation; after which his headless body was hung upon a tree. xxxix. 20; xl. 2, 21, 22; xliv. 10.

SECTION XVI. — SERVITUDE.

158. Noah predicted that Canaan should be a servant of servants. Abraham had three hundred and eighteen servants born in his house and trained in the art of war. Eleazer, Abraham's steward, was a servant, as the phrase "born in the house," is applied to him. He was prospective heir of the patriarch. He was the oldest servant and ruled over all his master had; and for this reason, he was selected to go and procure a wife for Isaac. He is called Eleazer of Damascus, and probably came with Abraham from the north, from Ur of the Chaldees; as Damascus was located in that region. ix. 25; xiv. 14; xv. 2, 3; xxiv. 2.

159. Hagar was a handmaid to Sarah, and is called an Egyptian. And it may be remembered that before this, Abraham had been down into Egypt and had sojourned there for a time, and maid servants are mentioned as among the presents he received from the Egyptian king. This Hagar was, at first, treated with great respect, and was assigned to Abraham as his concubine: and if her son was shut out from being heir, that was not because he was a servant; for the sons of the second wife of Abraham were treated in the same manner. xxv. 5. Servants were sometimes bought with money; and those born in the house, must have sprung from such as were at first bought. xvi. 1; xii. 10, 16; xxv. 5; xvii. 13.

160. The important mission entrusted to Eleazer, as well as the oath exacted of him, shows the confidence placed in him by his master. Nor could any one have been treated with more deference and respect, than was he, by the people to whom he was sent. The handmaids given to Leah and Rachel, and afterwards given by them to Jacob, were treated with considerable distinction. The sons of the handmaids are reckoned among the twelve patriarchs, as well as the sons of the wives; and though the sons of Rachel are treated with special affection, and for an obvious reason, no difference is apparent between the sons of the concubines and those of Leah. xxiv. 3, 31.

161. Servants were made such by being taken captive in war. Simeon and Levi, when they destroyed Shalem, took the wives and little ones as captives. They were made servants by the commission of crime. They were bought with money. xxxiv. 29; xliv. 17.

It may be added that there is no evidence that the relation of master and servant grew up among the patriarchs, nor do we find any divine requirement that men should have servants. The institution came into existence, like any other social custom, as the result of circumstances; and was allowed to remain without any special condemnation. It was, however, a very different thing from the system of servitude in our country, as several of the references already given will make sufficiently obvious.

SECTION XVII.—Oriental Hospitality.

162. Nothing is more interesting than to observe the hospitality of the ancients. They treated strangers and travellers with the greatest tenderness and respect. Let us notice some examples. As Abraham sat in the door of his tent, he saw three men approaching. Rising, he ran to meet them and said; "my lord, if now I have found favor in thy sight, pass not away, I pray thee, from thy servant; let a little water, I pray thee, be fetched; and wash your feet, and rest yourselves under this tree; and I will fetch a morsel of bread; and comfort ye your hearts." He then makes arrangements for their entertainment in the most expeditious and generous manner. It is true that these men were divine messengers; but it does not appear that Abraham at first knew them to be such, or that this fact had any influence on his conduct towards them. Indeed, the conduct of Abraham is only one instance, out of many, where the same generous hospitality is offered to strangers. The language of Lot to the angels that came to him in the evening, is of the same kind with that just noticed "Behold, now my lords, turn in, I pray you, into your servant's house, and tarry all night, and wash your feet; and ye shall rise up early and go on your ways." These men are indeed called angels, but this term is quite as applicable to human beings, as to those not human; and it is certain that Lot had no knowledge of their divine mission till a later period. The readiness with which Rebekah supplied the wants of Abraham's servant, by giving him drink and offering to water his camels, is quite in harmony with the generous sentiment that every where shows itself in those ancient times. Not less generous was the conduct of the sons of Heth, when they offered Abraham his choice, in regard to a burial place for his dead, and showed a delicate unwillingness to receive pay for such a privilege. And one cannot suppress the conviction that Abraham insisted on paying for a place of burial; with an ulterior purpose; presuming, it may be, that the amicable state of things then existing might not always continue. xviii. 4, 5; xix. 2; xxiv. 18-20; xxiii. 6.

SECTION XVIII.—Salutations.

163. The observances of friends on meeting and parting, may be noticed here. The language of Laban to Jacob, shows that parting with friends was sometimes attended with music and merriment. The parties kissed each other on meeting and separating. When Jacob first met Rachel, his future wife, he kissed her, and then informed her of the relation that existed between them. So Laban ran out to meet Jacob; and embracing, kissed him. When Jacob was about to meet his brother Esau, after a long separation, having a desire to show him special respect, he bowed seven times to the earth. Esau ran to meet him; and embracing him, fell on his neck and kissed him and both of them wept. A similar meeting is recorded of Joseph and Benjamin in Egypt, and afterwards of Joseph and his aged father. Bowing to the earth, or perhaps only towards the earth, was a common token of respect and deference. Abraham bowed himself to the people of the land when he was about to negotiate with the sons of Heth for Machpelah. So Jacob bowed himself before Esau, as seen above. xxxi. 27, 28, 55; xxix. 11, 12, 13; xxxiii. 3, 4; xlv. 14; xlvi. 29; xxiii. 7, 12.

SECTION XIX.—The Arts.

164. Of course what we call the arts of life, were in a very imperfect state, during the age of the patriarchs. Jubal was the father of such as handle the harp and the organ. The tabret and harp are also mentioned. These instruments of music were doubtless rudely constructed; but their existence shows that men were then not very unlike what they are now. Of course the mechanic art of constructing these instruments, as well as the fine art of playing on them, must have been known at that time. iv. 21; xxxi. 27.

165. Tubal-cain was instructor of every artificer in brass and iron; and though allusions to instruments of brass and iron are not numerous, there are enough such to show their existence. The knife and the sword must have been made of one of these metals. The manufacture of cloth must have been known, as references to the wool of their flocks, would indicate. Sackcloth may have been of this material, though of this there is no certainty. In Egypt fine linen is mentioned. Frequent references to gold and silver ornaments, indicate some knowledge of the art of refining silver and gold, and working them into such forms as are fitted to please the fancy. It is quite probable, however, that the gold and silver ornaments, mentioned in connection with the patriarchs and their families, were obtained from Egypt; as no mention is made of these things till Abraham had visited that country. Indeed, it is worthy of note that as soon as Abraham returned from Egypt, he is spoken of as being rich in cattle, in *gold and silver.* iv. 22; xii. 42; xliv. 2; xiii. 2.

166. The implements of agriculture were undoubtedly very rude, though they answered all the purposes of practical life at that time. The fields were sowed, it is said; and of course they must have been plowed; and some instrument for this purpose must have been in use. They bound sheaves in the field; then they must have had some instrument for cutting the grain. We read of the threshing floor of Atad; then Atad must have had some mode of threshing his grain, though it was not after the modern fashion. Bread, made of fine meal, was an article of food; of course there was some method of grinding the grain. We will not say that they separated the flour from the bran, as they probably lived on Graham principles. xxvi. 12; xxxvii. 7; l. 11; xviii. 6.

167. As early as the days of Noah, the art of building must have been carried to a great degree of perfection; else how could the ark have been built and fitted to carry its enormous burden over the turbulent abyss of waters. All the instruction given to Noah by the Divine Being would still leave many things, it is presumed, to the knowledge and skill of the architect. The making of tents and houses, at a later day, would require some skill. The manufacture of brick, with which to build the tower of Babel, is another instance of the skill of those primitive times.

168. There are a few references to carriages. Joseph rode in the second chariot of Egypt; and there went up to Canaan with him, both chariots and horsemen, at the burial of his father. Wagons were sent from Egypt to Canaan, to bring the patriarch and his family down to that country. It is probable that both wagons and chariots were used only in Egypt, or seldom elsewhere. In Canaan burdens were carried upon asses; and men and women rode on camels. xlvi. 29; l. 9.

SECTION XX.—Weights and Measures.

169. Time was then reckoned by days, weeks, months, and years, nearly in the same manner as with us. Forty days and forty nights, is the same kind of reckoning then as now. Months are mentioned as made up of days. Hence we read of the first day of the month, the seventeenth day of the month, and the seventh and twentieth day. We also read of the first month, the second month, and the seventh month. By comparing vii. 11 with viii. 4, it will be seen that five months is precisely 150 days, which make one month to be thirty days. A similar comparison of vii. 11 and viii. 13, will show that a Jewish year consisted of twelve months. vii. 4, 11; viii. 13, 14; viii. 4.

170. The seasons of the year were the same as with us, only that summer and winter are the only names by which they were designated, unless seed time and harvest be intended as denoting spring and autumn. viii. 22.

Length, in respect to short distances, was reckoned in cubits; long distances by the number of days journey. A "bow shot" is employed to denote a brief space over which an arrow might be sped. vi. 15; xxxi. 23; xxi. 16.

The points of the compass are named; but a careful observation will show that they are used with great indefiniteness. A place laying in a northerly direction was said to be north, though it might lay far east or west of that point. So of the other points. This makes it quite difficult to determine with accuracy the location or direction of places. xiii. 14; xxviii. 14.

The word "measure" has reference to a vessel of a certain capacity. Hence "three measures of meal," were not, as we might infer from our use of that term meal in three separate vessels; but it was a certain amount three times repeated. xviii. 6.

Isaac sowed his field, and received that year a "hundred fold;" that is, an hundred times as much as he sowed, which, though a great yield, was not unusual in that country. xxvi. 12.

Money was sometimes reckoned by pieces, and sometimes by shekels, or by weight. There were shekels of silver and shekels of gold. xxxiii. 19; xxiii. 15; xliii. 21; xlv. 22.

SECTION XXI.—Religion of the Hebrews.

171. It is obvious that the Hebrews recognized but one supreme Divinity, to whom a good and virtuous life was the most acceptable service. They prayed to him in times of need. They built altars and offered sacrifices thereon. It is remarkable that no mention is made of priests in connection with the patriarchs. Melchisedek was a priest of the most High God; but to what race he belonged does not appear, from the narrative; and the apostle Paul, referring to this personage, speaks of him as being "without father or mother," &c., meaning thereby, that we have no account of his parentage, his history, or his death. The patriarchs themselves offered sacrifices and officiated at the altar. This was done by Abel, Noah, Abraham, Isaac, and Jacob. There were priests in Egypt, who owned some real estate, and were supported, when occasion required, out of the public treasury. iv. 3, 4; viii. 20; xii. 8; xxvi. 25; xxviii. 18; xxxi. 54; xlvii. 22.

172. "Men began to call upon the name of the Lord," even before the flood — language that seems to imply at that time, some arrangement for the maintenance of public worship. Paying tithes is mentioned once or twice. Abraham paid the tenth of the spoils he had obtained in battle, to Melchisedek. Jacob promised to pay to the Lord the tenth of all he had, if he should be prospered in his way. The animals offered in sacrifice, were the heifer, she goat, ram, turtle dove and pigeon. Pouring oil on the top of a pillar, was understood, no doubt, as a religious offering. xiv. 20; xxviii. 22; xv. 9; xxviii. 18; xxxv. 14.

173. The worship of images is alluded to in connection with the family of Laban. The earrings of which we read in connection with these images, were appendages to the same worship, and not the usual ornaments worn by damsels. Abraham planted a grove in Beersheba, where the worship of God was observed. At a later day such groves became very obnoxious, as places where idol worship, accompanied by obscene and immoral rites, was practiced. The rite of circumcision was instituted as a perpetual memorial of religious obligation. xxxi. 19; xxxv. 4; xxiv. 30, 47; xvii. 10; xxi. 33.

CHAPTER IV.

GEOGRAPHY.

Contents:—General Divisions; Mountains; Valleys and Plains; Rivers; Groves and Wildernesses; Seas; Cities; National Designations.

SECTION I.—GENERAL DIVISIONS.

174. Canaan is often alluded to as the residence of the patriarchs, and the country that was to be the everlasting possession of their descendants. The boundaries are defined in a general way in x. 19, from which it appears that Sidon, Gerar, Gaza, Sodom, Gomorrah, Admah, Zeboim, and Lasha, lay on the outer borders around it.

175. When Abram came to Canaan he came from Ur of the Chaldees. Chaldea is, therefore, another country alluded to in the book. Assyria, that lay in the same general direction, is referred to; and as that name seems to have been given to the country by Asshur, the cities he built were probably in that country. xi. 31; xxv. 18; x. 11, 12.

176. Laban, into whose family Jacob married, is called a Syrian. Thus, by implication, Syria is referred to. The same country is called Mesopotamia and Padan Aram. xxviii. 5; xxiv. 10; xxviii. 2.

Mt. Seir was an extensive region, as is evident from what is said of it and the cities it contained. It was also called Edom. xxxvi. The land of the Philistines is referred to; but no name is given to it, though it is thought to have originated the name of Palestine. It was included in the gift to the seed of Abraham, as a part of their everlasting possession. xxi. 32; xxvi. 3.

177. Egypt is too often referred to, to require particular description. It embraced the land of Goshen or Rameses; and one of its principle cities, viz., On, is once or twice named. The "river" often alluded to in connection with Egypt, though not named, is understood to be the Nile. The "river of Egypt" may be the same, and it may not. xlvii. 6, 11; xli. 50; xli. 1; xv. 18.

SECTION II.—Mountains.

178. The first mountain named in the Bible is Mt. Ararat where the ark of Noah rested. Mesha and Sephar are mentioned in connection with a mountain of the East; but the passage is equivocal; and we cannot tell which of those names was intended to designate the mountain referred to; and perhaps the reference is to a mountain between the two. There is a reference to "a mountain on the east of Bethel," but its name is not given. It was between Bethel and Hai. viii. 4; x. 30; xii. 8.

179. There was a mountain in the land of Moriah, on which Abraham offered his son Isaac in sacrifice. It is called the "mountain of the Lord." We commonly refer to it as Mt. Moriah, but it is not so called in the book. It was in the land of Moriah. xxii. 2, 14.

Mt. Gilead lay in the direction of Syria, and is noted as being the place where an interesting conference was held between Laban and Jacob. xxxi. 21, 55. Mt. Seir was an extensive country and was the possession of Esau and his descendants. It was also called Edom. It was called Seir, from Seir who first governed the country, and Edom, from Esau, whose name was also Edom. xxxvi.

SECTION III.—VALLEYS AND PLAINS.

180. There was a plain in the land of Shinar where Babel was built. The plain of Jordan is several times mentioned. It was a very fertile region of country. The plain of Mamre was where Hebron was located, and was the principal residence of the patriarchs. The valley of Shaveh belonged to the king of Sodom, and is called the "king's dale." The vale of Siddim was where Sodom was located, and was afterwards the Salt Sea. The valley of Gerar was not far from a city of the same name in the land of the Philistines. xi. 2; xiii. 11, 18; xiv. 8; xiv. 3; xxvi. 17.

SECTION IV.—RIVERS.

181. Gihon, Pison, Hiddekel and Euphrates are mentioned in connection with Eden. The last named river is also alluded to in describing the eastern boundaries of the Abrahamic possessions. "River of Egypt" is mentioned in the same passage, in connection with the western boundary. It may be the Nile, or it may be some other river near to Egypt. The ford Jabbok was probably a ford across a river of the same name. A river is mentioned as being in the land of Edom, on which Rehoboth was situated; but the name is not given. The most important of all the rivers alluded to in Genesis, is the Jordan, running along the eastern border of Canaan. ii. 10–14; xv. 18; xxxii. 22; xxxvi. 37; xiii. 10.

SECTION V.—GROVES AND WILDERNESSES.

182. Abraham planted a grove in Beersheba. We also read of the wilderness of Beersheba and the wilderness of Paran. xxi. 33; xxi. 21.

SECTION VI.— SEAS.

183. The Salt Sea was once the Vale of Siddim. The sea where Sidon or Zidon was located is not named, but it is evidently the Mediterranean. xlix. 13. xiv. 3.

Isles. We read of the "Isles of the Gentiles;" but we cannot say whether there is an allusion to islands, as we now use that term, or to some other tracts of country. x. 5.

SECTION VII.—CITIES AND TOWNS.

184. A careful observation of passages will enable us to determine with considerable accuracy, the location of the principal cities mentioned in the book of Genesis; and from this method alone we may easily obtain more information concerning the Geography of Palestine, than is commonly possessed by most readers of the Bible. We shall reach our object best by speaking of places in groups; or regarding them from certain stand points, from which we can trace their relations with each other.

185. The first city mentioned in the Bible is the city of Enoch, built by Cain, and named after his son Enoch. iv. 17. Its location is not defined, except that it is spoken of as east of Eden. It was in the land of Nod;— so the passage seems to teach; but the word *Nod* means "vagabond," and may refer to Cain and not the place of his residence.

186. *Babel, Erech Accad, Calneh.* Speaking of Nimrod, a grandson of Ham, it is said, "the beginning of his kingdom was Babel, and Erech, and Accad, and Calneh, in the land of Shinar." x. 10. It will be remembered that Babel was the place where men attempted to build a tower that should reach to heaven and where their language was confounded. xi. 3–9. Nimrod it would seem was the principal leader in this attempt. This and the other places, mentioned with it, was the land of Shinar.

187. *Nineveh, Rehoboth, Calah, Resen.* " Out of that land [Shinar] went forth Asshur, and builded Nineveh. and the city of Rehoboth, and Calah, and Resen, between Nineveh and Calah; the same is a great city." x. 11, 12. It is generally understood that Assyria took its name from Asshur; and of course Nineveh and the other places mentioned with it, were in that country.

188. *Sidon, Gerar, Gaza, Sodom, Gomorrah, Admah, Zeboim, Lasha.* The border of the Canaanites — in other words, the boundary of Canaan, is thus given; it was from Sidon as thou comest to Gerar unto Gaza, as thou goest unto Sodom and Gomorrah and Admah and Zeboim, even unto Lasha. x. 19. These places lay at various points around what was then regarded as the land of the Canaanites. The traveller, commencing at Sidon, would pass by Gerar to Gaza, and thence to Sodom, &c. even unto Lasha; and from Lasha [it is implied] he would come again to Sidon, " the place of first beginning."

189. The location of these places, we can determine, with considerable certainty, both by direct statement, and by reasonable inference. Let us see. The location of Sidon seems to be settled within certain limits, by the following passage; — " Zebulon shall dwell at the haven of the sea; and he shall be a haven for ships; and his border shall be unto Zidon." xlix. 13. The inference is that Zidon [or Sidon] was on the sea coast. Of course the Mediterranean sea is had in view, as no other is known to border on Canaan that can at all answer the description here given. This is one point gained, as to one of the places by which Canaan was bounded.

190. Gerar is another of the places named in the boundary. The location of this may be determined by several references. It was " in the south country, and between Kadesh and Shur;" xx. 1; and the latter place is said to be "before Egypt." xxv. 18. Now as Egypt was in a south-west direction from Canaan, it follows that Kadesh, Gerar and Shur were near the south-west corner of that country. This settles the location of Gerar, the second point in the boundary line. Sidon, before mentioned, to answer the description, must be placed on the Mediterranean, in the north-west corner of Canaan. And as the boundary line is made to commence there, and proceed to Gerar at the south, we are prepared to infer the location of the next places named on the line.

191. We infer that Gaza lay east of Gerar, in the direction of Sodom and Gomorrah, Admah and Zeboim; and that the latter places were on the east border of the country. This inference we find to be correct.

It is said "the plain of the Jordan, was well watered &c., before the Lord destroyed Sodom and Gomorrah." xiii. 10. Abraham dwelled in the land of Canaan, and Lot dwelled in the cities of the plain, and pitched his tent toward Sodom. xiii. 12. Sodom and Gomorrah then, were on the Jordan, which we know ran on the east line of Palestine. Admah and Zeboim were doubtless near by, as they are not only mentioned in connection with Sodom and Gomorrah, in the boundary line, but also in the battle of the kings. xiv. 8. It cannot be doubted, then, that Lasha, the only remaining place in this boundary, was in the northeast corner of Canaan, opposite to Sidon, the place of beginning.

Notwithstanding the indirect way we arrive at the result, we feel almost as sure of its accuracy, as if we had visited those places. And having determined these principal points, we are better prepared to seek for others by the guidance of these. We can make no use of Sidon to determine the location of other places, as that place is not mentioned, except in the instances already quoted. The same is true of Gaza and Lasha. Not so of Gerar; nor Sodom and Gomorrah.

192. *Gerar, Kadesh, Shur, Zoar, Mamre or Hebron.* Gerar, we have seen, was "in the south country," and "between Kadesh and Shur." Isaac went down to that country, apparently with the intention of going on to Egypt; but was divinely admonished to remain in Gerar. Gerar was a city of the Philistines, and the capital of that country. There was a valley of the same name not far off. Of course Kadesh and Shur were not far from Gerar. The one place locates the others. xxv. 18; xxvi. 1, 6, 17.

We read of "Bela which is Zoar," and as Lot fled to Zoar, when he left Sodom, it was evidently near that city. It was a small place. xiv. 2; xix. 22, 23; xix. 20.

193. Abraham dwelt in the plain of Mamre, when the angels came and announced the destruction of Sodom. It is obvious from the circumstances that Mamre and Sodom were not very far apart. Abraham could see the smoke of the country, after its destruction. Mamre, however, was not *very* near to Sodom, as it appears that Abraham and Lot had separated thus far, to avoid collisions between their respective herdsmen. Neither was it so near that Abraham could know of Lot's captivity, till a messenger informed him. We will learn more of Mamre, [which, it will be remembered, is the same as Hebron,] in connection with other places. xix. 28; xiv. 13; xiii. 12.

194. *Shinar, Ellassar, Elam, Sodom, Gomorrah, Admah, Zeboim, Zoar, Ashteroth-Karnaim, Ham, Shaveh-Kiriathaim, Mt. Seir, Elparan, Vale of Siddim, Kadesh, Hazezon-tamer.* The kings of the first three places named, and one king whose place is not named, making four in all, make war with the kings of Sodom, Gomorrah, Admah, Zeboim, and Zoar. They fought in the vale of Siddim, afterwards called the "salt sea," meaning the same as the Dead sea. Prior to this celebrated battle, they had conquered all the other places mentioned in this list; and in this battle, too, they were successful, carrying away much spoil, and many captives, (including Lot and his family.) They extended their conquests as far as Kadesh, which, as we have seen, was not far distant from Egypt. The location of the other places is quite uncertain, though some other passages will be quoted, by and by, with reference to some of them, that will enable us to approximate to the truth.

195. Ashteroth-Karnaim is not located by any circumstance in the narrative, nor by any parallel passages in Genesis. Ham may have been named after the son of Noah, as we know that many of Ham's descendants settled in Canaan; and it is quite natural that they should name some place after him, but its location is not given. Mt. Seir has already been spoken of, and we shall have occasion to refer to it again. Hazezon-tamer appears to have been the residence of the Amorites and perhaps the Amalekites; but its location does not appear. Mamre, after whom the plain of Mamre was named, was an Amorite, and it is reasonable to presume that the residence of that tribe was not far from Mamre; and this places their residence in the direction of Kadesh, spoken of with it. Elparan was by the wilderness, perhaps the wilderness of Paran, and this, too, lay in the same direction towards Kadesh. xiv. 1–10.

196. *Dan, Hobah, Damascus, Salem, Valley of Shaveh.* Abraham, hearing that Lot had been taken captive and carried away, took his trained servants, and his confederates, Mamre, Eschol, and Aner, and pursued them unto Dan. He then attacked them and pursued them to Hobah, on the left hand of Damascus. These places, therefore, were all north of Canaan, and on the way to Shinar, and the other places to which these kings belonged and to which they were returning. On his return, Abraham was met by Melchisedek, king of Salem, an evidence that Salem was between Mamre and the other places just named; at least it was north of Mamre, as Abraham was on his way home toward the south. It is thought that this Salem, was the same as Jerusalem, so distinguished afterwards as the chief city of Judea.

197. The king of Sodom, too, went out to meet Abraham at the valley of Shaveh, which locates this place also in the same general direction as Salem. Besides, this valley was the " king's dale," or valley, and must have been near to Sodom. Furthermore, the spoils were there divided, Abraham's confederates taking their share, and the king taking the rest, Abraham himself declining to receive any. Place this valley a little north and west of Sodom and we have the proper location to suit the circumstances. Was not this Shaveh, the same as Shaveh-Kiriathaim, mentioned in the same account as being taken by the northern kings? The resemblance in the name would make this probable; for we shall have occasion to see that double names are often abridged. xiv. 14-18.

198. *Ur, Haran, Moreh, Bethel, Hai, Hebron, Lahai-roi, Gerar, Beersheba.* We will now take the patriarch Abraham as our guide, and follow him, and note the places he passes through, and the place of his residence. The first mention of Abraham is in connection with Ur of the Chaldees. Leaving this place with Terah, his father, and with Lot, his nephew, he is next seen in Haran, a place obviously taking its name from a brother of Abram, who had recently died in Ur. Of course Haran lay in the direction of Canaan, as Abram was on his way to that country. We shall find the same place mentioned in another passage, as the retreat of Jacob when he left home to escape the wrath of Esau. How natural that he should go to the former residence of his grandfather, where some of his relatives still resided.

199. Soon after this, Abram starts for the land of Canaan, and comes into that country. He came to Sichem unto the plain of Moreh. Soon thereafter he removed to a mountain on the east of Bethel, having Bethel on the west, and Hai on the east. This places Abraham's residence on the mountain, Bethel, and Hai, on an east and west line. But farther than this, their location does not appear. xii. 5, 6.

It is added that "Abram journeyed, going on still *toward the south*." This settles the point of his original residence. It was north of Palestine. Ur was far north; Haran not so far. Sichem, and the plain of Moreh, in Palestine, were north of Bethel and Hai. All these things are thus rendered certain. xii. 9.

200. After making a journey to Egypt, Abram returns to Bethel, and to his place between Bethel and Hai. xiii. 3. At this time Abram and Lot separated, to avoid unpleasant collisions between their respective herdsmen; and as Lot chose the plain of the Jordan, near Sodom; and as that was the eastern boundary of Canaan, the inference is, that Abram resided west of Sodom, though not very far off, as we have before seen. Besides, it is expressly said of Lot, when he separated from Abram, that he went *east*. xiii. 11. Abram's next residence is in the plain of Mamre, which is Hebron. Mamre, in whose plain was Hebron was one of Abram's confederates, and one of those who went with him in pursuit of the kings that had carried away Lot. Hebron was also called Kirjetharba. It was here that Sarah died, and near here was the cave of Machpelah, the place where she was buried.

Hebron, in Mamre, was a long time the abode of the patriarchs. Abram dwelt there, so did Isaac; and to the same place Jacob returned, when he came back from Padan-aram. Abram died in Hebron and was buried in Machpelah. xiii. 18; xiv. 13, 24; xxiii. 2, 17; xxxv. 27; xxv. 8 ,9.

201. Isaac had his abode near the well Lahai-roi, which must have been near Hebron. Afterwards, on account of a famine in the land, he went down to the country of the Philistines, and dwelt in Gerar. He afterwards went from there to Beersheba; and it was here that the unhappy conflict between Jacob and Esau occurred; and it was from this place that Jacob was sent away, to avoid the vengeance of his brother. xxiv. 62; xxv. 11; xxvi. 6, 23; xxviii. 10.

202. *Padan-aram, Haran, Bethel, Mt. Gilead, Mahanaim, Seir, Jabbok, Peniel, Succoth, Shalem, Ephrath, Arbah* or *Hebron.* We will now take another guide. We will follow Jacob on his excursion to the north. He was instructed to go to his uncle Laban at Padan-aram. This same Laban is called a Syrian. Padan-aram, then was Syria. The original of Syria is Aramea, which can at once be seen to have been derived from the last half of Padan-aram. xxviii. 5. Notice another circumstance. When Jacob left Beersheba, it is said he started for Haran, and when he arrived there he inquired of the men of Haran, whether they knew Laban, and was told that they did. This makes Haran, too, to be in Syria. Chaldea, it will be remembered, was still further north, as Abram came from that country to Haran, on his way to Canaan. xxviii. 10; xxix. 4, 5.

203. On his way to Haran from Beersheba, Jacob stopped over night at a place which he called Bethel, from a vision he had there. It was before called Luz. He visited the same place on his return from Haran. xxviii. 19; xxxv. 1. It may be recollected that this is mentioned in connection with Abraham, and called Bethel, though at that time, it had not received this name. The writer gives the modern name, and not the ancient one, a not uncommon occurrence in the Bible, as well as in other books. From Bethel Jacob went on his journey, and came into "the country of the people of the east."

The residence of Laban was evidently in a north-east direction from Canaan, and hence it is regarded as both north and east. xxix. 1.

204. As we are in search of places merely, and not transactions, we will pass over the experience of Jacob with Laban, and commence with his return from that country; which, as he moves slowly with his family, his flocks and herds, will naturally bring before us a number of places. It is quite probable, too, that he did not take the same route as when he came, since he seems to have wished to evade pursuit. At all events we first find him, on his return route, at Mt. Gilead, where Laban after a seven days' journey, had overtaken him. There, after some angry altercation, they entered into a solemn compact, set up a pillar of stones, as a memento thereof; and at length separated for their respective destinations. Laban called the place Jegar-sahadutha; but Jacob called it Galeed, or Gilead. He also named it Mizpah. xxxi. 47, 49.

205. The next place is called Mahanaim, on account of a vision of angels he saw there. It may be added here, that names given, like this, to celebrate some passing event or circumstance, were not always permanent, though they sometimes appear to have been so. Here it is said that Jacob sent messengers before him to Esau, his brother, unto the land of Seir, the country of Edom. It follows, then, that Seir or Edom lay between him and Canaan. It will be recollected that Mt. Seir is mentioned among the conquests of the kings, whose visit to Sodom has before been spoken of. This is very natural, for it lay right on their route. xxxii. 2, 3; xiv. 6. Still farther along, Jacob passed over the ford Jabbok, and near that place he wrestled with the angel, and called the place Peniel or Penuel. After the interview with Esau, Jacob journeyed to Succoth. He then came to Shalem, in the land of Canaan, and pitched his tent before the city, and there erected an altar which he called El-elohe-

Israel. From this place he goes again to Bethel, where he had a vision on his way *to* Haran. From Bethel he goes a little way to Ephrath, where his favorite wife Rachel is taken from him and where she is buried. Ephrath is described as the same as Bethlehem. Jacob, or Israel, as he is now called, journeyed and pitched his tent beyond the tower of Edar; and at last he came back to his father, now in Hebron, though, when Jacob left, he was in Beersheba. xxxii. 31; xxxiii. 17, 18; xxxv. 19, 21, 27.

206. The flight of Jacob has given us an interesting line of travel, from Syria, northeast of Canaan, to the patriarchal home in Hebron. The places that lie along this route, beginning at the north, are Haran, in Syria, Mt. Gilead, Mt. Seir or Edom, the ford Jabbok, Succoth, Shalem, Bethel, Ephrath or Bethlehem, tower of Edar, and finally Mamre or Hebron. Succoth and all the preceding places lay beyond the line of Canaan; the others *in* that country. That the route here spoken of was quite meandering, is obvious. Jacob probably went out of his way to visit his brother at Mt. Seir. He had to leave his return route too, when he visited Bethel, though his route *to* Syria was through that place.

207. *Gerar, Kadesh, Shur, Beersheba, Valley of Gerar.* The intercourse that the patriarchs held with the Philistines, will help us to locate some of the places mentioned in Genesis. Gerar was a city of the Philistines, and the residence of the king. It was near to Egypt and between Kadesh and Shur. Add to this, that the wilderness in the way to Shur, is the place where Hagar wandered when she left the home of her mistress, the first time. And as Shur was near Egypt, the wilderness must have been in that direction. Was not Hagar seeking her former home in Egypt? xvi. 7; xxvi. 1.

The second time she left, with Ishmael, her son, she was found in the wilderness of Beersheba. Was not this then in the same general direction? What confirms this opinion, is, that when Isaac left the valley of Gerar, he went up to Beersheba. When the people of those days went to Egypt, or towards that country, they went *down*. When they returned they went *up*. Going from Gerar *up* to Beersheba, locates the latter place in the direction of Hebron from Gerar. Of course Hagar might very naturally get lost in that wilderness, on her way to Egypt. xxi. 14; xxvi. 23.

This Beersheba was an important place. Abram planted a grove there and called on the name of the Lord. He afterwards dwelt at Beersheba for a time. There Abimelech, king of the Philistines, made a covenant with Abraham, and afterwards with Isaac. Indeed, it was called Beersheba or, *well of the oath*, because there a controversy concerning a well had been settled, and a solemn covenant entered into between the parties. xxi. 33; xxii. 19; xxvi. 33. At a subsequent period Jacob visited Beersheba on his way to Egypt, which is a very natural occurrence, as that had been the residence of his father and grandfather. The circumstance shows also that the place was in the direction of Egypt as we had before conjectured. xlvi. 1.

208. *Hebron, Shechem, Dothan, Mt. Gilead, On, Goshen, Rameses.* The history of Joseph will help us to locate some of the places alluded to in Genesis. When Joseph had his dreams, his father Jacob resided at the old paternal mansion in Hebron; and he sent Joseph to inquire after his brothers at Shechem where they were tending their flocks. It is obvious then that Shechem was not far from Hebron. The place was probably named after Shechem, son of Hamor, who is mentioned in another place. xxxvii. 13, 14; xxxiii. 19.

Joseph does not find his brethren at Shechem, and on inquiring he proceeds to Dothan. And here the plot of taking his life was formed, which resulted in selling him as a slave to the Midianites, or what is the same, the Ishmaelites, who were on their way from Mt. Gilead to Egypt, carrying thither balm, spicery and myrrh. xxxvii. 17, 25.

All this confirms our previous location of places. There seems to have been a well known route from Egypt to Syria, and so on to Chaldea. Along this route lay Gilead, Succoth and sundry other places before mentioned. The route passed near enough to Pothan to attract the attention of the sons of Jacob, as the merchantmen passed with their camels. In connection with Egypt, mention is made of On, of which place Potipherah was priest—of Goshen where the sons of Jacob resided—of Rameses, which seems only to be another name for Goshen. xli. 45; xlv. 10; xlvii. 11.

209. *Dinhabah, Bosrah, Temani, Avith, Masrekah, Rehoboth, Pau.* All these places were in Edom, the residence of Esau, the location of which has before been noticed. xxxvi. 32–39.

210. *Havilah, Shur, Mesha, Sephar, Jehovah-jireh, Chezib, Timnath, Shiloh.* These places we will notice without any particular stand-point of observation. The Ishmaelites are said to have their residence from Havilah to Shur. The latter place being near to Egypt, Havilah must have been in the other direction, on the Assyrian route, and a considerable way off, as the Ishmaelites were a numerous tribe. Mesha and Sephar are mentioned in defining the residence of the children of Jokshan, one of the descendants of Shem. Where they were, we cannot say, except that they are said to be in the east. Jehovah-jireh is the place where Isaac was taken for sacrifice. Chezib was the birthplace of Shelah, one of the sons of Judah, and Timnath is where Judah went to shear his sheep. Shiloh, we understand is a place in Canaan, and not as commonly regarded, a name of the promised Messiah. xxv. 18; x. 30; xxii. 14; xxxviii. 5, 12; xlix. 10.

SECTION VIII. — NATIONAL DESIGNATIONS.

211. It seems proper to note the national designations, in connection with the Geography of Palestine.

Canaanites. These were the descendants of Canaan, son of Ham, son of Noah. And as most of the people of Palestine were the children of Canaan, therefore, that land was called after his name. The term Canaanite is sometimes used in a more restricted sense, and denotes the people of a city or district. x. 15; xv. 21. The following tribes are expressly said to be descended from Canaan, viz., Jebusite, Amorite, Girgasite, Hivite, Arkite, Sinite, Arvadite, Zemarite, Hamathite. *Heth*, too, was a son of Canaan, and his tribe is called Hittites. x. 15–18.

The Rephaims, Zuzims, Emims, Horites, Amalekites and Amorites are mentioned as being conquered in the war of the kings. xiv. 4–7. So we have the Kenites, Kenizzites, Kadmonites, Perizzites, in addition to the above, as the people of Canaan. xv. 19, 20. The surrounding nations are sometimes referred to. Hence we read of the Chaldees, Syrians, Egyptians. So we have the Edomites or Horites, and Ishmaelites.

212. Some of these names have a derivation that is obvious, and some have not. The Hittites from Heth, were probably at first called Hethites, which was shortened into Hittites. Horites may have taken their name from Hori, son of Lotan, son of Seir. xxxvi. 22. Amalekites from Amalek, grandson of Esau. xxxvi. 16. Another grandson, Kenaz, may have originated the Kenizzites. xxxvi. 15. Edomites were called so from Edom, one of the names of Esau; and Ishmaelites from Ishmael; and Canaanites from Canaan. Adullamite is twice mentioned. xxxviii. 1, 12.

INTRODUCTION. 119

CHAPTER V.

CHRONOLOGY.

CONTENTS: — Dates from the Creation to the Deluge; Dates from the Deluge to Abraham; Dates from Abraham to the death of Joseph; Remarks.

213. Chronology treats of the dates of important events. In the present chapter we shall, of course, speak of only such events as are recorded in the book of Genesis. Three important periods are comprehended in the book. The first of these is from the Creation to the Flood; the second, from the Flood to the patriarch Abraham; and the last extends from Abraham to the death of Joseph. We subjoin a chronological table, having reference to each of these periods.

SECTION I.—FIRST PERIOD.

214.

From Adam to Seth, was	130 years.	Gen.	v.	3.
" Seth to Enos,	105	"	"	v. 6.
" Enos to Cainan,	90	"	"	v. 9.
" Cainan to Mahalaleel,	70	"	"	v. 12.
" Mahalaleel to Jared,	65	"	"	v. 15.
" Jared to Enoch,	162	"	"	v. 18.
" Enoch to Methusaleh,	65	"	"	v. 21.
" Methusaleh to Lamech,	187	"	"	v. 25.
" Lamech to Noah,	182	"	"	v. 28.
" Noah to Shem,	500	"	"	v. 32.
" Shem to Flood,	100	"	"	vii. 6.
Total from Adam to the Flood,	1656			

215. *Remarks.* The Septuagint adds one hundred years to each of the patriarchs, Adam, Seth, Enos, Cainan, Mahalaleel and Enoch, before the birth of their sons, while it takes twenty from the age of Methusaleh and adds six to that of Lamech. This of course lengthens out the time that must have intervened between the Creation and the Deluge, and makes it to have been 2242 years, instead of 1656, as we have

given it. All the copies of the Septuagint are not, however, precisely alike; the Vatican having 2242, as given above, and the Alexandrine 2262. So too, the Hebrew Samaritan text differs from the Jewish and makes the period only 1307.

SECTION II.—Second Period.

216.

From the	Flood to Arphaxad,	2 years.	Gen. xi. 10.
"	Arphaxad to Salah,	35 "	" xi. 12.
"	Salah to Eber,	30 "	" xi. 14.
"	Eber to Peleg,	34 "	" xi. 16.
"	Peleg to Rue,	30 "	" xi. 18.
"	Rue to Serug,	32 "	" xi. 20.
"	Serug to Nahor,	30 "	" xi. 22.
"	Nahor to Terah,	29 "	" xi. 24.
"	Terah to Abram,	70 "	" xi. 26.
Total from the Flood to Abram,		292 "	

217. *Remarks.* Instead of this reckoning the Samaritan copy makes this period to have been 942 years; the Vatican 1172; the Alexandrine 1072, and Josephus 1002. The mode of reckoning made use of by the ancient Hebrews was such as would very easily lead to mistakes in copying; for they made use of letters instead of figures, and some of these letters so nearly resembled each other, that one would often be mistaken for another, and would be so written down by the copyist. This would of course, change the reckoning. Hence, when the ancient translations are found to differ from our Hebrew copy of the Bible, the fact is best accounted for, perhaps, by supposing that the Hebrew Bible they translated from was different from ours, the difference having originated in the manner here indicated. Still some variations may have arisen since the translation was made.

INTRODUCTION.

SECTION III.—THIRD PERIOD.

218. From Abram to Isaac, 100 years. Gen. xxi. 5.
" Isaac to Jacob, 60 " " xxv. 26.
" Jacob to Joseph, probably, 91 " { " xli. 46, 47.
                                     { " xlv. 6.
                                     { " xlvii. 9.
" Joseph to his death, 110 " " l. 26.

Total from Abram to the death of Joseph, 361 "
Total from Creation to death of Joseph, 2309 "

SECTION IV.—DATES OF THE PRINCIPAL EVENTS OF THE LAST PERIOD.

219. Abram left Haran for Canaan, aged 75 years. Gen. xii. 4.
Age of Abram, when Ishmael was born, 86 " " xvi. 16.
Age of Abram, when Isaac was born, 100 " " xxi. 5.
Age of Ishmael, when circumcised, 13 " " xvii. 25.
Age of Abraham, when circumcised, 99 " " xvii. 24
Age of Sarah, when Isaac was born, 90 " " xvii. 17.
When Sarah died, she was 127 " " xxiii. 1.
When Abraham died, he was 175 " " xxv. 7.
When Ishmael died, he was 137 " " xxv. 17.
Isaac, when married, was 40 " " xxv. 20.
When Jacob was born, Isaac was 60 " " xxv. 26.
When Esau was married, he was 40 " " xxvi. 34.
When Isaac died, he was 180 " " xxxv. 28.
Joseph, when promoted in Egypt, was 30 " " xli. 46.
When Jacob went to Egypt, he was 130 " " xlvii. 9.
When Jacob died, he was 147 " " xlvii. 28.
When Joseph died, he was 110 " " l. 26.

PART II.

PHILOSOPHY AND THEOLOGY.

CHAPTER VI.

EXISTENCE OF GOD.

CONTENTS : — Preliminary Topics ; The World not Eternal ; Creation by Natural Causes, considered ; Necessity of a Creator.

GEN. i. 1. In the beginning God | created the Heaven and the Earth.

220. The subject for this chapter, is the Existence of God, as proved by the creation of the world ; and this seems a fit subject with which to introduce the Philosophy and Theology of the book of Genesis ; as it lies at the basis of all true Philosophy, and is essential to the existence of all Theological science, and is the first thing announced in the "Book of books."

SECTION I.—PRELIMINARY TOPICS.

221. (1.) When was the creative work performed? Assuming, what we shall hereafter prove, that God created the world, it is worthy of inquiry when the work was done. "In the beginning," is the only answer given in the record ; and though this expression is quite indefinite, the subject did not require it to be otherwise. If any limitations or qualifications are required, they may be derived from what follows. The six days or periods of creation, are the "beginning" referred to. The condition of matter farther back than the six days, is not touched upon by the writer of this book. We may speculate upon that subject, but we can decide nothing by divine authority. As to the time that has intervened between the creation and the present, dating from the creation of man, there are no facts with which we are acquainted, that can be urged as reliable proofs of a longer period than the one given in the Bible, which is understood to be about six thousand years. There is no evidence that men have lived on the earth longer than that period. Animals and plants have existed much longer, as is proven by their fossil remains, found imbedded in the solid rocks that compose the earth's crust — rocks that must have required ages to form. But no *human* fossil has ever been found in any situation indicating a longer period than we have supposed. We adhere to the Bible account, and must be excused for adopting no other, till we find something better sustained. We believe this account may be safely adhered to. We know of no facts that conflict with it. We believe there are none. True, apparent conflicts do exist; but a careful examination shows them to be only apparent.

222. It is well known, for example, that the Chinese and Hindoos have laid claim to a greater antiquity than is revealed in the Bible. So have the Egyptians. But those who are best qualified to judge of these pretensions, assure us that they are entirely unfounded.

223. (2.) What are we to understand by the phrase "heaven and earth." We understand the common idea to be, that this phrase was intended to include the whole universe, and that all material things were produced at the same time. The earth, sun, moon and stars, are mentioned, and must of course be included in the phrase. But we need not take in more than our solar system to justify this language. Less than this, will not answer the description; more than this, is not required. There is, besides, good natural reasons for extending the creative work to the whole of our system, as all parts are essentially connected; but we know of no natural reason for a larger application.

224. It is true that the solar system may be essentially connected with other systems, and may be a necessary part of the great universe. We believe it is. But it may have no office to perform that would require the present order and arrangement of its several bodies.

If the power of attraction, for example, be universal, the solar bodies may, by that law alone, be essential to the stability and permanency of the whole universe. But the strength of this power is not lessened or increased by placing these bodies in the order, and subjecting them to the motions, that now belong to them. The same power belongs to the mass of matter that makes up the system ; whether it exists in one body or in thirty ; whether it be permanent and stationary, or arranged into moving forms.

225. Here I wish to suggest an idea, to be thought of in connection with the creation of this world *out of nothing*. All matter has the power of attraction. There was a time, when, according to the popular theory, the matter that makes up this world, did not exist. What then must have been the effect upon the rest of the universe, of creating this world, and investing it with such tremendous power? Would it not have disturbed the balance of the other worlds and systems, and sent disorder and destruction throughout the whole range of creation? Nothing can be plainer than this ; and hence it is well to suppose all worlds to be created at one and the same moment ; for no other view can be reconciled with the theory of creation from nothing. So one error requires another, to sustain the harmony of the theory.

226. (3.) What was the condition of the planets before they assumed their present form? allowing that they existed before, which we assume to be not unphilosophical. We do not ask this question, because it is practically important ; but because it may be made to teach us a lesson that *is* practically important.

We are not satisfied to trace the unformed earth back to the sun, or to any other source. There is a tendency to push our inquiries still farther. Here, however, we have no certain guide. On questions of this nature we can only conjecture. It is not unreasonable to suppose that other worlds and systems may have been constituted of the same materials, before they were worked into the forms in which we now find them. We can hardly suppose that what admitted of being brought into forms, so wisely and benevolently fitted to promote the happiness of sentient creatures, should not be called into requisition, for this purpose, during the whole of past eternity. Still, if we go back of the present system, through thousands of anterior systems, each having a life of ages, we must at last come to the first; and back of that, will lie an eternity of unoccupied duration. This is a difficulty we cannot avoid; and if we suppose our system the first, and an unoccupied eternity beyond *it*, we have only the same difficulty; and to choose between two theories, when the objections to each are equally balanced, is an impossibility, and therefore we shall not attempt a choice. The only wisdom (and this is the practical lesson I wish to enforce) is, to restrain our inquiries when we can find no firm ground on which to stand — when we have no light of Philosophy or Revelation to guide us.

227. (4.) It may be well to contemplate the original creation, with reference to the *mode* by which the divine power was applied to the creative work.

We are apt I fear, to entertain ideas of this subject that make the Creator too much like one of us. We are apt to imagine that he had an immense physical form, and stood over the huge mass of materials, out of which the world was to be made, and by some mysterious power, unlike any thing that has ever been exhibited since, operated upon those materials, and brought them into their present form of order and beauty.

It is natural that some such ideas should be entertained, as assimilate the Deity to the form and processes of humanity; and much of the style and phraseology of the Bible, is accommodated to this tendency. Still we must guard against ideas that are too gross and unrefined. We must not forget that God is a spirit, and has a mode of operation peculiar to himself. He acts upon matter through the power of his spirit, and not as one physical body acts upon another. The Divine Being, as we understand the subject, was then no more obvious to human perception than he is now. He was no more directly active upon the vast bodies of matter that compose the solar system, than he is at this moment. When he said,

"Let there be light," "Let there be a firmament," "Let us make man," he uttered no audible voice that he does not now utter, in all the processes of the ever active universe. If one of us, with the physical organs we now possess, had been placed above the huge and chaotic masses that were to form our beautiful world, and had been permitted to look down upon the progressive work, we should have seen no more of God — we should have heard his voice no more than we do now. True, the all-pervading spirit would have been there — the power of the Almighty would have been felt upon the changing masses, as they assumed continually more of order, form and arrangement ; but it would have been a presence and power that are felt now, as well as then — a presence and power, felt by all other worlds, as much as by the one that was to be our own.

228. We regard the Deity as in some sense inherent in matter. He pervades it in every part. He is as present in the molecules that are inconceivably diminutive, as in the huge mass that forms the centre of our world. He is as present now, as he was at the morning of time ; he will be as present, in every part, through all the cycles of the future, as he is now. Indeed, if we look at the subject with clear philosophic vision, we shall discover that most of what are called the attributes of matter, are really the attributes of the Deity that dwells in and pervades all parts of the material creation. Here I propose to correct the notions of some men who are called Philosophers. They tell us that the central sun once sent forth the earth, and other planets, to their present positions, by a power or force inherent in itself. Was not this power the power of God, and not of matter ? They tell us that the earth and other planets are carried round the sun by the combined action of two forces, acting in different directions. This is making a matter complicated that is itself simple. This thing is not done by two forces, but by one ; and that is the power of God : and this is proved by the intelligence that always accompanies its exercise.

In a word, matter has no power of its own. It cannot cohere, nor separate ; it cannot move in a straight line, nor in a curve; it cannot change its position in one way, nor another; it cannot arrange itself in order, nor in disorder; in fine, it cannot do any of the things that are usually ascribed to it. The power of the universe is the power of God, as much as the intelligence of the universe is the intelligence of God; for both these attributes are forever conjoined, and cannot be separated; and it is not good reasoning to refer one of them to the Deity and the other to Nature. "All power is of God."

We are accustomed to speak of the "laws of nature;" and the phrase is not objectionable, if it does not mislead us. It may help us to illustrate the truths of natural science; but sound Philosophy knows of no such laws. The *sovereign will,* accompanied by an almighty power, and guided by wisdom and benevolence, is the true and only law. All forms of speech that do not imply this, or are not based on this idea, are fallacious and untrue. In theology they have done unspeakable mischief. The tendency of men to shut out a Deity from the universe, and to put Nature in the place of Nature's God, should be firmly withstood by all who would maintain a sound Philosophy or a consistent Theology; and especially by all who would keep unimpaired the substantial principles of morality and religion.

229. We have already yielded too much to the encroachments of infidel Philosophy. We have taken from God a portion of his divine power, and given it to Nature. We have allowed Nature to make her own laws; and many of us do not presume to think that the Deity is consulted in the matter. The revolutions of the planets, the changing of the seasons, the alternation of light and darkness, the growth of vegetation, the production of sunshine and showers, the support of animal life;—these, and many other things, have been handed over to Nature; and many good men, and Christians too, are ready to admit that the God they worship and whom they *call* Supreme, has no immediate or direct agency in any of them. Some even seem to regard it as a fine achievement of theological science, an indication of a high degree of divine knowledge, that they are able to elevate the Deity above many of the inferior operations of the universe. The sparrows used to fall to the ground by our heavenly Father; at present, this trifling affair is attended to by the laws of Nature.

We have only to say that we have no sympathy with this idea. It is not good Philosophy, it is still worse Theology. It lessens the sanctions of moral duty. It turns our thoughts away from God, and makes us worship the creature more than the Creator. The tendency of the theory is atheistic, unchristian and immoral.

230. We are not unaware of the fact that the theory is assumed by some, as enabling them the better to vindicate the divine character, by removing from the Deity the responsibility of certain evils that exist in the world; but the theory does not reach the object. It rather increases the difficulty: for while it makes him no less really the author of these evils, it attaches to him the disgrace of seeking to hide himself behind the laws of Nature, while the work is being done.

SECTION II.—The World not Eternal.

231. That matter is eternal, we may reasonably assume, as the author of the language placed at the head of this chapter, puts forth no opposing sentiment. The word *create* does not imply the production of the world from nothing, as we have shown in our criticism on that term, (pp. 56, 57.) But the question has sometimes been asked, whether it is not as reasonable to suppose that the *world* always existed, in an organized system, as to maintain the eternal existence of *matter* in any other form. If we admit the self-existence of any thing, may we not as well admit the self-existence of the world, as the self-existence of the materials out of which the world was made? We answer, No; and we offer our reasons for this decision:—A world of order and beauty, such as ours—an organized system, in which all the parts are wisely adjusted and benevolently fitted to administer to the wants of living creatures—contains the plainest indications of having been thus organized and arranged by an intelligent Creator. No piece of human mechanism contains clearer proofs of the workings of genius and skill, than the world in which we live. And as no one would think of accounting for the one of these things, without an intelligent author; so no one can suppose this of the other. Not so with unorganized matter. It shows no design. It indicates no previous intelligence. It has no mechanical structure; no systematic organization. That it may have existed forever, therefore, is not an unwarrantable supposition.

232. When we look upon a beautiful temple, we know it has been made by human hands and human genius; for such structures are never produced in any other way. No one doubts the correctness of our conclusion. When we look upon the trees of the forest, or the stones in the quarry, of which temples are constructed, we do not come to any such conclusion. We know that human hands and human skill are not necessary for the production of these things. We might not at first conclude that they had any maker at all. On a closer examination, however, we discover that the trees and stones, too, show evidence of design. They are composed of parts, nicely arranged, and must therefore have been made. Could we, however, go back to that condition of matter where no arrangement, or order, or system, could be perceived, the necessity of admitting a Creator would then cease. All organization must have an intelligent author; but back of all organization, no intelligent author need be supposed.

233. Again; another question, leading to the same result with the one we have just discussed, is the following: — Since, after admitting the creation of the world, we are compelled to admit an eternal Creator, does not this involve the same difficulty as to admit the world itself eternal: and if it does involve the same difficulty, why not as well adopt the one theory as the other? We answer that the two theories do *not* involve the same difficulties. That the world was made, we know from its mechanical arrangements and wise adaptations. It is strictly a machine, and must have been made by a wise mechanic. Not so, God. He does not consist of "body or parts." We cannot examine his structure, as we can that of the human body, or the solar system, or any other of his works; and we cannot of course detect in him the

same indications of design, as we see in the system of nature. The two things are quite unlike. Our conclusions must correspond;—the world was made; God was not made.

SECTION III.—CREATION BY NATURAL CAUSES.

234. Some Philosophers admit the fact of a creation, but they seek to account for it on natural principles, without the agency of a God. The solar system, for example, came into its present form, and assumed all of the beauty and harmony that belong to it, by the operation of natural laws that are inherent in matter itself.

According to one theory, advocated by these men, the solar bodies — the sun and all the planets — were originally but one body in a highly heated state. This immense mass of heated matter, was subject, as it naturally would be, to violent explosions, of which earthquakes on our globe are but miniature representations. By this explosive power, the planets were thrown off from the central mass, to the positions they now occupy; and some of these planets, in imitation of their illustrious parent, ejected smaller bodies that now constitute their moons. Thus all the great masses of the solar system were located. Add to this, that these bodies, turning on their axes, would naturally become round, or as nearly so as they are found to be. This was the commencement of the system; and as this was affected by natural laws, so all else that occurred then, or has occurred since, is, in like manner, brought about by principles inherent in nature.

235. There are some things that are favorable to this theory; and, associated with the doctrine of an all-pervading Deity, it may be admitted as the true interpretation of the origin of the world; but of itself, it does not account for all the facts of creation, and never can account for them. The sun is apparently, perhaps really, a highly heated body. As such it may have been, and may now be, explosive in its tendency. The other planets may have been the same. There are many geological facts which prove that the earth was originally so; and analogy would lead us to infer this of the other planets.

The idea, therefore, that the planets may have been ejected from the sun, and that the secondary planets may, in like manner, and by the same cause, have been thrown out from the primaries, is not unphilosophical.

236. Another thing may be urged in favor of the theory. The sun is known to turn upon its centre. If, therefore, the planets were thrown from it, the tendency would be, to throw them all in one general direction, that is, in the direction of its central motion. Hence, when all the planets are found to occupy the position here indicated, the fact affords confirmation to the theory.

Again; that the planets should be of different sizes, and be thrown to different distances, is what we might expect, and is what we all know to be true.

So far the work seems natural. It could all be done by forces now in existence. Farther than this. The sun and other bodies, turning as we know they do, on their axes, would, by a natural law, become round; not indeed exactly round, but as nearly so as they really are. This part of the work, too, is a natural process.

237. We will look now at some of the objections to the theory — objections to it, as disconnected from the idea of a Creator.

First, How did the planets, when thrown to the position in which we find them, happen to remain there? If a law of nature ejected them, why did not another law of nature bring them back again? We know there is such a law. When any body is thrown up from the earth, it comes back to the earth again; and philosophers tell us that this law is universal. How then did the law come to be evaded, when the planets were thrown off from the central body? This matter has not been explained. The theory recognizes one law of nature, and makes use of it to eject the planets, and send them off to their proper places; but, to keep them there, it is obliged to ignore another law, whose existence is no less certain.

238. Again; when the planets were thrown out into space, they not only did not return as we should expect them to do; but they commenced a motion that we should not expect. They began a revolution round the sun. What was the cause of this? What natural

law originated the annual revolution of the planets?

239. Philosophers tell us that the planets move round the sun by the action of two forces; one of which draws them toward the sun, and is therefore called the centripetal force; the other acts in a different direction, and tends to carry them away from the sun, and is therefore named the centrifugal force. Acted upon by these forces, they neither go *to* the sun, nor *from* it, but *round* it. One of these forces may be called natural — it is the power of attraction — the centripetal force; but nature does not supply the other; and we cannot account for its existence on any known principle. But suppose we could. How did these forces happen to be so exactly balanced, that the planets, vast as they are, and immense as are the distances they travel, do not vary a hair's breadth from the same track, year after year, and age after age? Nor this only; they come round, with each revolution, to the place of setting out, at precisely the same moment of time!

240. To appreciate the force of this reasoning, let us look at the subject a little more closely. The power with which the sun attracts the earth, (also the other planets,) is said to depend on two conditions. One is, the amount of matter in the attracting bodies; and the other is, the distance between them. This increases the difficulty of accounting for the revolution of the planets upon the natural theory. The earth for instance, is moved along in space by a certain force. Acted upon by this force alone, it would go forward in a straight line, till it passed entirely out of the system and disappeared in the far off regions of space. This not being the thing required, another force is instituted, that draws the earth toward the sun. Obeying neither force alone, it yields partly to both, and turns into a circular or eliptical path around the central body. The question then presents itself; — How did the sun happen to possess precisely that amount of matter, no more nor less, that would exert upon the earth the requisite attraction? If the sun had been larger than it is, its attraction upon the earth would have been too great; and the earth, yielding to it, would have been drawn into the central body. On the other hand, had the sun been smaller than it is, the attraction, being less, would have been too little; and the earth would have passed away, and been lost from the system. The same unhappy consequence would have followed, if the *earth* had been larger or smaller than it is.

241. Nor this only. The distance of these bodies from each other, is an important consideration. The amount of their attraction is determined as much by this, as by their size. How then did they happen to be just so far apart, as to ensure the requisite power, no more nor less? If they were farther separated, their attraction would be less, and would of course be too small—if they were not so far apart, the attraction would be greater, and of course would be too great. Now we say, it was a marvellous *chance* that adjusted their sizes and distances, with such exact precision, and did that, not only with reference to one planet, but with reference to a large number of bodies.

242. The wonder is increased by one other circumstance. Not only must the size and distances of the planets, be accurately determined, as they stand related to the sun; but a no less important adjustment is necessary as they stand related to each other; for they all attract each other, and in accordance with the same law of size and distance. What adds to the difficulty still more, is, that their relative distances are perpetually changing, as they move in different orbits, and with various velocities, around the central sun.

243. Another thing may be added that possesses some importance. It is the motion of the planets on their axes. Every planet turns on its centre, and presents its sides alternately to the central luminary. To throw the planet out from the sun, may be the action of a natural law; but to set it rolling on its centre, so as to warm and enlighten its several sides, required another power, and one that nature does not seem to supply. The theory of creation, without a Deity, fails to explain this difficulty.

244. The formation of the solar system has been explained differently by another class of theorists, alike disposed to shut out the agency of the divine spirit.

Their theory is this:—Originally all the matter that makes up the solar system, existed in a vapory or gaseous state, and was widely diffused throughout the regions of space. In process of time, this widely diffused substance began to consolidate at several different points, each point forming a nucleus around which the adjacent matter continued to collect, till a world, such as ours, or such as any one of the other planets, was produced. Thus, by mere accident, (for without a God it could be nothing else,) the planets were formed and located. This being done by a natural law, the same must be our conclusion, concerning other processes, whether we can explain all the facts of the case, in accordance with the theory, or not.

245. We reply that the theory leaves too many things unexplained. It does not account for the commencement of the creative work. It gives no reason for the beginning of each world. It does not account for the size and position of the heavenly bodies. Why did they happen to be formed in the best possible places, and grow to the best possible size? And in what way, or by what cause, did they commence the revolutions they perform, both on their axes and round the sun? These questions are not answered, and cannot be, by any merely natural theory that has ever been devised. We must seek an explanation of these things from some other source.

SECTION IV.—Necessity of a Creator.

246. The solar system is a most wonderful contrivance of the divine mind. The sun is the centre of the system. It is a large body, and, according to the acknowledged philosophy of the subject, it exerts a controlling power over the rest of the system. It could not have fulfilled its evident purpose, if it had been of different size or location. Without a Deity, it might have been different. Chance might have made it larger or smaller; it might have made it give too much light or too little. So, too, chance would have been quite as likely to place the sun outside the circle of bodies, to be lighted and warmed by it, as within that circle, where alone its work could be properly performed. Or, it would have been as likely to have made a sun of some other body, the Earth, for instance, or Venus, or Mars ; and who does not see, that, in such a case, the operations of the system would have been very imperfectly performed, if performed at all ?

247. Not only is the sun the only body that could perform its offices, and is located in the only proper place for doing its work ; but the work is done, so to speak, in the most economical and judicious manner. Observe ; the sun does not travel round the planets to warm them and give them light ; but it occupies a central and permanent position, and the planets, placed around it, are turned over, and so alternately offer their several sides to its light and heat. Could anything be more natural and admirable than this arrangement ? The old doctrine which taught that the earth was the centre of the system, and that the sun and stars revolved around *it*, was at once exploded, when the size and distance of the sun were ascertained. Men reasoned thus : — It is not to be supposed that an immense body, much larger than the earth, and ninety-five millions of miles from it, should make a circuit of such inconceivable extent, to accomplish an object that can be accomplished in a much better way. The better way, the true economy, is, to turn this little planet over every twenty-four hours, and thus permit all parts to enjoy the blessings of the parent luminary. But the force of this reasoning, which facts show to be conclusive, depends wholly on the idea that the affairs of the system are wisely and judiciously conducted. Reasoning upon the chance theory, the ancient doctrine is as likely to be true as the modern. The true plan was evidently chosen, because it was the best ; and this act of choosing, implies, of necessity, the existence of an intelligent Creator, as choosing the *best* method, shows his wisdom and goodness.

248. That God, in the beginning, did, therefore, create the heavens and the earth, as the Bible says, seems the most obvious and best sustained of all truths : and we are constrained to regard, as the most marvellous thing, among the wonders of the world, the unbelief of men, or even their doubts, in regard to this fact. We may be allowed to hope, then, that the arguments for a creating intelligence, that have been presented, more especially the objections to opposing theories, may be regarded as entirely conclusive, and may establish in the mind, this soundest of philosophical truths, and most practical of theological doctrines.

CHAPTER VII.

THE CREATION CONSIDERED WITH REFERENCE TO THE FACTS OF GEOLOGY.

CONTENTS: — Primitive Condition of the Earth; First Day of Creation; Second Day; Third Day; Fourth Day; Fifth day; Sixth Day; the Seventh Day.

SECTION I.—PRIMITIVE CONDITION OF THE EARTH.

2. And the earth was without form, and void; and darkness *was* upon the face of the deep; and the Spirit of God moved upon the face of the waters.

249. That the surface of the earth was originally water, is conceded by all respectable Geologists. The strata of rock, with vegetable and animal remains imbedded in them, were evidently formed in water. And there can be no doubt, that, what now constitute the highest mountains on the globe, was once beneath the surface of the ocean; and that they have been lifted up to their present position, by some power acting from below. There is reason to believe that such upheavals and depressions have occurred many times. Some of the witnesses of what is here stated will be introduced. Professor Jameson, of the University of Edinburgh, uses the following language; — "It is impossible to deny that the seas have formerly, and for a long time, covered the masses of earth that now constitute our highest mountains; and further, that these waters during a long time, did not support any living bodies." La Place, an infidel philosopher, gives his testimony to the same point. He says;

"There cannot be the least doubt, but that the sea covered a great part of our continents, on which it has left incontestable proof of its existence." Buffon, too, maintains that the earth was once in a liquid state. De Luc says: "It is unnecessary to stop to prove, that our continents have once formed the bed of the sea; there is no longer any diversion of opinion among naturalists upon this point." Buckland says the same thing;— "All observers admit the strata were formed beneath the waters." Professor Silliman, of Yale College says;— "The incumbent ocean is indispensable, equally so with the agency of internal fires, to the correct deductions of the theoretical Geologists." See Bakewell's Geology, p. 562. Turner's Sacred History, vol. I. p. 32. Buckland, vol. I. p. 42.

250. It is an extraordinary coincidence, that many of the pagan nations have had traditions, referring the present order of things to original chaos. Such traditions have been found among the Greeks and Romans, the Phœnicians, the Scandinavians, the Bramins of India, &c. &c.

SECTION II.—First Day of Creation.

3. And God said, Let there be light: and there was light.
4. And God saw the light, that *it was good*: and God divided the light from the darkness.

5. And God called the light Day, and the darkness he called Night: and the evening and the morning were the first day.

251 The statement that the Spirit of God moved upon the *face of the waters*, shows that the writer is speaking of the earth's surface. This was the place that was without form and void; and here the first effort of creative power is put forth. We do not understand the expression, "Let there be light," as relating to the actual creation of light, but to its production in a particular locality. "Let light be *there*," that is, on the face of the deep, or at the earth's surface, would convey the true idea, as we understand the subject. Till the time here referred to, the earth was surrounded by a thick mist or vapor, rising up many miles above its surface, and shutting out the sun's rays. The removal of this vapor by the Divine Spirit, or, if one prefers the expression, by a natural law, would allow the light to shine down upon the earth's surface, and drive away the surrounding darkness. The whole was a natural process, as far as anything is natural ; and it was, in a certain sense, supernatural, as all else, in the same sense, now is. That this view of the subject is correct, is proven, both by the language employed, and by the philosophy of the subject.

That darkness was upon the face of the deep, justifies the inference that elsewhere it was not dark ; and that the light may have shined above, though not at the earth's surface ; and hence, "Let there be light," must be explained with the limitation we have given the expression, and which the connection seems to require. The other clause, "face of the waters," where the Spirit of God moved, confirms the view we have given, by confining to that locality, this first effort of creative power.

Further than this : — It is well understood, and acknowledged, by all who have investigated the subject, that originally the earth's temperature was much greater than it is at present; the result of which would be, the production of the mist or vapor, and consequent darkness, implied in our interpretation ; and the removal or diminution of that, would *let the light be* where it had before been excluded.

252. The separation of light and darkness is easily explained. The light, coming from any fixed point, on one side of the earth, would produce darkness on the other side ; and thus a separation would take place. "Evening and morning" are occasioned by an alternation of light and darkness ; and the revolution of the globe on its axis, would produce this result. And it may be added, that the mention of evening and morning implies such a revolution ; and we know, moreover, that such a motion would have a tendency to bring our world into its present globular, or nearly globular form, in accordance with laws of matter now well understood.

If the views we have given of light be objected to, on the ground that the sun was not created till the fourth day, we simply ask that this objection be permitted to lie over till we come to that place in the record, when we trust we may be able to give to it a satisfactory answer. For the present we wish it assumed, that the sun *did* exist on the first day, and gave light then, as it gave light afterwards.

253. We will add here, as relating to the subject of this section, that many pagan nations have traditions that are in harmony with the Mosaic record. These traditions doubtless had their origin with the ancient Hebrews. Ellis, in his Polynesian Researches, says of the Otaheitans, that they "refer the first existence of their principal deities, to the state of darkness, which they make the origin of all things. These are said to be " fanau Po," born of Night. " Po, the world of darkness." The Anglo Saxons began their computation of time from darkness ; and the beginning of their year they call " Mother Night." Aristotle says of the Greeks :—" The theologians say, all things are born from night, the philosophers, that all things were mingled together." Were not both substantially correct, in these particulars? According to Ovid, the same opinion existed with the Romans: and Plutarch and Diodoros Siculus assert the same thing of the Egyptians. See Turner's Sacred History, vol. 1. p. 22, 23.

SECTION III.—Second Day of Creation.

6. ¶ And God said, Let there be a firmament in the midst of the waters, and let it divide the waters from the waters.

7. And God made the firmament, and divided the waters which *were* under the firmament from the waters which *were* above the firmament : and it was so.

8. And God called the firmament Heaven. And the evening and the morning were the second day.

254. The proper distribution of light and heat about the surface of the earth, as well as the separation of the waters, by evaporation, and sundry other purposes, required a firmament or atmosphere. The constituents of the atmosphere, already existed in the waters, and needed only to be evolved and compounded in the requisite proportion. This was done, like all the rest, by the Spirit of God, that brooded over the great deep. And it is worthy to be particularly noticed, that this part of the creative

THE CREATION CONSIDERED.   141

work was done at the only proper time for doing it. The light that now shined down upon the earth, required the agency of the atmosphere. The evaporation of water to form the clouds, required it. The growth of vegetation, and all the subsequent operations of the world required it. It was not needed till this time, and till this time, the surrounding space was otherwise occupied. It now became necessary, and could not be dispensed with, in conducting and completing the divine operations. That the firmament was made *in the midst of the waters*, is the clearest dictate of reason, in view of what we know of the condition of the earth at the time here referred to. The surrounding vapor, caused by the high temperature, had indeed been diminished, so as to allow the light to shine upon the earth, but it had not yet been wholly removed. In the midst, then, of this vapor, the atmosphere was formed. There was water below, within, and above the firmament.

SECTION IV.—THIRD DAY OF CREATION.

9. ¶ And God said, Let the waters under the heaven be gathered together unto one place, and let the dry *land* appear: and it was so.
10. And God called the dry *land* Earth; and the gathering together of the waters called he Seas: and God saw that *it was* good.
11. And God said, Let the earth bring forth grass, the herb yielding seed, *and* the fruit tree yielding fruit after his kind, whose seed *is* in itself, upon the earth: and it was so.
12. And the earth brought forth grass, *and* herb yielding seed after his kind, and the tree yielding fruit, whose seed *was* in itself, after his kind: and God saw that *it was* good.
13. And the evening and the morning were the third day.

255. Two prominent particulars are here brought to view. One is, the separation of the dry land and water; the other, the production of vegetation. We will notice each in its order.

That what is now dry land, was once below the surface of the water, is proved by the presence of vegetable and animal remains, found in the rocky strata that compose the earth's crust, as well as by the fact that these strata must have been formed under water. Many of these remains were dry land productions, that were placed in their position above water, and afterwards sunk with the general surface beneath the ocean, and still later, lifted up again into dry land, to be again depressed and raised indefinitely.

Plenty of Geological authorities can be adduced in favor of the Mosaic account. We have before seen that Professor Jameson regards the sea, as having once, and for a long time, covered the earth's surface, including those portions that now constitute the highest mountains. This of course implies the separation mentioned by the sacred writers; for these mountains, being elevated from under water, would form the dry land, and allow the waters to flow together into one place. Higgins speaks as follows, on this subject: — "The stratified rocks must originally have been horizontal, or nearly so; and many of them were formed in the same manner as the deposits which are always to be found in the beds of rivers, and in the basins of the oceans, but they were afterwards acted upon by mighty disturbing forces, which elevated and disrupted them, throwing their strata into a variety of forms. Some were upheaved in a mass, by an omnipotent agent acting from beneath them; and some were tilted into inclined positions: and others, acted upon in more than one point, were made to assume the form of a basin. These effects have been both local and general; at one time affecting a district not more than a few miles in extent, and at others, elevating entire continents and immense mountain chains. The agent, as we believe, that produced these mighty effects, was internal heat, the same cause, which, in the present day, mimics its former results, by the exhibition of volcanic action, and other phenomena." The same author says again: — "The relative position, and superficial extent of land and water, have been constantly changing; not slowly and imperceptibly, as at present, but by the action of causes, the effects of which have been almost instantaneous; upheaving the bed of the ocean, and deluging the dry lands. In some instances the cause, and consequently the effect has been local: but at certain periods there was probably a universal convulsive movement of the entire crust of the earth, when element, warring with element, involved all nature in one general ruin." Robert

Murdie has the following language: — "Those gigantic masses, which can have been produced by no surface action, are the result of energies, which, whatever they may have been, have had their origin and their plan of action, within the globe itself; whether the influence of that action were more general or more local, whether it went to the uplifting of a continent, or the building of a chain of mountains, or merely raised the point of a volcanic cone above the waters of the sea."

These authorities are sufficient, though many more might be produced — all showing that such revolutions have occurred, as described in the Mosaic account, by which a separation of dry land and water was effected. Higgins, p. 226, 274. Murdie's Popular Guide, p. 227.

256. The creation of vegetation is the next particular embraced in the record. But here I wish it to be observed that, according to the Bible account, there was a time when vegetation did not exist; and it is interesting to see that Geology teaches the same thing. Let us hear some of the witnesses to this fact. Bakewell says: — "The Primary Rocks were so called, because no fossil remains of animals or vegetables, nor any fragments of other rocks, were found embedded in them." Professor Jameson says that the waters that originally covered the earth, "did not, for a long time, support any living bodies." Dr. Good, in his Book of Nature, says of the Primary Formations, "Not a single relic of either animal or vegetable petrifaction, is found in any of them." Bakewell's Geology, p. 7, 562. Book of Nature, p. 67.

257. What Geologists call the Primary Formations, meaning the lowest, or those first deposited, do not, as they say, contain any vegetable or animal relics. There was a time, then, when no vegetable or animal existed. So say Geologists; and so says the Bible record. In Gen. ii: 5, we are informed that God made "every plant of the field, before it was in the earth, and every herb of the field, before it grew." The idea seems to be, that the germs of the vegetable kingdom, in their multifarious forms, were first created in the earth, and then grew, as the result of sunshine, and rain, and cultivation, as at subsequent times. There are certain "laws," as we call

them, that now regulate the vegetable kingdom; but what law of nature produced the original germs from which vegetation springs? We know that every form of vegetable life, has associated with it, an arrangement for securing its reproduction and perpetuity. This we call natural; but what natural law originated the first seeds or germs that were to be thus perpetuated?

The action of a divine power and intelligence, is the only supposition that can explain this phenomenon. And I would farther suggest: — if a divine agency first originated the arrangement, whether it be not the same agency, (though we call it a law of nature,) that now continues it.

258. The Primary Formations, we said, are such as lie the lowest in the earth's crust, and were of course the first deposited.

These having no vegetable or animal remains in them, were placed in their position, before the creation of vegetation on the third day. Those Formations that occupy a position next above these, are called Transition Rocks; receiving this name, because they intervene between the rocks below them, that have no relics, and the rocks above, where such relics are abundant. These Transition Rocks are interspersed sparingly with these remains, increasing with the advance upwards. This state of things is perfectly consistent with the Bible account. That account allows a long period for the Primitive Rocks to form, for we may suppose some part of this work was done before the Bible account begins, as there is nothing in the record to forbid this supposition, since that record commences with the surface, and does not relate to what may have been done far below. The account then tells us of the creation of the vegetable kingdom; and of course all deposits made afterwards, would contain, as we find they do, vegetable relics.

259. The Geologists speak of these Transition Rocks as follows — Buckland: — "In the interior region of this series, plants are few in number, and principally marine; but in the superior regions, the remains of land plants are accumulated in prodigious quantities." Higgins: — "In every period after the formation of the primitive rocks, it, [the earth,] appears to have been inhabited by a class of animals, and decorated with vegetation, suited to its physical condition : and the imbedded remains are sufficient evidence of this fact." Dr. Good says of the same Geological strata : — "It is in this second class of formations, that petrifactions first make their appearance : and it deserves particular attention, that they are uniformly confined, both in the animal and vegetable kingdoms, to those in the lowest links in the scale of organization. It is here also that the carbonaceous matter, which is chiefly of vegetable origin, first makes its appearance in any considerable quantity." Silliman : — "In regard to vegetables, there is good reason to believe that they were at least as early as animals. Vegetables are found more or less through the whole Transition Series." This author thinks that some vegetables have become so carbonized as to lose their identity, in which case, vegetable productions "will claim the highest rank in organic antiquity." Buckland, vol. I. p. 57. Higgins, p. 227. Good, p. 68. Bakewell, p. 555.

260. It has before been observed, that the earth possessed originally a much higher temperature than at present : a supposition indispensable to a correct and rational system of Geology. The proof of the fact, (or one of the proofs,) is derived from the vegetable and animal relics just referred to. They are such as could not have grown and lived in the climate that now prevails where they are found : and they are found too plentifully, and in too perfect a form, to have been transmitted to the place they now occupy, from some distant region. They required, and must have had, a much higher temperature; in other words, a much higher temperature must have prevailed, on that part of the globe, at that time. The fact doubtless is, that from the earth's primeval state, to the present time, the temperature has been constantly decreasing : sometimes very slowly, and at others very rapidly, depending on the convulsions and revolutions that have taken place.

7

SECTION V.—Fourth Day of Creation.

14. ¶ And God said, Let there be lights in the firmament of the heaven to divide the day from the night; and let them be for signs, and for seasons, and for days, and years:
15. And let them be for lights in the firmament of the heaven to give light upon the earth: and it was so.
16. And God made two great lights; the greater light to rule the day, and the lesser light to rule the night: he *made* the stars also.
17. And God set them in the firmament of the heaven to give light upon the earth,
18. And to rule over the day and over the night, and to divide the light from the darkness: and God saw that *it was* good.
19. And the evening and the morning were the fourth day.

261. We would suggest what seems to us a very rational theory, that what is stated of our planet, as to its progressive formation, was also true of the other planets that make up the system ; and no less true of the central body that controls and governs the rest. The sun, therefore, according to this theory, was in existence on the first day, and gave light then, as it gave light afterwards. It was not then a perfect sun, any more than the earth was a perfect earth. The one changed and improved as well as the other ; and the same was true of the whole system. In process of time the whole was completed ; and the system set in motion, as the writer informs us. And since it was not his purpose to give us a particular account of the other planets, but only of the earth, he therefore passes over the processes to which they were subjected ; and states, in a brief and general way, the fact of their creation, and the arrangement of the whole into one great system ; and he chooses the only proper time for making this statement, viz. : at the completion of the work on the fourth day ; though the bodies referred to, may have existed, in an imperfect state, as did the earth, at the very beginning.

262. It may be remarked, however, that the passage admits of a construction that will obviate the difficulty in another way. The past tense in the Hebrew language, was not divided, as in our own, into Imperfect, Perfect and Pluperfect ; but it expressed all these by one form only ; and in translating, the sense of the passage, and its connections, must determine what form of our verb to use. Hence, verse 16, of the passage now under consideration, may be put into brackets, and rendered thus ;—

[And God *had* made two great lights, the greater light to rule the day, and the lesser light to rule the night; the stars also] which would throw the creation of these bodies into the past, and make only the placing of them in the firmament of heaven, to have been done on the fourth day. We conceive that either mode of removing the difficulty is sufficient; and that the theory that would commend itself to our judgment, as most worthy of acceptance on the ground of reason, is also in harmony with the Bible account, when rightly construed.

263. Another difficulty may be noticed and removed by philosophical facts. The two great lights were placed "in the firmament of heaven;", but it will be objected that this cannot be true, as these bodies are far beyond our firmament or atmosphere. To this, it would be a sufficient reply, perhaps, to say, that the writer makes use of popular language, which is accommodated to appearances, rather than to facts, as when we speak of the sun rising and setting, though we know no such thing really occurs, but only appears to. But if the objector insists on a philosophical accuracy of language, on the part of the writer of the Bible account, we would remind him that the language here used is strictly accurate and philosophical. The *lights* are in the firmament of heaven, and indeed they are but a little way from us, else we could not see them, though the *bodies* that produce them are far away. I do not presume that our philosophical objector will claim that he can see to the distance of 95 millions of miles, or even 240 thousand miles.

As the mention of evening and morning, on the first day, proves the diurnal revolution of the globe at that time; so the reference to the seasons and years, proves the annual revolution of the earth, on the fourth day.

SECTION VI. — FIFTH DAY OF CREATION.

20. And God said, Let the waters bring forth abundantly the moving creature that hath life, and fowl *that* may fly above the earth in the open firmament of heaven.

21. And God created great whales, and every living creature that moveth, which the waters brought forth abundantly after their kind, and every winged fowl after his kind ; and God saw that it was good.

22. And God blessed them, saying, Be fruitful, and multiply, and fill the waters in the seas, and let fowl multiply in the earth.

23. And the evening and the morning were the fifth day.

264. The number of living creatures, great and small, that exist in the depths of the ocean, is beyond all human calculation. The waters have truly brought forth "abundantly," from the great whales, down through all forms of life to the minutest of living creatures, of which the naked eye does not take cognizance.

The statement of the writer seems to convey the idea that the waters brought forth the fowls, as well as the fishes ; and there seems to be some propriety in receiving the statement in this way ; for the two elements, water and air, are similar, and their respective inhabitants are constructed on similar principles. The passage, however, admits of a different construction. It may be construed thus : — Let the waters bring forth abundantly, &c., and [let] the fowl fly above the earth. Again ; God created great whales, which the waters brought forth, &c. ; and [God created] every winged fowl, &c.

This passage speaks of marine animals : and the account of the creation of land animals is subsequent to this ; and hence the relics of marine animals are found lowest in the earth, as men of science informs us. Bakewell says ; — " The lower series of the transition beds . . . . . contain almost exclusively the remains of marine animals." Speaking of the strata above the transition, called the Secondary Formations, the same author says : — " The fossil remains, in the upper secondary strata, are, with some exceptions, those of marine animals, but of different genera or species from those in the strata below them." Buckland : — " The first remains of animal life, yet noticed, are marine." Bakewell, p. 7. Buckland, vol. I. p. 340.

265. The Bible record says that God created great

whales; but the term "whale" denotes any large fish or marine animal. And it must not be passed in silence, that, among marine fossils, are found animals of immense magnitude. Geologically, such animals are called "reptiles." On this subject Mantell has the following statement:—"There was a period when the earth was peopled by oviporous quadrupeds of the most appalling magnitude. Reptiles were the lords of creation." Higgins:—"There was a time in the history of our world, when these animals (reptiles) attained an appalling magnitude, and rioting in the wide expanse of waters, swayed the sceptre of uncontrolled power over all other created beings. They all appear to have existed at a period when our earth enjoyed a much higher temperature than it now possesses. Judging from the antiquity of the rocks, in which the bones of reptiles are found, they appear to have been created a long period before the viviporous animals, and at a time when the earth was unfit for animals of a higher organization." Cuvier says:—"It will be impossible not to acknowledge, as a certain truth, the number, the largeness, and the variety, of the reptiles that inhabited the sea and the land at the epoch at which the strata of the Jura (mountains) were deposited." Sir Humphrey Davy, Von Bush, Ure, and others could be quoted in favor of the same thing. It is sufficient to say that no respectable scholar, having the least acquaintance with Geological science, assumes to deny the fact stated in the Bible, that the first animal existences were both abundant in quantity and monstrous in size; and that the element to which they principally belonged, was water. Higgins, p. 257.

We may add that there is a natural reason why marine animals were not created sooner than they were, which is, that the element in which they were to live, was not till then, in a condition to receive them. Its temperature was too high; and it held in solution too many mineral substances, as the rocky strata, formed above them, clearly indicate. Nor was this element in a condition then to support animals of a higher and more perfect organization. Hence, when it became so, the huge and unsightly monsters disappeared, and more perfect races took their place.

SECTION VII. — Sixth Day of Creation.

24. ¶ And God said, Let the earth bring forth the living creature after his kind, cattle, and creeping thing, and beast of the earth after his kind : and it was so.

25. And God made the beast of the earth after his kind, and cattle, after their kind, and every thing that creepeth upon the earth after his kind : and God saw that *it was* good.

26. ¶ And God said, Let us make man in our image, after our likeness : and let them have dominion over the fish of the sea, and over the fowl of the air, and over the cattle, and over all the earth, and over every creeping thing that creepeth upon the earth.

27. So God created man in his own image, in the image of God created he him ; male and female created he them.

CHAP. II.

4. ¶ These *are* the generations of the heavens and of the earth when they were created, in the day that the Lord God made the earth and the heavens.

5. And every plant of the field before it was in the earth, and every herb of the field before it grew : for the Lord God had not caused it to rain upon the earth, and *there was* not a man to till the ground.

6. But there went up a mist from the earth, and watered the whole face of the ground.

7. And the Lord God formed man *of* the dust of the ground, and breathed into his nostrils the breath of life ; and man became a living soul.

266. The manner in which the beasts of the field, and creeping things were formed at first, has been a troublesome question ; and no one has been able satisfactorily to decide it, and perhaps never will. The Bible says ; the earth brought them forth ; but further than this, it gives us no definite information. So far as this relates to the smaller animals, the insects, for example, there may not seem to exist the same difficulty as attends the creation of the larger species. The reason is, that we witness the same thing, or something analogous to it, at the present time : and we can the more readily suppose the same process at the outset. But concerning the larger animals ; the lion, the tiger, the elephant, &c., we derive from the present no light as to the mode of their creation at the first. " Perhaps they have advanced to their present size from very small beginnings." Perhaps they have. Perhaps at first they were mere animalcules, such as are now generated in the summer's sun, and have advanced, in the progress of ages, to their present stature. This does not remove the difficulty. It only changes it to a different position. Nature alone can no more produce a small animal, than a large one. It can no more generate life in the microscopic animalcule, than in the ox or the elephant. It can no more produce the result, by having ages for the work, than it can in the twinkling of an eye. We must associate a God with nature, to explain existing facts; and even then the exact mode of operation may not be rendered certain.

267. There is one argument for the progressive theory. It is the argument of analogy. All else in the creative process, seems to have been gradual and exceedingly slow. The condensation of the planets, the deposition of strata, and doubtless other processes, required long ages for their completion. Why not the same be true of the vegetable and animal productions? That God could create the world at once, and could fill it with inhabitants, with a single word, is not to be doubted. He has power enough to do this; but as he has not chosen this mode in other productions and processes, why should we suppose vegetable and animal life an exception to his ordinary method?

But, though we adopt the progressive theory, the idea sometimes put forth, that an animal or a vegetable of one kind, may have risen up from one of a different or inferior order, has no analogy or good sense to support it. Every plant and animal is made "after its kind;" and however long the time in producing them, the kinds must have been separate and distinct.

268. The passage now before us, brings to view the creation of land animals. Of course after their creation we may suppose them to have shared the fate common to all animal and vegetable existences before them. They must have perished, and left their bones to rot upon the plains, or to be buried in the earth, or to be sunk in the water. This has been done; and according to the Mosaic theory, they may be expected to be found in the earth, in the order laid down in the record. On this point what do Geologists say?

Bakewell:—" The co-existence of land animals, at the period when most of the secondary series were deposited, is proved by the occasional occurrences of terrestrial fossil plants, and the bones of fresh water and amphibious reptiles." Jameson : — "The bones of mammiferous land quadrupeds, are found only above the coarse limestone, which is above the chalk." The limestone and chalk are down as far as the transition strata. It is not until you get above these, says Professor Jameson, that land animals are found. Vegetables, and marine animals, we have seen, may be found lower. They should be ; for according to the Bible record, they were formed first. Cuvier has nearly the same language as Jameson. So has Buckland. Sir H. Davy says : — "The remains of quadrupeds of extinct species occur next above those of birds and oviporous reptiles. . . . It is only in the loose and slightly consolidated strata of gravel and sand, and which are usually called diluvial formations, that the remains of animals, such as now people the globe, are found." Bakewell, p. 7, 562.

269. The Bible tells us that man was created last. How does the testimony of Geologists agree with this statement? We have the satisfaction of knowing that they all agree with the Bible account ; not because they are glad to be found on the side of divine revelation, for some of them are not ; but because facts compel them to give in their testimony in its favor. The few we shall quote will represent the declarations of the many. Jameson : — "Man is found nowhere except at the surface." Bakewell : — "The absence of human bones in the stratified rocks, or in the undisturbed beds of gravel or clay, indicate that man, the most perfect of terrestrial beings, was not created till after those great revolutions which buried many different orders, and entire genera of animals, deep under the present surface of the earth." Cuvier : — "It is a fact, that, as yet, no human bones have been discovered among fossil remains."

270. Thus, all through the Bible account of creation there is the most perfect agreement with facts as they exist in the earth. It is the business of Geologists to search out these facts, and bring them before the world. They have done so ; and the result has been astonishingly in favor of the Bible account. On this point, Cu-

vier, the great French Naturalist, whom we have several times quoted, says:—"The books of Moses show us that he had very perfect ideas respecting several of the highest questions of Natural Philosophy. His Cosmogony .... is exactly the same as that which has been deduced from Geological considerations." Professor Silliman, of Yale College, one of the best instructed naturalists of this country, speaks as follows:—"The order of the physical events, discovered by Geology, is substantially the same, as that recorded by the sacred historian." Bakewell, 562, 17, 554, 538.

271. I would add that many of the earlier events, recorded in the Bible, are found imperfectly represented in the traditions of pagan nations. The most remarkable instance of this kind, relating to the creation of the world, is the account given in the Institutes of Menu, which Sir William Jones regards as nearly as ancient as the writings of Moses. The account of the six days of the creation, as there given, so obviously resembles that given in Genesis, that it is scarcely possible to doubt its being derived from the same patriarchal communication. There is a particular description given of the term "day," and it is expressly stated to be a period of several thousand years — a comment on the Mosaic use of that term, of no small importance, when its antiquity is considered. The sixth day of creation closes up the creative work. A few remarks on the whole subject will close the discussion.

272. (1.) It is worthy of notice, as an occasion of admiration, that the order of creation is the most natural of any that could have been devised. Everything is made at its proper time. Removing the superincumbent vapor from the earth's surface, allowing the light to shine down on the face of the deep, was the first work. The cooling process to which the earth was then subject would induce this state of things. An atmosphere is next in order. There is now a place for it: and it is needed to help carry on the subsequent work. Then a separation takes place between the dry land and water. Without this, vegetable and animal life, as it now exists, could not be. All that followed this separation, required it; nor was a different order possible. In other words, the

7*

plants and animals required the dry land and water; but the latter did not require the former. Again: The vegetable kingdom occupies the only place that could have been properly assigned it. Before this, it could not exist; it was indispensable afterwards. It required all that went before, the light, the atmosphere and the dry land; but it did not require anything that followed. Then comes the creation of animals. Where else could they have been placed?—not till there was light; not till there was an atmosphere; not till there was dry land; not till there was vegetation. Man is made last, to crown the work, as the most perfect of the creation, to have dominion over, and make use of all the rest. I would add another consideration. At first the temperature of the earth was not adapted to its present inhabitants, nor indeed to inhabitants of any kind. Neither was the atmosphere in a condition to subserve the purposes of the subsequent vegetable and animal creation. The high temperature filled it with too much mist or vapor; but at length, being removed by a diminution of temperature, there would arise a rich and luxuriant vegetation, such as we find to have been the case, from the first vegetable relics found in the earth. Under the state of things then existing, such vegetation could exist before the animals. And at length, when the temperature and the purity of the atmosphere, would admit of animals of some sort, it might still require a considerable period for the condition of things to be suited to such animals as now are, and especially to man.

273. (2.) There is supposed to be a discrepancy between the Bible account and the facts of Geology in regard to the creation of vegetables, and the creation of animals: the latter being placed subsequent to the former by the Bible, while Geology seems to regard them as cotemporary, both being found on a common level in the earth's crust. We remark in regard to this matter, that the point here involved is not a settled question among Geologists; and until it becomes so, no argument can be drawn from it.

Besides, we are to consider that vegetable relics may have existed on the surface of the dry land, long before animals were deposited there : and yet, as they could not be covered up so as to be imbedded in the solid rocks by aqueous deposits, till sunk beneath the water, they would occupy a common level with animals, and seem to have been placed in their position at the same time.

274. (3.) The question whether the days of creation were literal days, or periods of indefinite length : both interpretations being sustained by usage, is still open to discussion. That a special exercise of divine power could have created the world in six natural days is not doubted ; and as the first production of the earth's arrangements, must have been special, with any view we can take of the subject, there is perhaps no more difficulty in regarding it as special and peculiar, with respect to time, than with respect to mode. Analogy, more than any exegesis of terms, or facts of Geology, favor the idea of extending the term "day" to a long and indefinite period. If the condensation of the planets, from a gaseous to a solid state · the deposition of strata, forming the earth's crust : and other processes ; some of which must have occurred before the Mosaic account begins, and others may have occurred before that period, were slow, and required periods of great length, as seems indisputable ; then the production of light at the earth's surface, the formation of the atmosphere, the separation of dry land and water, etc., would most naturally be subject to the same law of progress, and require long periods for their completion. Some Geologists take this view of the term day, among whom may be mentioned, Jameson, Silliman, Good, Hitchcock, &c.

275. If it be objected to this view of "day," that it is described in the account as made up of an "evening," and a "morning," and must therefore have been a natural day of twenty-four hours ; we reply, that the passage may be differently construed, with equal fidelity to the original ; "There was evening and morning, the first day" — in other words, the earth turned on its axis, producing a succession of evening and morning during the first period, may be the true rendering. But if this does not meet the objection satisfactorily, there is another reply that may, and may not, be more satisfactory. It is this ; — Each *period* may be spoken of, with propriety, as having an evening and a morning; and it is worthy of remark that each Geological epoch is represented as being marked by a gradual approach, and then by a gradual decline, of what constitute its distinguishing features, not unlike the approach of light and its gradual decline in the natural day. The late Hugh Miller takes this view, and illustrates it beautifully.

276. It is worthy of special notice, in this connection, that the six days of creation are called " generations ;" and the whole period of creation is called " a day," ii. 4 — a pretty good evidence that the latter term is used in a very extended and indefinite sense — a usage the more satisfactory, in establishing this point, for being employed by the same writer, and in connection with the same subject.

277. In conclusion of this subject, it may be proper to recapitulate the main points of agreement, between the Mosaic account, and the well ascertained facts of Geology.

(1.) The earth was originally in a liquid state, made so, mainly, by the action of heat.

(2.) There was a time when no vegetable or animal life existed on the earth. Moses makes a considerable period to have elapsed before the creation of vegetables or animals. Geologists, too, assure us that there could have been no vegetable or animal, during the period the Primitive Rocks were being deposited.

(3.) The whole earth, being once covered with water, there must have been a time when the water and dry land were separated. Such separation, Moses informs us, took place by the fiat of Omnipotence. Geologists tell us there was such a separation, and that similar convulsions have been frequent in past ages.

(4.) The first living thing created, was vegetation. So says the Bible; and few Geologists have expressed any doubt on this point.

(5.) The first living animals created, were marine. Moses speaks thus, and so do Geologists, as these are found lowest among the deposites of animal remains.

(6.) Man was made last. So says the Bible; and

Geologists agree to this statement. All human relics are found at the surface. This is admitted as true now; but there is, with some men, a lingering *hope* that future discoveries will detect the existence of human bones in the rocks (of which there are yet no well attested examples,) that will prove the Bible false. We have only to wait and see.

278. These are the prominent points of the Bible record; and they are fully sustained by scientific investigations. These investigations, it should be added, belong to modern times; and so far as we know, only to modern times. Hence there was no source from which the ancients could have obtained such information, but from the Divine Being, who must, therefore, have revealed it to them.

SECTION VIII. — THE SEVENTH DAY.

CHAP. II.

1. Thus the heavens and the earth were finished, and all the host of them.
2. And on the seventh day God ended his work which he had made; and he rested on the seventh day from all his work which he had made.
3. And God blessed the seventh day, and sanctified it: because that in it he had rested from all his work which God created and made.

279. That God blessed the seventh day and sanctified it, because that on it he had rested (*ceased,* as the word means) from all his work, is simply a statement of the origin of the sabbath, as understood by the writer, and was probably not written at the time the account was, with which it is connected, but at a later period, when other Mosaic institutions were established. This is made obvious, both by a careful inspection of the place where it is found, showing clearly that it does not belong there; and also by the fact, that, no where in the book of Genesis, is there any allusion to such an institution as the sabbath.

280. The original record simply states that God ended his work which he had made; and he rested (ceased) on the seventh day from all his work which he had made: but it does not state that, on this account, God sanctified, or set apart, that day as a sabbath.

281. It may be added that the translators were evidnetly misled by this interpolation, and gave a rendering to the word "rest," which does not belong to it in this connection. True the original word means *rest*, and the term *sabbath*, as denoting a day of rest, is derived from it: but it also means, *rest from*, or cease to do a thing, and plainly has this meaning here. It is translated *cease* in viii. 22.

CHAPTER VIII.

CREATION OF MAN AND THE UNITY OF THE RACE.

CONTENTS:— Creation of Man; Unity of the Race as a Bible doctrine; Unity of the Race on Natural Grounds; Common Theory Considered; True Theory.

SECTION I.— CREATION OF MAN.

282. The creation of man is involved in great obscurity. The *fact* of his creation is asserted in the Scriptures, and the fact of his creation is proved by Geological phenomena: for there was a time when, according to Geology, man did not exist: as he does now exist, it follows that he must have been created. But the *manner* of his creation, is wholly unknown. He was made of the dust of the ground. This we know, independent of revelation. All the materials that make up the human body are found in the soil, the atmosphere, and other elements. Perhaps it is as true of man, as to his physical existence, as of other animals, that " the earth brought him forth." It is certain that he can be referred to no other source. We are not aware that " Philosophers " have ever assigned him any other origin: and therefore, in this particular, they should not object to the Bible doctrine.

283. But this being admitted, the mind is still unsatisfied, and must ever be, as to the mode by which these elements were combined into a human body. To derive man from the ape, and then from some other animal still lower, and so on back to the insect, does not remove the difficulty. The first starting point needs a God, as much as the full stature of a perfect man; and hence, were we to admit this theory, we could not get rid of a first intelligent cause that originated and conducted the long continued process. But admitting a God, the difficulty is removed only in part, since the *mode* of creation, he has not condescended to reveal, and philosophy throws no clear light upon the subject.

284. God made man male and female. The word "man" includes both sexes. This affords a conclusive argument against any theory that shuts out a Deity from the creative work. It would have been a singular *chance* that produced a man and a woman at the same time, especially if we adopt the theory that traces our existence back through untold generations to the smallest of earth-born creatures. Two operations, commencing at the same time, and continuing on in parallel lines through innumerable ages, and terminating at last in the perfect form of a male and a female, and coming at this result at the same time, is a chance phenomenon that few sensible men will be likely to adopt.

285. One truth, we think, is beyond dispute, that it is much more difficult to exclude a Deity from the creation, than to admit his agency, though we may see, or think we see, objections to the latter view. We ought not to reject propositions that are well sustained, though involving some difficulties, when, in so doing, we are compelled to admit others, at which common sense revolts and yet this is a common weakness, with a certain class of men, who call themselves philosophers, and who arrogate to themselves a much larger share of reason and common sense, than they are willing to allow to others.

286. Two things are asserted of man, having reference to his creation, that are worthy of special notice. One is, man's physical creation. God made him of the dust of the ground, and breathed into him the breath of life, and he became a living soul. Another is, his spiritual creation. God made him in his own image. The importance of this fact made the author repeat it, In the image of God made he him. The first of these passages can have no reference to the soul or spirit, as the term "soul" there, is not used in the modern sense of that word, but has the meaning of "creature." And the last passage can have no reference to the body, as that cannot be regarded, as in any sense, the image of God.

SECTION II. — UNITY OF THE RACE AS A BIBLE DOCTRINE.

287. The common opinion among men who take the Bible as their standard of faith, is, that all men had a common origin, and sprang from one human pair. Some few, however, have thought differently, and at the same time have professed adherence to the Bible history. They tell us that the Bible is not decisive on this point. It seems to them that the book mentions at least two creations of men, one in chapter first, verse 26, of Genesis, and the other, in chapter second, verse seventh. Some add to this opinion, that the man created in the second instance, was to till the ground; while such was not the purpose had in view in the first creation. On the contrary, the man first made, was to have dominion over the beasts of the field, the fowls of the air, and the fishes of the sea — a plain indication that he and his race were to subsist by hunting and fishing, and not by cultivating the ground. And we know there have always been men of this stamp, of which our American Indians are perhaps the most remarkable example.

288. Again: if there were not other creations besides Adam and Eve, where, it is asked, did Cain get his wife? since Adam, Eve and Cain were the only persons living, according to the Bible, at the time of his marriage, and, who were the inhabitants of the city that he built? and, how could Cain fear that those who should find him would slay him, while there were yet no persons living, from whom he could expect any hostile intentions?

289. Most men, however, who take the ground of different races, or different origins of the race, do so, either with open and undisguised disregard of the Bible, or with a disregard obviously implied: and they rely for proofs of their opinion, on the wide differences there are among men, in color, form, features, &c.

290. The question that divides inquirers on this subject is not one that can be decided with as much ease and dispatch as the casual observer may suppose. The allusions in the Bible, to one origin, or more than one, are not so decisive as to remove all doubts; and the facts of nature, are not such, as to admit of being brought into harmony with the one theory or the other, without considerable discussion. It is certain that much has been written upon the subject; and yet there is, by no means, a uniformity of opinion respecting it.

291. For ourself we see no substantial reasons for relinquishing the common view of one origin of the race, both as a Bible doctrine, and as most in harmony with the facts of nature. Still we may not explain either the Bible or facts, after the common mode, nor, perhaps after any mode but our own.

Of course our purpose does not require nor permit a long continued discussion. We hope, however, to give the reader as much satisfaction, as he would be likely to find, perhaps more, than if he were to read many volumes on the subject.

292. In regard to the statements of the Bible, we remark, first, that what are called two creations, are in fact but two statements of one creation. The careful reader will not, I think, fail to perceive this. The latter passage only need be quoted to make this obvious. "These are the generations of the heavens and the earth, when they were created, in the day that the Lord God made the earth and the heavens, and every plant of the field before it was in the earth, and every herb of the field before it grew; for the Lord God had not caused it to rain upon the earth, and there was not a man to till the ground. But there went up a mist from the earth, and watered the whole face of the ground; and the Lord God formed man from the dust of the ground, and breathed into his nostrils the breath of life, and man became a living soul." ii. 4–7. The statement that there was not a man to till the ground, refers back to the period when there was yet no vegetation on the earth. *At that time*, there was not a man to till the ground. The period referred to, was prior to what is called the first creation. Of course the second account is only a repetition of the first, and cannot possibly be referred to the creation of another and different race.

The language of the two passages is somewhat varied, but they are sufficiently alike to make their meaning obviously the same. To subdue the earth, in the one, and to till the ground, in the other, are sufficiently identical. And that the dominion over the animals, was not intended to indicate a particular mode of life, is proved by the fact, that the same dominion was given to Noah and his sons after the flood; and it was surely not then understood as shutting them out from the cultivation of the earth.

293. The oft repeated question;—Where did Cain get his wife, if there was no other branch of the human race but that of Adam, must be answered, as it has often been answered before;—he obtained her, from among other members of the Adamic family: for though none are mentioned up to that period of the history, the general statement that "Adam had sons and daughters," without assigning them any date, allows us to place some of these in advance of the time that Cain took his wife, there being nothing to exclude this idea, but some things that seem to demand it.

294. No one can fail to perceive, that the order of time is not observed by the sacred writer, nor are all events recorded, that are presumed to have taken place. Still no one need be misled at all, who sincerely desires to understand and rightly interpret the book. It is only such as have a favorite theory support, or such as wish to bring the book into disrepute altogether, that can fail to perceive and appreciate the facts as they are. The writer, having introduced the case of Cain, continues and finishes what he has to say of that personage, his residence, his marriage, the city he built, and his posterity for six generations. He then mentions the birth of Seth, in the place of Abel, whom Cain slew. Shall we say that things are here recorded in the order they occurred, and that Adam did not have Seth till six generations of Cain had made their appearance, and most of them, perhaps, had passed away? This would be preposterous. We all understand, that having disposed of Cain and his descendants, the writer *goes back*, and takes up the history of Adam

where he had left it, and speaks of the birth of Seth. There is nothing against the supposition, therefore, that the birth of Seth, and of many, if not all, of Adams' other sons and daughters, occurred before Cain took his wife. Add to this that Seth was to fill the place of Abel, and as such, there may have been some reason for the fears of Cain lest that brother might avenge the murderous act that had taken the life of Abel.

295. Let another thing be noticed. Cain was to be a fugitive and a vagabond in the earth; and yet the next thing we hear of him is, that he had a son and built a city. How could his sentence have been fulfilled, unless a considerable time elapsed, between the first and last of these events? While Cain was leading a fugitive and vagabond life, therefore, the "sons and daughters" of Adam might have become sufficiently numerous to have allowed him a fair opportunity for choosing a companion and bringing together inhabitants for the city that he built. Nor does it follow from this view, that Cain married his sister, though it does follow that some one or more of his brothers did; and as there was no law or custom to prevent such a union, as at a later day, the occurrence was not an unnatural and an improper one.

SECTION III.— UNITY OF THE RACE ON NATURAL GROUNDS.

296. The reasons for concluding that men had more than one origin, are quite as unsatisfactory on natural, as on Bible grounds. That the extremes of the race are widely separated, is certain; but the difference and shades of difference are so gradual, advancing from one extreme to the other, that no one can point out the dividing line that separates the different branches of the human family. Hence, as might be expected, there is very little uniformity of opinion, as to the number of races, some giving us three, some five, and some a larger number.

297. The plan of dividing men into different races, so as to favor the idea that they did not emanate from one parentage, is liable to serious objections on another account. There is no mark of difference that does not admit of infinite modifications. If it be the shape of the

head, there is every variety of form, from the upright forehead of the most intelligent and refined European, to the receding slope of the most ignorant and debased negro. If the hair is made the test, there is no less variety in this particular. Or if the thickness of the lips, or the prominent cheek bones, or the projecting heels, be chosen to mark the difference, there will be found the same difficulty: since the extremes of difference have infinite intervening modifications. There is the same difficulty here, that there is in dividing men into saints and sinners; for, though you can speak of them under these designations, having reference to persons widely separated in respect to character, yet the shades of character are so numerous, and run into each other so imperceptibly, that no point can be fixed upon, where a distinct line of separation can be drawn. The same is true of color. From the lightest to the darkest, there is a gradation so imperceptible, that no place can be selected, which, more than any other, can be regarded as the dividing line. We may divide men into races on the ground of intelligence, or character, as well as on the ground of color; and how, in such a case, shall we decide the number of races? The truth is, there are insuperable difficulties in the way of dividing men into races, many or few, by any clear and distinct indications, on any grounds that have yet been assumed.

298. Again, we know that what we call the races may mix; and the offspring of this union will possess, to a limited extent, the peculiarities of both races. We know they are thus mixed all over the world; and it is possible to conceive of them as being much more completely amalgamated than they are at present. And if this can be conceived of as possible, may not the converse of this be conceived of with equal consistency, in which case the races thus mixed would become again separated, and regain all the marked peculiarities they had at first?

If this be good reasoning, then it follows that all branches of the human family, may have proceeded from a common parentage, having a combination of the characteristics that are now seen more prominently in the different tribes and races that emanated therefrom. In what manner, and by what means, this could be done, will be shown before we close this discussion. But the usual mode of explaining the subject must first be noticed.

SECTION IV.— THE COMMON THEORY CONSIDERED.

299. The common theory, with those who acknowledge one parentage, is that the differences among men, are the result of climate, mode of life, peculiar diseases, &c.

Dr. Good, in his "Book of Nature," states and defends this theory, in a manner that may be given as a fair sample of others, having the same opinions. We will make some quotations from this author. In respect to color he says: "All the deepest colors we are acquainted with, are those of hot climates; and all the lighter colors of cold ones . . . . . The same remark will apply to plants, as well as to animals; . . . hence the beasts, birds, flowers, and even fishes, of the equatorial regions, are uniformly brighter, and deeper tinctured in their spots, their feathers, their petals, and their scales, than we find them in any other part of the world . . . . . Hence, too, the reason why the Asiatic and African women, confined to the walls of their seralios, are as white as Europeans : why Moorish children of both sexes are at first usually fair, and why the fairness continues among the girls, but is soon lost among the boys. As we approach towards the poles we find everything progressively whiten ; bears, foxes, hares, falcons, crows, and black-birds, all assume the same common livery. The immediate matter of color is the mucous pigment which forms the middle layer of the general integument of the skin : and upon this the sun in hot climates appears to act in a two-fold manner, at first, by the direct affinity of its calorific rays, with the oxygen of the animal surface in consequence of which, the oxygen is detached and flies off, and the carbon and hydrogen, being set at liberty, form a more or less perfect charcoal, according to the nature of their union : and next, by the indirect influence which its calorific rays, like many other stimulants, produce upon the liver, by exciting it to a secretion of more abundant bile, and of a deeper hue." p. 205.

300. Dr. Good adds, as showing the reason why in cold climates, some persons are more swarthy than others, that the pigment of the skin, above referred to, is more abundant in some persons than others. Besides the effect of climate on color, the same author remarks, that "oils and spirits produce a peculiar excitement of the liver, and like the calorific rays of the sun, usually become the means of throwing out an overcharge of bile into circulation." The difference in form and features, he thinks, may have been the result, to some extent, of lapsus naturæ. Hence he adds, "Even when accident, or a cause we may not discover, has produced a preternatural conformation, or defect, in a particular organ, it is astonishing to behold how readily it is often copied by the generative principle, and how tenaciously it adheres to the future lineage. A preternatural defect upon the hands or the feet, has been propagated for many generations. In like manner, in all probability, from some primary accident, resulted the peculiar shape of the head and face, in most nations, as well as most families." p. 208.

301. The effect of different habits and modes of life, upon the form and features, is alluded to as follows:— "The whole difference between the cranium of the negro and that of the European, is, in no respect, greater than that which exists between the cranium of the wild boar, and that of the domestic swine. M. Blumenback ... has completely succeeded in showing, that the swine genus, even in countries where we have historical and undeniable proofs, as especially in America, of its being derived from one common and imported stock, exhibits in its different varieties, distinctions, not only as numerous and astonishing, but, so far as relates to the exterior form, of the very same kind, as are to be met with in the different varieties of the human species." p. 208. The doctor humorously remarks that the argument for the plurality of races, is, at best, but *skin deep*.

302. That the climate, and especially the mode of life, do produce a marked effect upon men and animals, is well known and universally conceded. The same is true of trees and plants. But that this fact sufficiently accounts for all the differences in the human race, may not be quite so evident. A person residing at the north, will become darker, in a certain degree, by a residence in a southern climate; but the change is not great, nor continued, so far as we know, beyond certain limits. Nor indeed is the change greater than we all experience, in the same climate, by an unusual exposure to the sun and wind. Such change is very sudden, being produced in a single day or two, and obliterated nearly as soon.

303. The mode of life, too, has its effect, as the difference between the domestic and the wild horse, between the ox and the bison, the wild boar and the domestic swine, the fruit trees found in the wilderness, and those cultivated in our fields, does clearly indicate. But this, too, will not satisfy every one as explaining the varieties of the human race; for persons, very unlike in form and features, are possessed of very similar habits and mode of life; and when the mode of life has been substantially the same for centuries, the differences in other respects, have not been obliterated. The negro, who has lived in the same climate with the white man, for hundreds of years, and has had nearly the same mode of life, is still a negro, and so far as we can discover is unchanged and likely to remain so.

304. A writer in the Democratic Review for September, 1851, has some facts and arguments that seem worthy of serious consideration. They do not indeed exactly harmonize with those of Dr. Good, but we think they are more reliable in those particulars wherein they differ.

"Previous to the settlement of the Europeans on this continent throughout its whole length, from the cold regions of the north, to those of the southern continent, it was inhabited by a race, or a variety of races, nearly resembling each other, in color, and with few exceptions, in their general appearance, though differing widely in their mode of life and degree of civilization. The uniformity of color indeed approaches to monotony. Those who occupy the mountains, and those who occupy the plains, are the same." This author bases his statements on the authority of Humboldt, than which none can be better.

"The Indians that remain in the country, retain the marks that distinguished their ancestors, although an entire change has come over their condition."

305. What is here stated, will not be disputed by any one ; and if there was nothing else to refute the theory of varieties in the race, from climate and mode of life, this single fact would be sufficient. The Indians are everywhere the same, and have been so, for centuries, in spite of climate and mode of life. The same is true of the Spaniards in this country. "In the vast regions, peopled from Spain, from 40 degrees south to 40 north, the Spaniard is everywhere to be met with." And the Spaniard of this country, is precisely like the Spaniard of Europe, irrespective of climate and mode of life. It is obvious, too, that the climate of England, France, Spain and Italy, in Europe, is slightly unlike : but the people, it is well known, are more unlike than the climate. In Asia " we find the whole body of the population, of a dark color, not indeed resembling the negro, but very far from the complexion of the European, even in parallel latitudes. The Monguls, notwithstanding their high latitude, (40 to 50 north) are of a dingy complexion ; while the Tartars, extending south to the southern seas, are of a light complexion. In the southern part of the Mongul region, (say 40 north,) is Caucasus, the inhabitants of which, have the perfection of the European form and complexion. The Persians, between the tropic of Cancer and 40 north, are from an olive to a dark brown. The Chinese, same latitude, are a faint yellow. In Hindostan, (8 to 36 north,) there is a considerable variation of color, such as might be easily allowed to climate. The average complexion is darker than the region above, but it is lighter still than the average of Arabia, the bulk of which country is farther to the north than that of Hindostan. The peninsula of Malacca is inhabited by a people who are darker than the southern Arabs, being 20 degrees farther north, and are darker than the Malays at the equator."

306. This we suppose is a fair and reliable description of the people of Asia : and it will be seen that the complexion of the different tribes and nations, dwelling in that part of the globe, does not correspond with climate.

If in some instances the color varies with the temperature, as in Hindostan and Arabia, this circumstance is merely accidental, as no such thing can be affirmed of the country generally. The dark complexion is found in the north, as well as in the south : and in parallel latitudes, the complexion is very unlike ; and it not unfrequently occurs that a lighter complexion is joined with a hotter climate.

307. How is it with Africa ? The writer before quoted says ; — "Africa . . . . . has almost as great variation of color, as the other sections, and there mixed up with even less conformity to the degrees of temperature. There are found on the Slave Coast, as it is called, the blackest and most degraded of the negro tribes : yet in the same region we find tribes, as different from these, as any in Africa, except the Moorish races on the Mediterranean. The Ashantee people, near the Gold Coast, (6 to 8 north,) are lighter colored, and better featured, than most of the negro tribes of the whole continent. They have oval faces, and their hair curled rather than woolly. They have also some degree of civilization.

308. Senegambia is on the coast west of Soudan, and in the same latitude. The people are mostly full negroes. In the midst of them, however, are large tribes of Foulahs, extending from the Gambia river, in 10 degrees north, southward to Cape Palmas, (Liberia,) 5 south, in a nearly savage state, who have black, or, as some say, merely a tawny complexion, straight, silky hair, regular and pleasing features, totally unlike those of the negro. They are said even to resemble the symmetrical and delicate form of the Hindoos. *The higher classes are the blackest, the lower, or the slaves, are the whitest.*

309. Desert of Sahara. Here, though we meet with all the varieties, the prevailing character is the Arab, which all the severity of desert life, is not able to convert into a negro. The Touricks, who comprise the largest class of native Africans, are of the complexion of the Arabs, generally brown, or almost white. Egypt has always had different races. The Nubians have oval faces, curved nose, thick (but not negro) lips, frizzled (but not woolly) hair, brown complexion, and fine form. Abyssinians are the blackest people of Africa, excepting the negroes of the west coast."

Parkins (Life in Abyssinia,) says of these people :— "In color, some of them are perfectly black, but the majority are brown, or a very light copper or nut color; but men and women are remarkably well formed, and in general handsome, often strikingly so. In features, as in form, the young Abyssinian women are perhaps the most beautiful of any on earth." "Again, the people of Ajan (continues the author first quoted) have hair, long and black, dark eyes, brown skin, and European features.

310. East Coast of Africa, south of the equator. The people are next to brutes, but they are whiter than the Arabians or Hindoos. *The complexion here grows darker, in receding from the heat,* but there is no resemblance to negroes. Those in the southern part of this region, are of the Caffre race, and of elegant symmetry, almost European features. West Coast. The people of Congo, although black, have no sign of negro features. Their faces resemble the Caucassian, hair of a reddish brown color. This is pretty nearly the character of the rest of those regions. They are in a low state of civilization. Hottentots are of a yellowish brown, and some tribes are of a red or copper color.

311. In the Pacific Islands, the black and brown are both found, many times, in the same localities, but quite separate. The brown race have long, black, shiny hair, eyes brilliant and full of fire, great mental energy, and determined character. Van Diemen's Land is inhabited by regular negroes: New Zealand, by Malays, tall, well formed, black eyes, and intelligent. Marquesas, finely formed, and active population. Sandwich Islands, complexion dark olive. That the Oceanic races have long lived together, as they are found, is a fact admitting not the slightest doubt." Of course, the same climate and mode of life, ought to have made them alike, if such a result could be expected from such a cause.

312. It may be remarked in general, that though negroes have been traced from the north of Asia to the south, and thence to Egypt, and other parts of Africa, they are everywhere the same. In Egypt the whites and blacks have always kept distinct. The children of Israel in ancient times, after a sojourn in Egypt of two hundred years, went up out of that land every whit unchanged. So all over the world, the same Hebrew people, formerly and now, are easily distinguished. The Mamelukes in Egypt, after 260 years, were still very unlike the Egyptians. Tartars are the same in the north of Asia, and in the south. So the Arabs at home, and in the desert. The Moors, in the Barbary States, and the Moors in Spain, are the same, after a separation of a thousand years. The Normans and Saxons in England, not very unlike at first, retained their separate identity for a long time. So all European nations in America, are the same as they are at home.

313. In view of all these facts, what shall we say of the cause or causes that have produced the actual differences among men? Climate and mode of life will not suffice to answer this question; nor, on the other hand, need we suppose a different original parentage to each variety.

SECTION V.—True Theory.

314. We propose a theory for removing the difficulties of this subject, that is perhaps new. It is so at least to us. But we hope it may receive a candid examination, and not be rejected till a better is found. It seems to us to offer the best, and indeed the only satisfactory solution, of the great question we have been discussing.

We know that children are not entirely like their parents, nor like each other, and are not expected to be. Some will possess a lighter, and some a darker complexion; some will have a higher forehead, and some a lower; some will be taller, and some not so tall. The color and texture of the hair will differ, as well as the skin. And if this be true now, as we know it is, the same thing may be presumed of the first families of the earth. This being admitted, it is not unreasonable to conclude, that the differences, at first slight, would be enlarged, and become more marked in different individuals and families. If a son, for instance, were darker than his father, there would be just as good reason why the grandson should be darker still, as there was that the son should be. So we may go on, till we come to the darkest face to be found among men. The same may be concluded of any other peculiarity.

315. I know that what is here supposed would not be, without a special reason. If all colors and forms, slightly different, were kept continually mixed, the extremes would not be likely to be far separated. But such mixture has not been, and as men are, could not be expected. Sympathy, on the one hand, and prejudice on the other, would lead to classes or castes. "Birds of a feather will flock together;" and the principle has prevailed in the past, as far back as history goes, as much as it prevails in the present. And castes, once formed, to whatever peculiarity they might relate, would not be easily broken up. The tendency would be rather to raise the partition walls; and the peculiarity that first led to the separation, whatever it might be, would naturally become more and more prominent indefinitely. If it were color, the whitest would associate together, and so would the blackest; and the tendency would be to increase the whiteness on the one hand, and the blackness on the other. True, some would disregard existing prejudices; and this would throw in, between the extremes, shades of color that would lessen the contrast; as the same thing is done at the present day, still, the general tendency would not be broken up, as such instances would be, as they now are, rare exceptions to a general rule.

316. In our view, the main cause of existing varieties in the human race, is the influence of caste; though, of course, we must suppose, as before shown, an original tendency to produce slight differences. This, to us, appears to explain the whole thing. The animals are not like us, for the reason that they have no sympathy or prejudice, founded on such considerations. Our cattle associate together, irrespective of color, size, shape of the head, or length of the foot. Still, I can easily suppose, that, should they get a prejudice against each other, on account of color; the red for instance, declaring that they will not intermarry or associate with the brown, and should carry out this resolution for a few generations, each excluding at once, any and every unlucky new-comer, that was not red enough or brown enough, to suit the popular taste ; the result would at length be, that the offspring of the red, would be red, and that of the brown, would be brown ; and the tendency would finally become so fixed and permanent, that variations from the common standard, would be exceedingly rare or disappear altogether.

317. This theory harmonizes perfectly with the facts that have already been adduced. How can two races exist together, in the same locality for ages, except on the principle here laid down ? We know with certainty that if they should mingle together, their separate peculiarities would disappear. Such is the result, wherever such a cause exists to induce it, and to the extent to which it prevails ; and where it prevails sufficiently, all distinction is ultimately lost, as is illustrated by our ancestors, the Normans and Saxons, and as is being illustrated continually before our eyes, by the intermingling, in our country, of the nations and races from the old world.

It is well for us, as Christian believers, to hesitate a long time, before we give up, as unreliable, the teachings of the Bible, or put on those teachings a forced construction, not demanded by existing facts. The unity of the race, we think, imposes upon us no necessity of doing either of these things.

CHAPTER IX.

THE DELUGE CONSIDERED WITH REFERENCE TO THE FACTS OF GEOLOGY.

CONTENTS:—Moral Cause of the Deluge; Physical Cause of the Deluge; Possibility of the Deluge; Probability of the Deluge; Proofs of the Deluge; The Ark; Number of Animals in the Ark; Food during the Flood; Duration of the Flood; Mountains of Ararat.

318. The account of the deluge, as well as that of creation, will be sustained or set aside, in most minds, mainly, according as it may seem to agree or disagree with the facts of Geology. We believe that Geology, so far from setting aside the fact of a deluge, furnishes strong confirmation to that event: and this is one of the things we propose to show. There are several particulars connected with this event, that may be noticed separately, as the best mode of giving a complete view of the whole subject.

SECTION I.—MORAL CAUSE OF THE DELUGE.

This is stated by the writer thus:—

CHAP. VI.

5. ¶ And GOD saw that the wickedness of man *was* great in the earth, and *that* every imagination of the thoughts of his heart *was* only evil continually.

6 And it repented the LORD that he had made man on the earth, and it grieved him at his heart.

7. And the LORD said, I will destroy man whom I have created from the face of the earth; both man, and beast, and the creeping thing, and the fowls of the air; for it repenteth me that I have made them.

8. But Noah found grace in the eyes of the LORD.

11. The earth was also corrupt before God; and the earth was filled with violence.

12. And God looked upon the earth, and, behold, it was corrupt: for all flesh had corrupted his way upon the earth.

13. And God said unto Noah, The end of all flesh is come before me; for the earth is filled with violence through them; and, behold, I will destroy them with the earth.

319. That outward physical events are at all occasioned by moral considerations, on the part of the Creator, seems to be no part of the prevailing philosophy of modern times. Much of the philosophy of modern times, however, is philosophy "falsely so called." He who made the physical world, made also the moral ; and both are inseparable parts of one great system. Every physical event has its moral bearings ; and if this be true, it is a clear dictate of reason, that such moral bearings were intended by the Creator : and that the cause was set in operation with a view to the foreseen result. Who does not know that man's physical organization has much to do with his moral character? and that the latter has no less to do with his physical condition? Here, then, is an obvious connection, between the physical and the moral world, in respect to the individual ; and surely a no less real connection exists between the race, and the universe, outside and around us. It is not sound philosophy to separate what God has so obviously joined together. I apprehend that could we understand the counsels of the Most High, we should plainly discover, that most of what is done in the outward world, is induced by moral considerations. The sun shines, and the rain falls, not wholly to give seed to the sower and bread to the eater, but, through these benefactions, to lead intelligent minds up, through nature to nature's God, and thus to elevate them in the scale of moral and spiritual excellence. And if the outward blessings of life, have an ulterior moral purpose, it is quite as reasonable to conclude, that outward afflictions are employed for the punishment of sin, to correct our faults and improve our virtues.

SECTION II. — The Physical Cause of the Deluge.

320. This is expressed by the sacred writer thus, — "All the fountains of the great deep were broken up, and the windows of heaven were opened." vii. 11. The way in which the deluge is regarded by most people, is, that it was occasioned by a long continued outpouring from the skies. In their estimation it was the *rain* that caused the flood. Hence, when the opposers of the Bible have shown, that all the rain in the clouds could not have produced such a result, the honest, but uninformed believer has no sufficient reply to make. Fortunate indeed it is for such an one, if he comes to the conclusion that there may be some things, connected with this subject, that he does not fully understand, though he may not tell precisely what they are. In this case he will wisely hold on to his faith, and wait for more light; or rather not wait, but go in pursuit of it.

321. "All the fountains of the great deep were broken up." The true interpretation of this language, we conceive to be, that there was such a breaking up of the earth's crust, as to allow the waters of the ocean, or "great deep," to overflow the land. There was an upheaval of the bed of the ocean, and a depression, or subsidence, of the dry land; and thus the whole surface was covered with water — not perhaps at the same moment, but within the time during which the flood was continued. The effect was increased, to some extent, by the rain from heaven.

322. Now we take upon ourself to say, that there is nothing unreasonable in the idea that such an event, as here described, did really occur, aside from the positive testimony in favor of its truth. We know, indeed, that sundry objections have been brought against a universal deluge; and sundry expedients have been resorted to, to meet these objections. By some the language of the writer has been regarded as highly figurative: and we are told that we must understand it with reasonable and judicious limitations; and some analogous expressions, evidently employed in a limited sense, are referred to, for confirmation of this view. But we propose to show, that there is nothing unreasonable in a deluge, with the most extended construction that can be put upon the phraseology by which it is described.

SECTION III.— OF THE POSSIBILITY OF A DELUGE.

323. In the first place, we know abstractly, that all things are possible with God: but we do not rely on this abstract truth. We prefer to note particular facts that are fitted to make out our case. One of these facts is, that there was water enough in the clouds, and on the earth, to have produced a universal deluge. Some have thought otherwise, and have sought for various methods to account for the fact, on other grounds. One theory supposes a condensation of the atmosphere, which, we know, extends far above the earth, and may or may not be sufficient to produce the result. One eminent philosopher thinks that the tail of a comet, passing near the earth, at that time, became condensed, and occasioned the deluge, though I am not informed how the water was disposed of afterwards.

324. Leaving these theories, we will offer well attested facts in their place. We have before shown that Geologists give their testimony in favor of the Bible, in respect to another point, by saying that there was a time, when the whole surface of our globe was covered with water. The facts of Geology cannot be accounted for on any other supposition. It is plain, then, that the same water that covered the earth once, would be sufficient to cover it again The same Power from which issued the mandate, "Let the waters be gathered together into one place," could reverse this order — could depress the dry land, upheave the bed of the ocean, and overspread the whole earth with a flood.

325. Again ; it is well known that most of the earth's surface is now, and always has been, nearly overspread with water. The proportion of dry land to water, is less than one to two. A slight depression of the dry land, therefore, if such a thing be admitted as possible, would now occasion a universal deluge.

The common opinion seems to be, that the depth of the ocean corresponds with the height of the land — that the lowest depths and the highest mountains, are nearly equal in extent. But recent experiments have shown that the depth of the ocean far exceeds this estimate. A French author (Guyot, "Earth and Man") says on this subject; " The interior of the basins of the oceans, is unequal, generally deeper than toward the borders. The greatest observed depths are found in the middle region of the Atlantic. They equal, or surpass by several thousand feet, the elevation of the highest mountains of the globe. The mean depth of the basin of the oceans, seems to be much more considerable than the mean elevation of the continents above their surface." p. 91. This author gives the different soundings of experimenters as follows ; 7,200 feet, 6,000, 7,800, 13,000, 19,800, 27,000, 16,000, 34,200. This last number exceeds the highest mountain on the globe, by nearly 10,000 feet. La Place thinks that the greatest depth of the ocean, is about 11 miles. In view of these facts, it is not only obvious that there is water enough on the globe, to produce a universal deluge ; but a moderate elevation of the bed of the ocean, with a slight depression of the land, would produce this result.

SECTION IV. — THE PROBABILITY OF A DELUGE.

326. A deluge is not only possible ; but, in view of the statements of Geologists, it is an event that may be regarded as exceedingly probable. These men tell us that the depression of the dry land, and the upheaval of the bed of the ocean, has occurred many times, in the past history of our globe. The evidence of this is as conclusive and satisfactory as any facts of science. The rocky strata that compose the highest mountains, were formed under water. That they have been lifted up, and then depressed ; and that this has occurred many times, is proved by fossil remains found in them, which are sometimes those of the water and sometimes those of the land, and which exist at all heights, from the lowest transition strata, to the upper or diluvial formations. This up and down movement of the earth's surface is one of the processes that attended the early experience of our globe. It was one of these, the last important one, that produced the flood of Noah, though the same thing has been done, on a small scale, within the period of authentic profane history. A few quotations, some of which have been used in another place, will show what Geologists have said on this subject.

327. Buckland ; — " The debris of the first dry land, being drifted into the sea, and there spread out into extensive beds of mud, sand and gravel, would forever have remained beneath the surface of the water, had not other forces been subsequently employed to raise them into dry land. These forces seem to have been the same

THE DELUGE CONSIDERED. 179

expansive powers of heat and vapor, which, having caused the elevation of the first raised portions of the fundamental crystaline rocks, continued their energies through all succeeding Geological epochs, and still exert them in producing active volcanoes." This author adds: "All observers admit that the strata were formed beneath the water."

Higgins:—"The stratified rocks must originally have been horizontal, or nearly so; and many of them were formed in the same manner, as the deposits which are always found in the beds of rivers and the basins of the oceans; but they were afterwards acted upon by mighty disturbing forces that elevated and disrupted them. . . . . These effects have been both local and general, at one time, affecting a district not more than a few miles in extent, at others, elevating entire continents and immense mountain chains." Buckland, vol. I. p. 42. Higgins, p. 226.

328. No one can help seeing that the elevation of an entire continent would cause the water to flow over continents that had before been dry land; and the elevation of the latter, would, in their turn, throw the water back upon the other. What is this but a deluge, or rather a succession of deluges? And as all parts of the earth show marks of these changes, there must have been more or less of these inundations all over the surface of our globe.

329. Again:—The relative position and superficial extent of land and water, have been constantly changing, not slowly and imperceptibly as at present, but by the activity of causes, the effects of which, have been almost instantaneous, upheaving the bed of the oceans, and deluging the dry lands." Higgins, 274.

330. These quotations from men of eminence in the scientific world, will show that a flood, such as is described in Genesis, was a very probable event. From what the earth had undergone, it was not unreasonable that a similar event should occur in the days of Noah. The probability is increased, by what has often occurred since. Extensive surfaces have arisen up from beneath the water, and other surfaces have sunk and disappeared. The Island of

Hieri rose up from the sea, B. C. 193. Thia in A. D. 40. These became united in A. D. 726. Graham Island rose from the waters of the Mediterranean sea, in 1831. During the earthquake at Lisbon, in 1755, the seas in every part of Europe, were agitated ; and in some places became turbid and thick. Had the cause of this agitation been more active and powerful, as it would have been at an earlier day, the whole of Europe would have been submerged and formed the bed of the ocean. The poet, in allusion to such agitations, has the following graphic language ; —

> " Diseased Nature often times breaks forth
> In strange eruptions ; oft the teeming Earth
> Is, with a kind of colic, pinched, and vexed,
> By the imprisonment of unruly winds
> Within her womb, which, for enlargement striving,
> Shake the old bedlam Earth, and topple
> Down steeples and moss grown towers."

SECTION V.—Proofs of the Deluge.

331. The testimony of Geologists, in favor of similar changes with that of the flood of Noah, we have before given ; and reasoning from analogy, we have deduced the probability of such an event. It may be well to see what some of them say expressly concerning this event. Cuvier : — " I can concur with the opinion of M. DeLuc and Dolomieu, that, if there be anything determined in Geology, it is that the surface of our globe has been subject to a vast and sudden revolution, not longer ago than five or six thousand years ; that this revolution has buried and caused to disappear, the countries formerly inhabited by man, and the species of animals now most known ; that, on the contrary, it has left the bottom of the former sea dry, and has formed on it the countries now inhabited." Comstock's Geology, 1841.

Buckland : — " The Alps and Carpathian, as well as every other mountainous region which I have visited, bear the same evidence of having been modified by the force of waters, as do the hills of the lower regions." Ib.

Professor Hitchcock : — " The conclusion to which I am led irresistibly, formed by an examination of this

THE DELUGE CONSIDERED.   181

stratum, (in Massachusetts,) is, that all the diluvium which has been previously accumulated, has been modified by a powerful deluge, sweeping from the north and north-west, over every part of the state, not excepting the highest mountains." Report of the Geology of Massachusetts.

332. That the earth's surface has sometimes, not many thousands of years in the past, been overflowed by a mighty inundation, is proved by the position and location of many masses of rock, that have evidently been moved from one place to another by this agency. " In Sweden and Russia, large blocks of rock occur out of place in great numbers; and no doubt can be entertained, that they have been transferred southward from the north. Boulders have been transferred from the Savoy Alps, to the Jura, across what is now lake Geneva. Professor Buckland found amongst the transferred gravel of Durham, twenty varieties of slate and greenstone, which do not occur in places nearer than the lake district of Cumberland. Between the Thames and the Tweed are rocks that must have come from the coast of Norway. On the coast of Yorkshire are fragments of rocks that must have come from the coast of Norway, and such as came from the Highlands of Scotland. In East Lyme, Ct., near the road leading from Rope Ferry to Saybrook, is a huge block of granite, weighing, it is estimated, about 400 tons, that was evidently carried there from a mountain two miles distant. The boulders of Plymouth and Barnstable came from the vicinity of Boston and Cape Ann." Hitchcock.

333. Many other similar quotations might be made, but these are sufficient. Whether what is here described took place in the flood of Noah, may not be certain : but they certainly belong to the same class of changes, and by their analogy, they furnish evidence of that event. Lyell supposes that deluges are a part of the regular order of Providence; and he predicts an American deluge about 30000 years hence.

334. There is another branch of evidence, bearing upon this subject, to which we are inclined to attach considerable importance. I refer to the traditions of different nations, concerning the deluge. It is quite remark-

able that the traditions found among the most barbarous nations, as well as those more enlightened, should show a harmony, more or less exact, with the facts of Geology and the deductions of science. Yet, if the deluge be a reality, the existing state of things is only what we might reasonably expect; and it would be almost, if not quite, as difficult to account for these traditions, without a deluge to have originated them, as to account for the facts of Geology, without that event. Richard Watson (Theol. Dic. Art. *Deluge*,) has the following judicious remarks, touching this point. " Its magnitude and singularity could scarcely fail to make an indelible impression on the minds of the survivors, which would be communicated from them to their children, and would not be easily effaced from the traditions of their latest posterity. A deficiency of such traces of this awful event, though it might not serve entirely to invalidate our belief of its reality, would certainly tend considerably to weaken its claims to credibility; it being scarcely probable that the knowledge of it should be utterly lost to the rest of the world, and confined to the Jewish nation alone. What we might reasonably expect, has been actually and completely realized." Traditions of the flood are found among the Greeks, Egyptians, Phœnicians, Assyrians, Hindoos, Chinese, Otaheitans, Cubans, Peruvians, Brazilians, Mexicans, &c., &c.

335. Humboldt, speaking of these traditions, makes the following appropriate and forcible remarks:—"These ancient traditions of the human race, which we find dispersed over the surface of the globe, like the fragments of a vast shipwreck, are of the greatest interest to the philosophic study of our species. Like certain families of plants, which, notwithstanding the diversities of climate and the influence of heights, retain their impress of a common type, the traditions concerning the primitive state of the globe, present, among all nations, a resemblance that fills us with astonishment. So many different languages, belonging to branches which appear to have no connection with each other, transmit the same facts to us. The substance of the traditions respecting **the destroyed races, and the renovation of nature,** is everywhere almost the same, although each nation gives it a local coloring." Humboldt's Travels, School District Library, pp. 191, 192.

336. In ancient times the deluge was a matter of record in profane history, deemed authentic. Josephus affirms that Berosus, a Chaldean historian, relates the circumstances of a great deluge in which all mankind perished, except a few, and that Noachus, the preserver of the human race, was carried in an ark to the summit of an Armenian mountain. Josephus also states that Hieronimus, the Egyptian historian, who wrote the antiquities of the Phœnicians, and Nicholas of Damascus, together with other writers, speak of the same deluge. Likewise there is a fragment preserved of Abydemus, an ancient Assyrian historian, in which it is said, not only that there was a deluge, but that it was foretold before it happened, and that birds were sent forth from the ark, three different times, to see whether the waters were abated.

337. In addition to the opinion of Geologists, the traditions of all nations, and the testimony of ancient profane historians, we have another history that has never been impeached, to which we may do well to take heed: and this history is the *Bible*. And while we give credit to other ancient records, that have by no means been preserved with the same care, why should we not admit the statements of this record, so long as no natural or historical evidence can be adduced against it. If it be said that there *are* natural reasons against it, we meet the assertion with a prompt and vigorous denial, and appeal to facts to sustain our position.

338. Another question presents itself, in connection with the deluge, that some may think more difficult than the abstract reality of such an event. I refer to the preservation of Noah and his family, together with the number of animals that are said to have been saved at the same time. On this point several things will be noticed.

SECTION VI.—THE ARK.

CHAP. VI.

14. ¶ Make thee an ark of gopher wood; rooms shalt thou make in the ark, and shalt pitch it within and without with pitch.

15. And this *is the fashion* which thou shalt make it *of:* The length of the ark *shall be* three hundred cubits, the breadth of it fifty cubits, and the height of it thirty cubits.

16. A window shalt thou make to the ark, and in a cubit shalt thou finish it above; and the door of the ark shalt thou set in the side thereof; *with* lower, second, and third *stories* shalt thou make it.

339. A cubit is generally thought to be a foot and a half of our measure. Hence the ark must have been 450 feet in length, 75 feet in breadth, and 45 feet in height, a proportion of length, breadth and height, corresponding very nearly with vessels, at the present day, that are constructed on strictly scientific principles. That it was made in a similar form, need not be supposed. Probably it was not, as the object had in view was not to move from place to place, requiring a form fitted to move with the least resistance, but simply to preserve alive its inmates. A flat bottom would answer the purpose as well, perhaps better, and would be of simpler construction.

340. The three stories of the ark fitted it for containing more burden, and for its better distribution, than it otherwise could have been. Doubtless the common sense of Noah was allowed its proper exercise, in the arrangement and disposition of the lading, so that the heaviest would be placed below, and the lightest above. But whether the ark, large as it was, and conveniently arranged, would contain all that was put into it, is a question that is not very easily settled. We can approximate, we think, to a just conclusion.

SECTION VII.—NUMBER OF ANIMALS IN THE ARK.

CHAP. VI.

19. And of every living thing of all flesh, two of every *sort* shalt thou bring into the ark, to keep *them* alive with thee; they shall be male and female.
20. Of fowls after their kind, and of cattle after their kind, of every creeping thing of the earth after his kind, two of every *sort* shall come unto thee, to keep *them* alive.

CHAP. VII.

2. Of every clean beast thou shalt take to thee by sevens, the male and his female: and of beasts that *are* not clean by two, the male and his female.
3. Of fowls also of the air by sevens, the male and the female; to keep seed alive upon the face of all the earth. * * *

CHAP. VII.

8. Of clean beasts, and of beasts that *are* not clean, and of fowls, and of every thing that creepeth upon the earth.
9. There went in two and two unto Noah into the ark, the male and the female, as God had commanded Noah.
10. And it came to pass after seven days, that the waters of the flood were upon the earth.
* * * * *

14. They, and every beast after his kind, and all the cattle after their kind, and every creeping thing that creepeth upon the earth after his kind, and every fowl after his kind, every bird of every sort.
15. And they went in unto Noah into the ark, two and two of all flesh, wherein *is* the breath of life.
16. And they that went in, went in male and female of all flesh, as God had commanded him; and the Lord shut him in. * *

341. The opinion has been entertained by some, that all animals absolutely were not preserved in the ark — that some now extinct, and known to have lived only by their fossil remains, were then totally destroyed. The language above quoted does not seem to admit of any such limitation or exception. On this subject we remark, that the number of animals originally upon the earth, was very large. This we know from their fossil remains; but most of these lived and perished long before the flood, and indeed long before the creation of man. Those that were cotemporary with man were comparatively few in number: and though they might have become very numerous, at the time of the deluge, the number of *kinds* need not be so regarded. The kinds are not now numerous. Buffon, an eminent naturalist, says, that all existing species (aside from the fishes and fowls) can be reduced to 250.

This probably falls far below the true estimate ; but, with all reasonable additions, the ark could have contained them. But if this were proved to be impossible, there is no certainty that the number of kinds then, were equal to the present number: for it is not at all improbable that some kinds, perhaps many, have been created since the flood. Geologists tell us that, during the epochs of creation, there must have been several distinct creations of animals, each creation suited to the condition of the earth at the time, and succeeded by another, as the condition of things required it. And if this be so, analogy would favor the idea, that some animals may have received their existence since the deluge : and especially because there is reason to believe that the climate of the earth, underwent a great change, when the flood occurred.

342. "Dr. Hales has proved," says Comstock, "that the ark was of a burden of 42,413 tons, as we compute the tonnage of ships at the present day." We suppose that 250 pairs, and a much larger number, would find ample room in that immense structure. As to the largest animals, we may suppose, if we see reason for so doing, that the young of these, and not those full grown, were selected, as securing the result just as well. But animals of this kind are not numerous, as are those of a smaller size.

A few moments thought will convince any one, that the number of animals, said to have been saved in the ark, is really no objection to the truth or credibility of the deluge. And though seven of each kind of clean beasts were saved, and two of each kind of unclean, yet we know that the *kinds* of the former, are not numerous, and of the larger ones, the young and small could have been selected.

SECTION VIII. — Food during the Flood.

CHAP. VI.

21. And take thou unto thee of all food that is eaten, and thou shalt gather it to thee; and it shall be for food for thee, and for them.

22. Thus did Noah; according to all that God commanded him, so did he.

343. It has greatly puzzled interpreters to determine why seven of some animals were preserved, instead of two. That Noah required clean beasts for the sacrifice he offered to the Lord, on leaving the ark, which is the usual reason given for this procedure, is quite unsatisfactory. Noah did indeed require clean beasts for sacrifice, but that he required five of every kind, is a somewhat extravagant supposition. It does not seem to have occurred to these expounders, that many animals are carniverous, and must have been furnished with flesh to eat. And the clean beasts were chosen for this purpose, rather than unclean, for the reason that they could be more easily procured, as being less wild and voracious. It may be added here, that what was deemed an objection in one part of the account, the preservation of seven clean beasts instead of two, helps us to remove another objection, quite as formidable, arising from the amount of food required for their sustenance, since, with this understanding, a small amount only of vegetable food would be required.

SECTION IX. — Duration of the Flood.

344. At first view there seems to be a great want of consecutive order, in the account we have of the flood. The entrance of Noah and his family into the ark, is mentioned not less than four times. There is a reason for this, however, that may not at first appear. The passages that seem to be repetitions are not precisely alike: and though they might be greatly abridged, and every idea be retained, yet we must allow the writer to tell his story in his own way. We place below the passages side by side: —

CHAP. VI.

17. And behold I, even I, do bring a flood of waters upon the earth, to destroy all flesh, wherein *is* the breath of life, from under heavens; *and* every thing that *is* in the earth shall die.

18. But with thee will I establish my covenant; and thou shalt come into the ark, thou, and thy sons, and thy wife, and thy sons' wives with thee.

CHAP. VII.

5. And Noah did according unto all that the Lord commanded him.

6. And Noah was six hundred years old when the flood of waters was upon the earth.

7. ¶ And Noah went in, and his sons, and his wife, and his sons' wives with him, into the ark, because of the waters of the flood.

* * * * *

11. In the six hundredth year of Noah's life, in the second month,

CHAP. VII.

1. And the Lord said unto Noah, Come thou and all thy house into the ark; for thee have I seen righteous before me in this generation.

* * * *

4. For yet seven days, and I will cause it to rain upon the earth forty days and forty nights: and every living substance that I have made will I destroy from off the face of the earth.

the seventeenth day of the month, the same day were all the fountains of the great deep broken up, and the windows of heaven were opened.

12. And the rain was upon the earth forty days and forty nights.

13. In the selfsame day entered Noah, and Shem, and Ham, and Japheth, the sons of Noah, and Noah's wife, and the three wives of his sons with them into the ark.

345. The first of these passages contains an *announcement* of the flood and the preservation of Noah and his family. The next *commands* Noah to go into the ark. The writer next states that Noah and his family *went into* the ark. The statement is then repeated, in connection with the *exact time* when it occurred.

346. There is some indefiniteness as to the time the flood prevailed. We have the record as follows:—

CHAP. VII.

11. In the six hundredth year of Noah's life, in the second month, the seventeenth day of the month, the same day were all the fountains of the great deep broken up, and the windows of heaven were opened.

12. And the rain was upon the earth forty days and forty nights.

17. And the flood was forty days upon the earth; and the waters increased, and bare up the ark, and it was lift up above the earth.

18. And the waters prevailed, and were increased greatly upon the earth; and the ark went upon the face of the waters.

19. And the waters prevailed exceedingly upon the earth; and all the high hills that *were* under the whole heaven, were covered.

20. Fifteen cubits upward did the waters prevail; and the mountains were covered.

21. And all flesh died that moved upon the earth, both of fowl, and of cattle, and of beast, and of every creeping thing that creepeth upon the earth, and every man:

22. All in whose nostrils *was* the breath of life, of all that *was* in the dry *land*, died.

23. And every living substance

THE DELUGE CONSIDERED. 189

was destroyed which was upon the face of the ground, both man, and cattle, and the creeping things, and the fowl of the heaven; and they were destroyed from the earth: and Noah only remained *alive*, and they that *were* with him in the ark.
24. And the waters prevailed upon the earth an hundred and fifty days.

CHAP. VIII

1. And God remembered Noah, and every living thing, and all the cattle that *was* with him in the ark: and God made a wind to pass over the earth, and the waters assuaged.
2. The fountains also of the deep and the windows of heaven were stopped, and the rain from heaven was restrained.
3. And the waters returned from off the earth continually: and after the end of the hundred and fifty days the waters were abated.
4. And the ark rested in the seventh month, on the seventeenth day of the month, upon the mountains of Ararat.
5. And the waters decreased continually until the tenth month: in the tenth *month*, on the first *day* of the month, were the tops of the mountains seen.
6. ¶ And it came to pass at the end of forty days, that Noah opened the window of the ark which he had made:
7. And he sent forth a raven, which went forth to and fro, until the waters were dried up from off the earth.
8. Also he sent forth a dove from him, to see if the waters were abated from off the face of the ground;
9. But the dove found no rest for the sole of her foot, and she returned unto him into the ark, for the waters *were* on the face of the whole earth: then he put forth his hand, and took her, and pulled her in unto him into the ark.
10. And he stayed yet other seven days; and again he sent forth the dove out of the ark;
11. And the dove came in to him in the evening; and, lo, in her mouth *was* an olive leaf plucked off: so Noah knew that the waters were abated from off the earth.
12. And he stayed yet other seven days; and sent forth the dove; which returned not again unto him any more.
13. ¶ And it came to pass in the six hundredth and first year, in the first *month*, the first *day* of the month, the waters were dried up from off the earth: and Noah removed the covering of the ark, and looked, and, behold, the face of the ground was dry.
14. And in the second month, on the seven and twentieth day of the month, was the earth dried.
15. ¶ And God spake unto Noah, saying,
16. Go forth of the ark, thou, and thy wife, and thy sons, and thy sons' wives with thee.
17. Bring forth with thee every living thing that *is* with thee, of all flesh, *both* of fowl, and of cattle, and of every creeping thing that creepeth upon the earth; that they may breed abundantly in the earth, and be fruitful, and multiply upon the earth.
18. And Noah went forth, and his sons, and his wife, and his sons' wives with him:
19. Every beast, every creeping thing, and every fowl, *and* whatsoever creepeth upon the earth, after their kinds, went forth out of the ark.

347. A careful observation and comparison of passages, in this account, will make out the following par-

ticulars:— Noah went into the ark on the 17th day of the second month, when the flood commenced. The flood continued from that date, 40 days and 40 nights, at which time the waters exceeded the highest mountains by 15 cubits, or a little more than 22 feet. At this time all land animals, not shut up in the ark, had perished.

348. When it is added that the waters prevailed upon the earth 150 days, we must include in this reckoning, the 40 days before alluded to. This is evident from viii: 4, where it is said that the ark rested, in the seventh month, and on the 17th day of the month, upon the mountains of Ararat: for this period is just five months (from the 17th of the second month to the 17th of the seventh,) from the time the flood commenced: and five months of Jewish reckoning, is precisely 150 days. From the time the ark rested on Ararat, up to the first day of the tenth month, the waters continued to decrease, so that then the tops of the mountains were seen. Forty days later Noah sent forth a raven, and still later a dove. On the first day of the first month, of the next year, Noah removed the covering of the ark; and in the second month, on the 27th day of the month, the ground was dry, and Noah went forth from the ark, one Jewish year and ten days after he had entered it.

SECTION X.— Mountains of Ararat.

349. The ark rested on the mountains of Ararat. We know there are such mountains as are here named. They are two in number, and from their height are called the Greater and Lesser Ararat. It is not improbable that the ark first rested upon the one, and by degrees, as the water subsided, passed down to the other, or to the plain between the two. These mountains have been known and called by this name, from the most ancient times; and the traditions of the people in that country, fully sustain the fact that this was the place where the ark rested.

350. The author of "Earth and Man," in his admirable lectures, has the following remarks that seem appropriate in this connection. "Here .... is the original country of the white race, the most perfect in body and mind. If we take tradition for our guide, and follow, step by step, the march of the primitive nations, as we ascend to their point of departure, they irresistibly lead us to the very centre of this plateau. Now in this central part also, in Upper Armenia and in Persia . . . we find the purest type of the historical nations. Thence we behold them descend into the arable plains and spread toward all parts of the horizon." pp. 292, 293.

351. " Man presents to our view his purest, his most perfect type, at the very centre of the temperate continents, at the centre of Asia-Europe, in the region of Iran of Armenia and of Caucassus ; and departing from this Geographical centre, in the three grand directions of the lands, the types gradually lose the beauty of their forms, in proportion to their distance, even to the extreme points of the southern continents, where we find the most deformed and degraded of races, and the lowest in the scale of humanity." pp. 254, 255.

CHAPTER X.

THEOLOGICAL DOCTRINES.

CONTENTS:— God and his Attributes; Unity of God; Nature and Responsibility of Man; Rewards and Punishments; Final Triumph of Good; Garden of Eden.

352. One reason why the ideas of men respecting the teachings of the Bible, are so indefinite and confused, is, that they seek to comprehend the teachings of the whole book at once, whereas they would have much clearer conceptions, and a much better understanding of the subjects treated of, if they would bring their investigations at first to bear upon some distinct parts of the book, and advance to others, only after these were clearly understood. This is the method we now propose to follow. We will first ascertain, as far as we can, what doctrines are taught in the book of Genesis ; and at some other time, we will do the same thing, with other portions of the Scriptures.

353. If it be thought that we shall be liable to fall into errors, by taking so limited a view, the danger, we think, can exist only with reference to doctrines not clearly revealed in this part of the Bible; and with respect to these we should not be too confident. But the doctrines that are expressed in clear and unambiguous terms, may be learned and received with confidence; and if the Bible is a consistent book throughout, no part of it will be found adverse to these, but will fully confirm them. Our investigations will be most profitable to us by observing some methodical arrangement.

SECTION I. — God and his Attributes.

354. We know that expressions are found in the book of Genesis, that, literally understood, convey unworthy ideas of God; but we have elsewhere offered, what we hope may be regarded, as good reasons for not giving such interpretation to these expressions; not merely because *we* do not believe such things of God, as this language would indicate, but because we have no good reason for supposing that the author himself believes thus. Doubtless their ideas of God were not equal to ours; for, if they were, we might pertinently ask: What good has the Bible done us? But their ideas were not as low and puerile, as we might suppose, while looking only at certain forms of expression which they employ. This is evident from other representations found in the book. Hence, if we find some rude expressions, as doubtless we do, they should be so interpreted as to harmonize with other and higher representations. The best forms of speech should be chosen to represent their ideas, rather than other and ruder forms.

The author of a book on Natural Philosophy, for example, should not be charged with error, when he speaks of the rising and setting of the sun, so long as we know that he has maintained the contrary of what this language implies, while treating of the earth's motions. Nor do we deal fairly by him, if we say his book is inconsistent and contradictory; for while treating the subject of the diurnal revolution of our planet, he shows us plainly what are the facts: but, while treating other subjects, he makes use of popular language, which, though literally untrue, does not mislead or deceive us. May it not be assumed, then that the writers of the Bible will be treated with equal fairness, by the readers of that book. It is certain that they are entitled to the consideration here asked for them: and if it be not granted, the wrong must be charged on their impugners and not on themselves. We proceed then to show what are the ideas, inculcated in the book of Genesis, concerning God and his attributes.

355. First, the actions ascribed to God, show the views entertained of him. The work of creation, ascribed to the energy of the Almighty, will of itself, vindicate the book from the charge of narrow views, that might be inferred from other allusions. The heavens and the earth are the work of his hands. He spake and it was done: he commanded and it stood fast. All things are regarded as created by the simple word of God. "Let there be light, and there was light," has often been quoted as one of the sublimest forms of speech. The original is perhaps still better than the translation, "Light, Be; and light was," is a literal rendering. That the author of the book of Genesis regarded God as simply a national divinity, and had no higher conceptions of his character, is asserted by some; but the assertion has no proof.

356. That the providential care of the family of Abraham, should encourage some such narrow views in the minds of a rude people, in a low state of civilization, can easily be supposed, and need not be denied. That forms of expression, there used, may be so interpreted, we will not dispute. We may go farther and say, that God himself may have designed to address the patriarchs in a manner fitted to remind them of his *special* care and protection. But that these views were the highest conceptions entertained of God — much less, that these were the only views that were revealed to the people of those days, is contradicted by frequent references of a more elevated character, of which, what is said of the creation, is an obvious example.

357. What is said of the Deluge, is no less to our purpose. That event was sufficiently momentous to indicate the interposition of an Almighty Power; and to insist that the historian who gives us the Bible account of it, had none but low and unworthy conceptions of the character of God, to whose agency that event is referred, shows an entire misconception of the facts as they are. In the same spirit are the destruction of Babel and of Sodom ; though these events are not of the same magnificent character as the former. They show that the "God of the Jews is also the God of the Gentiles," and that the book so regards him, as it makes him to concern himself with their affairs, holding them responsible to him for their conduct, and punishing them for their sins. Nor are other references without significance, as inculcating the same sentiment. Abraham once fell into an error on this subject, and took what he thought were judicious measures to guard himself from the wrongs of a people, who as he supposed, had no fear of God before their eyes. The result showed his mistake. Isaac, too, did the same thing, with a like misapprehension, and with the same result ; and Jacob found the house of God and the gate of heaven, where he did not expect the divine presence.

358. In the second place, the book employs language, to set forth the divine attributes, fitted to give us exalted views of the Creator. The language of Melchisedek is to the point :—" Blessed be Abraham of the Most High God, possessor of heaven and Earth ; and blessed be the Most High God, who hath delivered thine enemies into thy hands." The language of Abram, on the same occasion is similar; " I have lifted up my hand unto the Lord, the Most High God, possessor of heaven and earth." The language of God to this patriarch, on another occasion, is quite as emphatic, and equally to our purpose ;—" I am the Almigty God ; walk before me, and be thou perfect." Similar is the language to Jacob ;— " I am God Almighty :" and this patriarch uses the same language to his sons. " God Almighty give you mercy before the man." xiv. 19, 20, 22 ; xvii. 1 ; xliii. 14 ; xlix. 25.

359. That the ancients had the same extended views of " heaven and earth" that now prevail, is not presumed. Doubtless their ideas of the physical universe were very limited ; and their views of the Creator and Governor of the universe, must have corresponded ; but it is certain

that all there was of the world, be it more or less, was the product of the Power they worshipped — was in his hands and subject to his control.

SECTION II. — UNITY OF GOD.

360. The unity of God is obviously the doctrine of the book of Genesis. This is sufficiently manifest from the absence of all conflicting doctrines. True, the name of God (Elohim) is in the plural form; but the use of synonymous words in the singular, the use of the singular verb, the singular pronoun, &c., in conjunction with it, shows clearly that the sense of the word is singular. This subject is fully discussed in our criticism on this word, and need not be enlarged upon here. Consult p. 53–55. Few that have any knowledge of the Hebrew Scriptures, will maintain that any other than the unity of God is therein revealed.

SECTION III. — NATURE AND RESPONSIBILITY OF MAN.

361. It is worthy of being noticed, as a most important fact of revelation, that man was made in the image of God. This image can have no reference to man's physical form. It was evidently his spiritual nature that has the divine image: and this fact is the best evidence, furnished in this part of the Bible, to prove our immortality. We may criticise the words "soul" and "spirit," as much as we please: and we shall still be in the dark; but in the fact of man's likeness to the Divine Being, we see good and substantial reasons for believing in the soul's immortality. We are like God — so the book clearly represents. We have the same original attributes; and they are as imperishable in us as they are in him.

362. Were we to seek for a philosophical interpretation of the likeness we possess to the Creator, we should find it in the language of the apostle to the Gentiles, who calls God the "Father of our spirits," in contradistinction to our earthly parents, whom he designates as the "fathers of our flesh." The human soul is the child of God; and as such it is presumed to be like its parent; and if we look closely to what man is, as a spiritual being, the resemblance will become quite too obvious to be mistaken. The spirit of man and the Spirit of God are alike — the one emanated from the other, as the child from a parent; and both have the same attributes. The wisdom and power of man, and the wisdom and power of God, are alike. The justice of man, and the justice of God, are the same. The benevolence of man, and of God, are identical. The difference is not in the nature of these attributes, but only in their extent. Man is finite, and God is infinite.

The first act of God's moral government over man, is based on the doctrine here announced. There is an assumption of human responsibility; and this can only belong to a moral nature, such as no being but God possesses, and those made in his likeness.

363. But did human nature and responsibility remain the same? That man was originally holy, is generally assumed. That he remained so, is generally denied. His nature was at first pure — he was indeed a child of God — but when he fell, in other words, when he sinned, he became wholly changed. This is the common opinion, from which we are compelled to dissent. We see no reason for the popular doctrine, that human nature underwent a change, when Adam sinned. We are sure that no intimation of such a change is given, in the account we have of that transaction. Adam's *condition* was changed. His character was changed. He was right before he disobeyed, he was wrong afterwards. He was innocent before, afterwards he was guilty. He was happy before, he was afterwards miserable. But this does not relate to the nature of Adam. His nature was unchanged. His reason and intellect were the same. His conscience was not destroyed. If conscience admonished him not to commit sin, it was no less faithful to rebuke him after he had committed it. His consciousness of guilt and condemnation, is far from indicating a totally corrupt condition. It is, on the contrary, a clear proof that he was sensible of his responsibility as a moral being, and therefore, not totally corrupt.

Nor can we see any reason why that one sin of Adam should be so much more heinous than other sins. Surely if Adam became totally corrupt by his first sin, all other sins could be of little consequence to him. He might now sin with an uplifted hand, as no farther effect could result from his iniquities. Is this the view we are to take of this subject? If we take this view, we must do so, on our own responsibility, as the divine record cannot be so interpreted.

364. It is worthy of being added, that the subsequent history of man, is opposed to the sentiment now under review. Cain was punished for his sins, because he could have avoided the crime for which he was made to suffer. He had no more excuse than Adam had. He could not plead his corrupt nature in extenuation of his guilt, more than Adam could. This does not harmonize with the common views. Indeed, if Cain was wholly corrupt, so that he could not think a good thought, speak a good word, or perform a good act, then he had the best reason, in the world, for what he did; and his punishment was plainly unjust. We shall find no less difficulty in accounting for the good conduct of his brother, if the common theory be true. Abel was acceptable for his righteousness; but how came he to be thus righteous, since he had inherited a corrupt nature from his parents? True, he may have "met with a change;" but if this be so, it is certain that the writer has omitted to give us the record of that event.

The only rational conclusion is, that Adam's sons were like himself, capable of sinning, or refraining from sin, as they pleased: that, before they sinned, they were as innocent as himself; and that, after they had sinned, they had no more excuse than he; in other words, that their nature, the divine image within them, was the same, as it was at first.

365. With the view that is commonly held of the sin of our first parents, and the consequent depravity, we shall find it difficult to account for some instances of virtue and piety that are found among men in those ancient times. Enoch walked with God; so did Noah; and in the days of Enos, a grand-son of Adam, it is

said that men began to call on the name of the Lord. How is this to be accounted for, in view of their native depravity? This we deem a pertinent question. And it is quite as pertinent to ask, how we are to account for other instances of good behavior that made their appearance, after the flood, even with those that did not belong to the chosen people. What could be more honorable than the conduct of Pharaoh towards Abram and his wife, or of Abimelech on another similar occasion? What more generous than the conduct of the sons of Heth, when Abram proposed to purchase of them the cave of Machpelah. The king of Sodom shows a becoming sense of obligation to Abraham, when, after the slaughter of the kings, he proposes to the patriarch: "Give me the persons, but take the goods to thyself." The king of Egypt, at a later period, could appreciate the virtues of Joseph, and was not slow to reward them. In all these instances we see goodness where we should least expect it; and they clearly show that the image of God in man, neither the sin of Adam, nor any other cause, had ever radically changed.

366. A few words in this connection, on the cause of sin, will not be out of place. And the first thing we would notice, is, that a corrupt nature is not necessary to account for its existence; for, were that so, we would be obliged to refer the same thing to our first parents. It is obvious that if they could sin without such a cause, so can others, and so can all. They were naturally pure, and yet they sinned: we then can sin, though naturally as pure as they. It is a little remarkable that men have accounted for the sin of Adam, without a corrupt nature to engender it: but have not been able to account for the sin of others in the same way.

367. When we look carefully at the mode of procedure in the temptation of the first human pair, we cannot help seeing that they were tempted precisely as we are, and sinned in the same way. The forbidden object looked to them desirable: it was good for food; it was pleasant to the eyes: it would make them wise. This was one view of the subject. "But death will ensue, if we eat," they may have said; and yet they may have

thought, "there is no certainty of this; we do not see how it can be; and it is possible we may escape." Thus they reasoned, and they acted according to this reasoning; thus we have reasoned, and thus we have acted. Say, if you will, that we do this, because we are naturally inclined to evil. The inclination was with Adam, as much as with us; and yet of him no such thing is affirmed. He sinned while acting from impulses and desires within, called into exercise by circumstances without. We do the same. The fact is indisputable, and all can understand it.

368. The case of Adam and Eve shows that sin results from an error in judgment, in regard to some forbidden object. They erred in believing that a good could be found in the way of transgression. They erred equally in supposing that the punishment of sin could be avoided. These are the two great mistakes they committed; and these are the two great mistakes we commit, whenever we sin. The whole theory of sinning is here laid out before us; and the way of safety is plain: It is to trust to no information but what we get from our rightful Sovereign. Had Adam and Eve done this, they would have been safe. There is no other safe way for us.

SECTION IV.— REWARDS AND PUNISHMENTS.

369. The doctrine of rewards and punishments comes properly before us in this discussion. The book we are explaining says something on this subject; and it is important for us to know what it says.

While Adam and Eve were innocent, they are represented as being in a beautiful and well-watered garden, where there was everything to please and delight them. When they became sinful, they were not only "driven out" from the garden, but their condition is indicated by images that imply a high degree of suffering. No one can mistake the general design of the representation. It associates with innocence, all that is beautiful and attractive, and with guilt, what is painful and vexatious.

370. Besides this obvious representation, we have the express declaration of the Almighty to the same effect. "In the day thou eatest thereof thou shalt surely die."

Two particulars, connected with punishment, are here stated. One is, that punishment is immediate: and another, that it is certain. "In the day" conveys the one idea; and "surely" the other. Instances to confirm the doctrine may be taken from the history of those early times. Cain slew his brother, and was punished with a present punishment that he thought was greater than he could bear. The antediluvians became corrupt: and it is presumed that they, like Adam, suffered for their sins a present retribution, as well as an ultimate destruction. So of the Sodomites; so of Joseph's brethren; so of all others that sinned. None committed a more heinous sin than Cain; and it is presumed that none were punished with a severer infliction; and his punishment we know was temporal.

371. There is no more instructive narrative, showing the nature of punishment, than that relating to Joseph's brethren. They committed a great sin; and they suffered greatly on account of it. They not only suffered what appears on the face of the narrative; but they must, from the nature of the case, have suffered much more than this. But when their punishment had properly humbled them, and had accomplished the purpose originally intended, it came to an end; and this brings to view another feature of punishment, as administered by the divine Being, viz., its salutary tendency, implying its ultimate termination.

SECTION V. — FINAL TRIUMPH OF GOOD.

372. There are, in the book of Genesis, some great and precious promises, that must not be overlooked, in treating the doctrines revealed therein. One of these is spoken of in connection with the sin of our first parents. "I will put enmity between thee and the woman, and between thy seed and her seed: it shall bruise thy head, and thou shalt bruise his heel." To bruise the heel, is a small evil; but to bruise the head, denotes absolute destruction. The language is obviously figurative; but its meaning will not be mistaken. It denotes the utter extinction of moral evil; and when the promise is fulfilled, there will be no more sin nor suffering in the universe.

I am unable to see what other meaning can be attached to this passage; and I am convinced, that, if it had received the attention it deserves, we should not now be called upon to expose the teachings of that gloomy system which announces the endless perpetuity of evil.

373. Another promise, worthy of being placed by the side of this, was addressed to Abraham, and repeated to Isaac and Jacob, that in their seed all the families and nations of the earth should be blessed. We know not how this promise can be understood in any limited sense; and there are no conditions associated with it, that can occasion a failure. Indeed, the promise is obviously being fulfilled at the present time. The world is being blessed in the seed of Abraham. The work is now going on; and it gives joyful assurance that it will be gloriously accomplished, according to the spirit and letter of the original declaration.

The whole subject of the divine government is beautifully illustrated in the allegory of the Garden of Eden, to which the reader's attention is now directed.

SECTION VI.—GARDEN OF EDEN.

CHAP. II.

8. ¶ And the LORD God planted a garden eastward in Eden; and there he put the man whom he had formed.
9. And out of the ground made the LORD God to grow every tree that is pleasant to the sight, and good for food; the tree of life also in the midst of the garden, and the tree of knowledge of good and evil.
10. And a river went out of Eden to water the garden; and from thence it was parted, and became into four heads.
11. The name of the first *is* Pison: that *is* it which compasseth the whole land of Havilah, where *there* is gold;
12. And the gold of that land *is* good: there *is* bdellium and the onyx stone.
13. And the name of the second river *is* Gihon: the same *is* it that compasseth the whole land of Ethiopia.
14. And the name of the third river *is* Hiddekel: that *is* it which goeth toward the east of Assyria. And the fourth river *is* Euphrates.
15. And the LORD God took the man, and put him into the garden of Eden, to dress it, and to keep it.
16. And the LORD God commanded the man, saying, Of every tree of the garden thou mayst freely eat:
17. But of the tree of the knowledge of good and evil, thou shalt not eat of it: for in the day that thou eatest thereof thou shalt surely die.

CHAP. III.

1. Now the serpent was more subtile than any beast of the field which the Lord God had made: and he said unto the woman, Yea, hath God said, Ye shall not eat of every tree of the garden?
2. And the woman said unto the serpent, We may eat of the fruit of the trees of the garden:
3. But of the fruit of the tree which is in the midst of the garden, God hath said, Ye shall not eat of it, neither shall ye touch it, lest ye die
4. And the serpent said unto the woman, Ye shall not surely die:
5. For God doth know, that in the day ye eat thereof, then your eyes shall be opened; and ye shall be as gods, knowing good and evil.
6. And when the woman saw that the tree *was* good for food, and that it *was* pleasant to the eyes, and a tree to be desired to make one wise; she took of the fruit thereof, and did eat; and gave also unto her husband with her, and he did eat.
7. And the eyes of them both were opened, and they knew that they *were* naked: and they sewed fig leaves together, and made themselves aprons.
8. And they heard the voice of the Lord God walking in the garden in the cool of the day: and Adam and his wife hid themselves from the presence of the Lord God amongst the trees of the garden.
9. And the Lord God called unto Adam, and said unto him, Where *art* thou?
10. And he said, I heard thy voice in the garden; and I was afraid, because I *was* naked; and I hid myself.
11. And he said, Who told thee that thou *wast* naked? Hast thou eaten of the tree whereof I commanded thee that thou shouldest not eat.
12. And the man said, The woman whom thou gavest *to be* with me, she gave me of the tree, and I did eat.
13. And the Lord God said unto the woman, What *is* this *that* thou hast done? And the woman said, the serpent beguiled me, and I did eat.
14. And the Lord God said unto The serpent, Because thou hast done this, thou *art* cursed above all cattle, and above every beast of the field: upon thy belly shalt thou go, and dust shalt thou eat all the days of thy life.
15. And I will put enmity between thee and the woman, and between thy seed and her seed: it shall bruise thy head, and thou shalt bruise his heel.
16. Unto the woman he said, I will greatly multiply thy sorrow and thy conception; in sorrow thou shalt bring forth children: and thy desire *shall be* to thy husband, and he shall rule over thee.
17. And unto Adam he said, Because thou hast hearkened unto the voice of thy wife, and hast eaten of the tree of which I commanded thee, saying, Thou shalt not eat of it: cursed *is* the ground for thy sake; in sorrow shalt thou eat *of* it all the days of thy life;
18. Thorns also and thistles shall it bring forth to thee; and thou shalt eat the herb of the field:
19. In the sweat of thy face shalt thou eat bread, till thou return unto the ground; for out of it wast thou taken: for dust thou *art*, and unto dust shalt thou return.
20. And Adam called his wife's name Eve, because she was the mother of all living
21. Unto Adam also and to his wife did the Lord God make coats of skins, and clothed them.
22. ¶ And the Lord God said, Behold, the man is become as one of us, to know good and evil: and now, lest he put forth his hand, and take also of the tree of life, and eat, and live for ever:
23. Therefore the Lord God sent him forth from the garden of Eden, to till the ground from whence he was taken.

24. So he drove out the man; and he placed at the east of the garden of Eden Cherubims, and a flaming sword which turned every way, to keep the way of the tree of life.

374. Various opinions have been entertained concerning the Garden of Eden ; nor is there any settled theory at the present time, more than there has been in past ages. The account we have in the Bible is generally regarded as literal ; and a theory of the trial, temptation, and fall of our first parents, has been based upon this interpretation, and made to assume a corresponding shape and form. That the account is literal, however, seems to us quite improbable. The balance of evidence is decidedly against that interpretation. We will give some of the reasons for differing from the generally received theory.

375. First, no such place as corresponds, in any proximate form, to the Garden of Eden, has ever been found, on the face of the earth. Men have thought they had found it ; and their several opinions would locate it in every part of the earth. Asia, Africa, Europe and America, have their respective claims, sustained by men of genius and education. The opinions that have been put forth, and the arguments in their defense, would fill volumes ; and yet the world is quite as much in the dark now, as it ever has been, as to the solution of this question. Did we believe in a literal interpretation, it would be well to state the various opinions of men, and to make a selection of the best one ; but, believing we have found a more excellent way, we do not think best to employ time in discussing theories, and deciding between them, when they are all and equally false. We repeat that no such place as the Garden of Eden has ever been found. If it be replied that time would obliterate many of the features of the garden ; so that an approximation to the Bible description, is all that we could expect, and that such approximation has been arrived at ; we reply, that no such thing can be claimed for any theory with which we are acquainted. This will be made the more evident as we advance.

376. In the second place, there have never been such rivers as are spoken of in connexion with the Garden of

Eden. One of the rivers was Pison that encompassed the whole land of Havilah. Another was Gihon that encompassed the whole land of Ethiopia. The third river was Hiddekel which goeth toward the east of Assyria; and the fourth was Euphrates. There was a place in Palestine, or near that country, by the name of Havilah ; but we know of no river Pison with which it was encompassed. Ethiopia was in Africa, and Assyria was in Asia ; and we all know that no two rivers, arising near the same source, could have encompassed the one of these countries, and gone to the east of the other. There is a river Euphrates ; but there are no rivers connected with it, that answer the description of the others mentioned in this account. But if it could be shown that somewhere near the Euphrates, four rivers are found, that *may have been* the ones mentioned by Moses, that would not locate the Garden of Eden there ; for we know that a thousand similar instances can be adduced from all parts of the world. It is quite common for elevated regions of country to send forth, not four only, but many, streams of water, that go off into different and distant lands.

Let another thing be observed in connection with these rivers. They were at first but one river, which afterwards separated and became four. This at least is the common view of the account ; and it involves a thing that is quite unnatural. That several streams should meet and form one, is natural, and what we all know to be the usual arrangement ; but that one stream should part into four streams, is unnatural, and not to be believed on any slight evidence. It is still more unnatural, if possible, for a river to *encompass* a land. It may pass through it, but it cannot encompass or surround it.

377. In the next place, there never were such literal trees as are mentioned in connection with the Garden. Indeed, the names given to two of the trees of the Garden, the one being called " the tree of life," and the other " the tree of knowledge of good and evil," make it as obvious as the light of day, that a moral and not a literal interpretation was intended. We marvel that this circumstance has not attracted attention before, and more generally, and saved interpreters from many absurdities into which they have fallen. It is quite certain that these two trees are to be understood figuratively; if so, why not the other trees of the Garden, and the Garden itself, and the rivers by which it was watered?

378. Again; there never was such a serpent as the one alluded to in the account before us. Did serpents talk in those days? and did they interest themselves in moral subjects, the obedience and disobedience of men? Did they know, and how, that our first parents would be as gods, knowing good and evil, if they ate of the tree? Did they walk upright, making it a punishment to crawl on the ground, as they now do, and as they are fitted to do, by their configuration? And what interpretation can we attach to the promise, literally understood, that the seed of the woman should 'bruise the serpent's head,' which, in that case, would be nothing more than the simple announcement, that Eve's descendants *would kill snakes*. If it be said that the serpent was only an instrument in the hands of an invisible tempter, we would reply: 1st, that no such idea is inculcated by the sacred writer: and 2d, if it were so, that would not militate against a moral application.

379. Another thing, equally difficult, as literally interpreted, is, that the partaking of the fruit of the forbidden tree, should induce such consequences as described in the account. How could Adam and Eve now know that they were naked, rather than before they partook of the fruit? How could such fruit make them know good and evil, or become as gods? Nearly allied to this objection, is, the consequences that followed disobedience. What connection between the penalty inflicted on the woman, and the fruit she ate; or the punishment the man was made to suffer, and the sin for which it was inflicted? All this is unnatural and unphilosophical, when interpreted literally; and yet it admits of a consistent and beautiful application when viewed allegorically.

380. Another thing is worthy of notice in this connection. That Adam and Eve should be put into a literal garden, to keep it and cultivate it, and to confine their labors to that; when they had before received from the Creator the dominion of the whole earth, and were com-

manded to replenish and subdue it; — in other words, that they should be cast out of the garden, and made to do as a punishment for sin, what they had been instructed to do at first, and before sin entered into the world — is a theory that introduces difficulty and contradiction into the record, without any just occasion for so doing. But that, having given us an account of man's creation and his physical relations, the writer should then, by the ancient and symbolic method, instruct us in regard to his moral condition. is a rational and natural supposition.

381. We understand the Garden of Eden as an allegory; and with this understanding, it reveals to us a sound philosophy, in respect to man's moral state; and the fitness of the several parts of the allegory, to represent temptation to sin, the act of transgression, and the consequences thereof will justify the interpretation.

It should be borne in mind that the most ancient form of writing was by hieroglyphics or pictures. The meaning of the picture depended, like any word or phrase in any other form of writing, not only on itself, its form and arrangement, but on other pictures that were associated with it. It is very easy to see how the innocence of our first parents in their primitive state, their subsequent temptation and fall, and the painful consequences of their sin, could be set forth in this way. In this way, in our judgment, it was set forth.

382. The first picture is that of a beautiful and well-watered garden, having every tree that is good for food and pleasant to the eye. In the midst of the garden are two trees that attract special attention. They are very unlike. Their respective names could be afterwards inferred from their results. In this garden are our first parents, with the evident intention that they shall cultivate it and enjoy its fruits. This is the picture. The meaning is not difficult. The Garden denotes a state of innocence. What could be more appropriate? The trees are human actions. One tree only denotes wrong doing. It is man's duty to cultivate his moral nature, and enjoy the fruits of well-doing.

383. The next picture is the same as the first, with the addition of a serpent, extending to Eve the fruit of the forbidden tree (which, from this circumstance, becomes known as the forbidden tree,) and Adam standing near by, ready to receive it at her hand. Nothing could more aptly represent temptation than this picture The serpent is the most subtile of all the beasts of the field, and is therefore better fitted to set forth the seductive power of sin than any other animal. The conversation of the serpent with the woman, is sufficiently indicated by the picture itself, without any other expedient to denote it. Besides, it is the language of human experience. Sin looks attractive, and it promises much good; and it suggests that the punishment it may deserve, is quite uncertain. It mixes up truth and error in its promises, and by that means, the more effectually leads us astray.

384. The next picture contains the same general features as the former ones, except that it shows our first parents as conscious of guilt, and seeking to hide themselves among the trees of the garden. That the serpent has been successful is obvious; that Adam, as well as Eve, has sinned, is indicated by his appearance. That they were tried and condemned by their lawful Sovereign, was a legitimate inference, and is fully confirmed by the next and last picture.

385. Finally; the Garden no longer appears, or if it does, our first parents are no longer its inmates. The woman is represented in a condition of great pain and distress, teaching us that great physical suffering is requisite to adequately represent the consequences of sin to her tender nature. The man is toiling in the midst of briars and thorns that torture and goad him on every hand, teaching him plainly that the way of the transgressor is hard. A flaming sword and cherubim are marked on this picture as standing between the offenders and the tree of life, lest they should partake of that, and not suffer the penalty that had been announced as the result of transgression. The serpent is no longer coiled about the tree of knowledge, from which he had reached out the fruit to Eve; but he lies prostrate in the dust, from which he is to derive his sustenance; and some mark indicates (or it is a reasonable inference) that he shall ultimately be destroyed by a descendant of the woman whom he had seduced from duty.

386. This is briefly the meaning of this beautiful allegory. The most important lessons are here taught. The representation gives us the experience of our first parents, and not less the experience of their descendants. It shows the responsibility of man, the process of temptation and disobedience, and the consequences of sin. We know the truth of what is here taught from our own experience; for we, as much as Adam and Eve, have been in the Garden of Eden, have had the same unfortunate interview with the serpent, have sinned and fallen as they did, and found the consequences to be what they experienced.

387. The theology of the church has not been satisfied with these simple and beautiful lessons. It has therefore added many things to the divine word, and has thus marred the beauty of the sacred record, and brought it into disrepute with many men, who take the common view as the true one, and have too much good sense to accept it.

We will enumerate briefly the errors that have been engrafted upon the Bible representation, and give a few of the reasons why they ought not to be regarded as any part of the divine teaching. First, men have made the sin of our first parents to have produced a change in the Deity, loving and blessing them before they sinned, and hating and cursing them afterwards. Next, they have believed and taught that human nature was wholly changed by the first sin. It was before immortal and immaculate; it was afterwards subject to dissolution and totally corrupt. Some have carried the idea of change, so far, that they have represented the animals, as well as men, as having undergone a similar transformation. They became cruel and voracious, while before, they had no such peculiarities.

Then again we are told that Adam's sin affected all his posterity, as it affected himself; giving them a nature wholly corrupt, and subjecting them to the wrath and curse of God. And in harmony with these doctrines, "all the miseries of this life, death itself, and the pains of hell forever," are made the penalty of transgression. All these evils are attributed to a malignant spirit, who concealed himself in the body of a serpent, and thereby deceived our mother Eve.

388. That these doctrines have been engrafted upon the divine record, without authority, and are no part of the record itself, will be evident, in part from what is said to the contrary, and in part from the entire absence of any thing to sustain them.

From what can we infer that God was angry with our first parents after they had sinned? The gentle voice of the Almighty, on that occasion does not seem to be prompted by wrath. No curse is spoken against Adam and Eve or their posterity. Man is changed, sadly changed, but it is not his nature that is changed. He is the same man, now, in all the essential attributes of his being, that he was before the transgression. His posterity are like their original progenitor. They sin as he sinned and they suffer as he suffered.

The beasts were not changed. Many of them were intended at first, for destroying and feeding upon other animals. Their configuration shows this; and they had this configuration before the fall, as their fossil remains clearly indicate. Men formed their theology without a knowledge of Geological facts; and now as they become acquainted with these facts, they are compelled to make corresponding changes in their religious systems. That eternal death was threatened to Adam, is wholly assumed. It was not eternal death, but simply *death* that was announced. Nor this only; it was a death that was to be suffered, and was suffered, in the day of transgression. If "all the miseries of this life" are the result of sin, it is certain that they are not the result of Adam's sin. "Death itself," referring to natural death, is not attributed to Adam's sin, in the record, but to the fact that he was of earth, and must therefore return to the earth again. "The pains of hell forever" are not mentioned. That an evil spirit was concerned in the transgression, is an assumption, unfounded and absurd.

389. The following doctrines we consider to be plainly inculcated : 1st, that man is an accountable being ; 2d, that a state of innocence is a state of happiness ; 3d, that sin brings immediate and certain punishment ; and 4th, that sin will ultimately be destroyed. All opposing doctrines are without authority.

PART III.

HISTORY AND BIOGRAPHY.

390. Much the largest part of the book of Genesis is comprehended in this division, though it may not require the largest amount of discussion. There are but few things of a historical character, that do not relate to the personal experience of the patriarchs or that of their families. Most of the record, therefore, is Biography, rather than History.

CHAPTER XI.

ADAM AND HIS FAMILY.

CONTENTS:— Creation of Adam and Eve; Their Nuptials; The Temptation; Family of Adam; Genealogy of Cain; Genealogy of Seth.

391. If it surprises us that more is not said of so important a personage as the father of the human race, our surprise will be diminished, if not wholly removed, by considering the imperfect mode of perpetuating the knowledge of events that must have existed at first, it being by tradition, or by writing in its rudest form. And though Moses had the means of writing a more extended history of Adam, the fact of his having omitted to do so, shows clearly that he obtained his knowledge from brief records then in existence, and could communicate only what he derived from that source. Hence it will be observed, that, as the history of early times progresses, it becomes more full and complete, for the obvious reason that the art of writing, like all other arts, had improved with time; and of course the facility of making out historical records had increased in the same proportion.

Several particulars connected with Adam and his family, contained in the sacred record, may be noticed separately.

SECTION I. — CREATION OF ADAM AND EVE.

CHAP. I.

26. And God said, Let us make man in our image, after our likeness; and let them have dominion over the fish of the sea, and over the fowl of the air, and over the cattle, and over all the earth, and over every creeping thing that creepeth upon the earth.

27. So God created man in his own image; in the image of God created he him; male and female created he them.

28. And God blessed them; and God said unto them, Be fruitful, and multiply, and replenish the earth, and subdue it: and have dominion over the fish of the sea, and over the fowl of the air, and over every living thing that moveth upon the earth.

29. ¶ And God said, Behold, I have given you every herb bearing seed, which *is* upon the face of all the earth, and every tree, in the which *is* the fruit of a tree yielding seed; to you it shall be for meat.

30. And to every beast of the earth, and to every fowl of the air, and to every thing that creepeth upon the earth, wherein *there is* life, *I have given* every green herb for meat: and it was so.

31. And God saw every thing that he had made, and, behold, *it was* very good. And the evening and the morning were the sixth day.

CHAP. II.

4. These *are* the generations of the heavens and of the earth when they were created, in the day that the LORD God made the earth and the heavens.

5. And every plant of the field before it was in the earth, and every herb of the field before it grew: for the LORD God had not caused it to rain upon the earth, and *there was*

not a man to till the ground.

6. But there went up a mist from the earth, and watered the whole face of the ground.

7. And the LORD God formed man *of* the dust of the ground, and breathed into his nostrils the breath of life; and man became a living soul.

392. The purpose of God in creating man, is said to be, that he might have dominion over all subordinate creatures. We infer that he was to subsist on such as were suitable for food ; as his dominion over them, can, so far as we can see, have no other practical advantage. In addition to the flesh of animals, which we understand to be given him by implication, he is expressly told that he is to have "every herb bearing seed" and "every tree in which is the fruit of a tree yielding seed ;" while "every green herb" simply, was to be food for other animals. A distinction between the food of men and animals seems to be had in view ; but this distinction is not very clearly marked ; and a general, rather than a specific and invariable rule, must have been intended.

393. The image of God, in which man was created, we have spoken of elsewhere. So also the usage of the expression, "Let us make man." p. 195, 54,55.

So much of the above passage as relates to man's creation from the dust of the ground, is simply a repetition of the account in chapter first, (Comp. § 292,) with this variation only ; that, while the first account comprehends both a spiritual and physical creation, the last makes allusion only to the latter. A "living soul" is not a spiritual and immortal being, in the Bible sense of that expression, but simply a living creature, and may apply to animals, and is applied to them, as well as to men. The creation of man *in the image of God*, is the only allusion to the spiritual and immortal part of our nature, contained in the account of man's creation.

394. Gen. ii. 4, contains an appellation of Deity that had not been before employed ; and this fact has been a matter of speculation with interpreters. In the previous account, the Deity is called "God ;" he is now designated as "Lord God ;" and this expression is continued through the second and third chapters, with two or three exceptions, and in some other passages. This matter is discussed in another place to which the reader is referred. pp. 18–20.

SECTION II.—Nuptials of Adam and Eve.

CHAP. II.

18. ¶ And the Lord God said, It is not good that the man should be alone; I will make him an help meet for him.
19. And out of the ground the Lord God formed every beast of the field, and every fowl of the air; and brought *them* unto Adam to see what he would call them: and whatsoever Adam called every living creature, that *was* the name thereof.
20. And Adam gave names to all cattle, and to the fowl of the air, and to every beast of the field; but for Adam there was not found an help meet for him.
21. And the Lord God caused a deep sleep to fall upon Adam, and he slept; and he took one of his ribs, and closed up the flesh instead thereof;
22. And the rib, which the Lord God had taken from man, made he a woman, and brought her unto the man.
23. And Adam said, This *is* now bone of my bones, and flesh of my flesh: she shall be called Woman, because she was taken out of Man.
24. Therefore shall a man leave his father and his mother, and shall cleave unto his wife: and they shall be one flesh.
25. And they were both naked, the man and his wife, and were not ashamed.

395. It will be observed by the careful reader, that, in the middle of the Bible account of the Garden of Eden and the Temptation, there is another subject introduced, that seems to have no immediate connection with it. The writer gives us a description of the Garden, and mentions the prohibition put upon man.

He then suspends the record, and introduces the naming of the beasts, and the making of a help meet for Adam. After this, he resumes the subject of the temptation and the attending circumstances. How is this singular procedure to be accounted for?

This matter is not without its difficulties. The common idea is, that the historian goes back to relate some circumstances that had taken place before, and that he describes the exact manner in which the woman was made, as he had before only given us the simple fact of her creation in connection with that of man. We have what we deem a better interpretation of this subject. The creation of woman had several times been referred to. She was created when man was, i. 27, and obviously in the same way. Both were made of the dust of the ground; for, though this language is found in chapter second, it refers to the same creation as that mentioned in chapter first, and like that relates to the female as well as the male ; the term *man* including both. And if it be true that woman was made of the dust, it is not true that she was made of one of the ribs of Adam. And when it is said that God breathed into man the breath of life, and he became a living soul, the reference is to both. So both were made in the image of God. And when God planted a garden, and placed there the *man* whom he had formed, the meaning is, that he placed there both the man and the woman. The prohibition was evidently given to both. God called "their name Adam (or man) in the day when they were created," v. 2 ; and of course what is said of Adam, or of man, in these preliminary statements, applies to both ; and this fact excludes the idea that woman was made by a process different from man.

396. Again ; there is nothing in the connection, where the creation of woman from one of man's ribs is mentioned, to require an allusion to her original creation, but only to the relation she sustained to Adam. Such relation seemed necessary to be understood, to account for man's ready yielding to her solicitations, as well as her subjection to the man alluded to afterwards. And it is this relation, and not her first creation, that we suppose the writer had in view in this passage.

397. We regard the whole of what is here said of the woman, (and we think the naming of the beasts should be included in the same view,) as a divine vision. Explained thus, it is easy to understand it. The deep sleep, brought upon Adam, was not designed, as the common opinion is, that he might not feel the pain of a surgical operation ; but it was a requisite condition for viewing, with his mental organs, the instructive scene that was to pass before him. With this view, we suppose the beasts of the field, the fowls of the air, &c., to have passed before him to receive their name ; (and in a vision, not unlike a dream, this could be done, in a very brief space, though to do it literally, would require a long period, as well as being altogether unnecessary :) but the whole line of subordinate creatures offers no one

suitable to be his companion. The Lord then takes from him one of his ribs, and makes a woman, or *wife*, as the word also means, and gives her to him, as a companion. Adam comprehends the purpose of the vision, takes the woman for a wife, calls her name Eve, as about to become the mother of the whole human race, and cherishes her as bone of his bones and flesh of his flesh.

398. It is worthy of inquiry whether the passage itself does not clearly require this construction. " A deep sleep fell upon Adam, and he slept." Is not this plainly tautological? After telling us that "a deep sleep fell upon him," why add, that " he slept." Such an addition is of course superfluous. Ought we not then to understand the term here rendered " deep sleep," as meaning something else or more, than simply sleep. The Septuagint uses a word for deep sleep, that properly denotes an ecstacy or vision ; and we find the same Hebrew word employed in this sense in other places. A deep sleep (the same word in the original) fell upon Abram, xv. 12; and while in that state, sundry communications were made to him, a covenant entered into, and the ratifying sacrifices performed.

399. If it be said that woman was made from one of man's ribs, for the purpose of teaching Adam the nature of the marriage relation. (the only reason for the procedure that we can conceive of,) we reply, that a vision, wherein these things were enacted, would be equally instructive, without involving any difficulty or absurdity. That God can perform wonders, by the exercise of his miraculous power, we cheerfully admit — that he has done this, in numerous instances, we firmly believe ; but that he exercises his power in any extraordinary way, to accomplish an object that can as well be accomplished by its ordinary exercise, we are not at liberty to suppose. We see no reason why the creation of woman should be peculiar, and arrived at by a process entirely unlike the creation of man ; and as the passage that seems to set forth such an idea, can be rationally explained in another way, such interpretation ought to be adopted.

SECTION III.—THE TEMPTATION.

400. The nature of the temptation, and the imagery with which it is set forth, we have discussed elsewhere. See p. 203–210. That our first parents were morally responsible to the Creator — that they could obey or disobey the divine requirements as they pleased — that they were tempted and yielded to temptation — sinned and were punished — are the clear and explicit statements of the sacred historian. The account we have of the fall, shows them to have been the exact representatives of men at the present day and of all past days. They were tempted as we are — they were led astray by a similar deception, that there is pleasure in sin, and that punishment is uncertain; and like us, too, they learned, too late, that the way of the transgressor is hard.

SECTION IV.—FAMILY OF ADAM AND EVE.

CHAP. IV.

1. And Adam knew Eve his wife; and she conceived, and bare Cain, and said, I have gotten a man from the LORD.
2. And she again bare his brother Abel. And Abel was a keeper of sheep, but Cain was a tiller of the ground.
3. And in process of time it came to pass, that Cain brought of the fruit of the ground an offering unto the LORD.
4. And Abel, he also brought of the firstlings of his flock and of the fat thereof. And the LORD had respect unto Abel and to his offering:
5. But unto Cain and to his offering he had not respect. And Cain was very wroth, and his countenance fell.
6. And the LORD said unto Cain, Why art thou wroth? and why is thy countenance fallen?
7. If thou doest well, shalt thou not be accepted? and if thou doest not well, sin lieth at the door. And unto thee *shall be* his desire, and thou shalt rule over him.
8. ¶ And Cain talked with Abel his brother: and it came to pass, when they were in the field, that Cain rose up against Abel his brother, and slew him.
9. ¶ And the LORD said unto Cain, Where *is* Abel thy brother? And he said, I know not: *Am* I my brother's keeper?
10. And he said, What hast thou done? the voice of thy brother's blood crieth unto me from the ground.
11. And now *art* thou cursed from the earth, which hath opened her mouth to receive thy brother's blood from thy hand.
12. When thou tillest the ground, it shall not henceforth yield unto thee her strength; a fugitive and a vagabond shalt thou be in the earth.
13. And Cain said unto the LORD

My punishment is greater than I can bear.

14. Behold, thou hast driven me out this day from the face of the earth; and from thy face shall I be hid; and I shall be a fugitive and a vagabond in the earth; and it shall come to pass, *that* every one that findeth me shall slay me.

15. And the LORD said unto him, Therefore whosoever slayeth Cain, vengeance shall be taken on him seven-fold. And the LORD set a mark upon Cain, lest any finding him should kill him.

16. ¶ And Cain went out from the presence of the LORD, and dwelt in the land of Nod, on the east of Eden.

401. The reason why God had respect unto Abel and his offering, was not that one offering was intrinsically better than the other; but because it was prompted by different motives, or was accompanied by a better disposition and character. This is plain from what follows:— "If thou doest well, shalt thou not be accepted?" The employment of both was equally honorable, and equally according to divine appointment. Man was to have dominion over the beasts, and he was to cultivate the earth. Abel did the first, and Cain the last. The fruits of the field, therefore, and the firstlings of the flock, were alike worthy of the divine approval. Both are made offerings under the law of Moses.

402. The right of primogeniture is recognized in this passage. Cain, as first born, was permitted to exercise authority over his brother. This afterwards became an established usage.

403. "And Cain talked with Abel his brother"—or "Cain *said* to Abel his brother"—But what did he say? There is evidently an omission in the Hebrew; but the Greek version supplies it thus:—And Cain said unto Abel his brother, *Let us go into the field*. The passage then proceeds as in our version.

404. The voice of thy brother's blood crieth unto me *from the ground*. Had not Cain sought to conceal his murderous act by burying his victim in the ground? and was not the language of God accommodated to this circumstance?

405. The punishment of Cain was, that he should be a fugitive and a vagabond in the earth. These two words, fugitive and vagabond, have nearly, if not exactly, the same meaning, and are here combined, according to a Hebrew idiom, for the sake of emphasis. The intention is to show how great a vagabond he would be; in other words, how forlorn and wretched would be his condition. He would be cursed from the earth, or by the earth —the earth would curse him — it would not yield unto him its strength; not that it would not bring forth its productions because he cultivated it; but because his vagabond and wandering life would not permit him to be sufficiently permanent to cultivate it and reap its fruits.

406. The mark placed upon Cain has puzzled interpreters. Some have thought he became black, and was the progenitor of the African race. This theory does not meet the case, unless we suppose that some of his descendants escaped the flood. A mark of guilt and condemnation that would make him an object of compassion, and thus prevent his being slain, is perhaps all that need be understood; and we need not suppose a deviation from the ordinary laws of the human mind, to account for all that is here said.

407. Cain dwelt in the land of Nod. The word Nod means a vagabond; and the passage may be rendered, either as it now is, in which case we may suppose the place to have been named from him, as being a vagabond; or it may be rendered that he "dwelt in the land, a vagabond," without designating where that land was, except that it was east of Eden.

Another of Adam's sons was Seth, who was in the likeness of Adam; but the particulars of his life are not given.

Besides these sons, Adam is said to have had sons and daughters; and tradition makes the number of them to be very great, but this is only conjecture.

SECTION V. — DEATH OF ADAM AND EVE.

408. Adam died at the age of 930 years; but the age of Eve is not given. v. 5.

We might speculate upon many things connected with the life and experience of the first human pair; and our speculations might not be far-fetched or unreasonable; but our business is with the simple record, and not with speculations and conjectures, however just and plausible they may be.

SECTION VI. — GENEALOGY OF CAIN.
CHAP. IV.

17. And Cain knew his wife: and she conceived, and bare Enoch: and he builded a city, and called the name of the city, after the name of his son, Enoch.

18. And unto Enoch was born Irad; and Irad begat Mehujael: and Mehujael begat Methusael: and Methusael begat Lamech.

19 ¶ And Lamech took unto him two wives: the name of the one *was* Adah, and the name of the other Zillah.

20. And Adah bare Jabal: he was the father of such as dwell in tents, and *of such as have* cattle.

21. And his brother's name *was* Jubal: he was the father of all such as handle the harp and organ.

22. And Zillah, she also bare Tubal-cain, an instructer of every artificer in brass and iron: and the sister of Tubal-cain *was* Naamah.

23. ¶ And Lamech said unto his wives, Adah and Zillah, Hear my voice, ye wives of Lamech, hearken unto my speech: for I have slain a man to my wounding, and a young man to my hurt.

24. If Cain shall be avenged sevenfold, truly Lamech seventy and sevenfold.

409. Of these persons but little is recorded. The name of the first son of Cain was given to the first city we read of in the Bible.

410. Lamech had two wives: and the mention of this circumstance leads us to infer that such a thing was not common, even with that branch of the family of Adam, which may, and may not, have been more corrupt than the other.

411. Each of the sons of Lamech is distinguished by a particular profession: in other words, he stood at the head of a clan: distinguished by the business here described. It is not improbable that Lamech had other sons, but not being thus distinguished, they are passed over in silence. Doubtless other persons on this list had sons; but, for the same reason, they are not mentioned.

412. The language of Lamech to his wives is somewhat ambiguous, and may require a word of explanation. It seems to have something of the form and spirit of poetry, and may be arranged thus: — And Lamech said unto his wives, Adah and Zillah —

> Hear my voice, ye wives of Lamech;
> Hearken unto my speech;
> For I have slain a man to my wounding,
> And a young man to my hurt.
> If Cain shall be avenged seven-fold,
> Surely Lamech, seventy and seven-fold.

Is not the meaning this : — I have slain a man for wounding me, and a young man for hurting me ; that is, I have killed a man in my own defence. If, therefore, he who should kill Cain, for having slain his brother without provocation, should be punished sevenfold ; surely, he that shall be avenged upon Lamech, who only killed a man in his own defence, ought to be punished seventy and seven-fold. This construction of the passage makes it convey a consistent sentiment; and the original is equally well rendered.

413. It may be added, as worthy of notice, that Lamech, though living several generations after Cain, was aware of the guilt of his ancestor, and of the language of God to him in view of his guilt. And though the language here quoted by Lamech had been transmitted only by tradition, it seems to be accurately represented.

SECTION VII. — GENEALOGY OF SETH.

CHAP. V.

1. This *is* the book of the generations of Adam. In the day that God created man, in the likeness of God made he him;

2. Male and female created he them; and he blessed them, and he called their name Adam, in the day when they were created.

3. ¶ And Adam lived an hundred and thirty years, and begat *a* son in his own likeness, after his image; and called his name Seth:

4. And the days of Adam after he had begotten Seth, were eight hundred years: and he begat sons and daughters:

5. And all the days that Adam lived were nine hundred and thirty years: and he died.

6. ¶ And Seth lived an hundred and five years, and begat Enos,

7. And Seth lived after he begat

Enos eight hundred and seven years, and begat sons and daughters:

8. And all the days of Seth were nine hundred and twelve years: and he died.

9. ¶ And Enos lived ninety years, and begat Cainan:

10. And Enos lived after he begat Cainan eight hundred and fifteen years, and begat sons and daughters:

11. And all the days of Enos were nine hundred and five years: and he died.

12. ¶ And Cainan lived seventy years, and begat Mahalaleel:

13. And Cainan lived after he begat Mahalaleel eight hundred and forty years, and begat sons and daughters:

14. And all the days of Cainan were nine hundred and ten years: and he died.

15. And Mahalaleel lived sixty and five years, and begat Jared:

16. And Mahalaleel lived after he begat Jared eight hundred and thirty years, and begat sons and daughters.

17. And all the days of Mahalaleel were eight hundred ninety and five years: and he died.

18. ¶ And Jared lived a hundred sixty and two years, and he begat Enoch:

19. And Jared lived after he begat Enoch eight hundred years, and begat sons and daughters:

20. And all the days of Jared were nine hundred sixty and two years: and he died.

21. ¶ And Enoch lived sixty and five years, and begat Methuselah:

22. And Enoch walked with God after he begat Methuselah three hundred years, and begat sons and daughters:

23. And all the days of Enoch were three hundred sixty and five years:

24. And Enoch walked with God: and he *was* not; for God took him.

25. ¶ And Methuselah lived an hundred eighty and seven years, and begat Lamech:

26. And Methuselah lived after he begat Lamech seven hundred eighty and two years, and begat sons and daughters:

27. And all the days of Methuselah were nine hundred sixty and nine years: and he died.

28. ¶ And Lamech lived an hundred eighty and two years, and begat a son:

29. And he called his name Noah, saying, This *same* shall comfort us concerning our work and toil of our hands, because of the ground which the LORD hath cursed.

30. And Lamech lived after he begat Noah five hundred ninety and five years, and begat sons and daughters:

31. And all the days of Lamech were seven hundred seventy and seven years: and he died.

32. ¶ And Noah was five hundred years old: and Noah begat Shem, Ham, and Japheth.

414. Seth is spoken of as being born in the image and likeness of Adam, which can have but one of two meanings. One is, that Seth had the same physical form as Adam; but a thing so obvious would not have been mentioned. It is much more reasonable to conclude, that there is a reference to his temper and disposition.

415. Seth is spoken of in another place thus : —

CHAP. IV.

25. ¶ And Adam knew his wife again; and she bare a son, and called his name Seth: for God, *said she,* hath appointed me another seed instead of Abel, whom Cain slew.

26. And to Seth, to him also there was born a son; and he called his name Enos; then began men to call upon the name of the LORD.

He was regarded, as appears from this passage, as intended to fill the place of Abel, whom Cain slew. The position of first born was assigned him, as Cain had justly forfeited that right; and there was no other on whom it could be conferred. Hence he is placed at the head of the permanent genealogical record. Enos, son of Seth, is spoken of in the same passage, and it is said that in his day men began to call on the name of the Lord, which may be understood as complimentary to that personage.

416. Enoch walked with God; and he was not, for God took him. This language obviously teaches that Enoch was a good man, but that he did not die a natural death, we do not consider quite so plain, though this has been the almost universal interpretation. He did not live to the usual age of the ancient patriarchs; and therefore it is said that God took him, or took him away, that is, by an early death. The importance attached to this one instance of piety and goodness, would lead us to infer that the other names on the list, were not worthy of any such commendation. Some of them, it is reasonable to presume were corrupt, as well as the rest of the world, and perhaps to the same extent. It is certain that Methuselah, the son of Enoch, died in the year of the deluge; but whether he was swept away by the deluge, does not appear.

417. That Lamech, the father of Noah, was impressed with the consciousness that his son was to fill an important place among the men of that degenerate age, is certain, from the language he uses concerning him : but whether he is to be understood literally or figuratively, does not certainly appear. We suppose the last, since the cursing of the earth in the time of Adam, to which reference is here made, is unquestionably to be so understood, as we have shown in another place.

418. The remark made respecting each person on this genealogical list, that "he had sons and daughters," besides the particular son named in the list, need not always be understood as referring to sons and daughters born *after* the one named; for we know that the first born was sometimes displaced, and a later son assigned his position. This was so with Cain, first son of Adam; and it is not an unreasonable conclusion that the same thing may have occurred with others.

419. Some interpreters have thought that men did not live to so great an age, as they are here represented; and they have conjectured that some different mode of reckoning time from ours, must have been employed; but we know of nothing to sustain the theory. It is quite certain that the writer had no mode of reckoning essentially different from ours. This is obvious from what he tells us of the commencement, duration and termination of the deluge. His months were thirty days, and his years twelve months: and though the weeks are not so distinctly marked, the mention of seven days, several times, renders it probable that they reckoned weeks also as we reckon them. Besides, if we suppose that a year was only a month, or some other short period, and thus avoid what we conceive to be a difficulty, shall we not, by this new mode of reckoning, involve ourselves in other difficulties no less formidable? It is obvious that while we reduce the age of the oldest of the patriarchs to such limits as may suit us, we must reduce the age of the younger ones in the same proportion. How will this plan succeed? Supposing a month to be regarded as a year, we make the age of Methuselah to be a trifle over eighty years. So far the plan works well, for we can easily believe men to have lived before the flood to that age, as we have known them to live so long in our day. But applying the rule to the father of Methuselah: it does not work so well: for Enoch begat Methuselah at the age of sixty five, which reduced in the same ratio, would make him a little over *five years* when his son was born!

420. The truth is, that the present duration of life, is to us more credible, simply because it is one to which we are accustomed, and not because there is any natural reason why it should be so. If the time ever comes, as possibly it may, when men are old at thirty, and seldom live beyond that age, there will not be wanting those who will endeavor to show that, never in the history of the world, have men lived to the incredible age of one hundred years, though, by a peculiar use of words, or mode of reckoning, historians may seem to so represent them. One impression that seems to prevail, relating to this subject, should be corrected in this place. The change from the great age of the first inhabitants of the world, to the present standard, was not sudden, as seems to be commonly thought, but was gradual, extending over a long period. The different ages from Adam to Joseph stand thus: — 930, 912, 905, 910, 895, 962, 365, 969, 777, 950, 600, 438, 433, 464, 239, 230, 148, 205, 175, 180, 147, 110.

421. Again; the understanding we have of vi. 1–4, helps to confirm the idea of the great longevity of those ancient times. The passage is as follows: —

CHAP VI.

1. And it came to pass, when men began to multiply on the face of the earth, and daughters were born unto them,
2. That the sons of God saw the daughters of men that they *were* fair; and they took them wives of all which they chose.
3. And the LORD said, My Spirit shall not always strive with man, for that he also *is* flesh: yet his days shall be an hundred and twenty years.
4. There were giants in the earth in those days; and also after that, when the sons of God came in unto the daughters of men, and they bare *children* to them, the same *became* mighty men, which *were* of old, men of renown.

The "sons of God" were simply men, and the "daughters of men," were simply women; and the giants of those days, we take to be men of great stature, as well as prolonged age. The meaning is, that the men of those days, as well as their immediate descendants, were of gigantic stature, in comparison with those who lived at a later day when the account was written. The phrase "of old" shows that the writer is speaking of times that were ancient to himself, and of course that he regards them in the way of contrast with those of his own times. With this view, which is an exceedingly natural one, we remove at once the vain and absurd speculations of men concerning this passage; and the whole subject becomes more consistent, as there seems great propriety in supposing that the stature and age of men should correspond. We may add one or two circumstances by way of confirmation. We know that animals and vegetables, during the fossil epochs, were much larger than any that are now found in the same regions of country where these existed. May we not then infer that when man was made, and for ages afterwards, they were of larger stature than they were at a later day — this being true of man as of other animals — the same principle prevailing that had prevailed before, requiring a gradual decrease in size to correspond with the decrease of temperature. Notice again, that as we might expect, not only individuals but whole tribes, of more than common size, are alluded to at a later day; and again that human relics of great magnitude, have been found in all parts of the world.

CHAPTER XII.

NOAH AND HIS FAMILY.

CONTENTS. — Incidental notices of Noah; Noah Blessed; Covenant with Noah; Noah's Prediction; Death of Noah; Genealogy of Shem; Of Ham; Of Japheth.

SECTION I.— INCIDENTAL REFERENCES TO NOAH.

422. Noah was son of Lamech in the lineage of Adam through Seth, and was five hundred years old when his sons were born. He was regarded by his father as one that should fill an important place in that age. v. 28–32. Other notices of Noah will be found in the following passages where he is spoken of in connection with the flood.

CHAP. VI.

8. But Noah found grace in the eyes of the LORD.
9. ¶ These *are* the generations of Noah: Noah was a just man, *and* perfect in his generations, *and* Noah walked with God.
10. And Noah begat three sons, Shem, Ham, and Japheth.

This is a noble commendation, to which it is several times added that "Noah did according to all that God commanded him." vi. 22; vii. 5.

CHAP. VII.

6. And Noah *was* six hundred years old when the flood of waters was upon the earth.

And his sons were about one hundred years old at this time. Compare v. 32.

423. The transactions of Noah in the ark hardly need a word of explanation. They are such as would naturally suggest themselves under the circumstances. The raven went to and fro till the waters were dried up from off the earth. That the raven returned to Noah, is not asserted. It was not necessary to do so, to obtain food, as the dead carcasses that floated upon the water, would afford it nourishment fitted to its nature and wants. The dove returned to Noah, and at length brought to him an olive leaf, from which he knew that the waters were greatly diminished, and that the land would soon be dry. It has been argued that the ark could not have rested on Mount Ararat, as, nowhere in that vicinity, is the olive to be found; but it may be replied that we have no statement where the olive leaf was obtained; and we know the dove could have obtained it, at a great distance, and not be gone long from Noah.

CHAP. VIII.

20. And Noah builded an altar unto the LORD; and took of every clean beast, and of every clean fowl, and offered burnt offerings on the altar.
21. And the LORD smelled a sweet savor; and the LORD said in his heart, I will not again curse the ground any more for man's sake; for the imagination of man's heart *is* evil from his youth; neither will I again smite any more every thing living, as I have done.
22. While the earth remaineth, seed-time and harvest, and cold and heat, and summer and winter, and day and night shall not cease.

424. The offering of sacrifices is mentioned in connection with Cain and Abel; and now in conformity with ancient custom, and on an occasion when it would seem specially fit to do so, Noah selects a suitable number of clean animals and offers them as an offering to the Lord.

SECTION II. — NOAH BLESSED.

CHAP. IX.

1. And God blessed Noah and his sons, and said unto them, Be fruitful, and multiply, and replenish the earth.
2. And the fear of you and the dread of you shall be upon every beast of the earth, and upon every fowl of the air, upon all that moveth *upon* the earth, and upon all the fishes of the sea; into your hand are they delivered.
3. Every moving thing that liveth shall be meat for you; even as the green herb have I given you all things.
4. But flesh with the life thereof, *which is* the blood thereof, shall ye not eat.
5. And surely your blood of your lives will I require; at the hand of every beast will I require it, and at the hand of man; at the hand of every man's brother will I require the life of man.
6. Whoso sheddeth man's blood, by man shall his blood be shed: for in the image of God made he man.
7. And you, be ye fruitful, and multiply; bring forth abundantly in the earth, and multiply therein.

425. "Be fruitful and multiply and replenish the earth," is the same language as that addressed to Adam and Eve at first, except that the clause "subdue it" is omitted, which was not now as necessary as then. The parallel reaches farther. The "fear and dread" that were upon every beast of the field, &c., is substantially the same as the "dominion" over the beasts given to Adam. And when it is added, in the same connection, "Every moving thing that liveth shall be meat for you," we infer that the same thing was implied in the original grant, and that animal food, as well as vegetable, was intended for Adam as well as for Noah.

426. "The flesh, with the life thereof, which is the blood thereof, shall ye not eat." The life was first to be taken by the shedding of the blood; after which the flesh was to be eaten. "And surely your blood of your lives will I require." Viewing this with reference to what goes before, and placing the emphasis properly, and we shall have the true sense of this difficult passage. It was the same as to say: — The blood of animals, in other words, the life of animals, is given over to you. You may slay and eat as you have occasion; but *your* life or blood *I* require. That is to be held sacred. At the hand of every beast will I require it, and at the hand of man; at the hand of every man's brother will I require the life of man. I command every man to respect the life of his brother, and to protect and defend it. Let the reader bear in mind that these statements are made with reference to man's relation to the beasts, and to the exposure of human life thereby implied.

427. This will prepare us to understand that much controverted passage : — " Whoso sheddeth man's blood, by man shall his blood be shed." We do not doubt that "whoso," (which, in the original, may refer to animals as well as to men, depending on the connection and circumstances,) has reference here to animals; and the meaning is, that wild and dangerous animals are to be destroyed, though not intended for food. Whoso (the animal that) sheddeth man's blood, by man shall his blood be shed. The reason given for what is here stated, is exceedingly appropriate, with this construction, " In the image of God made he man." Man, by his nature, is placed above the beasts.

428. Several reasons favor this view of the passage. One is, that God would not be likely to require us to act upon a principle on which he did not himself act, in a similar case. Cain committed murder, and under very aggravated circumstances. God sat in judgment upon the crime, and pronounced sentence of condemnation upon the criminal. But the punishment was banishment, and not death. This is not all. Whoever should slay the offender, should himself be punished with a severer infliction. Is it reasonable to conclude that a principle here approved, should so soon be repudiated : and a principle here condemned, should so soon be enjoined as a rule of action ? But the reason assigned, that man is made in the image of God, is opposed to the common views. Is not the murderer made in the image of God, as well as his victim ? and if so, the same reason should prevail against killing him, that should have restrained him from killing his brother. It may be added that the

life of man is required at the hand of the beast, as well as at the hand of man; and hence any violation of the command on the part of the former, should be punished with death, as well as with the latter. And those who adopt the common construction, show great inconsistency, in allowing the beast to escape, while they inflict the penalty upon man. If one should be hung up by the neck for the offence, we see no reason why the other should not be.

SECTION III. — THE COVENANT WITH NOAH.

CHAP. IX.

8. ¶ And God spake unto Noah, and to his sons with him, saying,

9. And I, behold, I establish my covenant with you, and with your seed after you;

10. And with every living creature that is with you, of the fowl, of the cattle, and of every beast of the earth with you; from all that go out of the ark, to every beast of the earth.

11. And I will establish my covenant with you; neither shall all flesh be cut off any more by the waters of a flood; neither shall there any more be a flood to destroy the earth.

12. And God said, This is the token of the covenant which I make between me and you and every living creature that is with you, for perpetual generations:

13. I do set my bow in the cloud, and it shall be for a token of a covenant between me and the earth.

14. And it shall come to pass, when I bring a cloud over the earth, that the bow shall be seen in the cloud:

15. And I will remember my covenant, which is between me and you and every living creature of all flesh; and the waters shall no more become a flood to destroy all flesh.

16. And the bow shall be in the cloud; and I will look upon it, that I may remember the everlasting covenant between God and every living creature of all flesh that is upon the earth.

17. And God said unto Noah, This is the token of the covenant, which I have established between me and all flesh that is upon the earth.

429. It is not necessary to suppose that the bow was set in the clouds at the time this covenant with Noah was entered into.

I *have* set my bow in the clouds: and it shall be for a token, &c., would be a better rendering. The bow had always been in the clouds, when the position of the sun and of the clouds was such as to produce it. It was hereafter to be looked upon as a memento of the divine promise, that there should no more be a flood upon the earth. The reason of this arrangement is found in the association of ideas. As often as the beautiful bow was seen, it would remind the beholder of the gracious promise of which it was the token.

430. That God, as well as men, would look upon the bow and remember his covenant, is language that can be understood only as accommodated to common modes of speech among men. It cannot be literally true of the Divine Being, who needs no such expedients to remind him of his promises. Compare p. 41–43.

SECTION IV. — NOAH'S PREDICTION.

CHAP. IX.

18. ¶ And the sons of Noah, that went forth of the ark, were Shem, and Ham, and Japheth: and Ham is the father of Canaan.

19. These *are* the three sons of Noah: and of them was the whole earth overspread.

20. And Noah began *to be* a husbandman, and he planted a vineyard:

21. And he drank of the wine, and was drunken; and he was uncovered within his tent.

22. And Ham, the father of Canaan, saw the nakedness of his father, and told his two brethren without.

23. And Shem and Japheth took a garment, and laid *it* upon both their shoulders, and went backward, and covered the nakedness of their father; and their faces *were* backward, and they saw not their father's nakedness.

24. And Noah awoke from his wine, and knew what his younger son had done unto him.

25. And he said, Cursed *be* Canaan; a servant of servants shall he be unto his brethren.

26. And he said, Blessed *be* the LORD God of Shem; and Canaan shall be his servant.

27. God shall enlarge Japheth, and he shall dwell in the tents of Shem; and Canaan shall be his servant.

431. Noah planted a vineyard and drank of the wine. That the juice of the grape would become wine and produce inebriety, could have been learned at first only by sundry experiments, assisted by mere accident, perhaps, as is not unfrequently the case. It is not improbable that wine existed before the flood, as the writer here does not seem to speak of it as a new thing ; but of this we know nothing certainly. The idea is entertained by some that Noah was the first one that used it, and not being fully acquainted with its qualities and effects, he became unintentionally intoxicated. This may be the correct opinion and it may not, as there seems to be no way of deciding this question.

432. His exposure in his tent, and the conduct of his sons, are circumstances, not mentioned because of their importance in themselves, but as showing the occasion of the prediction that followed which was important. Nor need we suppose that the curse upon Canaan for the sins of his father, was uttered merely as pointing out the punishment of that sin. Canaan was the father of the Canaanites; and the prediction of Noah points to the subjugation of that people by the Israelites, as well as their subjugation generally to the different branches of Noah's family.

That Noah was divinely inspired when he uttered this prediction, will doubtless be regarded by many as unquestionable. This may be a correct idea; but it is not an unwarrantable supposition that, when it became known by Abraham and others of his family, that Canaan should become their inheritance, any remark of Noah, indicating the subjection of the Canaanites, would be so applied, though it might not originally have been uttered with any such intention.

433. Ham is called the younger son, Japheth the elder; but this fact seems to have had no influence on the order in which they are mentioned. ix. 24; x. 21. Shem, Ham, and Japheth is the order in which they are named in the record, and the order in which we habitually refer to them.

SECTION V. — Death of Noah.

CHAP. IX.

28. ¶ And Noah lived after the flood three hundred and fifty years.
29. And all the days of Noah were nine hundred and fifty years; and he died.

434. The history of Noah's sons is not given us, except that each of them is represented as having several sons found on their genealogical records, to which reference may be had. That they had daughters, too, is a reasonable inference, and of Shem is expressly stated; but their names are omitted. The age of neither son is given us, except that we infer from what is said of Shem, that he died at the age of six hundred years. xi. 10, 11.

SECTION VI. — GENEALOGY OF SHEM.

CHAP. X.

21. ¶ Unto Shem also, the father of all the children of Eber, the brother of Japheth the elder, even to him were *children* born.
22. The children of Shem; Elam, and Asshur, and Arphaxad, and Lud and Aram.
23. And the children of Aram; Uz, and Hul, and Gether, and Mash.
24. And Arphaxad begat Salah; and Salah begat Eber.
25. And unto Eber were born two sons: the name of one *was* Peleg; for in his days was the earth divided; and his brother's name *was* Joktan.
26. And Joktan begat Almodad, and Sheleph, and Hazarmaveth, and Jerah,
27. And Hadoram, and Uzal, and Diklah,
28. And Obal, and Abimael, and Sheba,
29. And Ophir, and Havilah, and Jobab: all these *were* the sons of Joktan
30. And their dwelling was from Mesha, as thou goest unto Sephar a mount of the east.
31. These *are* the sons of Shem, after their families, after their tongues, in their lands, after their nations.
32. These *are* the families of the sons of Noah, after their generations, in their nations: and by these were the nations divided in the earth after the flood.

CHAP. XI.

10. ¶ These *are* the generations of Shem: Shem *was* an hundred years old, and begat Arphaxad two years after the flood:
11. And Shem lived after he begat Arphaxad five hundred years, and begat sons and daughters.
12. And Arphaxad lived five and thirty years, and begat Salah:
13. And Arphaxad lived after he begat Salah four hundred and three years, and begat sons and daughters.
14. And Salah lived thirty years, and begat Eber:
15. And Salah lived after he begat Eber four hundred and three years, and begat sons and daughters.
16. And Eber lived four and thirty years, and begat Peleg:
17. And Eber lived after he begat Peleg four hundred and thirty years, and begat sons and daughters.
18. And Peleg lived thirty years, and begat Reu:
19. And Peleg lived after he begat Reu two hundred and nine years, and begat sons and daughters.
20. And Reu lived two hundred and thirty years, and begat Serug:
21. And Reu lived after he begat Serug two hundred and seven years, and begat sons and daughters.
22. And Serug lived thirty years, and begat Nahor:
23. And Serug lived after he begat Nahor two hundred years, and begat sons and daughters.
24. And Nahor lived nine and twenty years, and begat Terah:
25 And Nahor lived after he begat Terah an hundred and nineteen years, and begat sons and daughters.
26. And Terah lived seventy years, and begat Abram, Nahor, and Haran.

435. That Shem was the father of all the children of Heber, is a remark that seems intended for a particular purpose; and by supposing that the Israelites, who belong to this lineage, took the name of Hebrews from Heber, here mentioned, that special reference to this individual, will be accounted for; nor is there any other so good reason for the reference, nor any other so good a way to account for the name Hebrews, being applied to that people.

436. Asshur, mentioned on this list, as one of the sons of Shem, we are told in x. 11, went out from the land of Shinar and builded Nineveh and the city Rehoboth and Calah and Resen, between Nineveh and Calah; and the first of these we know became a city of great magnificence. It is generally understood, too, that Assyria, the country where these cities were located, took its name from Asshur.

437. In the days of Peleg the earth was divided. The name *Peleg* (signifying division) was given him in view of this circumstance. But what division of the earth was here intended, cannot be determined with accuracy. The reference may be to some natural convulsion which the earth underwent in that country; and we know that such things were common in that early age. It is more probable, however, that there is an allusion to some civil division of the country, whereby each family or tribe had a definite portion assigned them. This is confirmed by some subsequent references. The sons of Joktan " had their dwelling from Mesha as thou goest unto Sephar, a mountain of the east." The meaning is, that this tract of country was assigned to these families in the division referred to. It is added again, with a more general reference : — " These are the sons of Shem, after their families, after their tongues, *in their lands*, after their nations." And again: " These are the families of the sons of Noah, after their generations, in their nations ; and by these were the nations *divided in the earth*, after the flood."

438. In this genealogy it is said that Arphaxad begat Salah; but the Septuagint or Greek version, says, that Arphaxad begat Cainan, and Cainan begat Salah. The

New Testament follows the Greek version. See Luke, iii. 35, 36.

SECTION VII. — GENEALOGY OF HAM.

CHAP. X.

6. ¶ And the sons of Ham; Cush, and Mizraim, and Phut, and Canaan.
7. And the sons of Cush; Seba, and Havilah, and Sabtah, and Raamah, and Sabtecha: and the sons of Raamah; Sheba, and Dedan.
8. And Cush begat Nimrod: he began to be a mighty one in the earth.
9. He was a mighty hunter before the LORD: wherefore it is said, Even as Nimrod the mighty hunter before the LORD.
10. And the beginning of his kingdom was Babel, and Erech, and Accad, and Calneh, in the land of Shinar.
11. Out of that land went forth Asshur, and builded Nineveh, and the city of Rehoboth, and Calah,
12. And Resen between Nineveh and Calah; the same is a great city.
13. And Mizraim begat Ludim, and Anamim, and Lehabim, and Naphtuhim,
14. And Pathrusim, and Casluhim, (out of whom came Philistim,) and Caphtorim.
15. ¶ And Canaan begat Sidon his first-born, and Heth.
16. And the Jebusite, and the Amorite, and the Girgasite,
17. And the Hivite, and the Arkite, and the Sinite,
18. And the Arvadite, and the Zemarite, and the Hamathite: and afterward were the families of the Canaanites spread abroad.
19. And the border of the Canaanites was from Sidon, as thou comest to Gerar, unto Gaza; as thou goest unto Sodom, and Gomorrah, and Admah, and Zeboim, even unto Lasha.
20. These *are* the sons of Ham, after their families, after their tongues, in their countries, *and* in their nations.

439. The most important personage on this list, is Nimrod, the mighty hunter. He was so distinguished in his profession as to be the occasion of a proverb : — " Even as Nimrod the mighty hunter before the Lord." The beginning of his kingdom, that is, its chief city, was Babel, afterwards called Babylon, to which the writer adds others of less importance, Erech and Accad and Calneh. They were all in the land of Shinar. It is probable that the confusion of tongues, is to be placed in the time of Nimrod, if not still earlier.

440. Canaan was the father of the Canaanites, as is evident from the names given to the tribes, mentioned in other places, as belonging to that country, and corresponding with those here designated. The names Jebusite, Amorite, Girgasite, &c., are not, as we might infer, the names of individual sons of Canaan, as were Sidon and Heth; but they are national designations. The meaning is, that these *tribes* came from Canaan, whatever may have been the name (which the writer might not have known) of the sons through whom they came. The same remark will apply to Mizraim, Ludim, Anamim, &c.; for these endings (*ite* and *im*) are the usual terminations when tribes and nations are designated. Mizraim is another name for Egyptians; and it is believed that these people are here intended. Philistim from Casluhim, is another name for Philistines, who are many times referred to in the subsequent history.

441. CONFUSION OF TONGUES. — It seems very proper to speak of the confusion of tongues in connection with the race of Ham, as Nimrod, one of this race, had Babel for the capital of his kingdom; and it is not certain but all that is said of that event has reference to this branch of the family of Noah. The confusion of tongues is described thus: —

CHAP. XI.

1. And the whole earth was of one language, and of one speech.
2. And it came to pass, as they journeyed from the east, that they found a plain in the land of Shinar; and they dwelt there.
3. And they said one to another, Go to, let us make brick, and burn them thoroughly. And they had brick for stone, and slime had they for mortar.
4. And they said, Go to, let us build us a city and a tower, whose top *may reach* unto heaven; and let us make us a name, lest we be scattered abroad upon the face of the whole earth.
5. And the LORD came down to see the city and the tower, which the children of men builded.
6. And the LORD said, Behold, the people *is* one, and they have all one language; and this they begin to do: and now nothing will be restrained from them, which they have imagined to do.
7. Go to, let us go down, and there confound their language, that they may not understand one another's speech.
8. So the LORD scattered them abroad from thence upon the face of all the earth: and they left off to build the city.
9. Therefore is the name of it called Babel; because the LORD did there confound the language of all the earth: and from thence did the LORD scatter them abroad upon the face of all the earth.

Josephus supposes that the purpose had in view, in building the tower of Babel, was to provide a place of refuge in case of another deluge; but why they should have built this tower upon a plain, rather than upon a mountain, and by that means, made themselves so much more labor, this author does not explain: and probably did not see the difficulty. Besides; this view seems hardly compatible with what is said in the passage itself. It was not to provide themselves a place of refuge, but to make themselves a name, that they undertook this work. It was also to keep themselves from being scattered abroad upon the earth. No evil intention is ascribed to the projectors of this scheme. Still, being adverse to the design of the Creator, which was that man *should* be scattered abroad upon the earth, the project was not allowed to succeed.

442. From the remark with which this account begins, that the whole earth was of one language and one speech, the inference has been drawn that the confounding of language here alluded to, consisted in breaking up the old forms of speech and introducing a great number and variety of tongues in the place of the one that had before prevailed. This is not a necessary conclusion. All being of one language, may be mentioned as the ground on which they *expected* to succeed; but the confusion introduced into that language, shows that their expectations were not well grounded. The ground of their confident expectation failed them by a divine providence. To confound their language, so that they may not understand one another's speech, does not necessarily, nor naturally imply the destruction of the old language and the introduction of new ones. Their language was confounded, not destroyed. They did not understand one another's speech; not because they spake different languages, but because of some difficulty in speaking their own, or in understanding it; (or *hearing* it, as the word may mean;) the cause of this difficulty not being stated. Sudden convulsions of the earth, induced by natural causes, but ascribed by the ancients to the immediate agency of God, inducing fear and agitation in the multitude of laborers, or the leaders in the work, and various and conflicting opinions in their counsels, would be all that would be necessary to bring about the result here announced. We do not deny that there was a miraculous interposition; but we deny the necessity of any unnatural cause to bring about an equally unnatural result. The miracle, if there were such, consisted in the occurrence of natural events, at a particular time, and to accomplish a specific purpose — a purpose that resulted very naturally from the cause that produced it.

The style of the language here employed has been discussed elsewhere to which the reader is referred, § 72-78.

SECTION VIII.—Genealogy of Japheth.

CHAP. X.

1. Now these *are* the generations of the sons of Noah; Shem, Ham, and Japheth: and unto them were sons born after the flood.
2. The sons of Japheth; Gomer, and Magog, and Madai, and Javan, and Tubal, and Meshech, and Tiras.
3. And the sons of Gomer; Ashkenaz, and Riphath, and Togarmah.
4. And the sons of Javan; Elishah, and Tarshish, Kittim, and Dodanim.
5. By these were the isles of the Gentiles divided in their lands; every one after his tongue, after their families, in their nations.

443. " By these were the isles of the Gentiles divided, in their lands, every one after his tongue, after their families, in their nations." The division here referred to, is probably the same as that before noticed, as taking place in the days of Peleg.

444. Josephus gives us the different nations that originated from the sons of Noah as follows ;—" Japheth, the son of Noah, had seven sons. They inhabited, so that, beginning at the mountains of Taurus and Amanus, they proceeded along Asia as far as the river Tanais, and along Europe to Cadiz ; and settling themselves on the lands they lighted upon, they called the nations by their own names. For Gomer founded those which the Greeks now call Gallatians, (Galls,) but were themselves called Gomerites. Magog founded those that from him were named Magogites, but who are by the Greeks called Scythians.

Josephus goes on to say that Madai was the founder of the Medeans or Medes ; Javan settled Ionia, and all the Grecians originated from him. The Iberes sprung from Tubal, and the Capadocians from Meshech. A city among them called Mazaca he thinks took its name from Meshech. Tiras originated the Thracians. He traces the Rheginians to Ashkenaz, son of Gomer, and the Paphligonians to Riphath, and the Phrigians to Togarmah.

445. The children of Ham, he says, possessed the land of Syria and Amanus and the mountains of Libanus. Cush ruled over the Ethiopians, sometimes called Cushites, Mizraim is another name for the Egyptians. Phut founded Lybia; Canaan gave name to Judea, once called Canaan. Saba founded the Sabeans, Havilah the Getulians, Sabta the Astaborians, Sabtekah settled Sabacteus, Raamah originated the Ragmans, &c. All the children of Mizraim, being eight in number, possessed the country from Gaza to Egypt: though it retained the name of one only, the Philistim; for the Greeks called part of the country Palestine. As for the rest, Ludim, Anamim, &c., we know nothing except their names.

446. The sons of Canaan, Josephus disposes of thus; — Sidon built Sidon; Hamathite settled Epiphania. Hivite possessed Acre. But for the seven others, Heth, Jebusite, Amorite, Girgasite, Sinite, Arvadite, and Zemarite, we have nothing in the sacred books; for the Hebrews overthrew their cities. That is, as we understand Josephus, there is nothing in the sacred books concerning them, after the Hebrews overthrew their cities; for, till that time, several of these tribes are often mentioned in the Jewish writings.

447. Shem had five sons who inhabited from the Euphrates to the Indian Ocean. Elam gave name to the Elamites or Persians; Asshur to the Assyrians; Arphaxad to the Chaldeans; Aram to the Syrians; Lud to the Lydians: Uz son of Aram, settled Trachonitis and Damascus; Hul founded Armenia; Gether originated the Bactreans; Mash the Messaneans. Heber gave name to the Hebrews. The sons of Joktan dwelt from Sepher an Indian river and that part of Asia adjoining it.

In most respects this account of Josephus may be relied upon as accurate. At least it no doubt agreed with the authorities and traditions then in existence and deemed reliable.

CHAPTER XIII.

ABRAHAM AND HIS FAMILY.

CONTENTS; — Parentage and Relations; Removes to Haran; Goes to Canaan; Goes down to Egypt and returns; Abram and Lot separate; Receives a Divine Communication; Battle of the Kings; Another Vision; Hagar given to Abram; Another Vision; Another; Sodom Destroyed; Lot and his Daughters; Sojourn in Gerar; Birth of Isaac; Hagar and her Son Rejected; Covenant with Abimelech; The Offering of Isaac; Nahor; Death of Sarah; A Wife procured for Isaac; Death of Abraham; Ishmael and his Family.

SECTION I. — PARENTAGE AND RELATIONS.

CHAP. XI.

27. ¶ Now these *are* the generations of Terah: Terah begat Abram, Nahor, and Haran; and Haran begat Lot.

28. And Haran died before his father Terah in the land of his nativity, in Ur of the Chaldees.

29. And Abram and Nahor took them wives: the name of Abram's wife was Sarai; and the name of Nahor's wife Milcah, the daughter of Haran, the father of Milcah, and the father of Iscah.

30. But Sarai was barren; she *had* no child.

448. It would seem from several circumstances, here named, that Ur of the Chaldees, was the residence of Terah and his family, for a long period. His three sons were born there, and were there married. This is implied in the case of Haran; and is expressed with reference to the others. The wife of Nahor was daughter of his brother Haran. The same Haran was father of Iscah. The opinion is not without foundation that this Iscah and Sarah are the same. If this supposition is not true, then we have the allusion to Iscah without any necessity; and who Sarah was, of which we should expect to be informed, we are not told. Besides, if Sarah and Iscah *are* the same, then Sarah and Milcah were sisters: and both were sisters of Lot; and this will give us a reason that might not otherwise be so manifest, why Abram should have taken Lot with him, and regarded him with so much interest; for in this case, Lot was not only a nephew of the patri-

arch, but a brother of Sarah; and his father, being dead, he united his interests with those of his sister and uncle. With this view the language of Abram concerning his wife : — " She is the daughter of my father, but not the daughter of my mother," xx. 12, may be explained by supposing that grand-daughter (as the word daughter often means) was had in view, and by the additional supposition that Terah had two wives, one of whom was the mother of Abram, and the other of Haran.

SECTION II. — REMOVAL TO HARAN.

CHAP. XI.

31. And Terah took Abram his son, and Lot the son of Haran his son's son, and Sarai his daughter-in-law, his son Abram's wife ; and they went forth with them from Ur of the Chaldees, to go into the land of Canaan; and they came into Haran and dwelt there.
32. And the days of Terah were two hundred and five years: and Terah died in Haran.

449. Terah being the head of the family, is said to have taken Abram and others, and gone to Haran, though it appears from another passage, that Abram had instigated this movement, being instructed so to do by a divine vision. xii. 1.

Haran was evidently named after Haran, the brother of Abram, who had died in Chaldee. It was not, therefore, so called, when Terah and his family went there, but received its name from them, in honor of their deceased friend. Nothing can be more natural than this circumstance ; and there is a multitude of such and similar ones, that tend strongly to confirm the truth of the narrative.

The death of Terah is mentioned here, though Abram's removal to Canaan, and many other events afterwards recorded, must have taken place before his decease.

SECTION III. — ABRAM GOES TO CANAAN.
CHAP. XII.

1. Now the LORD had said unto Abram, Get thee out of thy country, and from thy kindred, and from thy father's house, unto a land that I will shew thee:
2. And I will make of thee a great nation, and I will bless thee, and make thy name great; and thou shalt be a blessing:
3. And I will bless them that bless thee, and curse him that curseth thee: and in thee shall all families of the earth be blessed.
4. So Abram departed, as the LORD had spoken unto him; and Lot went with him: and Abram was seventy and five years old when he departed out of Haran.
5. And Abram took Sarai his wife, and Lot his brother's son, and all their substance that they had gathered, and the souls that they had gotten in Haran; and they went forth to go into the land of Canaan; and into the land of Canaan they came.
6. ¶ And Abram passed through the land unto the place of Sichem, unto the plain of Moreh. And the Canaanite was then in the land.
7. And the LORD appeared unto Abram, and said, Unto thy seed will I give this land: and there builded he an altar unto the LORD, who appeared unto him.
8. And he removed from thence unto a mountain on the east of Bethel, and pitched his tent, having Bethel on the west, and Hai on the east: and there he builded an altar unto the LORD, and called upon the name of the LORD.
9. And Abram journeyed, going on still toward the south.

450. The message from God to Abram, here referred to, was given to him while he was in Ur of the Chaldees. It does not appear that Abram knew what land was intended for him, till he came into the land of Canaan, and received another and more definite statement. That he should be greatly blessed, and that all men would be blessed through him, are the two items in this announcement.

451. How long Abram and Lot resided in Haran, is not stated. "The substance they had gathered, and the souls they had gotten in Haran," may be understood as implying a considerable period.

452. The Canaanite was then in the land. Abram, therefore, could not claim the country by right of discovery, nor as being the first settler. He could only claim it as a divine bestowment ; and on this ground it was claimed, and taken possession of, at a later day.

453. That Abram journeyed still toward the south, shows that he had come from the north, or more properly, from the north-east. Hence we must place Haran and Ur in that direction.

SECTION IV.—ABRAM GOES DOWN TO EGYPT.

CHAP. XII.

10. ¶ And there was a famine in the land: and Abram went down into Egypt to sojourn there; for the famine was grievous in the land.
11. And it came to pass, when he was come near to enter into Egypt, that he said unto Sarai his wife, Behold now, I know that thou *art* a fair woman to look upon:
12. Therefore it shall come to pass, when the Egyptians shall see thee, that they shall say, This *is* his wife; and they will kill me, but they will save thee alive.
13. Say, I pray thee, thou *art* my sister; that it may be well with me for thy sake: and my soul shall live because of thee.
14 ¶ And it came to pass, that when Abram was come into Egypt, the Egyptians beheld the woman that she *was* very fair.
15. The princes also of Pharaoh saw her, and commended her before Pharaoh; and the woman was taken into Pharaoh's house.
16. And he entreated Abram well for her sake: and he had sheep, and oxen, and he-asses, and men-servants, and maid-servants, and she-asses, and camels.
17. And the LORD plagued Pharaoh and his house with great plagues, because of Sarai, Abram's wife.
18 And Pharaoh called Abram, and said, What *is* this *that* thou hast done unto me? why didst thou not tell me that she *was* thy wife?
19. Why saidst thou, She *is* my sister? so I might have taken her to me to wife: now, therefore, behold thy wife, take *her*, and go thy way.
20. And Pharaoh commanded *his* men concerning him: and they sent him away, and his wife, and all that he had.

CHAP. XIII.

1. And Abram went up out of Egypt, he, and his wife, and all that he had, and Lot with him, into the south.
2. And Abram *was* very rich in cattle, in silver, and in gold.
3. And he went on his journeys from the south, even to Bethel, unto the place where his tent had been at the beginning, between Bethel and Hai;
4. Unto the place of the altar, which he had made there at the first: and there Abram called on the name of the LORD.

454. That there was a famine in Canaan, and not in Egypt, is easily accounted for: the one was watered by the clouds that descended upon the land, and it would suffer immediately if they were withheld: the other was watered by the overflowing of the Nile, and was not affected by slight changes, such as would affect other countries. The Nile did not often withhold its supplies, but when it did, the effect was long continued. Hence the seven years of plenty, followed by seven of famine, was perfectly in accordance with natural circumstances.

Going *down* to Egypt is a reference, slight in itself, but well fitted to strengthen our confidence in the narrative, by its agreement with facts. Egypt was lower than Canaan; and therefore, those who went there from the latter place, went *down*; and on their return they went *up* out of Egypt.

455. The deception instigated by Abram is recorded as a historical fact, though it does not reflect well upon the character of the patriarch; and it shows a lack of information concerning the place he was to visit. True, it was not a sin of the first magnitude, nor was it prompted by unworthy motives; but a sin it was, and no less a sin in the patriarch than it would have been in any other man under the same circumstances, though some biblical expounders have conceived the necessity of exonerating him from all blame, which they would not feel at liberty to do, in ordinary cases. One thing we ought not to forget, that, if our sense of right and obligation is greater than that of the patriarchs, it is mainly because we have privileges which they had not. And indeed, were we to find them as conscientious, as are well instructed Christians of the present day, one of two conclusions would follow that few of us would be willing to accept, either that the record we have of those early times is false, or that revealed religion has been of no use to the world.

456. The "plagues" that came upon Pharaoh in consequence of Abram's wife, are not described, and may have been only such "troubles," as would naturally arise from the circumstances, though not the less brought upon him by the Lord, on that account. Abram and Lot went up from Egypt "into the south," that is, into the south part of Canaan; though, in going thither, they went north or north-east.

SECTION V. — Abram and Lot Separate.

CHAP. XIII.

5. ¶ And Lot also, which went with Abram, had flocks, and herds, and tents.
6. And the land was not able to bear them, that they might dwell together: for their substance was great, so that they could not dwell together.
7. And there was a strife between the herdmen of Abram's cattle and the herdmen of Lot's cattle: and the Canaanite and the Perizzite dwelled then in the land.
8 And Abram said unto Lot, Let there be no strife, I pray thee, between me and thee, and between my herdmen and thy herdmen; for we be brethren.
9. *Is* not the whole land before thee? separate thyself, I pray thee, from me; if *thou wilt take* the left hand, then I will go to the right;
or if *thou depart* to the right hand, then I will go to the left.
10. And Lot lifted up his eyes, and beheld all the plain of Jordan, that it *was* well watered every where, before the LORD destroyed Sodom and Gomorrah, *even* as the garden of the LORD, like the land of Egypt, as thou comest unto Zoar.
11. Then Lot chose him all the plain of Jordan; and Lot journeyed east; and they separated themselves the one from the other.
12. Abram dwelt in the land of Canaan, and Lot dwelt in the cities of the plain, and pitched *his* tent toward Sodom.
13. But the men of Sodom *were* wicked and sinners before the LORD exceedingly.

457. This passage sets forth the character of Abram to great advantage. His friendly disposition and his generous treatment of Lot, are worthy of all commendation. The occupation of the patriarchs required an extensive territory, especially as the wealth of Abram and Lot, consisting mostly of flocks and herds, had become very great at the time here referred to. That differences would arise with their respective herdsmen, (for though Abram and Lot were together, they seem to have had separate interests,) was a very natural occurrence; and the suggestion of Abram was exceedingly judicious as fitted to prevent such occurrences.

458. The remark that the Canaanite and the Perizzite were then in the land, was designed to give an additional reason why Abram and Lot should keep on good terms, as they would thus be better prepared to defend themselves, if occasion should require, against the inhabitants of the land. It may be added that the term Canaanite generally refers to all the people of Palestine, in which case the Perizzites would be included; but here, as in some other instances, it refers only to a particular tribe.

459. The plain of the Jordan is compared to Egypt as to its fruitfulness; and its situation along the valley of that river, and watered by numerous smaller streams, coming down from the mountains, and bringing the richness of the soil with them, renders the comparison very fit and proper.

"As thou comest unto Zoar," in verse 10th, must be understood as connected with "the plain of Jordan" in the former part of the verse, and not with Egypt in the latter part, as the phrase now stands. The passage should be construed thus; — "And Lot lifted up his eyes and beheld all the plain of the Jordan, as thou comest unto Zoar, that it was well watered every where . . . . like the land of Egypt."

SECTION VI. — A Divine Communication.

CHAP XIII.

14. ¶ And the LORD said unto Abram, after that Lot was separated from him, Lift up now thine eyes, and look from the place where thou art northward, and southward, and eastward, and westward:

15. For all the land which thou seest, to thee will I give it, and to thy seed for ever.

16. And I will make thy seed as the dust of the earth: so that if a man can number the dust of the earth, *then* shall thy seed also be numbered.

17. Arise, walk through the land in the length of it and in the breadth of it; for I will give it unto thee.

18. Then Abram removed *his* tent, and came and dwelt in the plain of Mamre, which *is* in Hebron, and built there an altar unto the LORD.

460. This communication, given to Abram at this time, seems intended to assure him, not merely that the land of Canaan was to be his, but to be his exclusively; and that even Lot was not to participate in the possession.

461. Mamre was a long time the residence of this patriarch, as well as of Isaac and Jacob afterwards; and though all of them had temporary residences in other places, yet the associations of Hebron often brought them back to that endeared spot. Many interesting circumstances connected with Hebron will appear in the progress of patriarchal biography.

SECTION VII. — BATTLE OF THE KINGS.

CHAP. XIV.

1. And it came to pass, in the days of Amraphel king of Shinar, Arioch king of Ellasar, Chedorlaomer, king of Elam, and Tidal king of nations;
2. That *these* made war with Bera king of Sodom, and with Birsha king of Gomorrah, Shinab king of Admah, and Shemeber king of Zeboiim, and the king of Bela, which is Zoar.
3. All these were joined together in the vale of Siddim, which is the salt sea.
4. Twelve years they served Chedorlaomer, and in the thirteenth year they rebelled.
5. And in the fourteenth year came Chedorlaomer, and the kings that *were* with him, and smote the Rephaims in Ashteroth-Karnaim, and the Zuzims in Ham, and the Emims in Shaveh-Kiriathaim,
6. And the Horites in their mount Seir, unto Elparan, which *is* by the wilderness.
7. And they returned and came to Enmishpat, which *is* Kadesh, and smote all the country of the Amalekites, and also the Amorites that dwelt in Hazezontamar.
8. And there went out the king of Sodom, and the king of Gomorrah, and the king of Admah, and the king of Zeboiim, and the king of Bela, (the same *is* Zoar;) and they joined battle with them in the vale of Siddim:
9. With Chedorlaomer the king of Elam, and with Tidal king of nations, and Amraphel king of Shinar, and Arioch king of Ellasar; four kings with five.
10. And the vale of Siddim *was* full *of* slime-pits; and the kings of Sodom and Gomorrah fled, and fell there; and they that remained fled to the mountain.
11. And they took all the goods of Sodom and Gomorrah, and all their victuals, and went their way.
12. And they took Lot, Abram's brother's son, who dwelt in Sodom, and his goods, and departed.
13. ¶ And there came one that had escaped, and told Abram the Hebrew; for he dwelt in the plain of Mamre the Amorite, brother of Eschol, and brother of Aner: and these *were* confederate with Abram.
14. And when Abram heard that his brother was taken captive, he armed his trained *servants,* born in his own house, three hundred and eighteen, and pursued *them* unto Dan.
15. And he divided himself against them, he and his servants, by night, and smote them, and pursued them unto Hobah, which *is* on the left hand of Damascus.
16. And he brought back all the goods, and also brought again his brother Lot, and his goods, and the women also, and the people.
17. ¶ And the king of Sodom went out to meet him (after his return from the slaughter of Chedorlaomer, and of the kings that *were* with him,) at the valley of Shaveh, which *is* the king's dale.
18. And Melchizedek king of Salem brought forth bread and wine: and he *was* the priest of the most high God.
19. And he blessed him, and said, Blessed *be* Abram of the most high God, possessor of heaven and earth:
20. And blessed *be* the most high God, which hath delivered thine enemies into thy hand. And he gave him tithes of all.
21. And the king of Sodom said unto Abram, Give me the persons, and take the goods to thyself.
22. And Abram said to the king of Sodom, I have lifted up my hand unto the LORD, the most high God, the possessor of heaven and earth,
23. That I will not *take* from a thread even to a shoe-latchet, and that I will not take anything that

is thine lest thou shouldest say, I have made Abram rich: 24. Save only that which the young men have eaten, and the portion of the men which went with me, Aner, Eschol, and Mamre; let them take their portion.

462 It will be remembered that Shinar was the country in which men attempted to build the tower of Babel; and as Amraphael, king of Shinar, is the first mentioned on the list of kings, it is quite probable that he was the most important personage among them, though the war was excited by Cherdorlaomer, king of Elam, to whom the southern tribes had been subject, and from whom they had recently revolted. The other places, mentioned in connection with Shinar, were probably located in the same region of country which was north or north-east of Canaan. Tidal is called king of nations, for the reason perhaps that he ruled over several cities or tribes. Perhaps, however, the word for "nations" should be rendered as a proper name, in which case, Tidal would be called simply king of "Goyim," which may be the name of only one city or country. The king of Bela is not named, either because Bela or Zoar was a very small city, or for some other reason not apparent.

463. The confederate kings appear to have laid waste the country on their way towards Canaan, and indeed they must have gone past their former allies, whose subjection they had mainly in view; for they visited Elparan, which was far beyond them in the direction of Egypt. They then turned back and subdued Enmishpat or Kadesh, and smote the whole country of the Amalekites and Amorites.

It was at this juncture that the kings of Sodom, Gomorrah, Admah, Zeboim and Zoar, went out to meet them, and joined battle with them in the vale of Siddim, not far from Sodom. The result was that they were signally defeated. Lot and his family were made captives; and it was in view of this circumstance, and the part that Abram had in rescuing his friend, that the narrative is given us.

464. Mamre was one of Abram's confederates and it was evidently after him that Abram's residence was named. He was an Amorite, and as that tribe had suffered from the northern kings, this was a good and sufficient reason, as well as being a confederate with Abram, for joining in the pursuit. Abram pursued them unto Dan, a place in the north of Palestine as Beersheba was in the south; hence the common saying, "from Dan to Beersheba." He then pursued them unto Hobah on the left hand of Damascus. These places of course were in the direction of Shinar, whither the kings were returning.

465. On the return of Abram, having recovered Lot and his family, he was met by Melchizedek, king of Salem, to whom Abram paid the tenth part of the spoils. If this Salem is the same as Jerusalem, as there is some reason to believe, the existence of a priesthood here, and the payment of tithes, become interesting circumstances, as foreshadowing the Jewish priesthood in the same place. Who this Melchizedek was, we are not informed. That he was priest of the Most High, and worshipped God according to the principles of true religion, there can be no doubt, both from the respect shown him by the patriarch, and from other references. See Heb. vii.

466. The interview which the king of Sodom had with Abram, is interesting, as showing the justice of the one, and the generosity of the other. The conduct of the king shows that he was not wholly depraved, though he was the ruler of a very corrupt and wicked people. The proposition of Abram to give his confederates their share of the spoils, shows that there was some established rule for dividing the booty in such cases: but whether such division was equal to each person, or otherwise, we do not learn from this narrative.

For local references, see Geography, pp. 103–118.

11*

SECTION VIII. — ANOTHER VISION.

CHAP. XV.

1. After these things the word of the LORD came unto Abram in a vision, saying, Fear not, Abram: I am thy shield, and thy exceeding great reward.
2. And Abram said, Lord GOD, what wilt thou give me, seeing I go childless, and the steward of my house is this Eliezer of Damascus?
3. And Abram said, Behold, to me thou hast given no seed: and lo, one born in my house is mine heir.
4. ¶ And behold, the word of the LORD came unto him, saying, This shall not be thine heir; but he that shall come forth out of thine own bowels shall be thine heir.
5. And he brought him forth abroad, and said, Look now toward heaven, and tell the stars, if thou be able to number them: and he said unto him, So shall thy seed be.
6. And he believed in the LORD; and he counted it to him for righteousness.
7. And he said unto him, I am the LORD that brought thee out of Ur of the Chaldees, to give thee this land to inherit it.
8. And he said Lord GOD, whereby shall I know that I shall inherit it.
9. And he said unto him, Take me a heifer of three years old, and a she-goat of three years old, and a ram of three years old, and a turtle dove, and a young pigeon.
10. And he took unto him all these, and divided them in the midst, and laid each piece one against another: but the birds divided he not.
11. And when the fowls came down upon the carcases, Abram drove them away.
12. And when the sun was going down, a deep sleep fell upon Abram: and, lo, a horror of great darkness fell upon him.
13. And he said unto Abram, Know of a surety that thy seed shall be a stranger in a land that is not theirs, and shall serve them; and they shall afflict them four hundred years;
14. And also that nation, whom they shall serve, will I judge: and afterward shall they come out with great substance.
15. And thou shalt go to thy fathers in peace; thou shalt be buried in a good old age.
16. But in the fourth generation they shall come hither again: for the iniquity of the Amorites is not yet full.
17. And it came to pass, that, when the sun went down, and it was dark, behold a smoking furnace, and a burning lamp that passed between those pieces.
18. In that same day the LORD made a covenant with Abram, saying, Unto thy seed have I given this land from the river of Egypt unto the great river, the river Euphrates:
19. The Kenites, and the Kenizzites, and the Kadmonites,
20. And the Hittites, and the Perizzites, and the Rephaims,
21 And the Amorites, and the Canaanites, and the Girgasites, and the Jebusites.

467. This communication is called a vision : but where the vision ends — whether it embraces the whole of the passage, or only a part of it — seems to be a matter of some uncertainty. We suppose the whole passage to be

included ; and that going forth abroad to count the stars, was as much a part of the vision, as what precedes this. So was the sacrifice, where the animals were slain and parted. So was the deep sleep or trance that fell upon the patriarch. So was the smoking furnace and burning lamp.

It is added ; — " In that same day the Lord made a covenant with Abram, saying, unto thy seed have I given this land," &c.

The vision shows the occasion of this covenant, and the ceremonies by which it was ratified, and as such it is beautiful and instructive ; while to regard the greater part of this as real, is to make it inconsistent and absurd.

468. The reference of Abram to being childless, need not be regarded as murmuring at his lot. It simply suggests a difficulty in the way of the divine promise. He had twice before been told that his seed should become very numerous. What more natural than his reference to his childless condition, in view of these promises ? Hence the promise of a son is here given.

469. The sacrifice here described is expressly said to have been prepared for the confirmation of the divine promise, that Abram should inherit the land of Canaan. The animals are such as were used in sacrifices and offerings afterwards, according to the law of Moses.

470. The deep sleep and horror of great darkness that fell upon Abram, was a fit condition for the announcement that followed. The nation that Abram's seed were to serve, and by whom they would be oppressed, is not named : but no one can doubt, in view of subsequent history, that the allusion is to Egypt.

471. The statement that the iniquity of the Amorites is not yet full, in this connection, shows clearly, that though the seed of Abram were to inherit Canaan, according to the divine promise, the sin of the Canaanites would be the reason of their destruction.

472. The river of Egypt, used to define the limits of Canaan, may have been the Nile, which was emphatically *the* river of Egypt, in which case a near approach to that river, though not actually reaching it, may be all that is intended ; or some other stream may be had in view that separated the two countries. The Euphrates is a well known river, lying east of Palestine, and is in this passage made the boundary of Abram's possessions in that direction, as the river of Egypt, in the other.

473. The several tribes here named were the people of Canaan. All together they are called Canaanites, though that term is sometimes applied to a particular tribe. So the Amorites, being a large and powerful tribe, are sometimes, as in verse 16th, put for the whole people of Canaan.

SECTION IX.— HAGAR GIVEN TO ABRAM.

CHAP. XVI.

1. Now Sarai Abram's wife bare him no children: and she had an handmaid, an Egyptian, whose name *was* Hagar.

2. And Sarai said unto Abram, Behold now, the LORD hath restrained me from bearing: I pray thee, go in unto my maid; it may be that I may obtain children by her. And Abram hearkened to the voice of Sarai.

3. And Sarai Abram's wife took Hagar her maid, the Egyptian, after Abram had dwelt ten years in the land of Canaan, and gave her to her husband Abram to be his wife.

4. And he went in unto Hagar, and she conceived : and when she saw she had conceived, her mistress was despised in her eyes.

5. And Sarai said unto Abram, My wrong *be* upon thee : I have given my maid into thy bosom; and when she saw that she had conceived, I was despised in her eyes : the LORD judge between me and thee.

6. But Abram said unto Sarai. Behold, thy maid *is* in thy hand; do to her as it pleaseth thee. And when Sarai dealt hardly with her, she fled from her face.

7. ¶ And the angel of the LORD found her by a fountain of water in the wilderness, by the fountain in the way to Shur.

8. And he said, Hagar, Sarai's maid, whence camest thou ? and whither wilt thou go? And she said, I flee from the face of my mistress Sarai.

9. And the angel of the LORD said unto her, Return to thy mistress, and submit thyself under her hands.

10. And the angel of the LORD said unto her, I will multiply thy seed exceedingly, that it shall not be numbered for multitude.

11. And the angel of the LORD said unto her, Behold, thou *art* with child, and shalt bear a son, and shalt call his name Ishmael; because the LORD hath heard thy affliction.

12. And he will be a wild man ; his hand *will be* against every man, and every man's hand against him; and he shall dwell in the presence of all his brethren.

13. And she called the name of the LORD that spake unto her, Thou God seest me: for she said, Have I also here looked after him that seeth me?

14. Wherefore the well was called Beer-lahai-roi; behold, *it is* between Kadesh and Bered.

15 ¶ And Hagar bare Abram a son : and Abram called his son's name, which Hagar bare, Ishmael.

16. And Abram *was* fourscore and six years old, when Hagar bare Ishmael to Abram.

474. Hagar was an Egyptian ; and it will be remembered that handmaids were among the gifts Abram received from the king of Egypt, when he visited that country.

475. No one can read the patriarchal narrative, without noticing that the desire for offspring was one of the strongest passions of those days. But, as was very natural, it is with those to whom that favor was denied, that we find the expression of that desire, most emphatic.

476. When Hagar left her mistress, and was found in the wilderness, she appears to have been on her way to Egypt. It is quite natural that, being an Egyptian, she should proceed toward that country. She was found by a fountain of water in the wilderness. It will be remembered that, at a subsequent time, she and her son came near perishing for the want of such an accommodation. It was not safe to leave one fountain, in the hope of finding another, unless the traveller was well acquainted with the route, which Hagar could not be expected to be, as she had probably never passed along that route but once before, viz., when she first came with Abram from Egypt.

What is said of the angel of the Lord, in this passage, will be best understood by consulting our criticism on that word ; also our remarks upon the mode of divine communications in those days. pp. 67-70. 30, 31.

477. It is generally understood that the Arabs are the descendants of Ishmael ; and they clearly exemplify the character here ascribed to their illustrious progenitor. They exist, too, as a distinct race, " in the presence of all their brethren," notwithstanding the efforts made to exterminate them.

SECTION X. — ABRAM HAS ANOTHER VISION. — CIRCUMCISION INSTITUTED.

CHAP. XVII.

1. And when Abram was ninety years old and nine, the LORD appeared to Abram, and said unto him, I *am* the Almighty God; walk before me, and be thou perfect.
2. And I will make my covenant between me and thee, and will multiply thee exceedingly.
3. And Abram fell on his face; and God talked with him, saying,
4. As for me, behold, my covenant *is* with thee, and thou shalt be a father of many nations.
5. Neither shall thy name any more be called Abram, but thy name shall be Abraham; for a father of many nations have I made thee.
6. And I will make thee exceeding fruitful, and I will make nations of thee, and kings shall come out of thee.
7. And I will establish my covenant between me and thee and thy seed after thee in their generations for an everlasting covenant, to be a God unto thee, and to thy seed after thee.
8. And I will give unto thee, and to thy seed after thee, the land wherein thou art a stranger, all the land of Canaan, for an everlasting possession; and I will be their God.
9. ¶ And God said unto Abraham, Thou shalt keep my covenant therefore, thou, and thy seed after thee in their generations.
10. This *is* my covenant, which ye shall keep, between me and you and thy seed after thee; Every man child among you shall be circumcised.
11. And ye shall circumcise the flesh of your foreskin; and it shall be a token of the covenant betwixt me and you.
12. And he that is eight days old shall be circumcised among you, every man-child in your generations, he that is born in the house, or bought with money of any stranger, which *is* not of thy seed.
13. He that is born in thy house, and he that is bought with thy money, must needs be circumcised: and my covenant shall be in your flesh for an everlasting covenant.
14. And the uncircumcised man-child whose flesh of his foreskin is not circumcised, that soul shall be cut off from his people; he hath broken my covenant.
15. ¶ And God said unto Abraham, As for Sarai thy wife, thou shalt not call her name Sarai, but Sarah *shall* her name *be*.
16. And I will bless her, and give thee a son also of her: yea, I will bless her, and she shall be *a mother* of nations; kings of people shall be of her.
17. Then Abraham fell upon his face, and laughed, and said in his heart, Shall *a child* be born unto him that is a hundred years old? and shall Sarah, that is ninety years old, bear?
18. And Abraham said unto God, O that Ishmael might live before thee!
19. And God said, Sarah thy wife shall bear thee a son indeed: and thou shalt call his name Isaac; and I will establish my covenant with him for an everlasting covenant, *and* with his seed after him.
20. And as for Ishmael, I have heard thee: Behold, I have blessed him, and will make him fruitful, and will multiply him exceedingly; twelve princes shall he beget, and I will make him a great nation.
21. But my covenant will I establish with Isaac, which Sarah shall bear unto thee at this set time in the next year.

22. And he left off talking with him, and God went up from Abraham.

23. ¶ And Abraham took Ishmael his son, and all that were born in his house, and all that were bought with his money, every male among the men of Abraham's house; and circumcised the flesh of their foreskin in the self-same day, as God had said unto him.

24. And Abraham *was* ninety years old and nine, when he was circumcised in the flesh of his foreskin.

25. And Ishmael his son *was* thirteen years old, when he was circumcised in the flesh of his foreskin.

26. In the self-same day was Abraham circumcised, and Ishmael his son.

27. And all the men of his house born in the house, and bought with money of the stranger, were circumsised with him.

478. This communication is not said to have been given in a vision; but its resemblance to the vision described in chapter 15th, must remove all doubt, as to the question, whether the same mode was adopted in both cases.

479. The promise of a numerous seed is here repeated, and a change is made in the name of the patriarch, to make it correspond more exactly with the nature of the promise. It should be observed, however, that the change was not wholly to bring about this conformity. Any change, made in view of the promise, would have accomplished the same purpose, which obviously was, to remind him, every time his name was mentioned, of the divine assurance of his prosperity. This idea will obviate a difficulty connected with the change in the name of Abraham's wife: for no reason, aside from the one here suggested, can be assigned for the change. The one name does not connect itself with the divine promise, more than the other; though many conjectures have been resorted to, to make this out. Either name, being chosen expressly with that intention, would serve as a constant memorial of the promised blessing. The principle here involved, shows itself very frequently in those early times, and was a matter of necessity, while the art of writing was unknown, or was not generally prevalent.

480. The memory of important contracts, or other events, was thus often refreshed by outward memorials. And I may add, that the more important the thing to be remembered, the more intimate and constant the memorial selected. There is nothing, for example, that would more constantly remind Abraham of God's promise than his name. The promise was important, and the memorial would frequently bring it to mind. The same remark will apply to the name of Sarah. The bow in the clouds, that was to assure Noah, and succeeding generations, that there should no more be a flood of waters, has the same purpose; and the memento is as lasting as the promise. The gift of sheep and oxen by Abraham to Abimelech, when a covenant was entered into between them, had the same purpose in view; and though the memorial would not very long continue, yet its continuance, and the remembrance of it, would be as lasting as would be required. And the seven ewe lambs, given to Abimelech on the same occasion, were specially intended as proof that a certain well belonged to Abraham, about which some misunderstanding, now settled, had existed. So the stone set up for a pillar by Jacob, between his country and that of Laban, was not to be passed, by either party, with hostile intention; and surely nothing could have answered the purpose better. So, too, the names given to places, in view of important circumstances that occurred there, of which many instances may be found in this book.

481. The rite of circumcision was established on the same principle with the one just illustrated, and was chosen in view of the purpose to be accomplished. First, it was to remind the Hebrew of the divine promise of a numerous posterity. Second, it was to be early performed, as showing the necessity of teaching the divine covenant to their children. Third, the memorial would last as long as life, so should the remembrance of the divine promise. Fourth, it was to be repeated throughout their generations, and thus be co-extensive with the continuance of their covenant relation to Jehovah. Fifth, the servant and stranger, who would have the benefits of the covenant, must also be subject to the same rite.

482. The covenant, here alluded to, comprehended several particulars. First, that Abraham should be the father of many nations. Sarah, too, was to be the mother of nations. Second, it is said to Abraham, kings shall come out of thee, and of Sarah, kings of people shall be of her. Third, God would, in a special manner, be a God to Abraham and his seed after him. Fourth, the land of Canaan was to be an everlasting possession to him and his seed.

The soul uncircumcised was to be cut off from his people — he was to be shut out from the blessings and privileges of the covenant he refused to recognize. Some think that being put to death was here had in view but without sufficient reason.

483. Abraham laughed when told that he should have a son; and it was in view of this circumstance, that the name of the son was Isaac, which in the Hebrew, means to laugh. That the patriarch laughed in the face of a personal Jehovah, whom he saw with his natural eyes, and with whom he conversed, as one man converses with another, is quite unlikely, not to say absurd or blasphemous; though, that such a thing occurred in a vision, and only *seemed* to be, is a very reasonable supposition; and surely the object had in view, could as well be accomplished in this way, as the other.

484. Ishmael too, son of Hagar, was to be blessed, as well as Isaac, in answer to the prayer of the patriarch. He was to be the father of twelve princes. These are named in xxv. 13–15. But the covenant, before alluded to, was to be with Isaac; and the rite of circumcision was to be confined to that branch of the family of Abram, after they became separate.

485. The Lord left off talking with Abraham and went up from him. That this was a mere appearance, may be learned, from verse 1st, where it is said that the Lord appeared to Abraham. The language answers to the description of a vision, and can be rationally understood in no other way. The assurance the patriarch felt that the vision was divine, and that its instructions were to be complied with, induced him to comply immediately with its requisitions.

SECTION XI. — ANOTHER VISION.

CHAP. XVIII.

1. And the LORD appeared unto him in the plains of Mamre: and he sat in the tent door in the heat of the day;
2. And he lifted up his eyes and looked, and lo, three men stood by him: and when he saw *them*, he ran to meet them from the tent door, and bowed himself toward the ground,
3. And said, My Lord, if now I have found favor in thy sight, pass not away, I pray thee, from thy servant:
4. Let a little water, I pray you, be fetched, and wash your feet, and rest yourselves under the tree.
5. And I will fetch a morsel of bread, and comfort ye your hearts; after that ye shall pass on: for therefore are ye come to your servant. And they said, So do, as thou hast said.
6. And Abraham hastened into the tent unto Sarah, and said, Make ready quickly three measures of fine meal, knead *it*, and make cakes upon the hearth.
7. And Abraham ran unto the herd, and fetched a calf tender and good; and gave *it* to a young man; and he hastened to dress it.
8. And he took butter, and milk, and the calf which he had dressed, and set *it* before them; and he stood by them under the tree, and they did eat.
9. ¶ And they said unto him, Where *is* Sarah thy wife? And he said, Behold, in the tent.
10. And he said, I will certainly return unto thee according to the time of life; and, lo, Sarah thy wife shall have a son. And Sarah heard *it* in the tent door, which *was* behind him.
11. Now Abraham and Sarah *were* old *and* well stricken in age; *and* it ceased to be with Sarah after the manner of women.
12. Therefore Sarah laughed within herself, saying, After I am waxed old shall I have pleasure, my lord being old also?
13. And the LORD said unto Abraham, Wherefore did Sarah laugh, saying, Shall I of a surety bear a child, which am old?
14. Is any thing too hard for the LORD? At the time appointed I will return unto thee, according to the time of life, and Sarah shall have a son.
15. Then Sarah denied, saying, I laughed not; for she was afraid. And he said, Nay; but thou didst laugh.
16. ¶ And the men rose up from thence, and looked toward Sodom: and Abraham went with them to bring them on the way.
17. And the LORD, said Shall I hide from Abraham that thing which I do;
18. Seeing that Abraham shall surely become a great and mighty nation, and all the nations of the earth shall be blessed in him?
19. For I know him, that he will command his children and his household after him, and they shall keep the way of the LORD, to do justice and judgment: that the LORD may bring upon Abraham that which he hath spoken of him.
20. And the LORD said, Because the cry of Sodom and Gomorrah is great, and because their sin is very grievous
21. I will go down now, and see whether they have done altogether according to the cry of it, which is come unto me; and if not, I will know.
22. And the men turned their faces from thence, and went toward Sodom but Abraham stood yet before the LORD.
23. ¶ And Abraham drew near,

and said, Wilt thou also destroy the righteous with the wicked?

24. Peradventure there be fifty righteous within the city: wilt thou also destroy and not spare the place for the fifty righteous that *are* therein?

25. That be far from thee to do after this manner, to slay the righteous with the wicked; and that the righteous should be as the wicked, that be far from thee: Shall not the judge of all the earth do right?

26. And the LORD said, If I find in Sodom fifty righteous within the city, then I will spare all the place for their sakes.

27. And Abraham answered and said, Behold now, I have taken upon me to speak unto the LORD, which *am but* dust and ashes:

28. Peradventure there shall lack five of the fifty righteous: wilt thou destroy all the city for *lack of* five? And he said, If I find there forty and five, I will not destroy it.

29. And he spake unto him yet again, and said, Peradventure there shall be forty found there. And he said, I will not do *it* for forty's sake.

30. And he said *unto him*, Oh let not the Lord be angry, and I will speak: Peradventure there shall thirty be found there. And he said, I will not do *it*, if I find thirty there.

31. And he said, Behold now, I have taken upon me to speak unto the Lord: Peradventure there shall be twenty found there. And he said, I will not destroy *it* for twenty's sake.

32. And he said, Oh let not the Lord be angry, and I will speak yet but this once : Peradventure ten shall be found there. And he said, I will not destroy *it* for ten's sake.

33. And the LORD went his way, as soon as he had left communing with Abraham : and Abraham returned unto his place.

486. That this is really another vision, may be assumed from its resemblance to the former ones, and from the language and nature of the representation. God *appeared* to Abraham : but he never appears to the natural vision of man. So three men stood by him. The inference is, that they suddenly appeared to him, as an image in a dream. Abraham runs to meet them. This, and all else, until the Lord went his way, as stated at the close of the chapter, is of the same character. It all occurred in a vision that came upon Abraham, as he sat or reclined in his tent for rest, in the cool of the day. The tent was placed under a tree, verse 8, for the purpose doubtless of being better protected from the scorching rays of the sun ; and the tent door was selected as the place of repose, as being more exposed to the refreshing breeze. How fit the circumstances for the vision that was to follow ! The laughing of Sarah, and her denial of having laughed, seem much more fit and proper, when this is regarded as a vision, than with any other view.

487. The persons who stood by Abraham, as here

stated, are called *men*. They were three in number. It is not true that one of the three was the Lord, though there is confessedly some ambiguity in the way they are spoken of. The Lord *and* three men, is the more reasonable construction.

488. " And the Lord said ; Because the cry of Sodom and Gomorrah is great, and because their sin is very grievous, I will go down now and see," &c. We ought to render this And the Lord *had* said this ; as it is plainly the writer's intention to inform us of something that had been done, and not of what occurred at the time when this interview of Abraham took place. The way such language, as applied to God and indicating imperfection in his attributes, is to be understood, we have illustrated in another place. pp. 47–50.

The plea of Abraham, in favor of Sodom, is exceedingly natural, especially in view of the fact that Lot and his family resided in that city.

SECTION XII. — Sodom and Gomorrah Destroyed.

CHAP. XIX.

1. And there came two angels to Sodom at even; and Lot sat in the gate of Sodom; and Lot seeing *them* rose up to meet them; and he bowed himself with his face toward the ground;

2. And he said, Behold now, my lords, turn in, I pray you, into your servant's house, and tarry all night, and wash your feet, and ye shall rise up early, and go on your ways. And they said, Nay; but we will abide in the street all night.

3. And he pressed upon them greatly; and they turned in unto him, and entered into his house; and he made them a feast, and did bake unleavened bread, and they did eat.

4. ¶ But before they lay down, the men of the city, *even* the men of Sodom, compassed the house round, both old and young, all the people from every quarter:

5. And they called unto Lot, and said unto him, Where *are* the men which came in to thee this night? bring them out unto us that we may know them.

6. And Lot went out at the door unto them, and shut the door after him.

7. And said, I pray you, brethren, do not so wickedly.

8. Behold now, I have two daughters which have not known man; let me, I pray you, bring them out unto you, and do ye to them as *is* good in your eyes: only unto these men do nothing; for therefore came they under the shadow of my roof.

9. And they said, Stand back. And they said *again*, This one *fellow* came in to sojourn, and he will needs be a judge: now will we deal

ABRAHAM AND HIS FAMILY.

worse with thee, than with them. And they pressed sore upon the man, *even* Lot, and came near to break the door.

10. But the men put forth their hand, and pulled Lot into the house to them, and shut to the door.

11. And they smote the men that *were* at the door of the house with blindness, both small and great; so that they wearied themselves to find the door.

12. ¶ And the men said unto Lot, Hast thou here any besides? son-in-law, and thy sons, and thy daughters, and whatsoever thou hast in the city, bring *them* out of this place:

13. For we will destroy this place, because the cry of them is waxen great before the face of the LORD; and the LORD hath sent us to destroy it.

14. And Lot went out, and spake unto his sons-in-law, which married his daughters, and said, Up, get you out of this place; for the LORD will destroy this city. But he seemed as one that mocked unto his sons-in-law.

15. ¶ And when the morning arose, then the angels hastened Lot, saying, Arise, take thy wife, and thy two daughters, which are here; lest thou be consumed in the iniquity of the city.

16. And while he lingered, the men laid hold upon his hand, and upon the hand of his wife, and upon the hand of his two daughters; the LORD being merciful unto him: and they brought him forth, and set him without the city.

17. And it came to pass, when they had brought them forth abroad, that he said, Escape for thy life; look not behind thee, neither stay thou in all the plain; escape to the mountain, lest thou be consumed.

18. And Lot said unto them, Oh, not so, my Lord:

19. Behold now, thy servant hath found grace in thy sight, and thou hast magnified thy mercy, which thou hast shewed unto me in saving my life; and I cannot escape to the mountain, lest some evil take me, and I die:

20. Behold now, this city *is* near to flee unto, and it *is* a little one: Oh, let me escape thither, (*is* it not a little one?) and my soul shall live.

21. And he said unto him, See, I have accepted thee concerning this thing also, that I will not overthrow the city, for the which thou hast spoken.

22. Haste thee, escape thither; for I cannot do any thing till thou be come thither. Therefore the name of the city was called Zoar.

23. The sun was risen upon the earth when Lot entered into Zoar.

24. ¶ Then the LORD rained upon Sodom and upon Gomorrah brimstone and fire from the LORD out of heaven;

25. And he overthrew those cities, and all the plain, and all the inhabitants of the cities, and that which grew upon the ground.

26. ¶ But his wife looked back from behind him, and she became a pillar of salt.

27. ¶ And Abraham gat up early in the morning to the place where he stood before the LORD:

28. And he looked toward Sodom and Gomorrah, and toward all the land of the plain, and beheld, and lo, the smoke of the country went up as the smoke of a furnace.

29. ¶ And it came to pass, when God destroyed the cities of the plain, that God remembered Abraham, and sent Lot out of the midst of the overthrow, when he overthrew the cities in the which Lot dwelt.

489. I do not feel at all certain but that this chapter, as far as verse 26th, is to be regarded in the same light as the former chapter, either as a part of the same vision, or another that occurred during the night of the same day. The destruction of Sodom, the residence of Lot, had been announced; and it is certain that the mind of Abraham was excited with apprehensions on account of his friend, of whose fate the vision had not informed him. What more natural then than that he should be favored with another communication, wherein the fate of Lot should be indicated, as well as the principal circumstances connected with that signal overthrow.

490. Many of the circumstances here spoken of, agree much better with this theory, than with any other. The whole of the people of Sodom gathering themselves around the house of Lot, and though bent on securing the stranger, yet being unable to do so, the supernatural strength put forth by the angels, the proposition of Lot to give up his two daughters to the mob: the whole multitude being struck with blindness; the wife of Lot becoming a pillar of salt; and finally the cities of the plain being destroyed by fire, coming down from the Lord out of heaven, when it is evident that the cities were swallowed up by an earthquake, and if burned at all, burned with fire from the earth, rather than from heaven. These are circumstances that are more fit to be referred to a vision, than to be regarded as actual occurrences, and are with this view, no less instructive, as indicating to Abraham the main facts about which he was solicitous.

491. And I would add, that, with this view, the account following the vision comes in with great propriety:—"And Abraham got up early in the morning, (having had the vision the preceding night,) to the plain where he stood before the Lord: (in the first vision,) and he looked toward Sodom and Gomorrah, and toward all the land of the plain; and behold and lo the smoke of the country went up, as the smoke of a furnace. And it came to pass when God destroyed the cities of the plain, that God remembered Abraham, and sent Lot out of the midst of the overthrow, when he overthrew the cities in which Lot dwelt."

This seems a plain historical statement of the destruction of Sodom and the escape of Lot, while the preceding has in it many circumstances that, as matters of fact, are difficult to understand, but which may very fitly be brought in as appendages of a vision, and as such are not difficult or incredible. For we know that in dreams and visions, things natural and unnatural, possible and impossible, are frequently combined ; and we are to look at their significance, and not at their literal harmony or possibility. Besides ; the last passage, upon the common view, is only a repetition of the other, so far as it relates to the destruction of the cities and the escape of Lot, and is therefore wholly unnecessary; while, with our view, it is not a repetition, but a historical statement of what had before only been foreshadowed.

492. I would add, that, though the representation is a vision, and therefore unreal, the circumstances of the vision, constituting the drapery with which it is presented, arose out of existing facts. The hospitality of Lot was quite in harmony with the spirit of the times; the proposition of the angels to remain in the street, covered with their own tent only, it being a warm season, as we had been told in the previous chapter; the hostility of the men of the city toward Lot, because " he would need be a judge ;" the offer of Lot to give up his daughters to the mob, rather than violate the rites of hospitality held sacred in that country; the divine protection extended to the righteous man, especially in view of his being a relation of Abraham ; and finally, the overthrow of the cities being referred directly to God. All these, and other particulars, though changed somewhat from a literal consistency and harmony, and exaggerated above what would be expected as real occurrences, are nevertheless all derived from the circumstances of the age, and the prevailing habits and views of the people.

493. A few additional particulars, alluded to in the passage, may be briefly noticed.

The angels that came to Lot are called *men*, throughout the passage, whenever there is any allusion to them, except when they are first announced. They were both angels and men : angels as denoting their office, being *messengers*, as the word means, and men, as having all the attributes, as well as form of men; and hence they are spoken of as eating, sleeping, putting forth physical strength, &c.

Lot sat in the gate of the city. Whether Lot was really a judge in Sodom, as sitting in the gate would indicate, we cannot say, but it is certain that he is so represented in the passage; hence the complaint of the people, "This one fellow came in to sojourn, and he will needs be a judge."

The rites of hospitality have always been regarded, in the East, as peculiarly sacred; and are so regarded at the present day.

The sons-in-law of Lot, may have been the betrothed of his daughters, as no other than the two daughters that were saved with him, are mentioned in the narrative. Or the representation may be intended merely to show, that, out of regard to Lot, all his relations might be saved, if they would, though as a reality he might have had no sons-in-law.

SECTION XIII.—Lot and his Daughters in the Mountain.

CHAP. XIX.

30. ¶ And Lot went up out of Zoar, and dwelt in the mountain, and his two daughters with him; for he feared to dwell in Zoar: and he dwelt in a cave, he and his two daughters.

31. And the first born said unto the younger, Our father is old, and *there is* not a man in the earth to come in unto us after the manner of all the earth:

32. Come, let us make our father drink wine, and we will lie with him, that we may preserve seed of our father.

33. And they made their father drink wine that night; and the first born went in, and lay with her father; and he perceived not when she lay down, nor when she arose.

34. And it came to pass on the morrow, that the first born said unto the younger, Behold, I lay yesternight with my father: let us make him drink wine this night also; and go thou in, *and* lie with him, that we may preserve seed of our father.

35. And they made their father drink wine that night also: and the younger arose, and lay with him; and he perceived not when she lay down, nor when she arose.

36. Thus were both the daughters of Lot with child by their father.

37. And the firstborn bare a son, and called his name Moab; the same *is* the father of the Moabites unto this day.

38. And the younger, she also bare a son, and called his name Benammi; the same *is* the father of the children of Ammon unto this day.

494. Lot was unwilling to flee to the mountains when Sodom was destroyed; but afterwards, fearing to dwell in Zoar, he went up to the mountain near by, and dwelt in a cave. On what his fear was based, as to dwelling in Zoar, we are not informed. As the place was near to Sodom he may have feared lest it would yet share the same fate, and he concluded that the danger of the wild beasts of the mountain, would be the least of two evils.

495. The conduct of Lot's daughters can be excused only by one circumstance mentioned incidentally in the narrative. They supposed that the destruction of Sodom had swept away all the men in the country, and that the future continuance of the race depended only on themselves. But it may be asked; What need of recording at all their abominable wickedness? The answer is, that the Moabites and the Ammonites are tribes that make a conspicuous figure in the subsequent history; and it was deemed important to record their origin. They originated from Moab and Ben-ammi, sons of Lot by his daughters.

SECTION XIV.—Sojourn in Gerar.

CHAP. XX.

1. And Abraham journeyed from thence toward the south country, and dwelt between Kadesh and Shur, and sojourned in Gerar.
2. And Abraham said of Sarah his wife, She *is* my sister: and Abimelech king of Gerar sent and took Sarah.
3. But God came to Abimelech in a dream by night, and said to him, Behold, thou *art but* a dead man, for the woman which thou hast taken; for she *is* a man's wife.
4. But Abimelech had not come near her; and he said, Lord, wilt thou slay also a righteous nation?
5. Said he not unto me, She *is* my sister? and she, even she herself, said, He *is* my brother: in the integrity of my heart and innocency of my hands have I done this.
6. And God said unto him in a dream, Yea, I know that thou didst this in the integrity of thy heart; for I also withheld thee from sinning against me: therefore suffered I thee not to touch her.
7. Now, therefore restore the man *his* wife; for he *is* a prophet, and he shall pray for thee, and thou shalt live: and if thou restore *her* not, know thou that thou shalt surely die, thou, and all that *are* thine.
8. Therefore Abimelech rose early in the morning, and called all his servants, and told all these things in their ears: and the men were sore afraid.
9. Then Abimelech called Abraham, and said unto him, What hast thou done unto us? and what have I offended thee, that thou hast brought on me and on my kingdom a great sin? thou hast done deeds unto me that ought not to be done.

10. And Abimelech said unto Abraham, What sawest thou, that thou hast done this thing?

11. And Abraham said, Because I thought, Surely the fear of God is not in this place; and they will slay me for my wife's sake.

12. And yet indeed *she is* my sister; she *is* the daughter of my father, but not the daughter of my mother; and she became my wife

13. And it came to pass, when God caused me to wander from my father's house, that I said unto her, This *is* thy kindness which thou shalt shew unto me; at every place whither we shall come, say of me, He *is* my brother.

14. ¶ And Abimelech took sheep, and oxen, and men-servants, and women-servants, and gave *them* unto Abraham, and restored him Sarah his wife.

15. And Abimelech said, Behold, my land *is* before thee: dwell where it pleaseth thee.

16. And unto Sarah he said, Behold, I have given thy brother a thousand *pieces* of silver: behold, he *is* to thee a covering of the eyes, unto all that *are* with thee, and with all *other:* thus she was reproved.

17. ¶ So Abraham prayed unto God: and God healed Abimelech, and his wife, and his maid-servants; and they bare *children.*

18. For the LORD had fast closed up all the wombs of the house of Abimelech, because of Sarah, Abraham's wife.

496. It will be remembered that when Hagar fled from her mistress, she was found in the way to Shur. It appears that Kadesh, Gerar and Shur, were in the south country. Other passages make it evident that this south country was in the south-west part of Canaan, near to Egypt; and we before gave this as a reason why the Egyptian handmaid was going that way.

497. That dreams, inspired by the divine spirit, were not confined to the Hebrews, is shown in this passage: and it is not, we conceive, unreasonable, to suppose that divine communications have been given to other nations besides the Hebrews, if not to all nations; though they have not so clearly recognized them, or at least have not so faithfully recorded and preserved them.

498. Here Abraham practices the same deception he had formerly done in Egypt, and with the same success. He was of opinion that the people of Gerar were so corrupt, that they would not at all respect the marriage relation, and therefore, he was bound to deceive them, and so avoid bad consequences. He found, however, that the people were better than he expected. The same thing has often occurred with others. Men regarded as heathen and infidels, are found practising on better principles than they have the credit of doing.

499. The afflictions brought upon Abimelech on account of Abraham's wife, were such only perhaps, as might be expected from the circumstances, on natural grounds.

SECTION XV.—Birth of Isaac.

CHAP. XXI.

1. And the Lord visited Sarah as he had said, and the Lord did unto Sarah as he had spoken.
2. For Sarah conceived, and bare Abraham a son in his old age; at the set time of which God had spoken to him.
3. And Abraham called the name of his son that was born unto him, whom Sarah bare to him, Isaac.
4. And Abraham circumcised his son Isaac, being eight days old, as God had commanded him.
5. And Abraham was an hundred years old, when his son Isaac was born unto him.
6. ¶ And Sarah said, God hath made me to laugh, *so that* all that hear will laugh with me.
7. And she said, Who would have said unto Abraham, that Sarah should have given children suck? for I have borne *him* a son in his old age.
8. And the child grew, and was weaned : and Abraham made a great feast the *same* day that Isaac was weaned.

500. This passage contains several references to the time and occasion when the birth of Isaac was announced. The promise given, the time it was to be fulfilled, the name before indicated, the circumcision, &c., are all alluded to with reference to what had taken place on that occasion.

501. That feasts were common on the occasion of weaning children, cannot be justly inferred from this single reference. The peculiar circumstances, connected with that child, may have induced the father to practice some things that were not usual.

SECTION XVI. — HAGAR AND HER SON REJECTED.

CHAP. XXI.

9. ¶ And Sarah saw the son of Hagar the Egyptian, which she had borne unto Abraham, mocking.
10. Wherefore she said unto Abraham, Cast out this bond-woman and her son: for the son of this bond-woman shall not be heir with my son, *even* with Isaac.
11. And the thing was very grievous in Abraham's sight, because of his son.
12. And God said unto Abraham, Let it not be grievous in thy sight because of the lad, and because of thy bond-woman; in all that Sarah hath said unto thee, hearken unto her voice; for in Isaac shall thy seed be called.
13. And also of the son of the bond-woman will I make a nation, because he *is* thy seed.
14. And Abraham rose up early in the morning, and took bread, and a bottle of water, and gave *it* unto Hagar (putting *it* on her shoulder) and the child, and sent her away: and she departed, and wandered in the wilderness of Beersheba.
15. And the water was spent in the bottle, and she cast the child under one of the shrubs.
16. And she went, and sat her down over against *him* a good way off, as it were a bow-shot, for she said, Let me not see the death of the child. And she sat over against *him*, and lifted up her voice, and wept.
17. And God heard the voice of the lad; and the angel of God called to Hagar out of heaven, and said unto her, What aileth thee, Hagar? Fear not: for God hath heard the voice of the lad where he *is*.
18. Arise, lift up the lad, and hold him in thine hand; for I will make him a great nation.
19. And God opened her eyes, and she saw a well of water; and she went, and filled the bottle with water and gave the lad to drink.
20. And God was with the lad; and he grew, and dwelt in the wilderness, and became an archer.
21. And he dwelt in the wilderness of Paran: and his mother took him a wife out of the land of Egypt.

502. The feeling that Abraham had for his son Ishmael, was exceedingly natural; and it was perhaps quite as natural that Sarah should have a different feeling. But a divine command determined him in favor of carrying out the wishes of his wife; though he was obliged to sacrifice the tender feeling of paternal affection.

503. He made all the provision that the nature of the case admitted of, for Hagar and her son, in their journey and sent them away. As on a former occasion, so now, Hagar directs her way toward her former home in Egypt. The wilderness of Beersheba, where she wandered, lay in that direction. See Geography. It appears that she

lost her way; and as water was not easily obtained in that country, death from the want of it, seemed inevitable. In this emergency Hagar did what any mother might be expected to do, under the same circumstances; and the narrative recording the circumstances, is affecting in proportion to its simplicity. The manner in which the angel of the Lord appeared to Hagar, and communicated to her what is here recorded, we suppose to be the same as most other divine communications, contained in this book; that is, in a vision. See p. 30.

504. The mother took, for Ishmael, a wife from the land of Egypt, for the obvious reason that she was an Egyptian; and her rejection by the Hebrew patriarch, doubtless increased her desire to ally her son with the Egyptians rather than with the Hebrews.

SECTION XVII.—COVENANT WITH ABIMELECH.

CHAP. XXI.

22. ¶ And it came to pass at that time, that Abimelech and Phichol the chief captain of his host spake unto Abraham, saying, God *is* with thee in all that thou doest:
23. Now therefore swear unto me here by God that thou wilt not deal falsely with me, nor with my son, nor with my son's son: but according to the kindness that I have done unto thee, thou shalt do unto me, and to the land wherein thou hast sojourned.
24. And Abraham said, I will swear.
25. And Abraham reproved Abimelech because of a well of water, which Abimelech's servants had violently taken away.
26. And Abimelech said, I wot not who hath done this thing: neither didst thou tell me, neither yet heard I *of it*, but to-day.
27. And Abraham took sheep and oxen, and gave them unto Abimelech; and both of them made a covenant.
28. And Abraham set seven ewe lambs of the flock by themselves.
29. And Abimelech said unto Abraham, What *mean* these seven ewe lambs which thou hast set by themselves?
30. And he said, For *these* seven ewe lambs shalt thou take of my hand, that they may be a witness unto me, that I have digged this well.
31. Wherefore he called that place Beersheba; because there they sware, both of them.
32. Thus they made a covenant at Beersheba: then Abimelech rose up, and Phichol the chief captain of his host, and they returned into the land of the Philistines.
33. ¶ And *Abraham* planted a grove in Beersheba, and called there on the name of the LORD, the everlasting God.
34. And Abraham sojourned in the Philistines' land many days.

505. The oath has, in all ages, been regarded as placing men under the strongest obligations to carry out those engagements having its sanction. The obligation, in this instance, is rendered more binding by the bestowment of a valuable gift, which would remind Abimelech no less than the oath, of the necessity of fulfilling his engagements. The seven ewe lambs had a special design. They were a memento that the well, about which a misunderstanding had existed, was Abraham's and not Abimelech's. The circumstance of their being *lambs* and *ewes* would ensure their longer continuance, and thereby would render the memento more valuable as such.

506. The forming of this covenant, seems to have been recorded mainly to show the origin of the name Beersheba, (well of the oath,) as that place became somewhat noted in after times. When the name is associated with events that occurred before this time, it is given by anticipation; in other words, the writer gives the modern name, as better understood than the ancient one. It is not certain but that the wilderness of Beersheba and of Paran are the same. What is said of Hagar and Ishmael seems to favor the idea of their identity.

507. The grove planted by Abraham in Beersheba, had a good object in view; but groves were made the places of idolatrous worship at a later day, and are often alluded to in this connection, in other parts of the Bible.

SECTION XVIII.—Offering of Isaac.

CHAP. XXII.

1. And it came to pass after these things that God did tempt Abraham, and said unto him, Abraham: and he said, Behold, here I *am*.

2. And he said, Take now thy son, thine only *son* Isaac, whom thou lovest, and get thee into the land of Moriah; and offer him there for a burnt-offering upon one of the mountains which I will tell thee of.

3. And Abraham rose up early in the morning, and saddled his ass, and took two of his young men with him, and Isaac his son, and clave the wood for the burnt-offering, and rose up, and went unto the place of which God had told him.

4. Then on the third day Abraham lifted up his eyes, and saw the place afar off.

5. And Abraham said unto his young men, Abide you here with

the ass; and I and the lad will go yonder and worship and come again to you.

6. And Abraham took the wood of the burnt offering, and laid *it* upon Isaac his son; and he took the fire in his hand, and a knife: and they went both of them together.

7. And Isaac spake unto Abraham his father, and said, My father: and he said, Here *am* I, my son. And he said, Behold the fire and the wood; but where *is* the lamb for a burnt offering?

8. And Abraham said, My son, God will provide himself a lamb for a burnt-offering: so they went both of them together.

9. And they came to the place which God had told him of; and Abraham built an altar there, and laid the wood in order; and bound Isaac his son, and laid him on the altar upon the wood.

10. And Abraham stretched forth his hand, and took the knife to slay his son.

11. And the angel of the LORD called unto him out of heaven, and said, Abraham, Abraham: and he said, Here *am* I.

12. And he said, Lay not thine hand upon the lad, neither do thou any thing unto him: for now I know that thou fearest God, seeing thou hast not withheld thy son, thine only *son* from me.

13. And Abraham lifted up his eyes, and looked, and behold, behind *him* a ram caught in a thicket by his horns: and Abraham went and took the ram, and offered him up for a burnt-offering in the stead of his son.

14. And Abraham called the name of that place Jehovah-jireh: as it is said *to* this day, In the mount of the LORD it shall be seen.

15. ¶ And the angel of the LORD called unto Abraham out of heaven the second time.

16. And said, By myself have I sworn, saith the LORD, for because thou hast done this thing, and hast not withheld thy son, thine only *son;*

17. That in blessing I will bless thee, and in multiplying I will multiply thy seed as the stars of the heaven, and as the sand which *is* upon the sea-shore; and thy seed shall possess the gate of his enemies;

18. And in thy seed shall all the nations of the earth be blessed; because thou hast obeyed my voice.

19. So Abraham returned unto his young men, and they rose up and went together to Beersheba; and Abraham dwelt at Beersheba.

508. That Abraham should have shown a willingness to sacrifice his son, can be accounted for, only by his having the fullest assurance that the command to do so was truly divine. We may not be certain as to the exact mode by which that command was given; but whatever that mode may have been, the patriarch did not doubt its authenticity. Add to this consideration, that, for aught we know to the contrary, the practice of offering human sacrifices existed as early as the time of Abraham, and had been practiced by idolatrous nations around him ; and nothing had yet been made known to him, by which he could be sure that they were not to be a part of the worship of the true God. With some degree of familiarity with human sacrificing on the part of others, therefore; and having the fullest assurance of a divine command, we can the more readily yield assent to the historical fact here recorded, however unnatural it may seem to us, aside from these circumstances. Add to this, the reason given by Paul, that Abraham expected that Isaac would be raised from the dead — an expectation he had every reason for entertaining, since it was through Isaac, that the patriarch was to become the father of many nations — and the verity of the transaction becomes still more obvious. Make one more addition. The world needed precisely such an event to fix the seal of God's displeasure upon human sacrifices, and forever exclude them from his worship. And the effect is seen in the remarkable fact, that, while no other nation has been without such sacrifices, they have never been a part of the worship sanctioned by divine revelation.

SECTION XIX. — NAHOR.

CHAP. XXII.

20. ¶ And it came to pass after these things, that it was told Abraham, saying, Behold, Milcah, she hath also borne children unto thy brother Nahor:

21. Huz his firstborn, and Buz his brother, and Kemuel the father of Aram,

22. And Chesed, and Hazo, and Pildash, and Jidlaph, and Bethuel.

23. And Bethuel begat Rebekah: these eight Milcah did bear to Nahor, Abraham's brother.

24. And his concubine, whose name *was* Reumah, she bare also Tebah, and Gaham, and Thahash, and Maachah.

509. Aram, grandson of Nahor, evidently gave name to the country where Nahor resided, called Padan Aram; and the people are called Arameans, rendered in our translation Syrians. Even Nahor is called an Aramean or Syrian, though the name was derived from his grandson.

Bethuel begat Rebekah who afterwards became the wife of Isaac.

Nahor, it appears, had a concubine as well as his brother Abraham, though no reason for this is given, as is done in the other instance.

SECTION XX.— Death and Burial of Sarah.

CHAP. XXIII.

1. And Sarah was a hundred and seven and twenty years old: *these were* the years of the life of Sarah.
2. And Sarah died in Kirjath-arba; the same *is* Hebron in the land of Canaan: and Abraham came to mourn for Sarah, and to weep for her.
3. ¶ And Abraham stood up from before his dead, and spake unto the sons of Heth, saying,
4. I *am* a stranger and a sojourner with you: give me a possession of a burying-place with you, that I may bury my dead out of my sight.
5. And the children of Heth answered Abraham, saying unto him,
6. Hear us, my lord: thou *art* a mighty prince among us: in the choice of our sepulchres bury thy dead; none of us shall withhold from thee his sepulchre, but that thou mayest bury thy dead.
7. And Abraham stood up, and bowed himself to the people of the land, *even* to the children of Heth.
8. And he communed with them, saying, If it be your mind that I should bury my dead out of my sight; hear me, and entreat for me to Ephron the son of Zohar.
9. That he may give me the cave of Machpelah, which he hath, which *is* in the end of his field: for as much money as it is worth he shall give it me for a possession of a burying-place among you.
10. And Ephron dwelt among the children of Heth: and Ephron the Hittite answered Abraham in the audience of the children of Heth, *even* of all that went in at the gate of his city, saying,
11. Nay, my lord, hear me: the field give I thee, and the cave that *is* therein, I give it thee; in the presence of the sons of my people give I it thee: bury thy dead.
12. And Abraham bowed down himself before the people of the land.
13. And he spake unto Ephron in the audience of the people of the land, saying, But if thou *wilt give it*, I pray thee, hear me; I will give thee money for the field; take *it* of me, and I will bury my dead there.
14. And Ephron answered Abraham, saying unto him,
15. My lord, hearken unto me; the land *is worth* four hundred shekels of silver; what *is* that betwixt me and thee? bury therefore thy dead.
16 And Abraham hearkened unto Ephron; and Abraham weighed to Ephron the silver, which he had named in the audience of the sons of Heth, four hundred shekels of silver, current *money* with the merchant.
17. And the field of Ephron, which *was* in Machpelah, which *was* before Mamre, the field, and the cave which *was* therein, and all the trees that *were* in the field, that *were* in all the borders round about, were made sure
18. Unto Abraham for a possession in the presence of the children of Heth, before all that went in at the gate of his city.
19. ¶ And after this, Abraham buried Sarah his wife in the cave of the field of Machpelah before Mamre: the same *is* Hebron in the land of Canaan.
20. And the field, and the cave that *is* therein, were made sure unto Abraham for a possession of a burying-place by the sons of Heth.

510. It seems that Mamre, Hebron, and Kirjath-arba, were different names of the same place. Abraham is called a stranger and a sojourner in the land, though he had been in Canaan more than fifty years. The language is used comparatively. The sons of Heth had been there much longer, and were indeed the original settlers of the country. It is further evident that the land did not belong to the patriarch or his posterity, and became his afterwards, by gift from God, who has a rightful claim to the whole earth.

511. The generous conduct of the sons of Heth, and of Ephron in particular, is worthy of special notice. And the truthfulness of the narrative is made obvious by this and other examples, where the generous virtues of others that were not of the tribe of Abraham, are freely recorded. To the same effect are the recorded instances of the faults of the patriarchs, with no excuse or palliation.

512. The unwillingness of Abraham to receive the field of Machpelah as a gift may be interpreted as showing a desire to keep himself, as much as possible, separate and distinct from the people of the land, who, he plainly foresaw, as indicated to him by the divine assurance that their land would be his, would become his enemies. His unwillingness to be in any way allied to the people of the land, as shown in several instances, may be referred, in part if not altogether, to the same cause.

For many of the allusions in this passage, viz., Real Estate possessions, Money, Mode of burials, &c , See Archæology.

SECTION XXI.—A WIFE PROCURED FOR ISAAC.

CHAP. XXIV.

1. And Abraham was old, *and* well stricken in age: and the LORD had blessed Abraham in all things.
2. And Abraham said unto his eldest servant of his house, that ruled over all that he had, Put, I pray thee, thy hand under my thigh:
3. And I will make thee swear by the LORD, the God of heaven, and the God of the earth, that thou shalt not take a wife unto my son of the daughters of the Canaanites, among whom I dwell:
4. But thou shalt go unto my country, and to my kindred, and take a wife unto my son Isaac.
5. And the servant said unto him, Peradventure the woman will not be willing to follow me unto this land: must I needs bring thy son again unto the land from whence thou camest?
6. And Abraham said unto him, Beware thou that thou bring not my son thither again.
7. The LORD God of heaven, which took me from my father's house, and from the land of my kindred, and which spake unto me, and that sware unto me, saying, Unto thy seed will I give this land; he shall send his angel before thee, and thou shalt take a wife unto my son from thence.
8. And if the woman will not be willing to follow thee, then thou shalt be clear from this my oath: only bring not my son thither again.
9. And the servant put his hand under the thigh of Abraham his master, and sware to him concerning that matter.
10. ¶ And the servant took ten camels of the camels of his master, and departed; for all the goods of his master *were* in his hand: and he arose, and went to Mesopotamia, unto the city of Nahor.
11. And he made his camels to kneel down without the city by a well of water at the time of the evening, *even* the time that women go out to draw *water*.
12. And he said, O LORD God of my master Abraham, I pray thee, send me good speed this day, and shew kindness unto my master Abraham.
13. Behold, I stand *here* by the well of water; and the daughters of the men of the city come out to draw water:
14. And let it come to pass, that the damsel to whom I shall say, Let down thy pitcher, I pray thee, that I may drink; and she shall say, Drink, and I will give thy camels drink also: *let the same be* she *that* thou hast appointed for thy servant Isaac; and thereby shall I know that thou hast shewed kindness unto my master.
15. ¶ And it came to pass, before he had done speaking, that, behold, Rebekah came out, who was born to Bethuel, son of Milcah, the wife of Nahor, Abraham's brother, with her pitcher upon her shoulder.
16. And the damsel *was* very fair to look upon, a virgin; neither had any man known her: and she went down to the well, and filled her pitcher, and came up.
17. And the servant ran to meet her, and said, Let me, I pray thee, drink a little water of thy pitcher.
18. And she said, Drink, my lord: and she hasted, and let down her pitcher upon her hand, and gave him drink.
19. And when she had done giving him drink, she said, I will draw *water* for thy camels also, until they have done drinking.
20. And she hasted, and emptied her pitcher into the trough, and ran again unto the well to draw

water, and drew for all his camels.

21. And the man wondering at her held his peace, to wit whether the Lord had made his journey prosperous or not.

22. And it came to pass, as the camels had done drinking, that the man took a golden earring of half a shekel weight, and two bracelets for her hands of ten *shekels* weight of gold;

23. And said, Whose daughter *art* thou? tell me, I pray thee: is there room *in* thy father's house for us to lodge in?

24. And she said unto him, I *am* the daughter of Bethuel the son of Milcah, which she bare unto Nahor.

25. She said moreover unto him, We have both straw and provender enough, and room to lodge in.

26. And the man bowed down his head, and worshipped the Lord.

27. And he said, Blessed *be* the Lord God of my master Abraham, who hath not left destitute my master of his mercy and his truth: I *being* in the way, the Lord led me to the house of my master's brethren.

28. And the damsel ran, and told *them of* her mother's house these things.

29. ¶ And Rebekah had a brother, and his name *was* Laban: and Laban ran out unto the man, unto the well.

30. And it came to pass, when he saw the earring, and bracelets upon his sister's hands, and when he heard the words of Rebekah his sister, saying, Thus spake the man unto me; that he came unto the man, and behold, he stood by the camels at the well.

31. And he said, Come in, thou blessed of the Lord; wherefore standest thou without? for I have prepared the house, and room for the camels.

32. And the man came into the house: and he ungirded his camels, and gave straw and provender for the camels, and water to wash his feet, and the men's feet that *were* with him.

33. And there was set *meat* before him to eat: but he said, I will not eat, until I have told mine errand. And he said, Speak on.

34. And he said, I *am* Abraham's servant.

35. And the Lord hath blessed my master greatly, and he is become great: and he hath given him flocks, and herds, and silver, and gold, and men-servants, and maidservants, and camels, and asses.

36. And Sarah my master's wife bare a son to my master when she was old: and unto him hath he given all that he hath.

37. And my master made me swear, saying, Thou shalt not take a wife to my son of the daughters of the Canaanites, in whose land I dwell:

38. But thou shalt go unto my father's house, and to my kindred, and take a wife unto my son.

39. And I said unto my master, Peradventure the woman will not follow me.

40. And he said unto me, The Lord, before whom I walk, will send his angel with thee, and prosper thy way; and thou shalt take a wife for my son of my kindred, and of my father's house:

41. Then shalt thou be clear from *this* my oath, when thou comest to my kindred; and if they give not thee *one*, thou shalt be clear from my oath.

42. And I came this day unto the well, and said, O Lord God of my master Abraham, if now thou do prosper my way which I go:

43. Behold, I stand by the well of water; and it shall come to pass, that when the virgin cometh forth to draw *water*, and I say to her, Give me, I pray thee, a little water of thy pitcher to drink:

44. And she say to me, Both drink thou, and I will also draw for thy camels: *let* the same *be* the woman whom the Lord hath appointed out for my master's son.

45. And before I had done speaking in mine heart, behold, Rebekah came forth with her pitcher on her shoulder; and she went down unto the well, and drew *water:* and I said unto her, Let me drink, I pray thee.

46. And she made haste, and let down her pitcher from her *shoulder*, and said, Drink, and I will give thy camels drink also: so I drank, and she made the camels drink also.

47. And I asked her, and said, Whose daughter *art* thou? And she said, The daughter of Bethuel, Nahor's son, whom Milcah bare unto him: and I put the earring upon her face, and the bracelets upon her hands.

48. And I bowed down my head, and worshipped the LORD, and blessed the LORD God of my master Abraham, which had led me in the right way to take my master's brother's daughter unto his son.

49. And now if ye will deal kindly and truly with my master, tell me: and if not, tell me; that I may turn to the right hand, or to the left.

50. Then Laban and Bethuel answered and said, The thing proceedeth from the LORD: we cannot speak unto thee bad or good.

51. Behold, Rebekah *is* before thee, take *her*, and go, and let her be thy master's son's wife, as the LORD hath spoken.

52. And it came to pass, that, when Abraham's servant heard their words, he worshipped the LORD, *bowing himself* to the earth.

53. And the servant brought forth jewels of silver, and jewels of gold, and raiment, and gave *them* to Rebekah: he gave also to her brother and to her mother precious things.

54. ¶ And they did eat and drink, he and the men that *were* with him, and tarried all night; and they rose up in the morning, and he said, Send me away unto my master.

55. And her brother and her mother said, Let the damsel abide with us *a few* days, at the least ten; after that she shall go.

56. And he said unto them, Hinder me not, seeing the LORD hath prospered my way; send me away that I may go to my master.

57. And they said, We will call the damsel, and inquire at her mouth.

58. And they called Rebekah, and said unto her, Wilt thou go with this man? And she said I will go.

59. And they sent away Rebekah their sister, and her nurse, and Abraham's servant, and his men.

60. And they blessed Rebekah, and said unto her, Thou *art* our sister, be thou *the mother* of thousands of millions, and let thy seed possess the gate of those which hate them.

61. ¶ And Rebekah arose, and her damsels, and they rode upon the camels, and followed the man: and the servant took Rebekah, and went his way.

62. And Isaac came from the way of the well Lahairoi; for he dwelt in the south country.

63. And Isaac went out to meditate in the field at the eventide: and he lifted up his eyes, and saw, and behold, the camels *were* coming.

64. And Rebekah lifted up her eyes, and when she saw Isaac, she lighted off the camel.

65. For she *had* said unto the servant, What man *is* this that walketh in the field to meet us? And the servant *had* said, It *is* my master: therefore she took a vail, and covered herself.

66. And the servant told Isaac all things that he had done.

67. And Isaac brought her into his mother Sarah's tent, and took Rebekah, and she became his wife; and he loved her: and Isaac was comforted after his mother's *death*.

513. The important trust committed to the eldest servant of Abraham shows, both the position of servants in those days, and the confidence placed by Abraham in this one in particular. The whole narrative, laying before us the servant's mission, is related with great simplicity, and has every mark of truthfulness. It shows clearly a primitive state of society, when hospitality and simple honesty were the prevailing traits of human character. The mode of obtaining wives, here indicated, can the more readily be received as true, from its resemblance to what we know to have existed among other nations in their primitive state. The manner in which the servant's prayer was verified, is to be understood as a remarkable providence. It is evident from the circumstances that there were several damsels at the well, and the choice of one of them from the rest, was made by the servant himself; and his prayer was that he might select one suitable for the wife of Isaac. He made his choice, and it turned out to be a judicious and satisfactory one.

SECTION XXII.—Abraham's Second Marriage.
CHAP. XXV.

1. Then again Abraham took a wife, and her name was Keturah.
2. And she bare him Zimran, and Jokshan, and Medan, and Midian, and Ishbak, and Shuah.
3. And Jokshan begat Sheba, and Dedan. And the sons of Dedan were Asshurim, and Letushim, and Leummim.
4. And the sons of Midian; Ephah, and Epher, and Hanoch, and Abidah, and Eldaah. All these were the children of Keturah.
5. ¶ And Abraham gave all that he had unto Isaac.
6. But unto the sons of the concubines, which Abraham had, Abraham gave gifts, and sent them away from Isaac his son, (while he yet lived,) eastward, unto the east country.

514. It is worthy of notice that the sons of the second wife, were treated in the same manner, as the son of the concubine; and Isaac is made the sole heir to Abraham's estate. Thus the right of primogeniture receives the sanction of the patriarch. May we not add that it received the divine sanction long before, when the right to rule over his brother, was given to Cain, the first born son of Adam? We know that it subsequently became one of the patriarchal institutions.

SECTION XXIII.—DEATH OF ABRAHAM.

CHAP. XXV.

7. ¶ And these *are* the days of the years of Abraham's life which he lived, an hundred three score and fifteen years.

8. Then Abraham gave up the ghost, and died in a good old age, an old man, and full *of years;* and was gathered to his people.

9. And his sons Isaac and Ishmael buried him in the cave of Machpelah, in the field of Ephron the son of Zohar the Hittite, which *is* before Mamre;

10. The field which Abraham purchased of the sons of Heth: there was Abraham buried, and Sarah his wife.

11. And it came to pass after the death of Abraham, that God blessed his son Isaac; and Isaac dwelt by the well Lahairoi.

515. Abraham lived to be a hundred and seventy-five years old, and died thirty-eight years after the death of Sarah. Both were buried together in the cave of Machpelah near Hebron. Isaac and Ishmael, unlike as they were in their maternal parentage, and unlike as they were to be in the future history of their descendants; being both sons and no doubt affectionate sons of the patriarch, joined in the last tribute of respect to their departed parent.

516. That Abraham "was gathered to his people" at the time he died, we take to be evidence that a future life, and a re-union of friends there, were believed in by the ancient Hebrews.

517. It is worthy of remark that when Rebekah was brought to Isaac, he dwelt by the well La-hai-roi, which is said to be in the south country, xxiv. 62, xxv. 11. Observe that the well near which Hagar was found, the first time she left her mistress, was called Beer-lahai-roi, xvi. 14. It is said further, that she was found in the wilderness, in the way of Shur, xvi. 7. It is said, too, of the children of Ishmael, that they dwelt from Havilah to Shur. All these statements together, show that Ishmael and Isaac resided, at least for a time, not far apart, a circumstance that will show the reason why both were together at the burial of their father, at the same time that it indicates no unfriendly feeling between the two brothers.

SECTION XXIV. — Ishmael and his Family.

CHAP. XXV.

12. ¶ Now these *are* the generations of Ishmael, Abraham's son, whom Hagar the Egyptian, Sarah's handmaid, bare unto Abraham.

13. And these *are* the names of the sons of Ishmael, by their names, according to their generations; the first-born of Ishmael, Nebajoth; and Kedar, and Adbeel, and Mibsam,

14. And Mishma, and Dumah, and Massa,

15. Hadar, and Tema, Jetur, Naphish, and Kedemah:

16. These *are* the sons of Ishmael, and these *are* their names, by their towns, and by their castles; twelve princes according to their nations.

17. And these *are* the years of the life of Ishmael, an hundred and thirty and seven years: and he gave up the ghost, and died, and was gathered unto his people.

18. And they dwelt from Havilah unto Shur, that *is* before Egypt, as thou goest towards Assyria: *and* he died in the presence of all his brethren.

518. The name of Ishmael was given to him before his birth. The sons of Ishmael were twelve in number, as had been foretold; and they became very numerous and powerful as had been promised to Abram and to Hagar. Their dwelling was from Shur, before or near to Egypt, unto Havilah on the Assyrian route: and though we do not know the exact extent of the country here alluded to, we know, from the circumstances, that it was quite considerable. xvi. 11; xvii. 20; xvi. 10.

519. It was said of Ishmael, xvi. 12, " he shall dwell in the presence of all his brethren:" and now we are told that "he died in the presence of all his brethren"; the meaning of which is, that, though his hand was against every man, and every man's hand against him, he was too powerful to be overcome, both during his life and at the time of his death. It is generally believed that the Arabs are the descendants of Ishmael; and in them we find the character of their illustrious progenitor.

CHAPTER XIV.

ISAAC AND HIS FAMILY.

CONTENTS. — Birth of Esau and Jacob; Sale of Birthright; Sojourn in Gerar; Removal to Beersheba; Isaac's Blessing; Esau and Family; Sier.

The birth of Isaac, his being offered in sacrifice, the procuring for him a wife, &c., have all been recorded and commented upon in that part of the book that relates to Abram and his family. The narrative proceeds as follows :—

SECTION I. — BIRTH OF ESAU AND JACOB.

CHAP. XXV.

19. ¶ And these *are* the generations of Isaac, Abraham's son: Abraham begat Isaac:
20. And Isaac was forty years old when he took Rebekah to wife, the daughter of Bethuel the Syrian of Padan-aram, the sister to Laban the Syrian.
21. ¶ And Isaac entreated the LORD for his wife, because she *was* barren: and the LORD was entreated of him, and Rebekah his wife conceived.
22. And the children struggled together within her; and she said, If *it be* so, why *am* I thus? And she went to inquire of the LORD.
23. And the LORD said unto her, Two nations *are* in thy womb, and two manner of people shall be separated from thy bowels; and *the one* people shall be stronger than *the other* people; and the elder shall serve the younger.
24. And when her days to be delivered were fulfilled, behold, *there were* twins in her womb.
25. And the first came out red, all over like an hairy garment; and they called his name Esau.
26. And after that came his brother out, and his hand took hold on Esau's heel; and his name was called Jacob: and Isaac *was* threescore years old, when she bare them.

520. The cause of the difference, at their birth, between Esau and Jacob, is not given, nor can it be inferred from the circumstances. The fact, however, may be made instructive as illustrating a principle that may help us to account for other differences among men that have come up since that time. Indeed many of the peculiarities by which different branches of the human race, are distinguished, may have had the same origin. There is no doubt that great diversities among men have originated

in this way; and when once started, there is a strong tendency to permanency, though nature may at last resume her accustomed course.

SECTION II. — Esau Sells his Birthright.

CHAP. XXV.

27. And the boys grew: and Esau was a cunning hunter, a man of the field; and Jacob was a plain man, dwelling in tents.
28. And Isaac loved Esau, because he did eat of *his* venison; but Rebekah loved Jacob.
29. ¶ And Jacob sod pottage; and Esau came from the field, and he *was* faint.
30. And Esau said to Jacob, Feed me, I pray thee, with that same red *pottage;* for I *am* faint: therefore was his name called Edom.
31. And Jacob said, Sell me this day thy birth-right.
32. And Esau said, Behold, I *am* at the point to die, and what profit shall this birth-right do to me?
33. And Jacob said, Swear to me this day; and he sware unto him; and he sold his birth-right unto Jacob.
34. Then Jacob gave Esau bread and pottage of lentiles, and he did eat and drink, and rose up, and went his way. Thus Esau despised *his* birth-right.

521. This transaction has been made to reflect very unfavorably upon the conduct of Jacob. He should not, it is said, have taken advantage of his brother's necessities, so as to procure a valuable object to which he was not otherwise entitled. But the narrative plainly implies that Esau did not regard the birthright as a valuable possession. The language "he despised his birthright," evidently conveys this idea. It does not appear that Jacob refused his brother food, nor that Esau must have perished if Jacob had not supplied his wants. If this were so, then the language, "he despised his birthright," is out of place. A man does not give evidence of despising a thing, or placing a small value upon it, when he parts with it to save his life. The intention of the passage is to show that Esau regarded the birthright as of little value, and therefore parted with it for a small consideration. Jacob, however, thought differently : and surely there was no wrong in receiving from his brother, what the latter deemed of little consequence.

522. It may be well to ask here what value there really was in the birthright?

It appears from what is said of Cain and Abel, that one privilege enjoyed by the first-born, was that of pre-eminence over the rest of the family. Cain was to rule over his brother. The conduct of Abraham would lead us to infer that the first-born was heir to the estate of his father, while others only received gifts and were sent away. xxv. 6. From other references that will be considered hereafter, it becomes obvious that the dying blessing of the patriarch, upon the first-born, was expected to be fraught with greater good, than upon the other children. Esau seems to make a distinction between the blessing and the birthright, xxvii, 36; but this may have been only a pretence, and intended to justify himself, in seeking to appropriate to himself what he had parted with, and what he now could not justly claim.

SECTION III.—Isaac's Sojourn in Gerar.

CHAP. XXVI.

1. And there was a famine in the land, besides the first famine that was in the days of Abraham. And Isaac went unto Abimelech king of the Philistines unto Gerar.

2. And the LORD appeared unto him, and said, Go not down into Egypt; dwell in the land which I shall tell thee of:

3. Sojourn in this land, and I will be with thee, and will bless thee; for unto thee, and unto thy seed, I will give all these countries, and I will perform the oath which I sware unto Abraham thy father;

4. And I will make thy seed to multiply as the stars of heaven, and will give unto thy seed all these countries; and in thy seed shall all the nations of the earth be blessed;

5. Because that Abraham obeyed my voice, and kept my charge, my commandments, my statutes, and my laws.

6. ¶ And Isaac dwelt in Gerar:

7. And the men of the place asked *him* of his wife; and he said, She *is* my sister: for he feared to say, *She is* my wife; lest, *said he*, the men of the place should kill me for Rebekah; because she *was* fair to look upon.

8. And it came to pass, when he had been there a long time, that Abimelech king of the Philistines looked out at a window, and saw, and behold, Isaac *was* sporting with Rebekah his wife.

9. And Abimelech called Isaac, and said, Behold, of a surety she *is* thy wife: and how saidst thou, She *is* my sister? And Isaac said unto him, Because I said, Lest I die for her.

10. And Abimelech said, What *is* this thou hast done unto us? one of the people might lightly have lain with thy wife, and thou shouldest have brought guiltiness upon us.

11. And Abimelech charged all *his* people, saying, He that toucheth this man or his wife shall surely be put to death.

12. Then Isaac sowed in that land, and received in the same year a hundredfold: and the LORD blessed him.

13. And the man waxed great, and went forward, and grew until he became very great:
14. For he had possession of flocks, and possession of herds, and great store of servants: and the Philistines envied him.
15. For all the wells which his father's servants had digged in the days of Abraham his father, the Philistines had stopped them, and filled them with earth.
16. And Abimelech said unto Isaac, Go from us; for thou art much mightier than we.
17. And Isaac departed thence, and pitched his tent in the valley of Gerar, and dwelt there.
18. And Isaac digged again the wells of water, which they had digged in the days of Abraham his father; for the Philistines had stopped them after the death of Abraham: and he called their names after the names by which his father had called them.
19. And Isaac's servants digged in the valley, and found there a well of springing water.
20. And the herdmen of Gerar did strive with Isaac's herdmen, saying, The water *is* ours: and he called the name of the well Esek; because they strove with him.
21. And they digged another well, and strove for that also: and he called the name of it Sitnah.
22. And he removed from thence, and digged another well; and for that they strove not: and he called the name of it Rehoboth; and he said, For now the LORD hath made room for us, and we shall be fruitful in the land.

523. The narrative seems to imply an intention on the part of Isaac to go down to Egypt, as he expected he could there alone receive supplies during the famine: but a divine vision detained him in Gerar, a city of the Philistines. The Abimelech here mentioned may have been the one that entertained Abraham; but it is highly probable that another of the same name, perhaps a son of the former, is had in view. It is not improbable that this was a common designation of all the kings of that country, as Pharaoh was of Egypt, and Cæsar was of Rome.

524. It appears that the result of Abraham's deception, concerning his wife, did not deter his son from doing the same thing; and the result, with the latter, was no more fortunate than with the former. It is quite probable that there are no circumstances, when deception, for any purpose, can be justified. The narrative seems designed to show us how much better truth would have answered the purpose, in the case recorded, than falsehood; and if truth were better then, it is better now. Another purpose had in view by the narrator, may be to show, that, even among heathens, there is the consciousness of right, implanted in the heart by the Creator's hand.

525. Isaac went down to Gerar, and was expecting to go on to Egypt, on account of a famine; but being detained in Gerar by a divine command, his wants are soon supplied; for he sowed the ground that same year and received a hundred fold. verse 12.

The prosperity of the patriarch had, with the Philistines, its usual effect. They envied him. A further result was, that they sought to injure him by filling with earth the wells that Abraham had digged while residing in that land, and to which Isaac had a just claim. Isaac, therefore, by request of Abimelech, left that neighborhood, and dwelt in the "valley of Gerar," a place that must have been, from the circumstances, not far from his former residence.

526. It is worthy of notice, that what is said in verse 18th, properly belongs with verse 15th, and should have succeeded it. The wells that were filled up, and that were dug anew, were not in the valley of Gerar; but they were in the former locality, from which Isaac had now removed. Hence, it is added, that now Isaac's servants digged in the "valley," that is, the "valley of Gerar," his new residence. But envy follows the patriarch hither; and a strife arises about this well. Another is dug with the same result. Isaac now removes still farther away, and digs another, about which there is no strife. The names given to these wells are made to correspond with the circumstances; for Esek and Sitnah mean enmity and strife; and the last, which was not the occasion of contention, was called Rehoboth, signifying plenty of room.

SECTION IV.—Removal to Beersheba.

CHAP. XXVI.

23. ¶ And he went up from thence to Beersheba.

24. And the Lord appeared unto him the same night, and said, I am the God of Abraham thy father; fear not, for I am with thee, and will bless thee, and multiply thy seed for my servant Abraham's sake.

25. And he builded an altar there, and called upon the name of the Lord, and pitched his tent there: and there Isaac's servants digged a well.

26. ¶ Then Abimelech went to him from Gerar, and Ahuzzath one of his friends, and Phichol the chief captain of his army.

27. And Isaac said unto them, Wherefore come ye to me, seeing ye hate me, and have sent me away from you?

28. And they said, We saw certainly that the Lord was with thee: and we said, Let there be now an oath betwixt us, *even* betwixt us and thee, and let us make a covenant with thee;

29. That thou wilt do us no hurt, as we have not touched thee, and as we have done unto thee nothing but good, and have sent thee away in peace: thou *art* now the blessed of the Lord.

30. And he made them a feast, and they did eat and drink.

31. And they rose up betimes in the morning, and sware one to another: and Isaac sent them away, and they departed from him in peace.

32. And it came to pass the same day, that Isaac's servants came, and told him concerning the well which they had digged, and said unto him, We have found water.

33. And he called it Shebah: therefore the name of the city *is* Beersheba unto this day.

527. From the well Rehoboth, Isaac removes to another place, which was afterwards called Beersheba, though this removal does not seem, like the former, to have been occasioned by the hostility of the Philistine herdsmen. The circumstance that gave name to the place is here recorded, and recorded on this account, more than because it possessed any other importance. Abimelech, seeing the prosperity of Isaac, thought best to enter into an arrangement with him for mutual protection, to which the patriarch was not averse: and the oath that passed between them, gave name to a well that was being dug near the place. It was called Beersheba, or well of the oath; and from that the name was given to the surrounding country. The expression of Abimelech that he and his people "had done Isaac nothing but good and had sent him away in peace," must be referred to a former occasion and not to more recent occurrences.

SECTION V.—Isaac's Blessing.
CHAP. XXVII.

1. And it came to pass, that when Isaac was old, and his eyes were dim, so that he could not see, he called Esau his eldest son, and said unto him, My son: And he said unto him, Behold, *here am* I.

2. And he said, Behold now, I am old, I know not the day of my death:

3. Now therefore take, I pray thee, thy weapons, thy quiver and thy bow, and go out to the field, and take me *some* venison;

4. And make me savory meat, such as I love, and bring *it* to me, that I may eat; that my soul may bless thee before I die.

5. And Rebekah heard when Isaac spake to Esau his son. And Esau went to the field to hunt *for* venison, *and* to bring *it*.

6. ¶ And Rebekah spake unto Jacob her son, saying, Behold, I heard thy father speak unto Esau thy brother, saying,

7. Bring me venison, and make

me savory meat; that I may eat, and bless thee before the LORD before my death.

8. Now therefore, my son, obey my voice, according to that which I command thee:

9. Go now to the flock, and fetch me from thence two good kids of the goats; and I will make them savory meat for thy father, such as he loveth;

10. And thou shalt bring *it* to thy father, that he may eat, and that he may bless thee before his death.

11. And Jacob said to Rebekah his mother, Behold, Esau my brother *is* a hairy man, and I *am* a smooth man;

12. My father peradventure will feel me, and I shall seem to him as a deceiver; and I shall bring a curse upon me, and not a blessing.

13. And his mother said unto him, Upon me *be* thy curse, my son; only obey my voice, and go fetch me *them*.

14. And he went, and fetched, and brought *them* to his mother: and his mother made savory meat, such as his father loved.

15. And Rebekah took goodly raiment of her eldest son Esau, which *were* with her in the house, and put them upon Jacob her younger son:

16. And she put the skins of the kids of the goats upon his hands, and upon the smooth of his neck.

17. And she gave the savory meat and the bread, which she had prepared, into the hand of her son Jacob.

18. And he came unto his father, and said, My father: And he said, Here *am* I; who *art* thou, my son?

19. And Jacob said unto his father, I *am* Esau thy first-born; I have done according as thou badest me: arise, pray thee, sit and eat of my venison, that thy soul may bless me.

20. And Isaac said unto his son, How *is it* that thou hast found *it* so quickly, my son? And he said,

Because the LORD thy God brought *it* to me.

21. And Isaac said unto Jacob, Come near, I pray thee, that I may feel thee, my son, whether thou *be* my very son Esau or not.

22. And Jacob went near unto Isaac his father; and he felt him, and said, the voice *is* Jacob's voice, but the hands *are* the hands of Esau.

23. And he discerned him not, because his hands were hairy, as his brother Esau's hands: so he blessed him.

24. And he said, *Art* thou my very son Esau? And he said, I *am*.

25. And he said, Bring *it* near to me, and I will eat of my son's venison, that my soul may bless thee. And he brought *it* near to him, and he did eat: and he brought him wine, and he drank.

26. And his father Isaac said unto him; Come near now, and kiss me, my son.

27. And he came near, and kissed him: and he smelled the smell of his raiment, and blessed him, and said, See, the smell of my son *is* as the smell of a field which the LORD hath blessed:

28. Therefore God give thee of the dew of heaven, and the fatness of the earth, and plenty of corn and wine:

29. Let people serve thee, and nations bow down to thee: be lord over thy brethren, and let thy mother's sons bow down to thee: cursed *be* every one that curseth thee, and blessed *be* he that blesseth thee.

30. And it came to pass, as soon as Isaac had made an end of blessing Jacob, and Jacob was yet scarce gone out from the presence of Isaac his father, that Esau his brother came in from his hunting.

31. And he also had made savory meat, and brought it unto his father, and said unto his father, Let my father arise, and eat of

his son's venison, that thy soul may bless me.

32. And Isaac his father said unto him, Who *art* thou? And he said, I *am* thy son, thy firstborn, Esau.

33. And Isaac trembled very exceedingly, and said, Who? where is he that hath taken venison, and brought *it* me, and I have eaten of all before thou camest, and have blessed him? yea, *and* he shall be blessed.

34. And when Esau heard the words of his father, he cried with a great and exceeding bitter cry, and said unto his father, Bless me, *even* me also, O my father.

35. And he said, Thy brother came with subtility, and hath taken away thy blessing.

36. And he said, Is not he rightly named Jacob? for he hath supplanted me these two times: he took away my birthright; and behold, now he hath taken away my blessing. And he said, Hast thou not reserved a blessing for me?

37. And Isaac answered and said unto Esau, Behold, I have made him thy lord, and all his brethren have I given to him for servants; and with corn and wine have I sustained him: and what shall I do now unto thee, my son?

38. And Esau said unto his father, Hast thou but one blessing, my father? bless me, *even* me also, O my father. And Esau lifted up his voice, and wept.

39. And Isaac his father answered and said unto him, Behold, thy dwelling shall be the fatness of the earth, and of the dew of heaven from above:

40. And by thy sword shalt thou live, and shalt serve thy brother; and it shall come to pass when thou shalt have the dominion, that thou shalt break his yoke from off thy neck.

528. It is obvious, in the first place, that very great weight was attached to the dying blessing that a father might pronounce upon his sons. This will account for two things, in this narrative, that might not otherwise be so obviously rational. One is, the anxiety of Rebekah that her favorite son should receive the blessing : and the other is, the exceeding grief of Esau when he found himself supplanted. It will not do to interpret this matter by our impressions, at the present day : for if we do, we shall surely be misled. Nor is it necessary to attach all the importance to the subject that they attached to it. We may rationally suppose that it was with them a mere superstition. This does not alter the case, as bearing upon a true and just interpretation.

529. Another difficulty deserves some attention. We find it difficult to understand how Isaac could be imposed upon as he was : but to obviate this objection, we must consider, first, that all the care in preparing Jacob for deceiving his father, that time and circumstances would permit, would not fail to be exercised, in view of the great issues that were at stake. But in the next place, it is expressly said, that "Isaac was old and his eyes were dim, and he could not see;" and when it is considered that, in extreme old age, the hearing is apt to fail with the sight, we can the more easily understand how the deception could be made successful. The sight was wholly gone, the hearing was imperfect, and the feeling had been effectually guarded against. It appears from verse 27th, that Isaac was also misled by the odor of Jacob's garments; for it was only what he would expect of Esau, who, as he supposed, had just come from the field, and had prepared the wild meat for food. Indeed, this will illustrate a clause in that passage that might not otherwise be so well understood : — " The smell of my son is as the smell of a field which the Lord hath blessed." The smell of my son, is as the smell of one who has just returned from a prosperous hunt, and has been employed in preparing the game he has taken.

530. Again; we are not called upon to justify the course pursued by Rebekah or Jacob in this affair. No intimation is given in the book that the transaction was an innocent one. On the contrary Jacob felt that it was wrong and told his mother so. The only apology that occurs to us as in the least available, is, the one we have noticed in another place, viz., that the blessing sought for by Esau, was a part of the "birthright" which he had sold to Jacob, and which the latter could only obtain by stratagem. True, it had been announced to Rebekah that " the elder should serve the younger ;" but this did not excuse the deception. Doubtless her partiality for Jacob was the only motive by which she was influenced.

531. The nature of what is called a "blessing," in this passage, is a topic that ought to receive a few moment's attention. Was the blessing a divine impulse, indicating what would take place in the future, or was it a fervent prayer of the patriarch, indicating what he wished might take place? We take the latter view, and there are many other references that will sustain this opinion. When Isaac sent Jacob away from him, xxviii. 1, it is said that he blessed him, meaning obviously that he expressed his good wishes for his prosperity and happiness. So Laban, when about to part from his friends, xxxi. 55, kissed his
13

sons and his daughters and blessed them; in other words, he gave them his parting benediction; and it is not presumed that he was divinely inspired to utter this blessing. The blessing upon Rebekah, xxiv. 60, shows clearly the nature of this transaction. "They blessed Rebekah, and said unto her, Thou art our sister, Be thou the mother of thousands of millions; and let thy seed possess the gate of those which hate them." That this was a prediction, cannot well be supposed, as we have no evidence that those who uttered the language were divinely inspired. It was then simply an invocation; and the same, we infer, of the blessing upon Jacob and Esau.

532. When Isaac said, "Therefore, God give thee of the dew of heaven, and the fatness of the earth, and plenty of corn and wine," he simply desired that his son Jacob should be blessed with an abundance of the earth's productions. "Let people serve thee, and nations bow down to thee," was simply a desire that his son should be prospered in a national point of view. "Be lord over thy brethren, and let thy mother's sons bow down to thee," was due to the first born, by the usage of those ancient times; and Isaac, on the presumption that he was blessing the first born, assigns his son the customary position, and invests him with its appropriate rights and privileges. "Cursed be every one that curseth thee, and blessed be he that blesseth thee," is a form of speech justified by the usage of those times, and means no more than that his son should triumph over his enemies, and be a blessing to his friends.

533. The blessing upon Esau is similar to that upon Jacob, in some respects, and dissimilar in others. "Behold thy dwelling shall be the fatness of the earth, and the dew of heaven from above," is substantially the same as the blessing upon Jacob, having reference to the same subject.

. "And by thy sword shalt thou live," was a reasonable inference, from the character of the man of whom it is spoken, and did not require divine enlightenment to foresee, or at least to presume. "And shalt serve thy brother." This was due to the first born, and Jacob is now regarded as such, and Esau is required to yield to this demand. "And it shall come to pass, when thou shalt have dominion, that thou shalt break his yoke from off thy neck." It was due to Esau that he should be encouraged to look forward to the time when he should no longer be in subjection to his brother; and it was not a far-fetched inference, from the character of the two sons respectively, and from the circumstances in which they were placed, that the subserviency of Esau to Jacob would not always last.

It may be added that Isaac had divine authority for expecting substantially what he expresses in his blessing; for he had been divinely assured that Canaan, and all the adjacent countries, should be given to him, and his seed, and that his seed should be multiplied as the stars of heaven, and in his seed all nations should be blessed.

SECTION VI.—Esau and his Family.

CHAP. XXXVI.

1. Now these *are* the generations of Esau, who *is* Edom.

2. Esau took his wives of the daughters of Canaan; Adah the daughter of Elon the Hittite, and Aholibamah the daughter of Anah the daughter of Zibeon the Hivite;

3. And Bashemath Ishmael's daughter, sister of Nebajoth.

4. And Adah bare to Esau Eliphaz: and Bashemath bare Reuel;

5. And Aholibamah bare Jeush, and Jaalam, and Korah: these *are* the sons of Esau, which were born unto him in the land of Canaan.

6. ¶ And Esau took his wives, and his sons, and his daughters, and all the persons of his house, and his cattle, and all his beasts, and all his substance, which he had got in the land of Canaan; and went into the country from the face of his brother Jacob.

7. For their riches were more than that they might dwell together; and the land wherein they were strangers could not bear them, because of their cattle.

8. Thus dwelt Esau in mount Seir: Esau *is* Edom.

9. ¶ And these *are* the generations of Esau the father of the Edomites in mount Seir·

10. These *are* the names of Esau's sons; Eliphaz the son of Adah the wife of Esau, Reuel the son of Bashemath the wife of Esau.

11. And the sons of Eliphaz were Teman, Omar, Zepho, and Gatam, and Kenaz.

12. And Timna was concubine to Eliphaz, Esau's son; and she bare to Eliphaz, Amalek: these *were* the sons of Adah, Esau's wife.

13. And these *are* the sons of Reuel; Nahath, and Zerah, Shammah, and Mizzah: these were the sons of Bashemath, Esau's wife.

14. ¶ And these were the sons of Aholibamah, the daughter of Anah the daughter of Zibeon, Esau's wife: and she bare to Esau, Jeush, and Jaalam, and Korah.

15. ¶ These *were* dukes of the sons of Esau; the sons of Eliphaz, the firstborn *son* of Esau;

292   ISAAC AND HIS FAMILY.

duke Teman, duke Omar, duke Zepho, duke Kenaz,
16. Duke Korah, duke Gatam, and duke Amalek: these *are* the dukes *that came* of Eliphaz in the land of Edom; these *were* the sons of Adah.
17. ¶ And these *are* the sons of Reuel, Esau's son; duke Nahath, duke Zerah, duke Shammah, duke Mizzah: these *are* the dukes *that came* of Reuel in the land of Edom; these *are* the sons of Bashemath, Esau's wife.
18. ¶ And these *are* the sons of Aholibamah, Esau's wife; duke Jeush, duke Jaalam, duke Korah: these *were* the dukes *that came* of Aholibamah the daughter of Anah, Esau's wife.

19. These *are* the sons of Esau, who *is* Edom, and these *are* their dukes.

* * * *

40. And these *are* the names of the dukes *that came* of Esau, according to their families, after their places, by their names; duke Timnah, duke Alvah, duke Jetheth,
41. Duke Aholibamah, duke Elah, duke Pinon,
42. Duke Kenaz, duke Teman, duke Mibzar,
43. Duke Magdiel, duke Iram: these *be* the dukes of Edom, according to their habitations in the land of their possession: he *is* Esau the father of the Edomites.

534. The wives of Esau are spoken of in another place, but with some variations that may not be easily explained. The variations may be best understood by placing the passages side by side; and here may be a suitable place for noticing this subject:—

CHAP. XXVI.

34. ¶ And Esau was forty years old when he took to wife Judith the daughter of Beeri the Hittite, and Bashemath the daughter of Elon the Hittite:
35. Which were a grief of mind unto Isaac and to Rebekah.

CHAP. XXVIII.

9. Then went Esau unto Ishmael, and took unto the wives which he had, Mahalath the daughter of Ishmael, Abraham's son, the sister of Nebajoth, to be his wife.

CHAP. XXXVI.

1. Now these *are* the generations of Esau, who *is* Edom.
2. Esau took his wives of the daughters of Canaan; Adah the daughter of Elon the Hittite, and Aholibamah the daughter of Anah the daughter of Zibeon the Hivite;
3. And Bashemath Ishmael's daughter, sister of Nebajoth.

It would be easy to pass over the difficulty here seen, with the simple remark, which may or may not be true, that the writer has made a mistake, or that some careless copyist has committed a blunder; yet this is the last conclusion that a judicious critic will be willing to adopt.

535. The best solution we know of, is, that Esau had all the wives here mentioned:—
1. Judith, daughter of Beeri; 2. Bashemath, daughter of Elon; 3. Adah, another daughter of Elon; 4. Aholibamah, daughter of Anah; and 5. Bashemath, daughter of Ishmael. It is not at all unreasonable to suppose that Esau married two sisters, daughters of Elon, either at the same time or successively; nor is it a far fetched supposition, that he had two wives of the same name, one of them a daughter of Elon, and the other a daughter of Ishmael; nor again is it an extraordinary or unnatural supposition that one passage should name some of his wives and omit others. The wives last named, and not before, may not have been his wives, at the time to which the first passage relates; or when giving the genealogy of Esau, as in chapter xxxvi, those wives only would be named, who had children, while others that had none, would be omitted.

536. The removal of Esau from the land of Canaan, is an important circumstance, affecting the relation of the two brothers. It was a concession on the part of Esau, that the land of Canaan was more properly his brother's. And it is worthy of being considered whether this removal from Canaan, was not the fulfilment of the language of Isaac to Esau, xxvii. 40, and "it shall come to pass when thou shalt have dominion, that thou shalt break his yoke from off thy neck." Thou shalt escape from his dominion, and be no longer subject to his authority, which by a divine arrangement, belongs only to the land of Canaan. This removal by Esau, seems to be a final removal: for he had been at Mt. Seir before, and it was there that he seems to have been visited by Jacob, on his return from Padan-aram. It would appear from all the circumstances, that Esau had established himself at Mt. Seir, while Jacob was in Mesopotamia, and had acquired there large possessions. From that place he had made a visit to his brother, as the latter was returning from his sojourn with Laban; and in turn had been visited by Jacob, in his progress to Canaan. Still later, both brothers are found together with their aged father in Hebron; and by their united services, the old man is carried to his final resting place in Machpelah. It is then agreed that, as the possessions of both brothers are very great, and as the divine promise had designated Jacob for the possession and government of Canaan, Esau shall entirely leave that country and establish himself permanently at Mount Seir, where he had before had a temporary residence, and where he had married one or more of his wives. The passage now under consideration, relates to the carrying out of this plan, and the reason that induced it.

537. "Aholibamah, the daughter of Anah, the daughter of Zibeon." It is remarkable how many difficulties some men find in the Bible where there are none. And on the other hand, how exceedingly obtuse the vision of these men to any rational explanation of apparent difficulties when such explanation lies directly before their eyes. Here, says one, Anah is called the daughter of Zibeon; but in another place, in the same chapter, verse 24, the same Anah is called the *son* of Zibeon. The truth is, however, that, Anah is not called the daughter of Zibeon. The passage says that Aholibamah was daughter of Anah, daughter of Zibeon. It was Aholibamah that was daughter of Anah, and *also* daughter of Zibeon: that is, daughter of Anah, and grand-daughter of Zibeon; and as Anah was son of Zibeon, of course a daughter of the former, would be grand-daughter of the latter. I am not aware that grand-sons or grand-daughters are mentioned in the Bible, the words son and daughter expressing both relations. The examples of this usage are too abundant not to occur at once to the mind of the reader. In this same chapter, verse 12, the grand-sons of Adah, wife of Esau, are called her sons; and in verse 13, the grand-sons of Bashemath, another wife of Esau, are called her sons.

538. It will probably occur to the reader, as a very natural circumstance, that Esau, having before this, resided at Mt. Seir, should have formed connections with the people of that country; and having formed such connections, that he should finally make that his permanent residence, and at length succeed to the entire government of the country.

539. It is worthy of remark, that, as the sons of Seir, who had governed the country before it came into the

hands of Esau, are called dukes, the same name is applied to the sons and grand-sons of Esau. The former, however, were only seven in number, while the latter are fourteen, which may arise from the government being enlarged, so as to give each a province for his control ; or one portion of these dukes may have been the successors of the others.

540. For some reason, not apparent, another set of dukes is added, after tracing the lineage and government of Seir, eleven in number, and having some of the same names with the former ones. This passage has the appearance of a supplement, intended to supply some omissions ; and indeed this may have been its design. When the country was under the government of Seir and his family, it was first governed by dukes, who reigned conjointly, and afterwards by kings, who succeeded each other. But no mention is made of kings among the sons of Esau.

SECTION VII. — SEIR, KING OF EDOM.

CHAP. XXXVI.

20. ¶ These *are* the sons of Seir the Horite, who inhabited the land; Lotan, and Shobal, and Zibeon, and Anah,

21. And Dishon, and Ezer, and Dishan: these *are* the dukes of the Horites, the children of Seir in the land of Edom.

22. And the children of Lotan were Hori and Heman; and Lotan's sister *was* Timna.

23. And the children of Shobal *were* these; Alvan, and Manahath, and Ebal, Shepho, and Onam.

24. And these *are* the children of Zibeon; both Ajah, and Anah: this *was that* Anah that found the mules in the wilderness, as he fed the asses of Zibeon his father.

25. And the children of Anah *were* these; Dishon, and Aholibamah the daughter of Anah.

26. And these *are* the children of Dishon; Hemdan, and Eshban, and Ithran, and Cheran.

27. The children of Ezer *are* these; Bilhan, and Zaavan, and Akan.

28. The children of Dishan *are* these; Uz, and Aran.

29. These *are* the dukes *that came* of the Horites; duke Lotan, duke Shobal, duke Zibeon, duke Anah,

30. Duke Dishon, duke Ezer, duke Dishan: these *are* the dukes *that came* of Hori, among their dukes in the land of Seir.

31. ¶ And these *are* the kings that reigned in the land of Edom, before there reigned any king over the children of Israel.

32. And Bela the son of Beor reigned in Edom: and the name of his city *was* Dinhabah.

33. And Bela died, and Jobab the son of Zerah of Bozrah reigned in his stead.

34. And Jobab died, and Hush-

am of the land of Temani reigned in his stead.

35 And Husham died, and Hadad the son of Bedad, who smote Midian in the field of Moab, reigned in his stead: and the name of his city *was* Avith.

36. And Hadad died, and Samlah of Masrekah reigned in his stead.

37. And Samlah died, and Saul of Rehoboth *by* the river reigned in his stead.

38. And Saul died, and Baal-hanan the son of Achbor reigned in his stead.

39. And Baal-hanan the son of Achbor died, and Hadar reigned in his stead: and the name of his city *was* Pau; and his wife's name *was* Mehetabel, the daughter of Matred, the daughter of Mezahab.

541. The Seir here mentioned, held the land of Edom before it came into the possession of Esau and his descendants. He is called the Horite, though the name seems to have originated at a later day, and to have been derived from Hori his grand-son.

542. Anah that found the mules in the wilderness, is here associated with this circumstance, from some importance attached to it, that does not appear on the surface of the record. To find some stray mules in the wilderness, was a very small affair in itself; and unless there is something else understood by the writer, and presumed to be understood by the reader, we see no good reason for stating it. We would suggest whether the meaning is not, that this Anah *found out the way of raising mules*, as he fed or had charge of the *asses* of his father, in the wilderness. Such an invention is a circumstance worthy of notice, perhaps, while the other cannot be so regarded.

543. It will be observed that the immediate sons of Seir, are all called *dukes*. Each seems to have had a particular territory or province over which he exercised authority, not successively, but cotemporarily. At a subsequent period, the country was governed by kings, who reigned in succession, as is obvious from the language that one died and another reigned in his stead. It is farther obvious that the term of each reign was during life.

544. " These kings reigned in the land of Edom, before there reigned any king over the children of Israel." This passage is thought to be a gloss, and to have been inserted at a late day, when there were kings that reigned over the children of Israel; but I would suggest that another construction is possible; and the character of the passage renders it not improbable. Edom, the country here spoken of, was at first in the hands of one Seir and his family, whose sons had at first governed it conjointly; and afterwards it was governed by a succession of kings, from the same tribe. All this was before it came into the possession of Esau; and this is the fact the writer desires to inform us of. May not the passage, therefore, be construed thus:— These kings reigned in the land of Edom, before there reigned *there* any king over the children of Israel; meaning by the " children of Israel," the descendants of Esau; as that name, though strictly applicable only to the sons of Jacob, would be apt to be applied to all the descendants of Abraham. On the same principle, Nahor is called an Aramean, from his grand-son Aram; and Seir is called a Horite, from Hori, among his descendants.

545. Rehoboth by the River. There are several places called Rehoboth, mentioned in the book of Genesis; and hence some circumstance, to distinguish one from the other, had to be named. Rehoboth is the name of a city built by Asshur in Assyria, x. 11; and it is there called the *city* Rehoboth, to distinguish it, it may be, from the *well* Rehoboth, xxvi. 22, belonging to Isaac. The city Rehoboth in Edom, is said to be on the river, to distinguish it from the one in Assyria, or some other, not so located.

546. It is worthy of being added, that all the kings mentioned on this list, are spoken of, each in connection with a particular city, *with but one exception*. No city is named in connection with Baal-hanan; but he is called son of Achbor. Is not the meaning, that he was a citizen of Achbor, as *son* is often used in this sense. This would make the passages alike.

547. Why Mehetabel, wife of Hadar, is distinguished by being named in this connection, does not appear, though she was probably remarkable for some trait of character, or important transaction, that made her worthy of this distinction.

CHAPTER XV.

JACOB AND HIS FAMILY.

CONTENTS; — Jacob goes to Padan-aram; His Marriage; His Family; Contract with Laban; Leaves Laban; The Pursued; Interview at Mount Gilead; Prepares to meet Esau; Meeting of the Brothers; Sojourn at Shalem; Goes to Bethel; Returns to Isaac; Joseph sold into Egypt; Judah; Joseph Tempted; Dreams of the Butler and Baker; Pharaoh's Dreams; Joseph placed over the Land of Egypt; First Journey to Egypt; Second Journey; The Silver Cup; Joseph made known to his Brethren; Jacob sent for; Jacob goes to Egypt; Joseph meets his Father; Interview of the Brethren with Pharaoh; Interview of the Father with Pharaoh; The Famine; Israel about to die; He blesses the Sons of Joseph; Blesses his own Sons; Death of Jacob; Death of Joseph.

The birth of Jacob, and some other circumstances connected with his life, have been noticed in connection with the life of Isaac, as belonging more appropriately there. Other things belong more properly to the present chapter.

SECTION I. — JACOB GOES TO PADAN-ARAM.

CHAP. XXVII.

41. ¶ And Esau hated Jacob, because of the blessing wherewith his father blessed him: and Esau said in his heart, The days of mourning for my father are at hand, then will I slay my brother Jacob.
42. And these words of Esau her elder son were told to Rebekah. And she sent and called Jacob her younger son and said unto him, Behold, thy brother Esau, as touching thee, doth comfort himself, *purposing* to kill thee.
43. Now, therefore, my son, obey my voice: and arise, flee thou to Laban my brother, to Haran;

44. And tarry with him a few days, until thy brother's fury turn away;
45. Until thy brother's anger turn away from thee, and he forget *that* which thou hast done to him: then I will send and fetch thee from thence. Why should I be deprived also of you both in one day?
46. And Rebekah said to Isaac, I am weary of my life because of the daughters of Heth: if Jacob take a wife of the daughters of Heth, such as these *which are* of the daughters of the land, what good shall my life do me?

CHAP. XXVIII.

1. And Isaac called Jacob, and blessed him, and charged him, and said unto him, Thou shalt not take a wife of the daughters of Canaan.

2. Arise, go to Padan-aram, to the house of Bethuel thy mother's father, and take thee a wife from thence of the daughters of Laban, thy mother's brother.

3. And God Almighty bless thee, and make thee fruitful, and multiply thee, that thou mayest be a multitude of people;

4. And give thee the blessing of Abraham, to thee, and to thy seed with thee; that thou mayest inherit the land wherein thou art a stranger, which God gave unto Abram.

5. And Isaac sent away Jacob: and he went to Padan-aram, unto Laban, son of Bethuel the Syrian, the brother of Rebekah, Jacob and Esau's mother.

6. When Esau saw that Isaac had blessed Jacob, and sent him away to Padan-aram, to take him a wife from thence; and that, as he blessed him, he gave him a charge, saying, Thou shalt not take a wife of the daughters of Canaan;

7. And that Jacob obeyed his father and his mother, and was gone to Padan-aram;

8. And Esau seeing that the daughters of Canaan pleased not Isaac his father;

9. Then went Esau unto Ishmael, and took unto the wives which he had, Mahalath, the daughter of Ishmael, Abraham's son, the sister of Nebajoth to be his wife.

10. ¶ And Jacob went out from Beersheba, and went toward Haran.

11. And he lighted upon a certain place, and tarried there all night, because the sun was set: and he took of the stones of that place, and put *them for* his pillows, and lay down in that place to sleep.

12. And he dreamed, and, behold, a ladder set up on the earth, and the top of it reached to heaven: and, behold, the angels of God ascending and descending on it.

13. And, behold, the LORD stood above it, and said, I *am* the LORD God of Abraham thy father, and the God of Isaac: the land whereon thou liest, to thee will I give it, and to thy seed;

14. And thy seed shall be as the dust of the earth; and thou shalt spread abroad to the west, and to the east, and to the north, and to the south: and in thee, and in thy seed, shall all the families of the earth be blessed.

15. And, behold, I *am* with thee, and will keep thee in all *places* whither thou goest, and will bring thee again into this land: for I will not leave thee, until I have done *that* which I have spoken to thee of.

16. And Jacob awaked out of his sleep, and he said, Surely the LORD is in this place, and I knew *it* not.

17. And he was afraid, and said, how dreadful *is* this place: this *is* none other but the house of God, and this *is* the gate of heaven.

18. And Jacob rose up early in the morning, and took the stone that he had put *for* his pillows, and set it up *for* a pillar, and poured oil upon the top of it.

19. And he called the name of that place Bethel: but the name of that city *was called* Luz at the first.

20. And Jacob vowed a vow, saying, If God will be with me, and will keep me in this way that I go, and will give me bread to eat, and raiment to put on,

21. So that I come again to my father's house in peace; then shall the LORD be my God:

22. And this stone, which I have set *for* a pillar, shall be God's house: and of all that thou shalt give me I will surely give the tenth unto thee.

CHAP. XXIX.

1. Then Jacob went on his journey, and came into the land of the people of the east.
2. And he looked, and behold a well in the field, and lo, there *were* three flocks of sheep lying by it; for out of that well they watered the flocks: and a great stone *was* upon the well's mouth.
3. And thither were all the flocks gathered: and they rolled the stone from the well's mouth, and watered the sheep, and put the stone again upon the well's mouth in his place.
4. And Jacob said unto them, My brethren, whence *be* ye? And they said, Of Haran *are* we.
5. And he said unto them, Know ye Laban the son of Nahor? And they said, We know *him*.
6. And he said unto them, *Is* he well? And they said, *He is* well: and behold, Rachel his daughter cometh with the sheep.
7. And he said, Lo, *it is* yet high day, neither *is it* time that the cattle should be gathered together: water ye the sheep, and go *and* feed *them*.
8. And they said, We cannot, until all the flocks be gathered together, and *till* they roll the stone from the well's mouth; then we water the sheep.
9. And while he yet spake with them, Rachel came with her father's sheep: for she kept them.
10. And it came to pass, when Jacob saw Rachel the daughter of Laban his mother's brother, and the sheep of Laban his mother's brother, that Jacob went near, and rolled the stone from the well's mouth, and watered the flock of Laban his mother's brother.
11. And Jacob kissed Rachel, and lifted up his voice, and wept.
12. And Jacob told Rachel that he *was* her father's brother, and that he *was* Rebekah's son: and she ran and told her father.
13. And it came to pass, when Laban heard the tidings of Jacob his sister's son, that he ran to meet him, and embraced him, and kissed him and brought him to his house. And he told Laban all these things.
14. And Laban said to him, Surely thou *art* my bone and my flesh. And he abode with him the space of a month.

548. It does not appear that Isaac was informed as to the intention of Esau, to slay his brother. Rebekah does not seem to have desired to make known this circumstance to him. Hence the reason given him by Rebekah, for sending away Jacob, was her extreme unwillingness that he should marry among the people of Canaan. "Rebekah said to Isaac, I am weary of my life because of the daughters of Heth. If Jacob take a wife of the daughters of Heth, such as these which are the daughters of the land, what good shall my life do me." Isaac acted according to her wishes — he called his son Jacob to him, renews his blessing upon him, admonishes him not to take a wife of the daughters of Canaan, and sends him to Padan-aram, to select a wife from among his mother's relations. The reference made by Rebekah to the daughters of Heth, rather than to any other tribe of the land of

Canaan, was suggested, and is explained by the fact, that Esau had married into that tribe, and taken two of his wives therefrom. xxvi. 34.

549. The blessing pronounced on Jacob, on the occasion of his leaving, xxviii. 3, 4, contains a reference to the promise that had been made to Abraham. It was quite natural that a promise, so important, and coming from such a source, should be made known to Abraham's posterity, and should be regarded with special satisfaction by those who reckoned themselves as the subjects of its blessings.

550. A tribute is paid to the character of Esau, when it is said that, having discovered that Isaac was not pleased with his having married among the people of Canaan, he went and took another wife from the family of Ishmael. Indeed we shall find many things in the conduct of Esau, to admire, though he was not chosen to represent the family of Abraham.

551. It is worthy of being observed, that what Isaac had craved in his blessing upon Jacob, is now announced to Jacob himself by the divine Being; and the blessing of Abraham is declared to be his. xxviii. 10–15.

552. "Surely the Lord was in this place and I knew it not." That was truly an honest confession. The same mistake was common among the patriarchs. Abram had made that mistake, when he went down into Egypt; and from the apprehension that there was no God there, had felt himself called upon to guard against wrong and outrage by deception and fraud. Isaac had made the same mistake while he sojourned with the Philistines: and now Jacob labors under the impression, that, since he is far away from the sacred altar at Beersheba, he is therefore out of the reach of the divine presence. There was however a God in Egypt; and there was a God in the land of the Philistines: and the same was true of the country where Jacob reposed his head, for the night, upon a heap of stones, not daring, it may be, to ask the hospitality of the people of that (so regarded) godless land.

553. "This is none other but the house of God." The idea here conveyed, is, that this ladder reached up into the house of God, or the residence of the Almighty. The remark was probably a part of the dream; and it gave name to the place, for the meaning of Bethel is "house of God." It is quite probable that what is here called a city, was not such at the time when Jacob lodged there, but became a city at a later day. It was at first called Luz.

554. The promise of Jacob to give God the tenth of all he had, was suggested, perhaps, by the conduct of Abraham on a former occasion; xiv. 20; and may be the ground on which the system of tithes was instituted, at a subsequent period, among the children of Israel.

555. The meeting at the well, the friendly kiss, the hospitable reception, and all the circumstances recorded in the same connection, are the characteristics of that primitive age; and one is half inclined, while reading this narrative to wish himself away from what are called the refinements of civilized society, and among the honest and simple hearted people of those early days.

SECTION II.—JACOB'S MARRIAGE.

CHAP. XXIX.

15. And Laban said unto Jacob, Because thou *art* my brother, shouldest thou therefore serve me for nought? tell me, what *shall* thy wages *be*?

16. And Laban had two daughters: the name of the elder *was* Leah, and the name of the younger *was* Rachel.

17. Leah *was* tender-eyed; but Rachel was beautiful and well-favored.

18. And Jacob loved Rachel; and said, I will serve thee seven years for Rachel thy younger daughter.

19. And Laban said, It is better that I give her to thee, than that I should give her to another man: abide with me.

20. And Jacob served seven years for Rachel; and they seemed unto him *but* a few days, for the love he had to her.

21. ¶ And Jacob said unto Laban. Give *me* my wife, for my days are fulfilled, that I may go in unto her.

22. And Laban gathered together all the men of the place, and made a feast.

23. And it came to pass in the evening, that he took Leah his daughter, and brought her to him; and he went in unto her.

24. And Laban gave unto his daughter Leah, Zilpah his maid *for* an handmaid.

25. And it came to pass, that in the morning, behold, it *was* Leah: and he said to Laban, What *is* this thou hast done unto me? did not I serve with thee for Rachel? wherefore then hast thou beguilded me?

26. And Laban said, It must not be so done in our country, to give the younger before the first-born.

JACOB AND HIS FAMILY.

27. Fulfil her week, and we will give thee this also, for the service which thou shalt serve with me yet seven other years.
28. And Jacob did so, and fulfilled her week: and he gave him Rachel his daughter to wife also.
29. And Laban gave to Rachel his daughter, Bilhah his handmaid, to be her maid.
30. And he went in also unto Rachel, and he loved also Rachel more than Leah, and served with him yet seven other years.

556. The deception practiced upon Jacob by Laban, as a moral transaction, cannot be justified : and we are not called upon to justify it. The same remark applies to the deceptive practices of others alluded to in the book. If it be said that these things are not condemned in the narrative, we reply that the writer is a historian, and as such it was his business to give us facts, and not to moralize upon the transactions he records.

The social customs brought to view in this passage are treated of in the chapter on Archæology.

SECTION III. — JACOB'S FAMILY.

557. Jacob had four classes of children ; and the passages that relate to their birth, may be arranged with reference to this circumstance.

CHAP. XXIX.
CHILDREN OF LEAH.

31. ¶ And when the LORD saw that Leah *was* hated, he opened her womb: but Rachel *was* barren.
32. And Leah conceived, and bare a son, and she called his name Reuben: for she said, Surely the LORD hath looked upon my affliction; now therefore my husband will love me.
33. And she conceived again, and bare a son; and said, Because the LORD hath heard that I *was* hated, he hath therefore given me this *son* also: and she called his name Simeon.
34. And she conceived again, and bare a son, and said, Now this time will my husband be joined unto me, because I have borne him three sons: therefore was his name called Levi.

CHAP. XXX.
CHILDREN OF RACHEL.

22. ¶ And God remembered Rachel, and God hearkened to her, and opened her womb.
23. And she conceived, and bare a son; and said, God hath taken away my reproach:
24. And she called his name Joseph; and said, The LORD shall add to me another son.

JACOB AND HIS FAMILY.

Children of Leah.

35. And she conceived again, and bare a son: and she said, Now will I praise the LORD: therefore she called his name Judah; and left bearing.

CHAP. XXX.

14. ¶ And Reuben went in the days of wheat harvest, and found mandrakes in the field; and brought them unto his mother Leah. Then Rachel said to Leah, Give me, I pray thee, of thy son's mandrakes.

15. And she said unto her, *Is it* a small matter that thou hast taken my husband? and wouldest thou take away my son's mandrakes also? And Rachel said, Therefore he shall lie with thee to-night for thy son's mandrakes.

16. And Jacob came out of the field in the evening, and Leah went out to meet him, and said, Thou must come in unto me; for surely I have hired thee with my son's mandrakes. And he lay with her that night.

17. And God hearkened unto Leah, and she conceived, and bare Jacob the fifth son.

18. And Leah said, God hath given me my hire, because I have given my maiden to my husband: and she called his name Issachar.

19. And Leah conceived again, and bare Jacob the sixth son.

20. And Leah said, God hath endowed me *with* a good dowry; now will my husband dwell with me, because I have borne him six sons: and she called his name Zebulon.

21. And afterwards she bare a daughter, and called her name Dinah.

CHAP. XXXV.

Children of Rachel.

16. ¶ And they journeyed from Bethel, and there was but a little way to come to Ephrath; and Rachel travailed, and she had hard labor.

17. And it came to pass, when she was in hard labor, that the midwife said unto her, Fear not; thou shalt have this son also.

18. And it came to pass, as her soul was in departing, (for she died) that she called his name Ben-oni: but his father called him Benjamin.

558. That the Lord intended the fruitfulness of Leah to offset against the beauty of Rachel, as the writer represents, may be set down as one of his inferences: though the principle from which it is derived, is one of general application, so that the advantages of individuals are more evenly balanced than is commonly supposed. The conclusion of Leah that she bore children because

God *had heard* she was hated, is of the same character, as the one just noticed.

559. Several expressions contained in these passages, show how intense was the desire for offspring in those days, the more intense, perhaps, where they were most denied.

560. The mandrakes, we may infer, were regarded as medicine, and good for the infirmity to which the wives were both at times subject. With this view, the allusion to them is significant, and appropriate in this connection, though indicating a simplicity that we find it difficult to appreciate at the present day.

CHAP. XXX.

CHILDREN OF LEAH'S MAID.

9. When Leah saw that she had left bearing, she took Zilpah, her maid, and gave her Jacob to wife.

10. And Zilpah, Leah's maid, bare Jacob a son.

11. And Leah said, A troop cometh: and she called his name Gad.

12. And Zilpah, Leah's maid, bare Jacob a second son.

13. And Leah said, Happy am I, for the daughters will call me blessed: and she called his name Asshcr.

CHAP. XXX.

CHILDREN OF RACHEL'S MAID.

1. And when Rachel saw that she bare Jacob no children, Rachel envied her sister; and said unto Jacob, Give me children, or else I die.

2. And Jacob's anger was kindled against Rachel: and he said, *Am* I in God's stead, who hath withheld from thee the fruit of the womb?

3. And she said, Behold my maid Bilhah, go in unto her; and she shall bear upon my knees, that I may also have children by her.

4. And she gave him Bilhah her handmaid to wife: and Jacob went in unto her.

5. And Bilhah conceived, and bare Jacob a son.

6. And Rachel said, God hath judged me, and hath also heard my voice, and hath given me a son: therefore called she his name Dan.

7. And Bilhah, Rachel's maid, conceived again, and bare Jacob a second son.

8. And Rachel said, With great wrestlings have I wrestled with my sister, and I have prevailed: and she called his name Naphtali.

561. "She shall bear upon my knees" — she shall bear me children, to be tended upon my knees, is probably the true meaning.

The remark of Rachel that she would die if she had no children, may be regarded as a singular contrast to the actual result of having them. It often occurs that what we most desire, will end in our greatest injury.

562. All the names of Jacob's sons and daughters are significant, and were suggested by some circumstance connected with their birth. We give here the names and their definition, together with the remark of the mother suggesting it.

Names.	Definitions.	Remarks.
Reuben.	See a son.	Surely the Lord hath looked upon my affliction.
Simeon.	Hearing.	The Lord had heard that I was hated.
Levi.	Joined.	This time will my husband be joined unto me.
Judah.	Praise.	Now will I praise the Lord.
Dan.	Judge.	God hath judged me.
Naphtali.	Wrestling.	With great wrestling have I wrestled with my sister.
Gad.	A Troop.	A troop cometh.
Asher.	Blessed.	The daughters will call me blessed.
Issachar.	Wages.	God hath given me my hire.
Zebulon.	Dwelling.	Now will my husband dwell with me.
Joseph.	Adding.	The Lord shall add to me another son.
Benjamin.	Son of my right hand.	
Dinah.	Judgment.	

563. *Remark.* — Benjamin was at first called Ben-oni, son of my sorrow, for an obvious reason; but the reason for changing this to Benjamin is not so obvious. Dinah is called judgment, for a reason that does not appear. May be she was born about the time Dan was, a son of Rachel, and was named with a similar name: for Dan and Dinah differ in Hebrew, only that one has the masculine form, and the other the feminine.

564. The list of Jacob's children is repeated in another passage thus:—

CHAP. XXXV.

23. The sons of Leah: Reuben, Jacob's first born, and Simeon, and Levi, and Judah, and Issachar, and Zebulon.
24. The sons of Rachel: Joseph, and Benjamin:
25. And the sons of Bilhah, Rachel's handmaid: Dan, and Naphtali:
26. And the sons of Zilpah, Leah's handmaid: Gad, and Asher. These *are* the sons of Jacob, which were born to him in Padan-aram.

Benjamin was not born in Padan-aram or Mesopotamia, as the passage states; but the place and circumstances of his birth, having been just referred to by the writer, no one could be misled by his being associated with the others who *were* born in that country. Such discrepancies belong to all historical documents.

565. Another list, including Jacob's grand-children, as well as children, is found in another connection, and is given as follows:—

CHAP. XLVI.

8. ¶ And these *are* the names of the children of Israel, which came into Egypt: Jacob and his sons: Reuben, Jacob's first-born.

9. And the sons of Reuben; Hanoch, and Phallu, and Hezron, and Carmi.

10. ¶ And the sons of Simeon: Jemuel, and Jamin, and Ohad, and Jachin, and Zohar: and Shaul, the son of a Canaanitish woman.

11. ¶ And the sons of Levi: Gershon, Kohath, and Merari.

12. ¶ And the sons of Judah: Er, and Onan, Shelah, Pharez, and Zarah: but Er and Onan died in the land of Canaan. And the sons of Pharez were Hezron and Hamul.

13. ¶ And the sons of Issachar; Tola, and Phuvah, and Job, and Shimron.

14. ¶ And the sons of Zebulon; Sered, and Elon, and Jahleel.

15. These *be* the sons of Leah, which she bare unto Jacob in Padan-aram, with his daughter Dinah: all the souls of his sons and his daughters *were* thirty and three.

16. And the sons of Gad: Ziphion, and Haggi, Shuni and Ezbon, Eri, and Arodi, and Areli.

17. And the sons of Asher; Jimnah, and Ishuah, and Isui, and Beriah, and Serah their sister: And the sons of Beriah; Heber, and Malchil.

18. These *are* the sons of Zilpah, whom Laban gave to Leah his daughter: and these she bare unto Jacob, even sixteen souls.

19. The sons of Rachel, Jacob's wife; Joseph and Benjamin.

20. And unto Joseph, in the land of Egypt, were born Manasseh and Ephraim, which Asenath, the daughter of Poti-pherah priest of On, bare unto him.

21. And the sons of Benjamin *were* Belah, and Becher, and Ashbel, Gera, and Naaman, Ehi, and Rosh, Muppim, and Huppim, and Ard.

22. These *are* the sons of Rachel, which were born to Jacob; all the souls *were* fourteen.

23. And the sons of Dan; Hushim.

24. And the sons of Naphtali; Jahzeel, and Guni, and Jezer, and Shillem.

25. These *are* the sons of Bilhah, which Laban gave unto Rachel his daughter: and she bare these unto Jacob: all the souls *were* seven.

26. All the souls that came with Jacob into Egypt, which came out of his loins, besides Jacob's sons' wives, all the souls *were* threescore and six:

27. And the sons of Joseph, which, were born him in Egypt, *were* two souls; all the souls of the house of Jacob, which came into Egypt, *were* threescore and ten.

566. It will be seen that all the sons of Jacob had

children that are named on this list. Some of their grand-children are also mentioned.

567. It appears that some of the sons had wives, outside of the tribe to which they belonged. Shaul, one of the sons of Simeon, is spoken of as son of a Canaanitish woman. All the sons of Judah, too, as we learn from another passage, xxxviii. 2, were the fruit of a similar marriage. The wife of Joseph was daughter of Potipherah, priest of On, who from his position, must have been a man of eminence. Of course she was an Egyptian.

568. It will be regarded perhaps, as not a little remarkable, that so few daughters are found on this list. Jacob had but one, namely, Dinah. Asher, too, had one daughter, Serah. It is possible, however, that some others among these names were daughters, for I take it that the term "sons," in giving a family list, does not exclude this idea; and if this be admitted it will remove a difficulty in verse 15th, where the sons and daughters of Jacob by Leah and her handmaid, are spoken of, while apparently no daughters are mentioned but Dinah. I conclude that some of the names, among the grand-children, were daughters.

569. The number of 33 includes not only the children and grand-children of Leah, but Jacob the father, and two sons that died in Canaan, Er and Onan. The number 66 leaves out Er and Onan, and the two sons of Joseph born in Egypt; but it includes Jacob himself and Joseph.

570. It is remarkable that Benjamin the youngest had the largest number of children; but the Septuagint regards some of them as his grand-children. With either view, there seems a little difficulty. Just before this, Benjamin is spoken of as a mere lad, too young to be trusted from home. He is now the father of several children, and perhaps some grand-children. The probability is, that some of the persons named as his children were born *in* Egypt, and belong to a later period.

571. It will readily be seen that the nicest accuracy of language is not observed in making out this list. "These are the names of the children of Israel that came into Egypt. xlvi. 8;" but in giving the names, Israel himself, as well as his children, are included. Verse 7th mentions his sons and daughters, while the enumeration contains but one daughter. It is said they " came into Egypt," but two are mentioned on the list, and are necessary to make out the full number, that died in Canaan, and of course did not come into Egypt. " All the souls that came with Jacob into Egypt. . . . . were three score and six;" but this number includes Jacob himself, as well as those that came *with* him ; it also includes Joseph that came before and not *with* Jacob. The candid and honest reader will not be disposed to find fault with these trifling inaccuracies. It is only the captious that seek to use them against the truth of the Bible record.

SECTION IV.—Jacob's Contract with Laban.

CHAP. XXX.

25. ¶ And it came to pass, when Rachel had borne Joseph, that Jacob said unto Laban, Send me away, that I may go unto mine own place, and to my country.

26. Give *me* my wives and my children, for whom I have served thee, and let me go ; for thou knowest my service which I have done thee.

27. And Laban said unto him, I pray thee, if I have found favor in thine eyes, *tarry: for* I have learned by experience that the Lord hath blessed me for thy sake.

28. And he said, Appoint me thy wages, and I will give *it.*

29. And he said unto him, Thou knowest how I have served thee, and how thy cattle was with me.

39. For *it was* little which thou hadst before I came, and it is *now* increased unto a multitude; and the Lord hath blessed thee since my coming: and now when shall I provide for mine own house also ?

31. And he said, What shall I give thee ? And Jacob said, Thou shalt not give me any thing: if thou wilt do this thing for me, I will again feed *and* keep thy flock.

32. I will pass through all thy flock to day, removing from thence all the speckled and spotted cattle, and all the brown cattle among the sheep, and the spotted and speckled among the goats: and *of such* shall be my hire.

33. So shall my righteousness answer for me in time to come, when it shall come for my hire before thy face: every one that *is* not speckled and spotted among the goats, and brown among the sheep, that shall be counted stolen with me.

34. And Laban said, Behold, I would it might be according to thy word.

35. And he removed that day the he-goats that were ring-streaked and spotted, and all the she-goats that were speckled and spotted, *and* every one that had *some* white in it, and all the brown among the sheep, and gave *them* into the hand of his sons.

36. And he set three days' journey betwixt himself and Jacob: and Jacob fed the rest of Laban's flocks.

37. ¶ And Jacob took him rods of green poplar, and of the hazel and chestnut tree; and pilled white streaks in them, and made the

white appear which *was* in the rods.

38. And he set the rods which he had pilled before the flocks in the gutters in the watering troughs when the flocks came to drink, that they should conceive when they came to drink.

39. And the flocks conceived before the rods, and brought forth cattle ring-streaked, speckled, and spotted.

40. And Jacob did separate the lambs, and set the faces of the flocks toward the ring-streaked, and all the brown in the flock of Laban; and he put his own flocks by themselves, and put them not unto Laban's cattle.

41. And it came to pass, whensoever the stronger cattle did conceive, that Jacob laid the rods before the eyes of the cattle in the gutters, that they might conceive among the rods.

42. But when the cattle were feeble, he put *them* not in: so the feebler were Labans, and the stronger Jacob's.

43. And the man increased exceedingly, and had much cattle, and maid-servants, and men-servants, and camels, and asses.

572. That the mode adopted by Jacob to increase his flocks and herds, is possible, is, we believe, conceded. It is founded upon a principle in nature that is well known, however mysterious and inexplicable it may be. But here one suggestion, as to the credibility of this and similar wonders, may not be out of place. Suppose, then, we had never seen any such thing as is here described, is there any other marvel recorded in the Bible, that would have been more difficult to receive as true? We receive this record as credible, because it implies the action of a law with which we are acquainted. May not other wonders be as much the result of natural laws, though we may not be acquainted with them? We believe that all miracles are the result of law (if one prefers that term) as much as any other event.

573. The morality of the transaction is to be decided upon, as we would decide upon any other in similar circumstances.

SECTION V. — JACOB LEAVES LABAN.

CHAP. XXXI.

1. And he heard the words of Laban's sons, saying, Jacob hath taken away all that *was* our father's; and of *that* which *was* our father's hath he gotten all this glory.
2. And Jacob beheld the countenance of Laban, and behold, it *was* not toward him as before.
3. And the LORD said unto Jacob, Return unto the land of thy fathers, and to thy kindred; and I will be with thee.
4. And Jacob sent and called Rachel and Leah to the field unto his flock,
5. And said unto them, I see your father's countenance, that it *is* not toward me as before: but the God of my father hath been with me.
6. And ye know that with all my power I have served your father.
7. And your father hath deceived me, and changed my wages ten times; but God suffered him not to hurt me.
8. If he said thus, The speckled shall be thy wages; then all the cattle bare speckled: and if he said thus, The ring streaked shall be thy hire; then bare all the cattle ring-streaked.
9. Thus God hath taken away the cattle of your father, and given *them* to me.
10. And it came to pass at the time that the cattle conceived, that I lifted up mine eyes, and saw in a dream, and behold, the rams which leaped upon the cattle *were* ring-streaked, speckled and grizzled.
11. And the angel of God spake unto me in a dream, *saying*, Jacob: And I said here *am* I.
12. And he said, Lift up now thine eyes and see, all the rams which leap upon the cattle *are* ring-streaked, speckled, and grizzled: for I have seen all that Laban doeth unto thee.
13. I *am* the God of Beth-el, where thou anointedst the pillar, *and* where thou vowedst a vow unto me; now arise, get thee out from this land, and return unto the land of thy kindred.
14. And Rachel and Leah answered and said unto him, *Is there* yet any portion or inheritance for us in our father's house?
15. Are we not counted of him strangers? for he hath sold us, and hath quite devoured also our money.
16. For all the riches which God hath taken from our father, that *is* ours and our children's: now then, whatsoever God hath said unto thee do.
17. Then Jacob rose up, and set his sons and his wives upon camels:
18. And he carried away all his cattle, and all his goods which he had gotten, the cattle of his getting, which he had gotten in Padan-aram, for to go to Isaac his father in the land of Canaan.
19. And Laban went to shear his sheep: and Rachel had stolen the images that *were* her father's.
20. And Jacob stole away unawares to Laban the Syrian, in that he told him not that he fled.
21. So he fled with all that he had, and he rose up, and passed over the river, and set his face toward the mount Gilead.

574. There seem to have been some transactions, between Laban and Jacob, of which we have no account. There is a hint of this kind, in the remark of Jacob that Laban had changed his wages ten times; and also in that

of his wives " Is there yet any portion or inheritance for us in our father's house? Are we not counted by him strangers; for he hath sold us and hath quite devoured also our money?" The conduct of Jacob may receive some mitigation, from the injustice that had been practiced upon him by Laban. So the taking of the images on the part of Rachel, may have been regarded only as seeking restitution for what her father had unjustly taken from her. And, though one wrong does never justify another, yet we cannot look upon a wrong act, when done in self-defence, as we do when it is done without any such reason. And, if in those days deception and fraud were not regarded in the same light they are now, the fact is one of many illustrations, of what Christianity has done for the world.

575. It is well for us to remark here, as very plainly shown in the book of Genesis, by many examples that might be cited, and especially by what Jacob says in verse 9th, and his wives in verse 16th, that God is said to do many things that can be ascribed to him only indirectly. God took from Laban his flocks and gave them to Jacob, only by allowing Jacob to do it, by an expedient that cannot be excused by any strictly just and righteous principle.

576. The country of Laban is called Padan-aram. His residence was Haran. It is a coincidence worthy of note, that one of the grand-sons of Nahor was called Aram: and as it was customary in those days to name places from persons, there can be little doubt that Aram was named after Aram, son of Kemuel, son of Nahor, brother of Abraham. It was called Padan-aram or *Plain* of Aram, as that is the meaning of Padan. It should be farther observed, that, in the Hebrew, what the translators call Syrian, is Aramean, (evidently from the same Aram) though it is believed that both terms are equally appropriate for the country referred to.

577. The river, here referred to, is understood to be the river Euphrates, as that is often called by way of distinction *the river*. The passage of this river seems to have occurred more than once, before Jacob reached his destination, owing, we suppose, either to some bend in the river, or perhaps, to the meanderings of the accustomed route. Comp. xxxii. 16, 21; xxxiii. 3.

578. That Laban was an idolator, is obvious from the images that were stolen by Rachel, as these images are expressly called Laban's gods, in verse 30. See also xxxv. 2. The reason why Rachel stole them, may have been from an idolatrous veneration that she entertained for them, having been thus educated; or, what is more probable, from their value as composed of gold or silver. And if the last, the disposition made of them afterwards, and other valuables connected with them, may be regarded as an indication of Jacob's abhorence of idol worship, since he would not retain even the precious metal that composed them, but buried it under a tree.

SECTION VI. — The Pursuit.

CHAP. XXXI.

22. And it was told Laban on the third day, that Jacob was fled.
23. And he took his brethren with him, and pursued after him seven days' journey; and they overtook him in the mount Gilead.

24. And God came to Laban the Syrian in a dream by night, and said unto him, Take heed that thou speak not to Jacob either good or bad.

SECTION VII. — The Interview in Mount Gilead.

CHAP. XXXI.

25. ¶ Then Laban overtook Jacob. Now Jacob had pitched his tent in the mount: and Laban with his brethren pitched in the mount of Gilead.
26. And Laban said to Jacob, What hast thou done, that thou hast stolen away unawares to me, and carried away my daughters, as captives *taken* with the sword?

27. Wherefore didst thou flee away secretly, and steal away from me; and didst not tell me, that I might have sent thee away with mirth, and with songs, with tabret, and with harp?
28. And hast not suffered me to kiss my sons and my daughters? thou hast now done foolishly in *so* doing.

29. It is in the power of my hand to do you hurt; but the God of your father spake unto me yesternight, saying, Take thou heed that thou speak not to Jacob either good or bad.

30. And now, *though* thou wouldest needs be gone, because thou sore longedst after thy father's house, *yet* wherefore hast thou stolen my gods?

31. And Jacob answered and said to Laban, Because I was afraid: for I said, Peradventure thou wouldest take by force thy daughters from me.

32. With whomsoever thou findest thy gods, let him not live: before our brethren discern thou what *is* thine with me, and take *it* to thee. For Jacob knew not that Rachel had stolen them.

33. And Laban went into Jacob's tent, and into Leah's tent, and into the two maid-servants' tents; but he found *them* not. Then went he out of Leah's tent, and entered into Rachel's tent.

34. Now Rachel had taken the images, and put them in the camel's furniture, and sat upon them. And Laban searched all the tent, but found *them* not.

35. And she said to her father, Let it not displease my lord that I cannot rise up before thee; for the custom of women *is* upon me. And he searched, but found not the images.

36. ¶ And Jacob was wroth, and chode with Laban: and Jacob answered and said to Laban, What *is* my trespass? what *is* my sin, that thou hast so hotly pursued after me?

37. Whereas thou hast searched all my stuff, what hast thou found of all thy household stuff? set *it* here before my brethren, and thy brethren, that they may judge betwixt us both.

38. This twenty years *have* I *been* with thee; thy ewes, and thy she-goats have not cast their young, and the rams of thy flock have I not eaten.

39. That which was torn *of beasts* I brought not unto thee; I bare the loss of it; of my hand didst thou require it, *whether* stolen by day, or stolen by night.

40. *Thus* I was; in the day the drought consumed me, and the frost by night, and my sleep departed from mine eyes.

41. Thus have I been twenty years in thy house; I served thee fourteen years for thy two daughters, and six years for thy cattle: and thou hast changed my wages ten times.

42. Except the God of my father, the God of Abraham, and the Fear of Isaac, had been with me, surely thou hadst sent me away now empty. God hath seen my affliction, and the labor of my hands, and rebuked *thee* yesternight.

43. ¶ And Laban answered and said unto Jacob, *These* daughters *are* my daughters, and *these* children *are* my children, and *these* cattle *are* my cattle, and all that thou seest *is* mine: and what can I do this day unto these my daughters, or unto their children which they have borne?

44. Now therefore come thou, let us make a covenant, I and thou; and let it be for a witness between me and thee.

45. And Jacob took a stone, and set it up *for* a pillar.

46. And Jacob said unto his brethren, Gather stones: and they took stones, and made an heap; and they did eat there upon the heap.

47. And Laban called it Jegarsahadutha: but Jacob called it Galeed.

48. And Laban said, This heap *is* a witness between me and thee this day. Therefore was the name of it called Galeed;

49. And Mizpah; for he said, The LORD watch between me and thee, when we are absent one from another.

50. If thou shalt afflict my daughters, or if thou shalt take *other* wives besides my daughters, no

man *is* with us; see, God *is* witness betwixt me and thee.

51. And Laban said to Jacob, Behold this heap, and behold *this* pillar, which I have cast betwixt me and thee;

52. This heap *be* witness, and *this* pillar *be* witness, that I will not pass over this heap to thee, and that thou shalt not pass over this heap and this pillar unto me, for harm.

53. The God of Abraham, and the God of Nahor, the God of their father, judge betwixt us. And Jacob sware by the fear of his father Isaac.

54. Then Jacob offered sacrifice upon the mount, and called his brethren to eat bread: and they did eat bread, and tarried all night in the mount.

55. And early in the morning Laban rose up, and kissed his sons and his daughters, and blessed them: and Laban departed, and returned unto his place.

579. It is not unreasonable to suppose that what Laban says of his willingness to send away Jacob and his wives, was a mere pretence. It is much more reasonable to conclude that Jacob was right, in his apprehensions, that Laban would seek to retain his daughters, than that he would send them away "with mirth and with songs, with tabret and with harp."

580. It is plain from Jacob's protestations, that he was not conscious of having taken the least thing from Laban unjustly: and when Laban had made a thorough search and had found nothing, it was quite natural that Jacob should be angry, and show his displeasure by well merited reproaches. The fidelity with which he had attended to his duty, while with Laban, was no vain boast, as is evident from Laban's own acknowledgment. 30: 27. And the expedient made use of to increase his possessions, during his last engagement, was no more than an offset for the fraud Laban had practiced upon him, and the additional service of seven years, thereby obtained.

581. Jacob felt conscious of being specially under the Providence of the God of Abraham: and this consciousness, connected, as it was, with the "fear of Isaac," or the veneration he had for his father, had inspired him with a desire to act well his part, to guard against frauds sought to be practiced upon him, and to accumulate wealth by a prudent care of what was intrusted to his hands.

582. The meaning of Laban, in verse 43, is not quite obvious, unless it be this, which seems most probable:—

"These daughters are my daughters; and these children are mine, &c. I can have no interest in inflicting injury on them, while they retain this relation." There was a better way; and that he very wisely suggests in the next verse.

583. As soon as a covenant is proposed, Jacob proceeds to the usual ceremonies—he gathers a heap of stones, as a witness of the contract, and prepares a feast for the mutual gratification and pleasure of both parties. The heap of stones, Laban called Jegar-Sahadutha; but Jacob called it Galeed, both terms having substantially the same meaning; but the latter, being preferred, became the permanent name of the mount.

The place was also called Mizpah, or "watch tower," as if to indicate that there God would watch the movements of both parties, and take cognizance of any injustice that the one might do to the other.

584. The language of Laban:—"The God of Abram, the God of Nahor, the God of their father, judge betwixt us," is quite significant. Abram and Nahor are placed side by side, as the latter sustained the same relation to Laban that the former did to Jacob; and "their father," that is, the father of Abram and Nahor, was Terah. It may be added that the wives of Abram, Isaac and Jacob, could be traced to the same parentage in Terah.

SECTION VIII.—JACOB PREPARING TO MEET ESAU.

CHAP. XXXII.

1. And Jacob went on his way, and the angels of God met him.

2. And when Jacob saw them, he said, This is God's host: and he called the name of that place Mahanaim.

3. ¶ And Jacob sent messengers before him to Esau his brother, unto the land of Seir, the country of Edom.

4. And he commanded them, saying, Thus shall ye speak unto my lord Esau; Thy servant Jacob saith thus, I have sojourned with Laban, and stayed there until now:

5. And I have oxen, and asses, flocks, and men-servants, and women-servants: and I have sent to tell my lord, that I may find grace in thy sight.

6. ¶ And the messengers returned to Jacob, saying, We came to thy brother Esau, and also he cometh to meet thee, and four hundred men with him.

7. Then Jacob was greatly afraid and distressed: and he divided the people that *was* with him, and the flocks, and herds, and the camels, into two bands;

8. And said, If Esau come to the one company, and smite it, then the other company which is left shall escape.

9. ¶ And Jacob said, O God of my father Abraham, and God of my father Isaac, the LORD which saidst unto me, Return unto thy country, and to thy kindred, and I will deal well with thee:

10. I am not worthy of the least of all the mercies, and of all the truth, which thou hast shewed unto thy servant; for with my staff I passed over this Jordan; and now I am become two bands.

11. Deliver me, I pray thee, from the hand of my brother, from the hand of Esau: for I fear him, lest he should come and smite me, *and* the mother with the children.

12. And thou saidst, I will surely do thee good, and make thy seed as the sand of the sea, which cannot be numbered for multitude.

13. ¶ And he lodged there that same night; and took of that which came to his hand a present for Esau his brother;

14. Two hundred she-goats, and twenty he-goats, two hundred ewes, and twenty rams.

15. Thirty milch camels with their colts, forty kine, and ten bulls, twenty she-asses, and ten foals.

16. And he delivered *them* into the hand of his servants, every drove by themselves; and said unto his servants, Pass over before me, and put a space betwixt drove and drove.

17. And he commanded the foremost, saying, When Esau my brother meeteth thee, and asketh thee, saying, Whose *art* thou? and whither goest thou? and whose *are* these before thee?

18. Then thou shalt say, *They be* thy servant Jacob's; it *is* a present sent unto my lord Esau: and behold, also he *is* behind us.

19. And so commanded he the second, and the third, and all that followed the droves, saying, On this manner shall ye speak unto Esau, when ye find him.

20. And say ye moreover, Behold, thy servant Jacob *is* behind us. For he said, I will appease him with the present that goeth before me, and afterward I will see his face; peradventure he will accept of me.

21. So went the present over before him: and himself lodged that night in the company.

22. And he rose up that night, and took his two wives, and his two women-servants, and his eleven sons, and passed over the ford Jabbok.

23. And he took them, and sent them over the brook, and sent over that he had.

24. And Jacob was left alone; and there wrestled a man with him until the breaking of the day.

25. And when he saw that he prevailed not against him, he touched the hollow of his thigh; and the hollow of Jacob's thigh was out of joint as he wrestled with him.

26. And he said, Let me go, for the day breaketh. And he said, I will not let thee go, except thou bless me.

27. And he said unto him, What *is* thy name? And he said Jacob.

28. And he said, Thy name shall be called no more Jacob, but Israel: for as a prince hast thou power with God and with men, and hast prevailed.

29. And Jacob asked *him*, and said, Tell *me*, I pray thee, thy name. And he said, Wherefore *is* it *that* thou dost ask after my name! And he blessed him there.

30. And Jacob called the name of the place Peniel: for I have seen God face to face, and my life is preserved.

31. And as he passed over Penuel, the sun rose upon him, and he halted upon his thigh.

32. Therefore the children of

Israel eat not *of* the sinew which shrank, which *is* upon the hollow of the thigh, unto this day: because he touched the hollow of Jacob's thigh in the sinew that shrank.

585. The meeting of the angels of the Lord with Jacob, is an allusion to some dream or vision, that gave name to a place, on that route; and this is its only significance, so far as we can discover.

586. The tone and manner with which Jacob would have the messengers address Esau, may be attributed to his pacific disposition, or to his fears, or to both. There is nothing in the account we have of this patriarch, that can lead us to any other conclusion, than that he was a man of peace. The difficulty that had arisen between him and his brother, was not to be attributed to his fault, unless a too great fidelity to maternal authority was his fault. And now that he is about to return, and must pass through the region of country occupied by Esau, he shows his pacific disposition by sending him a friendly message.

587. The return of the messengers, announcing the approach of Esau, with four hundred men, creates considerable alarm, as the messengers seem to have presumed that he was coming with hostile intention; and Jacob, in doubt whether his brother would approach him in a friendly manner or otherwise, makes his arrangements to suit either emergency. Dividing his company into two bands, so that if one is attacked, the other may escape, he then selects from his flocks and herds a well assorted and liberal present, to be sent forward to his brother, with the hope of thus appeasing his wrath, in the meantime, offering an earnest prayer to God for his protection.

588. The present being prepared and divided into several droves, each being instructed to advance in regular order, it is then sent over the Jordan, with specific instructions, in what manner to address the approaching brother. Himself, with his wives and children, and whatever else he had with him, passed over the ford of Jabbok, a small stream emptying into the Jordan. That night was one of great excitement with Jacob. He wrestled with a man, and the wrestling was long continued; but in the end, as the morning approached, he was successful, and obtained a blessing from his antagonist. Was not this an answer to the prayer of the patriarch, and significant of the next days' experience? The passage is evidently a vision as indicated by several circumstances. It was in the night. Jacob saw God face to face. No man hath literally seen God at any time; but it was common in those ancient times for God to *appear* to men.

589. The place where this vision occurred, was called Peniel or Penuel, meaning the "face of God." We think, however, that verse 31, should be differently rendered. "As the divine presence, or face of God, passed away, the sun rose and he halted upon his thigh." The effect upon Jacob, for the time being, was the same as if the vision had been real.

590. The custom of not eating the sinew that shrank, we believe is nowhere else alluded to in the Bible, and is one that probably did not long continue among that people.

SECTION IX. — MEETING OF THE BROTHERS.

CHAP. XXXIII.

1. And Jacob lifted up his eyes, and looked, and behold, Esau came, and with him four hundred men. And he divided the children unto Leah, and unto Rachel, and unto the two handmaids.
2. And he put the handmaids and their children foremost, and Leah and her children after, and Rachel and Joseph hindermost.
3. And he passed over before them, and bowed himself to the ground seven times, and he came near to his brother.
4. And Esau ran to meet him, and embraced him, and fell on his neck, and kissed him: and they wept.
5. And he lifted up his eyes, and saw the women and the children; and said, Who *are* those with thee? And he said, The children which God hath graciously given thy servant.
6. Then the handmaidens came near, they and their children, and they bowed themselves.
7. And Leah also with her children came near, and bowed themselves: and after came Joseph near and Rachel, and they bowed themselves.
8. And he said, What *meanest* thou by all this drove which I met? And he said, *These are* to find grace in the sight of my lord.
9. And Esau said, I have enough, my brother: keep that thou hast unto thyself.
10. And Jacob said, Nay, I pray thee; if now I have found grace in thy sight, then receive my present at my hand: for therefore I have seen thy face, as though I had seen the face of God, and thou wast pleased with me.
11. Take, I pray thee, my blessing that is brought to thee; because

God hath dealt graciously with me, and because I have enough. And he urged him and he took *it*.

12. And he said, Let us take our journey, and let us go, and I will go before thee.

13. And he said unto him, My lord knoweth that the children *are* tender, and the flocks and herds with young *are* with me; and if men should overdrive them one day, all the flock will die.

14. Let my lord, I pray thee, pass over before his servant; and I will lead on softly, according as the cattle that goeth before me, and the children be able to endure, until I come unto my Lord, unto Seir.

15. And Esau said, Let me now leave with thee *some* of the folk that *are* with me. And he said, What needeth it? let me find grace in the sight of my Lord.

16. So Esau returned that day on his way unto Seir.

17. And Jacob journeyed to Succoth, and built him an house, and made booths for his cattle: therefore the name of the place is called Succoth.

591. The division of his company into different bands, had the same object in view with that before given, xxxii. 7, 8; the choicest being placed in the rear so as to have the best chance to escape, if Esau should show a hostile intention. Still, to conciliate his brother as much as possible, Jacob approaches him in the most respectful manner, according to the custom of that ancient time. We cannot doubt that he was happily disappointed when his brother approached, and in a most affectionate manner, embraced and kissed him. And indeed the whole conduct of Esau on that occasion, is fitted to give us a favorable view of his character. In how delicate and generous a manner does he decline the offer of a present from his brother, and accepts it at last only, when to have objected farther, might have been construed into a misconception of his kind feelings. His proposition to go forward, and lead the way to his home at Mt. Seir, was in harmony with his disposition as shown by other circumstances.

And when this proposition was declined by Jacob, on account of the slow progress he would be obliged to make, the additional proposition on the part of Esau, to leave some of his company as companions and guides, shows the great kindness that was felt by that brother.

592. The allusion to Succoth was simply to account for the name of that place. The name means "booths," and was taken from the fact that Jacob had made a temporary stop at that place, and had constructed booths for his cattle.

SECTION X.—SOJOURN AT SHALEM.

CHAP. XXXIII.

18. ¶ And Jacob came to Shalem, a city of Shechem, which is in the land of Canaan, when he came from Padan-aram; and pitched his tent before the city.

19. And he bought a parcel of a field where he had spread his tent, at the hand of the children of Hamor, Shechem's father, for an hundred pieces of money.

20. And he erected there an altar, and called it El-elohe-Israel.

CHAP. XXXIV.

1. And Dinah the daughter of Leah, which she bare unto Jacob, went out to see the daughters of the land.

2. And when Shechem the son of Hamor the Hivite, prince of the country, saw her, he took her, and lay with her, and defiled her.

3. And his soul clave unto Dinah the daughter of Jacob, and he loved the damsel, and spake kindly unto the damsel.

4. And Shechem spake unto his father Hamor, saying, Get me this damsel to wife.

5. And Jacob heard that he had defiled Dinah his daughter: (now his sons were with his cattle in the field: and Jacob held his peace until they were come.)

6. ¶ And Hamor the father of Shechem went out unto Jacob to commune with him.

7. And the sons of Jacob came out of the field when they heard it: and the men were grieved, and they were very wroth, because he had wrought folly in Israel in lying with Jacob's daughter; which thing ought not to be done.

8. And Hamor communed with them, saying, The soul of my son Shechem longeth for your daughter: I pray you give her him to wife.

9. And make ye marriages with us, and give your daughters unto us, and take our daughters unto you.

10. And ye shall dwell with us: and the land shall be before you; dwell and trade ye therein, and get you possessions therein.

11. And Shechem said unto her father and unto her brethren, Let me find grace in your eyes, and what ye shall say unto me I will give.

12. Ask me never so much dowry and gift, and I will give according as ye shall say unto me: but give me the damsel to wife.

13. And the sons of Jacob answered Shechem and Hamor his father deceitfully, and said, (because he had defiled Dinah their sister,)

14. And they said unto them, We cannot do this thing, to give our sister to one that is uncircumcised; for that were a reproach unto us:

15. But in this will we consent unto you: if ye will be as we be, that every male of you be circumcised;

16. Then will we give our daughters unto you, and we will take your daughters to us, and we will dwell with you, and we will become one people.

17. But if ye will not hearken unto us, to be circumcised; then will we take our daughter, and we will be gone.

18. And their words pleased Hamor, and Shechem, Hamor's son.

19. And the young man deferred

not to do the thing, because he had delight in Jacob's daughter; and he *was* more honorable than all the house of his father.

20. ¶ And Hamor and Shechem his son came unto the gate of their city, and communed with the men of their city saying,

21. These men *are* peaceable with us; therefore let them dwell in the land, and trade therein; for the land, behold, *it is* large enough for them: let us take their daughters to us for wives, and let us give them our daughters.

22. Only herein will the men consent unto us for to dwell with us, to be one people, if every male among us be circumcised, as they *are* circumcised.

23. *Shall* not their cattle and their substance and every beast of theirs *be* ours? only let us consent unto them, and they will dwell with us.

24. And unto Hamor and unto Shechem his son, hearkened all that went out of the gate of his city; and every male was circumcised, all that went out of the gate of his city.

25. ¶ And it came to pass on the third day, when they were sore, that two of the sons of Jacob, Simeon and Levi, Dinah's brethren, took each man his sword, and came upon the city boldly, and slew all the males.

26. And they slew Hamor and Shechem his son with the edge of the sword, and took Dinah out of Shechem's house, and went out.

27. The sons of Jacob came upon the slain, and spoiled the city, because they had defiled their sister.

28. They took their sheep, and their oxen, and their asses, and that which *was* in the city, and that which *was* in the field.

29. And all their wealth, and all their little ones, and their wives, took they captive, and spoiled all even all that *was* in the house.

30. And Jacob said to Simeon and Levi, Ye have troubled me to make me to stink among the inhabitants of the land, amongst the Canaanites and the Perizzites: and I *being* few in number, they shall gather themselves together against me, and slay me; and I shall be destroyed, I and my house.

31. And they said, Should he deal with our sister as with an harlot?

593. We got the impression from the preceding narrative, that Jacob would pass by Mount Seir, on his way to Canaan: but nothing being said of this, we suspect that he did not take that route. It may be, however, that Succoth was near to Seir, and that was the reason of the temporary stay at that place. It may be, too, that Seir was not on or near the regular route; and this circumstance will place the conduct of Esau in a still more favorable light; since it shows how much pains he took to declare his kind disposition to his brother by going a long way to meet him.

Our knowledge of localities, obtained only from the book of Genesis, (for it does not fall in with our plan to go beyond this book at present,) though much more accurate and extensive than would at first be supposed, must still be limited; and some questions of this sort must be left till we advance into the other books ; and even then we may not be able to solve them all with accuracy.

594. The hundred pieces of silver, paid by Jacob for the parcel of ground before the city, is, in the Greek version, a hundred *lambs*, which suits what we know to have been ancient usage, better than our translation. It may be added, however, that the expression " a hundred pieces of silver," need not be, of necessity, interpreted to mean that Jacob paid for the land in *silver* money ; but it may be understood as simply indicating the *value* of the consideration.

As an illustration, it is said of Abimelech, xx. 14, that he gave Abraham, " sheep and oxen and men servants and women servants ;" and it is afterwards said, with apparent reference to this same present, that he had given him " a thousand pieces of silver." The meaning of our version and that of the Greek is, therefore, substantially the same ; the hundred lambs of the one, being equal to the hundred pieces of silver in the other.

595. The circumstance of Dinah's misfortune, is mentioned by the writer, as a matter connected with the biography of the patriarch, and as the occasion of the treachery and cruel massacre enacted by his two oldest sons and brothers of Dinah, and the farther occasion of the malediction of these sons found in the last " blessing" of their dying father. That malediction would not be understood without a knowledge of the disposition and conduct that merited it ; and the latter required the occasion of their treachery and cruelty to be recorded, and the excuse they urged in its justification, to be distinctly stated.

596. The unwillingness of the sons of Jacob to be allied with the people of Canaan, was a natural result of circumstances ; and if it was not a true interpretation of a divine command, it was at least a correct deduction from the example of their fathers. This feeling, however, did not justify the treacherous conduct of the two sons of Jacob ; nor is it justified in the narrative, but clearly condemned.

597. The destruction of the whole city of Shalem by the two sons of Jacob, would seem incredible, except for the following circumstances: —

One is mentioned in the narrative. Another is, that *cities* in those days were only small towns, many of them containing only a few scores of inhabitants. Another, that Simeon and Levi are to be regarded as the *leaders* in the attack; while doubtless the servants of Jacob, and perhaps some of his other sons, were joined with them in the enterprise. It is quite common with all writers, in recording such enterprises, to name only the leaders, although it is presumed that they were assisted by others.

For social customs, see Archæology.

SECTION XI. — GOING TO BETHEL.

CHAP. XXXV.

1. And God said unto Jacob, Arise, go up to Bethel, and dwell there: and make there an altar unto God, that appeared unto thee when thou fleddest from the face of Esau thy brother.

2. Then Jacob said unto his household, and to all that *were* with him, Put away the strange gods that *are* among you, and be clean, and change your garments:

3. And let us arise, and go up to Bethel; and I will make there an altar unto God, who answered me in the day of my distress, and was with me in the way which I went.

4. And they gave unto Jacob all the strange gods which *were* in their hand, and all *their* earrings which *were* in their ears; and Jacob hid them under the oak which *was* by Shechem.

5. And they journeyed: and the terror of God was upon the cities that *were* round about them, and they did not pursue after the sons of Jacob.

6. ¶ So Jacob came to Luz, which *is* in the land of Canaan, that *is*, Bethel, he and all the people that *were* with him.

7. And he built there an altar, and called the place El-bethel: because there God appeared unto him, when he fled from the face of his brother.

8. But Deborah, Rebekah's nurse, died, and she was buried beneath Bethel under an oak; and the name of it was called Allon-bachuth.

9. ¶ And God appeared unto Jacob again, when he came out of Padan-aram, and blessed him.

10. And God said unto him, Thy name *is* Jacob: thy name shall not be called any more Jacob, but Israel shall be thy name: and he called his name Israel.

11. And God said unto him, I *am* God Almighty: be fruitful and multiply; a nation and a company of nations shall be of thee, and kings shall come out of thy loins:

12. And the land which I gave Abraham and Isaac, to thee I will give it, and to thy seed after thee will I give the land.

13. And God went up from him in the place where he talked with him.

14. And Jacob set up a pillar in the place where he talked with him,

even a pillar of stone; and he poured a drink-offering thereon, and he poured oil thereon.

15. And Jacob called the name of the place, where God spake with him, Beth-el.

598. The strange gods here alluded to, were those that Rachel had brought with her from her father's house, of which we have heard before. It appears that Jacob had some way been made acquainted with the larceny of his wife: and he is now taking means to rid himself of the evil that was likely to grow into an idolatrous worship with his family. But who were the "people" implicated in the same charge of idolatry? The reference may be to the wives of some of Jacob's sons, or to his servants, of which we know he had many, or perhaps to the "wives and children" that had been made captives in the sacking of Shalem.

599. It may be remembered that when Jacob fled from the wrath of his brother, he tarried over night at Bethel, and had there erected a rude altar of stone; and had promised a tithe of all his possessions, provided the Lord would prosper him in his way, and return him to his father's house. Now the Lord *had* prospered him. giving him "bread to eat and clothing to wear," and had returned him to his own land, and had (as will soon appear) brought him near to his father's house. And under these circumstances, it seemed exceedingly proper, that he should go again to Bethel, and renew the altar and make suitable thank-offerings for the blessings he had received.

600. The Shechem here named, may be the same as Shalem before alluded to, or it may be a neighboring city, taking its name evidently from Shechem, son of Hamor, alluded to in the narrative.

601. The "terror of God" is a Hebraism, meaning a great terror: and the allusion is to the recent sacking of Shalem which Jacob supposed would provoke a war against him by the neighboring tribes; and the design of the narrative is to inform us that no such result followed, as *a great fear* had taken possession of the neighboring people.

602. As God had once appeared to Jacob in Bethel, so now we are told that he appeared to him again; though it is not said, in this case, as in the other, that this appearance was in a dream; yet we would suggest whether this is not a fair conclusion; and if so, it will help to sustain our views of this subject proposed in another place. p. 30.

603. Jacob is again told that his name should be changed to Israel, as he had been told on a former occasion, xxxii. 28 : and the reason of repeating the statement now, is probably to connect the new name with the promise given him, as a perpetual memento, for the same reason that Abram was changed to Abraham, when the same promise was given to him. And here we may suggest, that this change in the name, was not merely on account of the significancy of the name itself, but with a view to bring the divine promise more frequently before the mind. This is evident from the change in the name of Abram's wife, from Sarai to Sarah, for which no reason can be given from the difference between the names, though the reason we have suggested would apply here as well as to that of her husband. The same purpose was had in view in this case, as when a present was exchanged between two parties, to ratify a treaty, or a pillar of stones set up for the same purpose. The difference was only in this, that the one was a transient occurrence, and was commemorated by a monument equally transient; the other was more important and enduring, and was kept in memory by a monument more intimate and longer continued.

604. We remember to have seen the opinion expressed by some writer, that the account here given of Jacob's visit to Bethel, is only another version of the visit made there on his going *to* Padan-aram ; but the reason for this opinion drawn from some likeness of the two narratives, is not conclusive. The likeness is such as could not well be avoided, and such only as it would be expected, allowing both to have occurred. That God, having appeared to him before, and promised his protection, should now appear to him again, is what might be expected; and with such appearance, that Jacob should build again the altar, and pour thereon a drink-offering, in testimony of his gratitude, was a natural occurrence. From both passages, too, compared, it is evident that Bethel was on the route to Padan-aram, and that it could not have been far from the return route. And from the circumstances that occurred there at first, Jacob would be quite likely to visit the same place the second time.

SECTION XII. — JACOB'S RETURN TO ISAAC.
CHAP. XXXV.

16. ¶ And they journeyed from Bethel, and there was but a little way to come to Ephrath; and Rachel travailed, and she had hard labor.

17. And it came to pass, when she was in hard labor, that the midwife said unto her, Fear not; thou shalt have this son also.

18. And it came to pass, as her soul was in departing, (for she died) that she called his name Benoni: but his father called him Benjamin.

19. And Rachel died, and was buried in the way to Ephrath, which is Bethlehem.

20. And Jacob set a pillar upon her grave: that is the pillar of Rachel's grave unto this day.

21. And Israel journeyed, and spread his tent beyond the tower of Edar.

22. And it came to pass, when Israel dwelt in that land, that Reuben went and lay with Bilhah his father's concubine: and Israel heard it. Now the sons of Jacob were twelve.

23. The sons of Leah; Reuben, Jacob's first-born, and Simeon, and Levi, and Judah, and Issachar, and Zebulon:

24. The sons of Rachel; Joseph, and Benjamin:

25. And the sons of Bilhah, Rachel's handmaid; Dan, and Naphtali:

26. And the sons of Zilpah, Leah's handmaid; Gad, and Asher. These *are* the sons of Jacob, which were born to him in Padan-aram.

27. And Jacob came unto Isaac his father unto Mamre, unto the city of Arbah, which is Hebron, where Abraham and Isaac sojourned.

605. The death of Rachel, we may well suppose, was a sad bereavement to Jacob. The notice of this event, and of the occasion of it, is exceedingly brief. At first, we are surprised that this favorite wife should have been buried in the way to Ephrath, and not in the cave of Machpelah, where other members of the family had been laid, and which had by that means acquired a sanctity that did not belong to any other place. Still, when we consider the circumstances of her death, and the distance to Hebron that yet remained, our surprise is removed. One token of respect that appears not to have been usual, was shown to the burial place; and that was a monument over the grave, that remained for a considerable period afterwards.

606. "That is the pillar of Rachel's grave *unto this day.*" There are some who would make us believe that the book of Genesis was written nearly or quite a thousand years after the event here recorded, during many hundreds of years of which period, the land was in the hands of stangers, who could have no motive for preserving the monument over Rachel's grave, and a part of the time in the hands of enemies that might feel inclined to desecrate it. At all events the regular changes that might be expected to come over that locality, without any hostile intention, would obliterate all traces of the burial place and the monument, in much less time than is here supposed. The truth is, the circumstance of Rachel's death was recorded, while it was fresh in the memory of the family, and the fact that the pillar being set up over her grave; and a subsequent writer, not certainly later than Moses, added the clause that the pillar remained to this day.

607. What is contained in the 21st verse, is probably misplaced. It belongs more properly within the 16th verse, and is so placed in the Septuagint version.

608. The conduct of Reuben has, in the Greek, a clause, not found in our version, representing the wickedness of his son as "grevious in the sight of Jacob," as doubtless it must have been.

609. The twelve sons of Jacob are said to have been born to him in Padan-aram, while the youngest, it had just been stated, received his birth near Bethlehem. This circumstance shows that the nicest accuracy was not intended by the writer. Infidelity has sought to make something out of this circumstance. It seems to us quite evident, that an impostor would have avoided discrepancies so obvious, while the honest writer, presuming on the candor of others, would be very likely to have some such upon his pages, where no one could be misled by them.

610. When Jacob left home, Isaac, his father, was at Beersheba, xxviii. 10; but during his absence he had resumed the ancestral residence at Hebron, to which place Jacob now returns, and finds his father still alive, having attained an age beyond that of Abraham.

SECTION XIII. — Death of Isaac.

CHAP. XXXV.

28. And the days of Isaac were an hundred and fourscore years.
29. And Isaac gave up the ghost, and died, and was gathered unto his people, *being* old and full of days: and his sons Esau and Jacob buried him.

611. That Isaac "gave up the ghost," has nothing in the original to justify precisely that rendering. He *expired* would have been more accurate. That he " was gathered to his people" is a correct rendering, and seems plainly to imply the belief of a conscious personal existence beyond this life. Observe, that being gathered to his people, has no reference to his burial. He was gathered to his people, and afterwards buried by his sons, in the cave of Machpelah.

612. The presence of Esau at the burial of his father leads to two conclusions. One is, that the two branches of Isaac's family were not hostile to each other. Another is, that Mt. Seir, Esau's residence, was probably not very far from Hebron. Or, if one is disposed to think so, he may believe, what is quite natural under the circumstances, that Esau was with his father in his extreme old age, awaiting his expected departure, and that the arrival of Jacob was hastened by the same consideration.

SECTION XIV. — Joseph sold and carried to Egypt.

CHAP. XXXVII.

1. And Jacob dwelt in the land wherein his father was a stranger, in the land of Canaan.
2. ¶ These *are* the generations of Jacob. Joseph, *being* seventeen years old, was feeding the flock with his brethren; and the lad *was* with the sons of Bilhah, and with the sons of Zilpah, his father's wives: and Joseph brought unto his father their evil report.
3. Now Israel loved Joseph more than all his children, because he *was* the son of his old age: and he made him a coat of *many* colors.
4. And when his brethren saw that their father loved him more than all his brethren, they hated him, and could not speak peaceably unto him.
5. And Joseph dreamed a dream, and he told *it* his brethren: and they hated him yet the more.
6. And he said unto them, Hear, I pray you, this dream which I have dreamed:
7. For, behold, we *were* binding sheaves in the field, and, lo, my sheaf arose, and also stood upright; and, behold, your sheaves

stood round about and made obeisance to my sheaf.

8. And his brethren said to him, Shalt thou indeed reign over us? or shalt thou indeed have dominion over us? And they hated him yet the more for his dreams, and for his words.

9. And he dreamed yet another dream, and told it his brethren, and said, Behold, I have dreamed a dream more ; and, behold, the sun, and the moon, and the eleven stars, made obeisance to me.

10. And he told it to his father and to his brethren; and his father rebuked him, and said unto him, What is this dream that thou hast dreamed? Shall I, and thy mother, and thy brethren, indeed come to bow down ourselves to thee to the earth.

11. And his brethren envied him; but his father observed the saying.

12 ¶ And his brethren went to feed their father's flock in Shechem.

13. And Israel said unto Joseph, Do not thy brethren feed *the flock* in Shechem? come, and I will send thee unto them. And he said to him, Here *am* I.

14. And he said to him, Go, I pray thee, see whether it be well with thy brethren, and well with the flocks: and bring me word again. So he sent him out of the vale of Hebron, and he came to Shechem.

15. And a certain man found him, and, behold, *he was* wandering in the field : and the man asked him, saying, What seekest thou?

16. And he said, I seek my brethren: tell me, I pray thee, where they feed *their flocks*.

17. And the man said, They are departed hence; for I heard them say, Let us go to Dothan. And Joseph went after his brethren and found them in Dothan.

18 And when they saw him afar off, even before he came near unto them, they conspired against him to slay him.

19. And they said one to another, Behold this dreamer cometh.

20. Come now, therefore, and let us slay him, and cast him into some pit; and we will say, Some evil beast hath devoured him; and we shall see what will become of his dreams.

21. And Reuben heard *it*, and he delivered him out of their hands; and said, Let us not kill him.

22. And Reuben said unto them, Shed no blood, *but* cast him into this pit that *is* in the wilderness, and lay no hand upon him; that he might rid him out of their hands, to deliver him to his father again.

23. And it came to pass, when Joseph was come unto his brethren, that they stript Joseph out of *his* coat, *his* coat of *many* colors, that *was* on him.

24. And they took him, and cast him into a pit: and the pit *was* empty, *there was* no water in it.

25. And they sat down to eat bread: and they lifted up their eyes, and looked, and, behold, a company of Ishmaelites came from Gilead, with their camels bearing spicery and balm and myrrh, going to carry *it* down to Egypt.

26. And Judah said unto his brethren, What profit *is it* if we slay our brother, and conceal his blood?

27. Come, and let us sell him to the Ishmaelites, and let not our hand be upon him, for he *is* our brother *and* our flesh: And his brethren were content.

28. Then there passed by Midianites, merchantmen; and they drew and lifted up Joseph out of the pit, and sold Joseph to the Ishmaelites for twenty *pieces* of silver; and they brought Joseph into Egypt.

29. And Reuben returned unto the pit: and, behold, Joseph *was* not in the pit; and he rent his clothes:

30. And he returned unto his

brethren, and said, The child is not; and I, whither shall I go?

31. And they took Joseph's coat, and killed a kid of the goats, and dipped the coat in the blood:

32. And they sent the coat of *many colors*, and they brought *it* to their father; and said, This have we found; know now whether it *be* thy son's coat or no.

33. And he knew it, and said, *It is* my son's coat: an evil beast hath devoured him: Joseph is without doubt rent in pieces.

34. And Jacob rent his clothes, and put sackcloth upon his loins, and mourned for his son many days.

35. And all his sons and all his daughters rose up to comfort him; but he refused to be comforted: and he said, For I will go down into the grave unto my son mourning. Thus his father wept for him.

36. And the Midianites sold him into Egypt, unto Potiphar, an officer of Pharoah's, *and* captain of the guard.

613. "Jacob dwelt in the land wherein his father was a stranger, in the land of Canaan." One would suppose that Isaac, the father of Jacob, having dwelt in the land of Canaan the whole of his life of 180 years, could not well be called a stranger in the land. But, in the sense of that term here employed, and elsewhere in this book, he was a stranger: since he was not one of the original settlers, but came from a distant land. And it may be added that the frequent references of this kind, seem to furnish a formidable objection to the theory of some, that would make the land of Canaan to have belonged originally to the Hebrew people. This theory is adopted to furnish justification to the Israelites, when they returned from Egypt, for retaking Canaan and putting its inhabitants to the sword. The people of Canaan, it is said, were not the original settlers, but only occupied certain points as trading posts; and therefore, they could set up no opposing claim to the Israelites. This idea is set aside by several circumstances. The first grant of the land to Abram, contains a mention of its several tribes, viz: the Kenites, and Kenizzites, and Kadmonites, and Hittites, and Perizzites, and Rephaims, and Amorites, and Canaanites, and Girgashites, and Jebusites. So, too, in the account we have of the war of the confederate kings, mention is made of the Amorites and other tribes; and that these kings and their armies, were employed in laying waste a few trading posts, does not accord with the spirit of the narrative.

614. The best explanation we know of, of the conduct of the children of Israel when they came from

Egypt to Canaan, is, that He who owns all lands, had given them this country, and instructed them to regain its possession. Again; what meaning shall be attached to the circumstance of Abram's purchase of Machpelah for a burial place, xxiii. 16, and of Jacob buying a tract of land of Hamor near Shalem, xxxiii. 19, if the country was not the possession of the people?

The true explanation of this subject seems to be, that the Canaanites, including all the tribes before named, were the true inhabitants of Canaan — that the ground was theirs, as much as any land belongs to any man or set of men — that Abram and his family could settle there only by the consent of the people — that in process of time, when the iniquity of the Amorites was full, they would forfeit all claim to the land, and it would then become the possession of the Israelites, and that it was in view of this prospective possession, that the land was given to them by God. It is certain that the patriarchs so understood the gift, else why offer to purchase what was already theirs, and of which they held the title from the original owner. And with this view; and with the fullest confidence that the grant of the country to them was divine, they went up from Egypt to take possession of the country. Besides: if the Israelites had a just title to Canaan, on natural grounds, what fitness was there in making a formal gift of it to them on the part of Jehovah. The gift is offered on the presumption that, without it, they could not claim the possession.

615. Bilhah and Zilpah are here mentioned as Jacob's *wives*, not because they were such in the highest sense of that term; but, as the mothers of a portion of his children, they were such. And when it is added, that Joseph brought home their evil report, the reference seems to be, and perhaps is, only to the sons of the handmaids, who might have been, and would naturally be, more incensed at Jacob's partiality for Joseph, than the rest of his sons, and might have been the instigators of the cruel plot formed against him.

616. The coat of many colors has been the occasion of considerable discussion, but without bringing us to any other conclusion, than that it was a coat of many colors. The form of the coat, what it was that constituted its many colors, are questions that we cannot answer; and moreover they are questions that do not require an answer. The effect of the partiality of Jacob was as natural, as was the partiality itself, and as unfortunate, for the time being at least, as it was natural.

617. The dreams of Joseph were either natural, and were subsequently verified as a remarkable Providence, like many dreams at the present day; or they were a divine impulse, indicating his future elevation and fulfilled accordingly. Either supposition is not inconsistent with the spirit of the times. The last dream was understood to include his mother, among those that were to bow down to Joseph, but his mother was dead and buried in the way to Ephrath. How then could the dream be fulfilled? Perhaps the reference was to Leah, as we have yet had no account of her death. This could not be ; for though we have no account of her death, yet it is certain that she did die before the dream was fulfilled, and was buried in the cave of Machpelah, according to a subsequent statement.

618. The explanation is that dreams, as well as parables, must not be made " to go on all fours." We may interpret them with a greater strictness than they were intended to be interpreted. The design of the dreams of Joseph, allowing them the claim to inspiration, was to indicate the elevation of Joseph over the rest of the family; and this design was truly fulfilled, though every item in the dream, may not find its corresponding particular in the fulfilment.

619. The feeding of the flocks in Shechem, was a natural circumstance, from the fact that they had occupied that region of country on a former occasion, xxxv. 4 ; and that having exhausted the pasturage there, they should go to another place, was another natural circumstance attaching itself to their mode of life. The location of Dothan can only be determined by two circumstances. One is, that it was not far from Shechem ; and another is, that it lay on the route from Gilead to Egypt, a route that Jacob and his family had recently passed over in coming from Padan-aram to Hebron. The place is made sufficiently memorable, by the plot against Joseph, here brought to view.

620. It will be seen that Reuben, the oldest of Jacob's sons, joined in the conspiracy, only with an ultimate purpose of saving the boy, and delivering him to his father. And the suggestion of Judah seems to have been dictated by the same spirit, when he proposed to sell him as a slave to the Ishmaelites, that being the choice of two evils.

621. The merchantmen are called Ishmaelites, from being the descendants of Ishmael; and they are called Midianites, probably from the country to which they belonged.

622. It appears that, after the determination to cast Joseph into the pit, suggested by Reuben, the latter had returned to his own flocks, and had not known the change of purpose on the part of his brethren: and when he finds the pit empty, at the time when he expected to deliver him from their malice and return him to his father, he is greatly distressed, supposing, it would seem, that he had been destroyed by wild beasts, or taken out and killed by his brethren. And it does not appear that he was informed of the true state of the case, till after the disclosure in Egypt. At least his language to his brethren in Egypt, clearly conveys this idea:—" Spake I not unto you, saying, Do not sin against the child; and ye would not hear; therefore behold also *his blood is required.*" xlii. 22.

623. "All Jacob's sons and all his daughters went up to comfort him." But, says one, all his daughters were only Dinah, as we read of no others. We remark that the wives of his sons may be here referred to, and we so find them designated, xlvi. 15. It is also evident that he had grand-daughters when he went down to Egypt; and may have had such, at the time of this occurrence with Joseph; and in Scripture parlance these would be called his daughters.

624. Joseph was sold to Potiphar, an officer of Pharaoh and captain of the guard. Slaves were common in Egypt, at least we find them there, on the first visit of Abraham to that country; and they were among the presents he received from the king. The present of servants to

Abraham on his departure from Egypt, and the selling of Joseph to Potiphar, are two circumstances quite unlike, and both are introduced very naturally in the narrative, and with no apparent relation to each other; yet they harmonize perfectly in respect to the fact of servants or slaves beng bought and sold, and regarded as property in that country;— an undesigned coincidence going to establish the truth of the narrative. Compare pp. 34–37.

SECTION XV. — DIGRESSION CONCERNING JUDAH.

CHAP. XXXVIII.

1. And it came to pass at that time, that Judah went down from his brethren, and turned in to a certain Adullamite, whose name *was* Hirah.

2. And Judah saw there a daughter of a certain Canaanite, whose name *was* Shuah; and he took her, and went into unto her.

3. And she conceived, and bare a son; and he called his name Er.

4. And she conceived again, and bare a son; and she called his name Onan.

5. And she yet again conceived, and bare a son; and called his name Shelah: and he was at Chezib, when she bare him.

6. ¶ And Judah took a wife for Er his firstborn, whose name *was* Tamar.

7. And Er, Judah's firstborn, was wicked in the sight of the LORD; and the LORD slew him.

8. And Judah said unto Onan, Go in unto thy brother's wife, and marry her, and raise up seed to thy brother.

9. And Onan knew that the seed should not be his; and it came to pass, when he went in unto his brother's wife, that he spilled *it* on the ground, lest that he should give seed to his brother.

10. And the thing which he did displeased the LORD: wherefore he slew him also.

11. Then said Judah to Tamar his daughter-in-law, Remain a widow at thy father's house, till Shelah my son be grown: (for he said, Lest peradventure he die also, as his brethren *did:*) and Tamar went and dwelt in her father's house.

12. ¶ And in process of time the daughter of Shuah, Judah's wife died; and Judah was comforted, and went up unto his sheep-shearers to Timnath, he and his friend Hirah the Adullamite.

13. And it was told Tamar, saying, Behold thy father-in-law goeth up to Timnath to shear his sheep.

14. And she put her widow's garments off from her, and covered her with a veil, and wrapped herself, and sat in an open place, which *is* by the way to Timnath; for she saw that Shelah was grown, and she was not given unto him to wife.

15. When Judah saw her, he thought her *to be* an harlot; because she had covered her face.

16. And he turned unto her by the way, and said, Go to, I pray thee, let me come in unto thee: (for he knew not that she *was* his daughter-in-law;) And she said, What wilt thou give me, that thou mayest come in unto me?

17. And he said, I will send *thee* a kid from the flock. And she said, Wilt thou give *me* a pledge, till thou send *it?*

18. And he said, What pledge

shall I give thee? And she said, Thy signet, and thy bracelets, and thy staff that *is* in thy hand. And he gave *it* her, and came in unto her, and she conceived by him.

19. And she arose, and went away, and laid by her veil from her, and put on the garments of her widowhood.

20. And Judah sent the kid by the hand of his friend the Adullamite, to receive *his* pledge from the woman's hand: but he found her not.

21. Then he asked the men of that place, saying, Where *is* the harlot, that *was* openly by the way side? And they said, There was no harlot in this *place*.

22. And he returned to Judah, and said, I cannot find her; and also the men of the place said, *that* there was no harlot in this *place*.

23. And Judah said, Let her take *it* to her, lest we be shamed: behold, I sent this kid, and thou hast not found her.

24. ¶ And it came to pass about three months after, that it was told Judah, saying, Tamar thy daughter-in-law hath played the harlot; and also, behold, she *is* with child by whoredom. And Judah said, Bring her forth, and let her be burnt.

25. When she *was* brought forth, she sent to her father-in-law, saying, By the man, whose these *are*, am I with child: and she said, Discern, I pray thee, whose *are* these, the signet, and bracelets, and staff.

26. And Judah acknowledged *them*, and said, She hath been more righteous than I; because that I gave her not to Shelah my son. And he knew her again no more.

27. ¶ And it came to pass in the time of her travail, that, behold, twins *were* in her womb.

28. And it came to pass, when she travailed, that, *the one* put out *his* hand: and the midwife took and bound upon his hand a scarlet thread, saying, This came out first.

29. And it came to pass, as he drew back his hand, that, behold, his brother came out: and she said, How hast thou broken forth? *this* breach *be* upon thee: therefore his name was called Pharez.

30. And afterward came out his brother, that had the scarlet thread upon his hand: and his name was called Zarah.

625. "It came to pass *at that time.*" We need not suppose a reference here to the particular time of Joseph's being sold into Egypt. Joseph was seventeen years old when the difficulty occurred with his brethren. He was thirty when promoted in Egypt. Then succeeded seven years of plenty and two years of famine, before Jacob went down with his family to that country. This was twenty-two years from the time that Joseph was sold; and at the time of going to Egypt, we learn that Judah had some sons and grand-sons, which may oblige us to refer the transactions of this chapter farther back than the selling of Joseph.

And we feel the more at liberty to adopt this view, because, what is here recorded, is not a part of the regular narrative, but a sort of episode, and need not, therefore, be very intimately connected, by dates or otherwise, with the record which it interrupts.

626. The custom here referred to, with respect to marriage, is simply stated, while the reasons are left to conjecture. It will doubtless be remembered that this custom was the basis of an objection to the resurrection, once urged against the Saviour, by the Sadducees.

627. The scarlet thread was intended to show which of the twins was first born; that being an important circumstance with the people of those days, as we have often had occasion to remark. And though the occasion of the birth of these twins, might have been omitted, the omission would have occasioned a break in the genealogy of our Saviour. Matt. i. 3.

SECTION XVI. — JOSEPH TEMPTED.

CHAP. XXXIX.

1. And Joseph was brought down to Egypt; and Potiphar, an officer of Pharaoh, captain of the guard, an Egyptian, bought him of the hands of the Ishmaelites, which had brought him down thither.

2. And the LORD was with Joseph, and he was a prosperous man; and he was in the house of his master the Egyptian.

3. And his master saw that the LORD *was* with him, and that the LORD made all that he did to prosper in his hand.

4. And Joseph found grace in his sight, and he served him: and he made him overseer over his house, and all *that* he had he put into his hand.

5. And it came to pass from the time *that* he had made him overseer in his house, and over all that he had, that the LORD blessed the Egyptian's house for Joseph's sake; and the blessing of the LORD was upon all that he had in the house, and in the field.

6 And he left all that he had, in Joseph's hand; and he knew not aught he had, save the bread which he did eat. And Joseph was *a* goodly *person*, and well-favored.

7. ¶ And it came to pass after these things, that his master's wife cast her eyes upon Joseph; and she said, Lie with me.

8. But he refused, and said unto his master's wife, Behold, my master wotteth not what *is* with me in the house, and he hath committed all that he hath to my hand;

9. *There is* none greater in the house than I: neither hath he kept back any thing from me but thee, because thou *art* his wife: how then can I do this great wickedness, and sin against God?

10. And it came to pass, as she spake to Joseph day by day, that he hearkened not unto her, to lie by her, *or* to be with her.

11. And it came to pass about this time, that *Joseph* went into the house to do his business; and *there was* none of the men of the house there within.

12. And she caught him by his garment, saying, Lie with me: and he left his garment in her hand, and fled, and got him out.

13. And it came to pass, when

she saw that he had left his garment in her hand, and was fled forth,

14. That she called unto the men of her house, and spake unto them, saying, See, he has brought in an Hebrew unto us to mock us; he came in unto me to lie with me, and I cried with a loud voice:

15. And it came to pass, when he heard that I lifted up my voice and cried, that he left his garment with me, and fled, and got him out.

16. And she laid up his garment by her until his lord came home.

17. And she spake unto him according to these words, saying, The Hebrew servant, which thou hast brought unto us, came in unto me to mock me:

18. And it came to pass, as I lifted up my voice and cried, that he left his garment with me, and fled out.

19. And it came to pass, when his master heard the words of his wife, which she spake unto him, saying, After this manner did thy servant to me; that his wrath was kindled.

20. And Joseph's master took him, and put him into the prison, a place where the king's prisoners *were* bound: and he was there in the prison.

21. ¶ But the LORD was with Joseph, and shewed him mercy, and gave him favor in the sight of the keeper of the prison.

22. And the keeper of the prison committed to Joseph's hand all the prisoners that *were* in the prison: and whatsoever they did there, he was the doer *of it*.

23. The keeper of the prison looked not to any thing *that was* under his hand; because the LORD was with him, and *that* which he did, the LORD made *it* to prosper.

628. The promotion of Joseph in the house of Potiphar, was a natural result of his faithfulness; nor was there any thing in the state of society in Egypt, that would interfere with his promotion. Indeed the state of society was precisely such as would lead to this result. The labor being done mostly by servants, it would be a very gratifying circumstance to find one that could take charge of the rest, and conduct all the affairs in his hands, with wisdom and prudence. But his promotion was only the promotion of a servant, and must be so understood.

629. The crime charged upon Joseph by the wife of Potiphar, one would suppose, would have subjected the offender to a severer punishment than was here inflicted. We feel surprised that Joseph was not immediately executed; and we are inclined to suspect that there was some good reason for this lenity. I apprehend we shall not be far from the truth, if we regard Potiphar as entertaining some suspicions of Joseph's innocence, or at least presuming on some palliating circumstances of which his wife did not inform him. A woman, so far gone in crime, as she must have been, could hardly have been regarded by her husband as perfectly reliable. Add to this, that Joseph's former conduct would naturally incline the master to exercise towards his servant some degree of lenity. What confirms this opinion, is, the promotion of Joseph in prison; since this same Potiphar, we infer from another passage, had charge of the prison. Compare xl. 3, 4. It is hardly supposable that Joseph, for such a crime, would have been only imprisoned, in such a country, and under such a government as Egypt, unless there were strong suspicions of his innocence. It is quite as hard to believe, that the same officer he had offended, should place him over all the prisoners in his hands.

SECTION XVII. — DREAMS OF THE BUTLER AND BAKER.

CHAP. XL.

1. And it came to pass after these things, *that* the butler of the king of Egypt and *his* baker had offended their lord the king of Egypt.
2. And Pharaoh was wroth against two *of* his officers, against the chief of the butlers, and against the chief of the bakers.
3. And he put them in ward in the house of the captain of the guard, into the prison, the place where Joseph *was* bound.
4. And the captain of the guard charged Joseph with them, and he served them: and they continued a season in ward.
5. ¶ And they dreamed a dream, both of them, each man his dream in one night, each man according to the interpretation of his dream, the butler and the baker of the king of Egypt, which *were* bound in the prison.
6. And Joseph came in unto them in the morning, and looked upon them, and behold, they *were* sad.
7. And he asked Pharaoh's officers that *were* with him in the ward of his lord's house, saying, Wherefore look ye *so* sadly to-day?

8. And they said unto him, We have dreamed a dream, and *there is* no interpreter of it. And Joseph said unto them, *Do* not interpretations *belong* to God? tell me *them,* I pray you.
9. And the chief butler told his dream to Joseph, and said to him, In my dream, behold, a vine *was* before me;
10. And in the vine *were* three branches: and it *was* as though it budded, *and* her blossoms shot forth; and the clusters thereof brought forth ripe grapes:
11. And Pharaoh's cup *was* in my hand: and I took the grapes, and pressed them into Pharaoh's cup, and I gave the cup into Pharaoh's hand.
12. And Joseph said unto him, This *is* the interpretation of it: The three branches *are* three days:
13. Yet within three days shall Pharaoh lift up thy head, and restore thee unto thy place: and thou shalt deliver Pharaoh's cup into his hand, after the former manner when thou wast his butler.
14. But think on me when it shall be well with thee, and shew kindness, I pray thee, unto me,

and make mention of me unto Pharaoh, and bring me out of this house:

15. For indeed I was stolen away out of the land of the Hebrews: and here also have I done nothing that they should put me into the dungeon.

16. When the chief baker saw that the interpretation was good, he said unto Joseph, I also *was* in my dream, and, behold, *I had* three white baskets on my head:

17. And in the uppermost basket *there was* of all manner of bakemeats for Pharaoh; and the birds did eat them out of the basket upon my head.

18. And Joseph answered and said, This *is* the interpretation thereof: The three baskets *are* three days:

19. Yet within three days shall Pharaoh lift up thy head from off thee, and shall hang thee on a tree; and the birds shall eat thy flesh from off thee.

20. And it came to pass the third day, *which was* Pharaoh's birthday, that he made a feast unto all his servants: and he lifted up the head of the chief butler and of the chief baker among his servants.

21. And he restored the chief butler unto his butlership again; and he gave the cup into Pharaoh's hand:

22. But he hanged the chief baker, as Joseph had interpreted to them.

23. Yet did not the chief butler remember Joseph, but forgat him.

630. It was the business of one of these men to superintend the *drinking* department of Pharaoh's court, and the other the *eating* department. And as they were chiefs in these departments, the inference is, that they had a number of subordinates ; and this fact indicates the magnificence of the court which they served.

631. That the dreams here mentioned were divine, need not, I apprehend, be supposed : though it is difficult to understand how Joseph could have known the future of these men, without divine aid. The result verified his interpretation, and was the distant cause of his own deliverance. I infer that the chief baker was first decapitated, and then his body suspended to a tree. Compare verses 19 and 22.

632. The request of Joseph to be remembered by the butler, was very natural : and it was quite unnatural that he should have been forgotten. There are many supposable circumstances, however, that render the forgetfulness of the butler a credible event. He was doubtless quite delighted with his own liberty. There might have been circumstances rendering it dangerous for him to interfere in a matter of that kind. Besides, the man asking the favor, was only a servant ; and though his position in prison might make his favor an object, yet out of prison no such motive could avail.

633. That Joseph was stolen from his own land, has reference to the secret manner in which he was disposed of, with reference to his father, and is not to be considered an implication of those who bought him as a slave.

SECTION XVIII.— Pharaoh's Dreams.

CHAP. XLI.

1. And it came to pass at the end of two full years, that Pharaoh dreamed: and behold, he stood by the river.
2. And behold, there came up out of the river seven well-favored kine and fat-fleshed; and they fed in a meadow.
3. And behold, seven other kine came up after them out of the river, ill-favored and lean-fleshed; and stood by the *other* kine upon the brink of the river.
4. And the ill-favored and lean-fleshed kine did eat up the seven well-favored and fat kine. So Pharaoh awoke,
5. And he slept and dreamed the second time: and behold, seven ears of corn came up upon one stalk, rank and good.
6. And behold, seven thin ears and blasted with the east wind sprung up after them.
7. And the seven thin ears devoured the seven rank and full ears. And Pharaoh awoke, and behold, *it was* a dream.
8. And it came to pass in the morning that his spirit was troubled; and he sent and called for all the magicians of Egypt, and all the wise men thereof: and Pharaoh told them his dream; but *there was* none that could interpret them unto Pharaoh.
9. ¶ Then spake the chief butler unto Pharaoh, saying, I do remember my faults this day:
10. Pharaoh was wroth with his servants, and put me in ward in the captain of the guard's house, *both* me and the chief baker:
11. And we dreamed a dream in one night, I and he; we dreamed each man according to the interpretation of his dream.
12. And *there was* there with us a young man, an Hebrew, servant to the captain of the guard; and we told him, and he interpreted to us our dreams; to each man according to his dream he did interpret.
13. And it came to pass, as he interpreted to us, so it was; me he restored unto mine office, and him he hanged.
14. ¶ Then Pharaoh sent and called Joseph, and they brought him hastily out of the dungeon: and he shaved *himself*, and changed his raiment, and came in unto Pharaoh.
15. And Pharaoh said unto Joseph, I have dreamed a dream, and *there is* none that can interpret it: and I have heard say of thee, *that* thou canst understand a dream to interpret it.
16. And Joseph answered Pharaoh, saying, *It is* not in me : God shall give Pharaoh an answer of peace.
17. And Pharaoh said unto Joseph, In my dream, behold, I stood upon the bank of the river:
18. And behold, there came up out of the river seven kine, fat-fleshed and well-favored; and they fed in a meadow:
19. And behold, seven other kine

came up after them, poor and very ill-favored and lean-fleshed, such as I never saw in all the land of Egypt for badness:

20. And the lean and the ill-favored kine did eat up the first seven fat kine:

21. And when they had eaten them up, it could not be known that they had eaten them; but they *were* still ill-favored, as at the beginning. So I awoke.

22. And I saw in my dream, and behold, seven ears came up in one stalk, full and good:

23. And behold, seven ears, withered, thin, *and* blasted with the east wind, sprung up after them:

24. And the thin ears devoured the seven good ears: and I told *this* unto the magicians; but *there was* none that could declare *it* to me.

25. ¶ And Joseph said unto Pharaoh, The dream of Pharaoh *is* one: God hath shewed Pharaoh what he *is* about to do.

26. The seven good kine *are* seven years; and the seven good ears *are* seven years: the dream *is* one.

27. And the seven thin and ill-favored kine that came up after them *are* seven years; and the seven empty ears blasted with the east wind shall be seven years of famine.

28. This *is* the thing which I have spoken unto Pharaoh: What God *is* about to do he sheweth unto Pharaoh.

29. Behold, there come seven years of great plenty throughout all the land of Egypt:

30. And there shall arise after them seven years of famine; and all the plenty shall be forgotten in the land of Egypt; and the famine shall consume the land;

31. And the plenty shall not be known in the land by reason of that famine following; for it *shall be* very grievous.

32. And for that the dream was doubled unto Pharaoh twice; *it is* because the thing *is* established by God, and God will shortly bring it to pass.

33. Now therefore let Pharaoh look out a man discreet and wise, and set him over the land of Egypt.

34. Let Pharaoh do *this*, and let him appoint officers over the land, and take up the fifth part of the land of Egypt in the seven plenteous years.

35. And let them gather all the food of those good years that come, and lay up corn under the hand of Pharaoh, and let them keep food in the cities.

36. And that food shall be for store to the land against the seven years of famine, which shall be in the land of Egypt; that the land perish not through the famine.

634. "At the end of two full years," refers probably to the time Joseph had been in prison. The "river" is not named, for the reason that every body would know what river was intended. The Nile was had in view without doubt. The seven lean kine, devouring the fat kine, is in perfect keeping with the nature of dreams, wherein things natural and unnatural are brought before the mind. The reference to the magicians and wise men shows that there was a class of men in Egypt, thought to be skilled in the interpretation of dreams; and the confidence placed in them, may be the reason why this should have been made the instrument of Joseph's elevation.

Nothing could have introduced him sooner to the confidence of the king.

635. Pharaoh's spirit was troubled at his dreams. They were well fitted to trouble him. They showed a bad result; and that was understood as an omen of evil. And the interpretation Joseph gave, commended itself so obviously to his understanding, and his suggestions as to what was best to be done, so exactly met the emergency, that the king did not hesitate to adopt the plan and enter upon its execution.

636. "He shaved himself and changed his raiment." From that time to this, it has been common to treat prisoners in a manner somewhat peculiar, in regard to their clothing and personal habits. It would seem that, in the prison in Egypt, men did not shave; and besides that they wore some peculiar garment. Still nothing more may be intended than that Joseph prepared himself to make a respectable appearance before the king, without justifying the inference above drawn.

637. It is worthy of being noticed that, while Joseph has an opportunity of getting to himself some credit for his sagacity, he disclaims all knowledge of dreams, except what God is pleased to communicate to him.

638. That a fifth part of the product of the seven years of plenty, would suffice during the seven years of famine, might seem to us incredible; but it must be remembered that the seven plenteous years were *very* productive; and the amount raised might have been greater on account of the expectation that a famine would succeed: for if the king and court believed that a famine was coming, and were making preparations for it, it is reasonable to conclude that many of the people would have the same opinion, and would make their arrangements accordingly. If it be said that the people seem not to have made any extra provision, we reply that there is a *seeming* of this kind. But I suspect that "that year" xlvii. 17, and "the second year," verse 18, were not the first and second of the seven, but the last two. This is made evident from the fact that the food for the "second year" was bought with the only thing the people had left, "their bodies and lands;" and the continuance of the famine after that, is not mentioned. Another circumstance, showing the same thing, is, that the Israelites came into Egypt at the end of two years of the famine; and their being nourished by Joseph, during the famine, is mentioned in advance of the two years called "that year" and the "second."

Another thing. The Canaanites were in distress before two years came round, and had been twice to Egypt for food, the reason of which is, that, with them, no famine was expected. But the Egyptians were not pressed with want till a later period, which is readily accounted for upon our view that, being admonished, they made preparations accordingly, not the one fifth merely, as required by Joseph, but a larger amount, on their own account.

SECTION XIX.—JOSEPH PLACED OVER THE LAND.

CHAP. XLI.

37. ¶ And the thing was good in the eyes of Pharaoh, and in the eyes of all his servants.

38. And Pharaoh said unto his servants, Can we find *such an one* as this *is*, a man in whom the spirit of God *is?*

39. And Pharaoh said unto Joseph, Forasmuch as God hath shewed thee all this, *there is* none so discreet and wise as thou *art:*

40. Thou shalt be over my house, and according unto thy word shall all my people be ruled: only in the throne will I be greater than thou.

41. And Pharoah said unto Joseph, See, I have set thee over all the land of Egypt.

42. And Pharaoh took off his ring from his hand, and put it upon Joseph's hand, and arrayed him in vestures of fine linen, and put a gold chain about his neck;

43. And he made him to ride in the second chariot which he had: and they cried before him, Bow the knee: and he made him *ruler* over all the land of Egypt.

44. And Pharaoh said unto Joseph, I *am* Pharaoh, and without thee shall no man lift up his hand or foot in all the land of Egypt.

45. And Pharaoh called Joseph's name Zaphnath-paaneah: and he gave him to wife Asenath the daughter of Poti-pherah priest of On: and Joseph went out over *all* the land of Egypt.

46. ¶ And Joseph *was* thirty years old when he stood before Pharaoh king of Egypt: and Joseph went out from the presence of Pharaoh, and went throughout all the land of Egypt.

47. And in the seven plenteous years the earth brought forth by handfuls.

48. And he gathered up all the food of the seven years which were in the land of Egypt, and laid up the food in the cities: the food of the field which *was* round about every city, laid he up in the same.

49. And Joseph gathered corn as the sand of the sea, very much, until he left numbering, for *it was* without number.

50. And unto Joseph were born two sons before the years of famine came; which Asenath the daughter of Poti-pherah priest of On bare unto him.
51. And Joseph called the name of the first born Manasseh; for God, *said he*, hath made me forget all my toil, and all my father's house.
52. And the name of the second called he Ephraim: For God hath caused me to be fruitful in the land of my affliction.
53. ¶ And the seven years of plenteousness that was in the land of Egypt, were ended.
54. And the seven years of dearth began to come, according as Joseph had said; and the dearth was in all lands: but in all the land of Egypt there was bread.
55. And when all the land of Egypt was famished, the people cried to Pharaoh for bread: and Pharaoh said unto all the Egyptians, Go unto Joseph, what he saith to you, do.
56. And the famine was over all the face of the earth: and Joseph opened all the store-houses, and sold unto the Egyptians; and the famine waxed sore in the land of Egypt.
57. And all countries came into Egypt to Joseph for to buy *corn;* because that the famine was *so* sore in all lands.

639. "There is none so discreet and wise as thou." We do not think that Pharaoh's reasoning is entirely sound, if he had in view, as the basis of his conclusion, the single fact that Joseph had interpreted his dreams; for we see no necessary connection between that, and a fitness to manage the affairs of state. But the suggestions of Joseph, as to what was best under the circumstances, were such as to commend themselves to the judgment of any man: and this, in connection with his former management, both in the house of Potiphar, and in the prison, may have had an influence to determine the course of the king.

640. The ring, and fine linen, and gold chain, were badges of authority; and were necessary to establish his authority with the people. So with the second chariot, and the injunction to "bow the knee." The chariot is probably called "second," as having some mark to indicate that Joseph was only second to the king.

641. The name given to Joseph was probably significant of his position; but its exact meaning is not well determined. It was probably an Egyptian designation, and is to be known only by reference to the language of that country.

642. "The priest of On." On is, in the Septuagint, Heliopolis. It is mentioned only once or twice in Genesis;

and its location cannot be determined by these instances.

643. We infer that the food, said to be gathered up in all the land, was not merely the one-fifth mentioned before, but all that could be spared; while the fifth part was reserved for the king, and it was this last that helped to supply the people after the rest was gone, during the last two or three years of the famine.

SECTION XX. — First Journey to Egypt.

CHAP. XLII.

1. Now when Jacob saw that there was corn in Egypt, Jacob said unto his sons, Why do ye look one upon another?

2. And he said, Behold, I have heard that there is corn in Egypt: get you down thither, and buy for us from thence; that we may live, and not die.

3. ¶ And Joseph's ten brethren went down to buy corn in Egypt.

4. But Benjamin, Joseph's brother, Jacob sent not with his brethren; for he said, Lest peradventure mischief befall him.

5. And the sons of Israel came to buy *corn* among those that came: for the famine was in the land of Canaan.

6. And Joseph *was* the governor over the land, *and* he *it was* that sold to all the people of the land: and Joseph's brethren came and bowed down themselves before him *with* their faces to the earth.

7. And Joseph saw his brethren, and he knew them, but made himself strange unto them, and spake roughly unto them; and he said unto them, Whence come ye? And they said, From the land of Canaan to buy food.

8. And Joseph knew his brethren, but they knew not him.

9. And Joseph remembered the dreams which he dreamed of them, and said unto them, Ye *are* spies; to see the nakedness of the land ye are come.

10. And they said unto him, Nay, my lord, but to buy food are thy servants come.

11. We *are* all one man's sons; we *are* true *men*, thy servants are no spies.

12. And he said unto them, Nay, but to see the nakedness of the land ye are come.

13. And they said, Thy servants *are* twelve brethren, the sons of one man in the land of Canaan; and behold, the youngest *is* this day with our father, and one *is* not.

14. And Joseph said unto them, That *is it* that I spake unto you, saying, Ye *are* spies:

15. Hereby ye shall be proved: By the life of Pharaoh ye shall not go forth hence, except your youngest brother come hither.

16. Send one of you, and let him fetch your brother, and ye shall be kept in prison, that your words may be proved, whether *there be any* truth in you: or else by the life of Pharaoh surely ye *are* spies.

17. And he put them all together into ward three days.

18. And Joseph said unto them the third day, This do and live; *for* I fear God:

19. If ye *be* true *men*, let one of your brethren be bound in the

house of your prison; go ye, carry corn for the famine of your houses: 20. But bring your youngest brother unto me; so shall your words be verified, and ye shall not die. And they did so.

21. And they said one to another, We *are* verily guilty concerning our brother, in that we saw the anguish of his soul, when he besought us, and we would not hear; therefore is this distress come upon us.

22. And Reuben answered them, saying, Spake I not unto you, saying, Do not sin against the child; and ye would not hear? therefore, behold, also his blood is required.

23. And they knew not that Joseph understood *them ;* for he spake unto them by an interpreter.

24. And he turned himself about from them, and wept; and returned to them again, and communed with them, and took from them Simeon, and bound him before their eyes.

25. ¶ Then Joseph commanded to fill their sacks with corn, and to restore every man's money into his sack, and to give them provision for the way: and thus did he unto them.

26. And they laded their asses with the corn, and departed thence.

27. And as one of them opened his sack to give his ass provender in the inn, he espied his money; for, behold, it *was* in his sack's mouth.

28. And he said unto his brethren, My money is restored; and lo, *it is* even in my sack: and their heart failed *them*, and they were afraid, saying one to another, What *is* this *that* God hath done unto us?

29. ¶ And they came unto Jacob their father unto the land of Canaan, and told him all that befell unto them, saying,

30. The man, *who is* the lord of the land, spake roughly to us, and took us for spies of the country.

31. And we said unto him, We *are* true *men ;* we are no spies:

32. We *be* twelve brethren, sons of our father; one *is* not, and the youngest *is* this day with our father in the land of Canaan.

33. And the man, the lord of the country, said unto us, Hereby shall I know that ye *are* true *men ;* leave one of your brethren *here* with me, and take *food for* the famine of your households, and be gone:

34. And bring your youngest brother unto me; then shall I know that ye *are* no spies, but *that* ye *are* true *men ; so* will I deliver you your brother, and ye shall traffic in the land.

35. ¶ And it came to pass as they emptied their sacks, that behold, every man's bundle of money *was* in his sack: and when *both* they and their father saw the bundles of money, they were afraid.

36. And Jacob their father said unto them, Me have ye bereaved *of my children :* Joseph *is* not, and Simeon *is* not, and ye will take Benjamin *away :* all these things are against me.

37. And Reuben spake unto his father, saying, Slay my two sons, if I bring him not to thee: deliver him into my hand, and I will bring him to thee again.

38. And he said, My son shall not go down with you; for his brother is dead, and he is left alone: if mischief befall him by the way in the which ye go, then shall ye bring down my grey hairs with sorrow to the grave.

644. It appears from several instances recorded in Genesis, that going to Egypt for supplies during famine, was not an unusual occurrence. And the reason why Egypt was more highly favored, in this respect, than Canaan and other lands, was that its fertility did not depend upon rains falling directly upon the land, but upon the overflowing of the Nile. And though the lack of rain, at its source, would in time lessen its waters and prevent the overflowing of the land, and thereby occasion a famine, yet this would require a considerable period ; and when such an event occurred, it would evidently last a no less period. Hence, a seven years of plenty, when the Nile overflowed the land, and made its productions abundant, followed by as long a period of dearth, was a natural occurrence for that country ; though there is probably no other land on the earth where such a thing would be likely to occur, except by a miracle.

645. That Joseph should know his brethren, and they not know him, may seem at first a little strange : but Joseph was of an age to change more than most of his brethren who were older ; and besides, the fashion of his clothing was probably quite different from theirs ; to which we may add the ornaments he wore, as badges of authority, all which would tend to disguise him in the presence of his brethren. He was familiar with their dress and appearance ; but they were not familiar with his.

646. The suspicion that the brethren may have come "to see the nakedness of the land," was one of the best devices that was possible, as the existence of a famine there would seem to justify the charge : for it was not to be presumed, by Joseph's brethren, that there had been any special preparations for supplying the country, in such an emergency.

647. " One is not," — that is, one is dead. That was the story they had all along told ; and they tell it now, to keep up the appearance of consistency. There are two additional reasons for this. One is, that the eldest brother Reuben, and perhaps some of the others, had not yet known but that Joseph was killed ; and it was not best to inform them. Another is, that the facts of the case would not be likely to increase the good opinion they would have the Egyptian ruler entertain of them.

648. "By the life of Pharaoh," was the strongest form of oath known in Egypt. It was equivalent to saying, — "The life of the king be sacrificed, rather than what I say prove untrue."

649. Joseph says that he fears God; and he therefore suggests retaining one of the brethren as a hostage, and allowing the rest to go back to Canaan, and carry food to their families; whereas he might, in view of his suspicions, have kept them all, save one to go and bring the youngest brother, as he had first proposed.

650. "We are verily guilty." Observe, that when they allude to the anguish of Joseph, they are careful not to drop a word about his fate; and Reuben, hearing them, supposes they allude to his death, and makes his remarks according to this supposition.

651. The language of Egypt was different from the language of Canaan. Therefore the "interpreter" alluded to.

652. Why Simeon was selected as the hostage rather than either of the others may not be certain. It may be on account of his being the oldest, except Reuben; and the latter Joseph would be disposed to favor for his good intentions, while the rest were plotting his destruction. Besides, the absence of this brother might be less distressing to the father, as he had greatly incurred the old man's displeasure in the sacking of Shalem.

653. This is the only place where inns are mentioned in this book. The character of the establishment cannot be justly inferred from this single instance. That the travellers fed their own provender, is expressly stated; and being furnished in Egypt with provisions for the way, would also indicate that these things were not expected to be obtained at the inns along the route. Still, the circumstances were extraordinary, and extraordinary arrangements had to be made. In times of plenty the inns may have supplied these accommodations.

654. It would seem that one only had the money "in the mouth of the sack," while, with the rest, it was at the bottom, where they would not be likely to find it, till they reached home.

655. "Slay my two sons." When Reuben went down to Egypt he had four sons; but when this language occurred he may have had but two. The proposition was an emphatic way of giving the old man the assurance that Benjamin should be returned.

656. With sorrow to the grave, to *Sheol,* the place of the dead. See pp. 65–67.

SECTION XXI. — SECOND DESCENT TO EGYPT.

CHAP. XLIII.

1. And the famine *was* sore in the land.
2. And it came to pass, when they had eaten up the corn which they had brought out of Egypt, their father said unto them, Go again, buy us a little food.
3. And Judah spake unto him, saying, The man did solemnly protest unto us, saying, Ye shall not see my face, except your brother *be* with you.
4. If thou wilt send our brother with us, we will go down and buy thee food:
5. But if thou wilt not send *him* we will not go down: for the man said unto us, Ye shall not see my face, except your brother *be* with you.
6. And Israel said, Wherefore dealt ye *so* ill with me, *as* to tell the man whether ye had yet a brother?
7. And they said, The man asked us straitly of our state, and of our kindred, saying, *Is* your father yet alive? have ye *another* brother? and we told him according to the tenor of these words: Could we certainly know that he would say, Bring your brother down?
8. And Judah said unto Israel his father, Send the lad with me, and we will arise and go; that we may live, and not die, both we, and thou, *and* also our little ones.
9. I will be surety for him; of my hand shalt thou require him: If I bring him not unto thee, and set him before thee, then let me bear the blame for ever:
10. For except we had lingered, surely now we had returned this second time.
11. And their father Israel said unto them, If *it must be* so now, do this; take of the best fruits in the land in your vessels, and carry down the man a present, a little balm, and a little honey, spices, and myrrh, nuts, and almonds:
12. And take double money in your hand; and the money that was brought again in the mouth of your sacks, carry *it* again in your hand; peradventure it *was* an oversight:
13. Take also your brother, and arise, go again unto the man.
14. And God Almighty give you mercy before the man, that he may send away your other brother, and Benjamin. If I be bereaved *of my children,* I am bereaved.
15. ¶ And the men took that present, and they took double money in their hand, and Benjamin; and rose up, and went down to Egypt, and stood before Joseph.
16. And when Joseph saw Benjamin with them, he said to the ruler of his house, Bring *these* men home, and slay, and make ready; for *these* men shall dine with me at noon.
17. And the man did as Joseph bade; and the man brought the men into Joseph's house.

JACOB AND HIS FAMILY. 351

18. And the men were afraid, because they were brought into Joseph's house; and they said, Because of the money that was returned in our sacks at the first time are we brought in; that he may seek occasion against us, and fall upon us, and take us for bondmen, and our asses.

19 ¶ And they came near to the steward of Joseph's house, and they communed with him at the door of the house.

20. And said, O sir, we came indeed down at the first time to buy food:

21. And it came to pass, when we came to the inn, that we opened our sacks, and behold, *every* man's money *was* in the mouth of his sack, our money in full weight: and we have brought it again in our hand.

22. And other money have we brought down in our hands to buy food: we cannot tell who put our money in our sacks.

23. And he said, Peace *be* to you, fear not: your God, and the God of your father, hath given you treasure in your sacks: I had your money. And he brought Simeon out unto them.

24. And the man brought the men into Joseph's house, and gave *them* water, and they washed their feet; and he gave their asses provender.

25. And they made ready the present against Joseph came at noon: for they heard that they should eat bread there.

26. And when Joseph came home, they brought him the present which *was* in their hand into the house, and bowed themselves to him to the earth.

27. And he asked them of *their* welfare, and said, *Is* your father well? the old man of whom ye spake, *is* he yet alive?

28. And they answered, Thy servant our father *is* in good health, he *is* yet alive: and they bowed down their heads, and made obeisance.

29. And he lifted up his eyes, and saw his brother Benjamin, his mother's son, and said, *Is* this your younger brother, of whom ye spake unto me? And he said, God be gracious unto thee, my son.

30. And Joseph made haste; for his bowels did yearn upon his brother: and he sought *where* to weep; and he entered into *his* chamber, and wept there.

31. And he washed his face, and went out, and refrained himself, and said, Set on bread.

32. And they set on for him by himself, and for them by themselves, and for the Egyptians which did eat with him by themselves; because the Egyptians might not eat bread with the Hebrews: for that *is* an abomination unto the Egyptians.

33. And they sat before him, the first-born according to his birthright, and the youngest according to his youth: and the men marvelled one at another.

34. And he took *and sent* messes unto them from before him: but Benjamin's mess was five times so much as any of theirs. And they drank and were merry with him.

657. The conversation between Jacob and his sons, as preliminary to their second journey, is what might have been expected on such an occasion. The old man is grievously distressed with the idea of parting with Benjamin; but still he sees no other way in view of the circumstances. Reuben had given him the strongest pledges that his darling boy should not be harmed; and now Judah does

the same; and as we have yet found nothing in the conduct of Judah, as he stood related to his father, to incur the old man's displeasure, as we have with the three older sons, we may conclude that his influence was more available on that account. The consent is at last obtained; and the sons start for Egypt with their father's solemn benediction on their heads; and a few articles, the choicest things they had, as a present to the king.

658. There seems a discrepancy between xlii. 35 and xliii. 21, and there may be this discrepancy; as, in the latter passage, the brethren seem to have been somewhat excited, and were not very exact, in their statements. Besides, it was not important that they should be exact, in making the last statement, as it was not made to Joseph, but to one of his servants.

659. The suspicions of the brethren that they are brought into Joseph's house for bad purposes, was only one of the results of a guilty conscience. They had been guilty of an enormous wrong; and though several years had passed, since they committed the act, yet their guilt still clung to them; and whatever of misfortune befell them, or was likely to befall them, they were ready to attribute to their former conduct. It shows the necessity of keeping clear from crime that is followed by such consequences.

660. The feeling of Joseph towards his brother Benjamin, was a natural state of things, as this was indeed his only brother by the same mother, and that mother was dead. And though we find Joseph at last unable to restrain his feelings, in regard to all his brethren, and he treated them most affectionately, yet Benjamin all along is evidently regarded as the favorite one; as very naturally he would be.

SECTION XXII. — THE SILVER CUP.

CHAP. XLIV.

1. And he commanded the steward of his house, saying, Fill the men's sacks *with* food, as much as they can carry, and put every man's money in his sack's mouth.

2. And put my cup, the silver cup, in the sack's mouth of the youngest, and his corn money. And he did according to the word that Joseph had spoken.

3. As soon as the morning was light, the men were sent away, they and their asses.

4. And when they were gone out of the city, and not yet far off, Joseph said unto his steward, Up, follow after the men; and when thou dost overtake them, say unto them, Wherefore have ye rewarded evil for good?

5. Is not this it in which my lord drinketh, and whereby indeed he divineth? ye have done evil in so doing.

6. ¶ And he overtook them, and he spake unto them these same words.

7. And they said unto him, Wherefore saith my lord these words? God forbid that thy servants should do according to this thing:

8. Behold, the money, which we found in our sacks' mouths, we brought again unto thee out of the land of Canaan: how then should we steal out of thy lord's house silver or gold?

9. With whomsoever of thy servants it be found, both let him die, and we also will be my lord's bondmen.

10. And he said, Now also let it be according unto your words; he with whom it is found shall be my servant; and ye shall be blameless.

11. Then they speedily took down every man his sack to the ground, and opened every man his sack.

12. And he searched, and began at the eldest, and left at the youngest: and the cup was found in Benjamin's sack.

13. Then they rent their clothes, and laded every man his ass, and returned to the city.

14. ¶ And Judah and his brethren came to Joseph's house, for he was yet there: and they fell before him on the ground.

15. And Joseph said unto them, What deed is this that ye have done? wot ye not that such a man as I can certainly divine?

16. And Judah said, What shall we say unto my lord? what shall we speak? or how shall we clear ourselves? God hath found out the iniquity of thy servants: behold, we are my lord's servants, both we, and he also with whom the cup is found.

17. And he said, God forbid that I should do so; but the man in whose hand the cup is found, he shall be my servant; and as for you, get you up in peace unto your father.

18. ¶ Then Judah came near unto him, and said, Oh my lord, let thy servant, I pray thee, speak a word in my lord's ears, and let not thine anger burn against thy servant: for thou art even as Pharaoh.

19. My lord asked his servants, saying, Have ye a father, or a brother?

20. And we said unto my lord, We have a father, an old man, and a child of his old age, a little one; and his brother is dead, and he alone is left of his mother, and his father loveth him.

21. And thou saidst unto thy servants, Bring him down unto me, that I may set mine eyes upon him.

22. And we said unto my lord, The lad cannot leave his father: for if he should leave his father, his father would die.

23. And thou saidst unto thy servants, Except your youngest brother come down with you, ye shall see my face no more.

24. And it came to pass when we came up unto thy servant my father, we told him the words of my lord.

25. And our father said, Go again, and buy us a little food.

26. And we said, We cannot go down: if our youngest brother be with us, then will we go down: for we may not see the man's face, except our youngest brother be with us.

27. And thy servant my father said unto us, Ye know that my wife bare me two sons:

28. And the one went out from me, and I said, Surely he is torn in pieces; and I saw him not since;

29. And if ye take this also from me, and mischief befall him, ye shall bring down my gray hairs with sorrow to the grave.

30. Now therefore when I come to thy servant my father, and the lad *be* not with us, (seeing that his life is bound up in the lad's life:)

31. It shall come to pass, when he seeth that the lad *is* not *with us*, that he will die: and thy servants shall bring down the gray hairs of thy servant our father with sorrow to the grave.

32. For thy servant became surety for the lad unto my father, saying, If I bring him not unto thee, then I shall bear the blame to my father for ever.

33. Now therefore, I pray thee, let thy servant abide instead of the lad, a bondman to my lord; and let the lad go up with his brethren.

34. For how shall I go up to my father, and the lad *be* not with me? lest peradventure I see the evil that shall come on my father.

661. "Whereby he divineth." An allusion, it would seem, to some practice of the magicians, and the reference to it, was intended to intimate that he could detect them in their guilt, by some virtue belonging to that cup. In another verse, (15th) this idea is conveyed directly.

662. It is reasonable to suppose that Benjamin would protest his innocence, and doubtless he did, but to no effect, for, not only Joseph, but even Judah, assumed that the larceny had been committed. But what they should do, under the circumstances, they did not know. True, they could leave Benjamin in Egypt as a slave, and go back to Canaan, but they had given the strongest assurances that Benjamin should be returned in safety; and how, in view of their pledges, could they meet their aged father and Benjamin be not with them? This was truly a sad case.

663. The plea of Judah that follows, is the most perfect argument under the circumstances, that it was possible for any mortal man to utter. We do not wonder that it took effect.

SECTION XXIII.—JOSEPH MADE KNOWN TO HIS BRETHREN.

CHAP. XLV.

1. Then Joseph could not refrain himself before all them that stood by him: and he cried, Cause every man to go out from me. And there stood no man with him, while Joseph made himself known unto his brethren.

2. And he wept aloud; and the Egyptians and the house of Pharaoh heard.

3. And Joseph said unto his brethren, I *am* Joseph: doth my father yet live? and his brethren could not answer him; for

JACOB AND HIS FAMILY. 355

they were troubled at his presence.
4. And Joseph said unto his brethren, Come near to me, I pray you. And they came near. And he said, I am Joseph your brother, whom ye sold into Egypt.
5. Now therefore be not grieved, nor angry with yourselves, that ye sold me hither; for God did send me before you to preserve life
6. For these two years *hath* the famine *been* in the land; and yet *there are* five years, in the which *there shall* neither *be* earing nor harvest.
7. And God sent me before you to preserve you a posterity in the earth, and to save your lives by a great deliverance.
8. So now *it was* not you *that* sent me hither, but God: and he hath made me a father to Pharaoh, and lord of all his house, and a ruler throughout all the land of Egypt.
9. Haste ye, and go up to my father, and say unto him, Thus saith thy son Joseph, God hath made me lord of all Egypt: come down unto me, tarry not.
10. And thou shalt dwell in the land of Goshen, and thou shalt be near unto me, thou, and thy children, and thy children's children, and thy flocks, and thy herds, and all that thou hast:
11. And there will I nourish thee: (for yet *there are* five years of famine:) lest thou, and thy household, and all that thou hast, come to poverty.
12. And, behold, your eyes see, and the eyes of my brother Benjamin, that *it is* my mouth that speaketh unto you.
13. And ye shall tell my father of all my glory in Egypt, and of all that ye have seen; and ye shall haste, and bring down my father hither.
14. And he fell upon his brother Benjamin's neck, and wept; and Benjamin wept upon his neck.
15. Moreover, he kissed all his brethren, and wept upon them, and after that his brethren talked with him.

664. The scene here brought to view is intensely exciting. Nothing could be more natural, and nothing could be more affecting. If human language was ever dictated by divine inspiration, we should say that the language of Joseph on this occasion was so uttered. And the doctrine inculcated is so beautifully expressed, "Not you, but God, sent me here." The whole thing is a divine Providence. The salvation of the people from destruction, is the purpose accomplished, and God is deserving of all the praise. If such were the purpose of God with respect to Joseph's brethren, is it not reasonable to conclude, that all sins are overruled, in like manner, for good?

665. It is reasonable to presume that if Joseph had been at liberty to go up to Canaan, he would have done so, and not required his father's family to come down into Egypt. The latter arrangement was the one adopted, mainly on account of the famine. Still, Joseph, if not retained in Egypt of necessity, had many reasons for remaining there; and the change to that country, he doubtless regarded as a great advantage to his father's family.

666. The special affection of Joseph for Benjamin, here and elsewhere shown, was quite natural; not only as being nearly of the same age; but as being the sons of the same mother, while the other brethren were not so.

SECTION XXIV.—JACOB IS SENT FOR.

CHAP. XLV.

16. ¶ And the fame thereof was heard in Pharaoh's house, saying, Joseph's brethren are come: and it pleased Pharaoh well, and his servants.

17. And Pharaoh said unto Joseph, Say unto thy brethren, this do ye; lade your beasts, and go, get you unto the land of Canaan.

18. And take your father and your households, and come unto me: and I will give you the good of the land of Egypt, and ye shall eat the fat of the land.

19. Now thou art commanded, this do ye; Take you wagons out of the land of Egypt for your little ones, and for your wives, and bring your father, and come.

20. Also regard not your stuff: for the good of all the land of Egypt *is* yours.

21. ¶ And the children of Israel did so: and Joseph gave them wagons, according to the commandment of Pharaoh, and gave them provision for the way.

22. To all of them he gave each man changes of raiment; but to Benjamin he gave three hundred *pieces* of silver, and five changes of raiment.

23. And to his father he sent after this *manner;* ten asses laden with the good things of Egypt, and ten she asses laden with corn and bread and meat, for his father by the way.

24. So he sent his brethren away, and they departed: and he said unto them, See that ye fall not out by the way.

25. ¶ And they went up out of Egypt, and came into the land of Canaan unto Jacob their father.

26. And told him, saying, Joseph *is* yet alive, and he *is* governor over all the land of Egypt. And Jacob's heart fainted, for he believed them not.

27. And they told him all the words of Joseph, which he had said unto them; and when he saw the wagons which Joseph had sent to carry him, the spirit of Jacob their father revived.

28. And Israel said, *It is* enough: Joseph my son *is* yet alive: I will go and see him before I die.

667. The liberality of Pharaoh, as here exhibited, is worthy of our admiration; nor must we withhold it, though it be bestowed upon a heathen ruler. That wagons were to be taken from Egypt to bring down the patriarch and his household, indicates clearly that these vehicles were an Egyptian convenience, and that they were not used in Canaan. The "good things of Egypt," are not here described. They may have consisted of garments and ornaments. They were obviously not provisions, as these are specially named afterwards : and the provisions sent, though said to be for "his father" by the way, were evidently intended for all the household, consisting of many families, and a large company of servants.

668. "See that ye fall not out by the way:"—a very fit and timely admonition, since, in view of the circumstances, a "falling out" would be very apt to occur; each one being disposed to reproach the others for the cruel treatment of Joseph when they sold him to the Ishmaelites.

669. The effect of the intelligence that Joseph was yet living, upon his aged father, is precisely what we should expect. The first shock was nearly overwhelming. The news was too good to be true. At length, however, when the evidence was such as could not be well resisted, he yields a joyful faith to the message, and enters at once upon the necessary arrangements for the journey.

SECTION XXV.—JOURNEY TO EGYPT.

CHAP. XLVI.

1. And Israel took his journey with all that he had, and came to Beersheba, and offered sacrifices unto the God of his father Isaac.
2. And God spake unto Israel in the visions of the night, and said, Jacob, Jacob! And he said, Here am I.
3. And he said, I am God, the God of thy father: fear not to go down into Egypt; for I will there make of thee a great nation:
4. I will go down with thee into Egypt; and I will also surely bring thee up again: and Joseph shall put his hand upon thine eyes.
5. And Jacob rose up from Beersheba; and the sons of Israel carried Jacob their father, and their little ones, and their wives, in the wagons which Pharaoh had sent to carry him.
6. And they took their cattle, and their goods, which they had gotten in the land of Canaan, and came into Egypt, Jacob, and all his seed with him:
7. His sons, and his sons' sons with him, his daughters, and his sons' daughters, and all his seed brought he with him into Egypt.

670. The temporary stop at Beersheba, was exceedingly natural, as Jacob had resided there, (and so had Abram and Isaac,) on a former occasion; and we learn from this passage, as well as from others, that Beersheba lay in the direction of Egypt from Hebron.

671. "God spake to Israel in the visions of the night." And the reason of the communication seems to be, that Jacob was now leaving the promised land, which had been given to him and his seed ; and he may have had doubts whether or not it was the divine pleasure that he should do so ; and to assure him on this point, he is encouraged to go down into Egypt with the promise that he should again be brought up from that country, and should at length come into possession of the long promised inheritance. The announcement to Abram, (chap. xv.) that his seed should be a stranger in a land that was not theirs, and should be afflicted four hundred years, seemed now in the way of being fulfilled, though it does not appear that Jacob understood the prediction as having reference to his sojourn in Egypt, nor could it be certain that such was its design, till a later period, as the prediction did not specify the country where the servitude should be suffered.

SECTION XXVI. — Joseph's meeting with his Father.

CHAP. XLVI.

28. And he sent Judah before him unto Joseph, to direct his face unto Goshen; and they came into the land of Goshen.
29. And Joseph made ready his chariot, and went up to meet Israel his father to Goshen, and presented himself unto him, and he fell on his neck, and wept on his neck a good while.
30. And Israel said unto Joseph, Now let me die, since I have seen thy face, because thou *art* yet alive.

672. Judah was sent in advance to inform Joseph, and see to the requisite preparations. Joseph goes forward to meet his father, and to mingle his tears of joy with those of the old man whose happiness on earth is now complete.

673. The location of Goshen is sufficiently indicated by this passage. It was the nearest part of Egypt to Canaan. The Septuagint calls it "Goshen of Arabia," which sustains the same opinion. It must have extended far enough to the East, beyond the northern point of the

Red Sea, to have joined Arabia and thereby to have received this designation.

674. Joseph had a special chariot called "the second chariot;" and with this he goes to meet his father, accompanied, it may be, with his customary attendants.

SECTION XXVII.—INTERVIEW OF THE BRETHREN WITH PHARAOH.

CHAP. XLVI.

31. And Joseph said unto his brethren, and unto his father's house, I will go up and shew Pharaoh, and say unto him, my brethren, and my father's house, which *were* in the land of Canaan, are come unto thee.

32. And the men *are* shepherds, for their trade hath been to feed cattle; and they have brought their flocks, and their herds, and all that they have.

33. And it shall come to pass, when Pharaoh shall call you, and shall say, What *is* your occupation?

34. That ye shall say, Thy servants' trade hath been about cattle from our youth even until now, both we *and* also our fathers; that ye may dwell in the land of Goshen; for every shepherd *is* an abomination unto the Egyptians.

CHAP. XLVII.

1. Then Joseph came and told Pharaoh, and said, My father, and my brethren, and their flocks, and their herds, and all that they have, are come out of the land of Canaan: and, behold, they *are* in the land of Goshen.

2. And he took some of his brethren, *even* five men, and presented them unto Pharaoh.

3. And Pharaoh said unto his brethren, What *is* your occupation? And they said unto Pharaoh, Thy servants *are* shepherds, both we, *and* also our fathers.

4. They said moreover unto Pharaoh, For to sojourn in the land are we come, for thy servants have no pasture for their flocks; for the famine *is* sore in the land of Canaan; now therefore, we pray thee, let thy servants dwell in the land of Goshen.

5. And Pharaoh spake unto Joseph, saying, Thy father and thy brethren are come unto thee:

6. The land of Egypt *is* before thee: in the best of the land make thy father and thy brethren to dwell; in the land of Goshen let them dwell: and if thou knowest *any* men of activity among them, then make them rulers over my cattle.

675. That the children of Israel were shepherds, would incline Pharaoh to give them a separate part of the country, in view of the prevailing prejudice, against that class of men; and this was precisely what the sons of Jacob desired, as they could thus preserve their separate identity and their separate customs. The reason why shepherds were an abomination to the Egyptians, does not appear from the narrative, though it may be found in the history of that country at a former period. That there were no shepherds in Egypt, however, we must not conclude; for the proposition of Pharaoh, xlvii. 6, to make some of Joseph's brethren rulers over his cattle, would refute this idea. And at a later day there are numerous references to cattle in Egypt. But evidently this was not the main business of the people; and being uncommon it was not regarded with favor; and not being regarded with favor, it became uncommon.

676. The result of this interview was what had been desired — the land of Goshen was assigned to the Israelites; and we infer from what is said of it, that it was literally the best of the land. And being watered by the Nile, the land would be productive, while such would not be the case with the country of Canaan. And though, at this time, we may conclude the land was less productive than common, on account of the famine, we may also infer, that there was still some pasturage for the cattle.

SECTION XXVIII.— INTERVIEW OF ISRAEL WITH PHARAOH.

CHAP. XLVII.

7. And Joseph brought in Jacob his father, and set him before Pharaoh: and Jacob blessed Pharaoh.
8. And Pharaoh said unto Jacob, How old art thou?
9. And Jacob said unto Pharaoh, The days of the years of my pilgrimage are an hundred and thirty years: few and evil have the days of the years of my life been, and have not attained unto the days of the years of the life of my fathers in the days of their pilgrimage.
10. And Jacob blessed Pharaoh, and went out from before Pharaoh.

677. We cannot doubt that much more occurred in this interview than what is here recorded; but allusion is made to the age of the patriarch, as one important circumstance that seemed to be worthy of preservation in the record.

Jacob blessed Pharaoh when the interview began, and the same thing is repeated at the close. We infer that this was customary, especially on important occasions. The "blessing" was evidently nothing more than a benediction, or an expression of good wishes toward the king.

678. Isaac had lived to the age of 180 years, and Abraham to the age of 175; so that Jacob, at 130 years, had indeed not yet attained to the age of his fathers. There is no reference to the longevity of the patriarchs before the time of Abraham.

SECTION XXIX.—THE FAMINE.

CHAP. XLVII.

11. And Joseph placed his father and his brethren, and gave them a possession in the land of Egypt, in the best of the land, in the land of Rameses, as Pharaoh had commanded.

12. And Joseph nourished his father, and his brethren, and all his father's household, with bread, according to *their* families.

13. ¶ And *there was* no bread in all the land; for the famine *was* very sore, so that the land of Egypt, and *all* the land of Canaan, fainted by reason of the famine.

14. And Joseph gathered up all the money that was found in the land of Egypt, and in the land of Canaan, for the corn which they bought: and Joseph brought the money into Pharaoh's house.

15. And when money failed in the land of Egypt, and in the land of Canaan, all the Egyptians came unto Joseph, and said, Give us bread: for why should we die in thy presence? for the money faileth.

16. And Joseph said, Give your cattle; and I will give you for your cattle, if money fail.

17. And they brought their cattle unto Joseph: and Joseph gave them bread *in exchange* for horses, and for the flocks, and for the cattle of the herds, and for the asses: and he fed them with bread for all their cattle for that year.

18. When the year was ended, they came unto him the second year, and said unto him, We will not hide *it* from my lord, how that our money is spent; my lord also hath our herds of cattle: there is not aught left in the sight of my lord, but our bodies and our lands:

19. Wherefore shall we die before thine eyes, both we and our land? buy us and our land for bread, and we and our land will be servants unto Pharaoh, and give *us* seed, that we may live and not die, that the land be not desolate.

20. And Joseph bought all the land of Egypt for Pharaoh: for the Egyptians sold every man his field, because the famine prevailed over them; so the land became Pharaoh's.

21. And as for the people, he removed them to cities from *one* end of the borders of Egypt even to the *other* end thereof.

22. Only the land of the priests bought he not; for the priests had a portion *assigned them* of Pharaoh, and did eat their portion which Pharaoh gave them; wherefore they sold not their lands.

23. Then Joseph said unto the people, Behold I have bought you this day, and your land for Pharaoh: lo, *here is* seed for you, and ye shall sow the land.

24. And it shall come to pass, in the increase, that ye shall give the fifth *part* unto Pharaoh: and four parts shall be your own, for seed of the field, and for your food, and for them of your households, and for food for your little ones.

25. And they said, thou hast

saved our lives; let us find grace in the sight of my lord, and we will be Pharoah's servants.

26. And Joseph made it a law over the land of Egypt unto this day, *that* Pharaoh should have the fifth *part;* except the land of the priests only, *which* became not Pharaoh's.

27. ¶ And Israel dwelt in the land of Egypt, in the country of Goshen; and they had possessions therein, and grew, and multiplied exceedingly.

679. The settlement in Goshen, requires no comment, as this was the conclusion of an arrangement that has already been sufficiently noticed.

680. We have suggested, in another place, that the Egyptians, expecting a famine, would be apt to lay in an extra store, besides the fifth exacted of them by the king. Hence it appears that the special distress of the people, was not felt till the last two years of the seven; for I understand these to be the two years referred to in the foregoing passage.

"That year," verse 17, we take to be the sixth year; and "when that year was ended they come unto him the second year," not the second year of the famine, but the year following the one just alluded to, and "second" with reference to that, but in fact the last of the famine. This view is sustained, as before shown, by the fact that no mention is made of any other years of famine succeeding this. This is one circumstance. Another is, that the people are now represented as parting with all they possess, and becoming themselves the servants of Pharaoh; of course they had nothing to pay for other years of famine. And finally, the people are here furnished with seed to sow the land, as if the famine were at an end.

681. Joseph "removed the people to the cities, from one end of the borders of Egypt to the other end thereof." The Septuagint says that he made the people servants, from one end of Egypt to the other. The latter construction is in harmony with the context, while the other gives us no intimation of the intention of what is there stated.

682. The priests in Egypt have always been the most influential class of the citizens of that country. They not only presided over the arrangements of religion : but the sciences were in their hands; and it was in view of their importance to the state, that they were granted special privileges. They were not required, therefore, to sell their lands ; but were furnished with a supply of provisions, without any such consideration.

683. The fifth part of the products of the land, which was the proportion exacted of the people during the seven years of plenty, to prepare for the famine, was afterwards made a permanent arrangement, and continued so, the writer tells us, " unto this day ;" but when that period was, we cannot say. It may be Moses, and it may be some later writer, that added this clause.

SECTION XXX.—ISRAEL ABOUT TO DIE.

CHAP. XLVII.

28. And Jacob lived in the land of Egypt seventeen years: so the whole age of Jacob was an hundred forty and seven years.
29. And the time drew nigh that Israel must die: and he called his son Joseph, and said unto him, If now I have found grace in thy sight, put, I pray thee, thy hand under my thigh, and deal kindly and truly with me; bury me not, I pray thee, in Egypt:
30. But I will lie with my fathers, and thou shalt carry me out of Egypt, and bury me in their burying-place. And he said, I will do as thou hast said.
31. And he said, Swear unto me: And he sware unto him. And Israel bowed himself upon the bed's head.

684. Abram required the same form of oath of his eldest servant, on an important occasion, and we may reasonably infer that it was the customary form.

The great aim of the patriarch was to be carried back to Canaan ; and he puts his son under the strongest possible obligation to execute his wishes ; and the reason of applying to him, rather than to either of his other sons, was not alone the affection he had for him ; but because there was a reasonable probability that he would possess an ability to do thus, that the others would not.

685. We may add, that, to be carried back to Canaan and buried there, was not only the common feeling of all men to be buried in one's own land, and among his own kindred ; but, that country is looked upon as the promised inheritance of the seed of Abraham ; and the patriarch would be buried where his future seed were to occupy and control the country.

" I will do as thou hast said," was not enough to satisfy the patriarch. "Swear unto me," he says, and Joseph does swear accordingly; and we learn that the oath was faithfully executed.

SECTION XXXI.—ISRAEL BLESSES THE SONS OF JOSEPH.

CHAP. XLVIII.

1. And it came to pass, after these things, that *one* told Joseph, Behold, thy father *is* sick: and he took with him his two sons, Manasseh and Ephraim.

2. And *one* told Jacob, and said, Behold, thy son Joseph cometh unto thee: And Israel strengthened himself, and sat upon the bed.

3. And Jacob said unto Joseph, God Almighty appeared unto me at Luz in the land of Canaan, and blessed me.

4. And said unto me, Behold, I will make thee fruitful, and multiply thee, and I will make of thee a multitude of people; and I will give this land to thy seed after thee *for* an everlasting possession.

5. And now thy two sons, Ephraim and Manasseh, which were born unto thee in the land of Egypt, before I came unto thee in the land of Egypt, *are* mine; as Reuben and Simeon, they shall be mine.

6. And thy issue which thou begettest after them, shall be thine, *and* shall be called after the name of their brethren in their inheritance.

7. And as for me, when I came from Padan, Rachel died by me in the land of Canaan, in the way, when yet *there was* but a little way to come unto Ephrath: and I buried her there in the way of Ephrath; the same *is* Bethlehem.

8. ¶ And Israel beheld Joseph's sons, and said, Who *are* these?

9. And Joseph said unto his father, They *are* my sons, whom God hath given me in this *place.* And he said, Bring them, I pray thee, unto me, and I will bless them.

10. (Now the eyes of Israel were dim for age *so that* he could not see.) And he brought them near unto him: and he kissed them, and embraced them.

11. And Israel said unto Joseph, I had not thought to see thy face, and, lo, God hath shewed me also thy seed.

12. And Joseph brought them out from between his knees, and he bowed himself with his face to the earth.

13. And Joseph took them both, Ephraim in his right hand toward Israel's left hand, and Manasseh in his left hand toward Israel's right hand, and brought *them* near unto him.

14. And Israel stretched out his right hand, and laid *it* upon Ephraim's head, who *was* the younger, and his left hand upon Manasseh's head, guiding his hands wittingly; for Manasseh *was* the first-born.

15. And he blessed Joseph, and said, God, before whom my fathers Abraham and Isaac did walk, the God which fed me all my life long unto this day,

16. The angel which redeemed me from all evil, bless the lads; and let my name be named on them, and the name of my fathers Abraham and Isaac; and let them grow into a multitude in the midst of the earth.

17. And when Joseph saw that his father laid his right hand upon the head of Ephraim, it displeased him: and he held up his father's hand, to remove it from Ephraim's head unto Manasseh's head.

18. And Joseph said unto his father, Not so, my father: for this *is* the first-born; put thy right hand upon his head.

19. And his father refused, and said, I know *it* my son, I know *it:* he also shall become a people, and

he also shall be great: but truly his younger brother shall be greater than he, and his seed shall become a multitude of nations.

20 And he blessed them that day, saying, in thee shall Israel bless, saying, God make thee as Ephraim and as Manasseh. And he set Ephraim before Manasseh.

21. And Israel said unto Joseph, Behold, I die; but God shall be with you, and bring you again unto the land of your fathers.

22. Moreover, I have given to thee one portion above thy brethren; which I took out of the hand of the Amorite with my sword and with my bow.

686. Luz was the ancient name of Bethel; and we have seen that God had appeared to Jacob, several times, in that place, and had, each time, given him substantially the promise here referred to. It was obvious, therefore, that the children of Israel would not always remain in Egypt; and when they returned to Canaan, it was the wish of the patriarch that his two grand-sons, Ephraim and Manasseh, should have a portion of the country assigned to them, as well as to his other sons. He therefore says "they are mine, as Reuben and Simeon;" and "they shall be called after the name of their brethren in their inheritance."

687. The allusion to the death of Rachel, and to the place of her burial, in this connection, seems to intimate the portion of Canaan he would have the two sons of Joseph occupy. I had not thought to see thy face; and lo, God hath showed me also thy seed. How exceedingly natural and paternal.

688. That Jacob was impressed with the fact that Ephraim would become much more numerous and powerful than Manasseh, may be the true interpretation of the preference here signified; and it may be explained as simply the desire of the patriarch, that it should be so, which providentially came about, or which God graciously accomplished, in answer to the patriarch's prayer.

689. "He blessed Joseph," that is, by blessing the sons of Joseph; for the blessing of Joseph directly, occurred in the general blessing on all his sons, recorded in the next chapter. That Joseph's sons might grow into a multitude is the burden of the prayer here recorded; and that is substantially the burden of all the prayers of ancient times;—a plain proof that a numerous posterity was the most desirable object which could be presented to the mind in those days.

690. It seems plain from what is said of the hands of Israel, that the right hand had more importance attached to it than the left; and hence, the placing of that upon the head of Ephraim, indicated his pre-eminence over his brother. "I know it," "I know it," is equivalent to, "I very well know it." It is a part of a Hebrew idiom elsewhere treated of.

"In thee shall Israel bless." — It shall be thought a great favor to become as Ephraim or Manasseh; and it is here declared that his posterity would incorporate this form into their established expressions for such occasions.

691. The portion given to Joseph, above the rest of his sons, seems to refer to the parcel of ground lying near to Shalem, xxxiii. 19, which Jacob bought of the children of Hamor; and hence the bones of Joseph were buried there, on the arrival in Canaan. Josh. xxiv. 32. The Evangelist makes allusion to the same parcel of ground in John iv. 5.

692. "Which I took out of the hand of the Amorite, with my sword and with my bow," seems to declare that this tract was not obtained by purchase, but by war. The most natural way of removing the apparent contradiction, is, that the sword and bow have no connection with the acquisition. The passage should be construed thus; — "I have given thee one portion of the country, above thy brethren, namely, the parcel of ground I obtained of the children of Hamor, near to Shalem; and in addition to this gift, I bequeath to you my sword and my bow, as memorials of me."

SECTION XXXII. — JACOB BLESSES HIS SONS.

CHAP. XLIX.

1. And Jacob called unto his sons, and said, Gather yourselves together, that I may tell you *that* which shall befall you in the last days.

2. Gather yourselves together, and hear, ye sons of Jacob; and hearken unto Israel your father.

3. ¶ Reuben, thou *art* my firstborn, my might, and the beginning of my strength, the excellency of dignity, and the excellency of power:

4. Unstable as water, thou shalt not excel; because thou wentest up to thy father's bed; then defiledst thou *it:* he went up to my couch.

5. ¶ Simeon and Levi *are* brethren; instruments of cruelty *are in* their habitations.

JACOB AND HIS FAMILY.

6. O my soul, come not thou into their secret; unto their assembly, my honor, be not thou united: for in their anger they slew a man, and in their self-will they digged down a wall.
7. Cursed *be* their anger, for *it was* fierce; and their wrath, for it was cruel: I will divide them in Jacob, and scatter them in Israel.
8. ¶ Judah, thou *art he* whom thy brethren shall praise: thy hand *shall be* in the neck of thy enemies; thy father's children shall bow down before thee.
9. Judah *is* a lion's whelp: from the prey, my son, thou art gone up: he stooped down, he couched as a lion, and as an old lion; who shall rouse him up?
10. The sceptre shall not depart from Judah, nor a lawgiver from between his feet, until Shiloh come; and unto him *shall* the gathering of the people *be*.
11. Binding his foal unto the vine, and his ass's colt unto the choice vine; he washed his garments in wine, and his clothes in the blood of grapes:
12. His eyes *shall be* red with wine, and his teeth white with milk.
13. ¶ Zebulon shall dwell at the haven of the sea; and he *shall be* for a haven of ships; and his border *shall be* unto Zidon.
14. ¶ Issachar *is* a strong ass couching down between two burdens:
15. And he saw that rest *was* good, and the land that *it was* pleasant; and bowed his shoulder to bear, and became a servant unto tribute.
16. ¶ Dan shall judge his people, as one of the tribes of Israel.
17. Dan shall be a serpent by the way, an adder in the path, that biteth the horse heels, so that his rider shall fall backward.
18. I have waited for thy salvation, O LORD.
19. ¶ Gad, a troop shall overcome him: but he shall overcome at the last.
20. ¶ Out of Asher his bread *shall be* fat, and he shall yield royal dainties.
21. ¶ Naphtali *is* a hind let loose: he giveth goodly words.
22. ¶ Joseph *is* a fruitful bough, *even* a fruitful bough by a well; *whose* branches run over the wall:
23. The archers have sorely grieved him, and shot *at him,* and hated him:
24. But his bow abode in strength, and the arms of his hands were made strong by the hands of the mighty *God* of Jacob; (from thence *is* the shepherd, the stone of Israel:)
25. *Even* by the God of thy father, who shall help thee; and by the Almighty, who shall bless thee with blessings of heaven above, blessings of the deep that lieth under, blessings of the breasts, and of the womb:
26. The blessings of thy father have prevailed above the blessings of my progenitors unto the utmost bound of the everlasting hills: they shall be on the head of Joseph, and on the crown of the head of him that was separate from his brethren.
27. ¶ Benjamin shall raven *as* a wolf: in the morning he shall devour the prey, and at night he shall divide the spoil.
28. ¶ All these *are* the twelve tribes of Israel: and this *is it* that their father spake unto them, and blessed them; every one according to his blessing he blessed them.

693. The blessing here pronounced upon the sons of Jacob, by that aged and venerable patriarch, deserves a particular exposition; since, as we believe, it has very generally been misapprehended.

Though we firmly believe and maintain, that God graciously revealed many things to the patriarchs, of which they had no means of being otherwise informed; yet we do not agree with those interpreters who regard this "blessing" of Jacob, as a divinely inspired prediction, by which theory they have subjected themselves to unnecessary embarrassment, in the interpretation of the future events of Hebrew history.

694. The particulars contained in this blessing, (so far as they relate to the future at all,) are to be referred to a reasonable inference, based upon what was known of the temper and disposition of his sons; or to his dying requests, which his sons, or other descendants might, and probably would carry out; or finally, to his wishes, which the divine Being would be likely to regard with favor.

695. It is worthy of special notice, that the past temper and disposition of his sons, were specially had in view, and are made the basis of what would be likely to overtake them.

696. Reuben had been guilty of a heinous offence against his father; and on that account, could not expect the paternal benediction; and hence no benediction, properly so called, is here expressed; and all that is here announced, is, that he should not excel; and the reason given, is, that he was unstable as water. I am not quite sure but this language refers to his having fallen, like water, from the high position to which, as first born, he was entitled : and therefore he could not excel, that is excel his brethren, or have a pre-eminence over them, as he would have had, if he had not thus fallen.

697. Simeon and Levi are called brethren, as indicating a similarity in their dispositions; and the reference to their cruelty is made in allusion to the sacking of Shalem, so treacherously conceived and so barbarously executed. "I will divide them in Jacob, and scatter them in Israel." It is my wish, that in the division of the promised land, they should be so far separated as never more to be able to concoct and execute such a nefarious scheme.

698. The authority is given to Judah that properly belonged to the first-born; but the first-born had forfeited that right, and so had the second and third. It was to Judah, then, that the birthright belonged; and the father here invests him with its authority, and requires the other sons to yield obedience thereto. His prowess is described by the sagacity and dexterity of a lion seeking his prey.

699. "The sceptre shall not depart from Judah." Judah had just been invested with authority over his brethren; in other words, the sceptre had been given into his hands, and was not to be taken from him until Shiloh come — until the people should come to Shiloh, a noted place in the land of Canaan, of which we have frequent notices at a later day. "And unto him shall the gathering of the people be." The authority shall be in his hands, and the people shall gather to him with a view to its proper exercise, till the final settlement in the promised land. Farther than this, the patriarch does not express his wishes.

700. That there is here an allusion to the coming of the Messiah, at which time the sceptre should depart from Judah, or the authority over the Jews transferred to other hands, has not the slightest evidence in its favor. That the phrase "until Shiloh come" will bear the construction we put upon it, is proved by two facts. One is that the original is not violated by this rendering. Another, that the language of this "blessing" is poetic, and it is quite in harmony with the spirit of poetry, to make that *come* to us to which we are *going*.

The rest of the blessing upon Judah is simply an expression of the patriarch's wish that this son might be allowed to occupy the richest part of the country to which he was to lead the people; or it may be construed as indicating that, wherever he settled, he would be likely to make it very fruitful.

701. The language concerning Zebulon is to be construed as pointing to a locality of Canaan best fitted to the disposition and character of the man; and though we cannot refer to circumstances in his life that would have led to this arrangement, yet we must bear in mind that but few things are recorded of the sons of Jacob, except Joseph. Still, as what is said of the other sons, is based on what is known of them, we feel authorized to believe the same of Zebulon.

16*

702. Issachar is represented as a quiet and laborious man, and more willing to be subject to tribute than to make the requisite resistance to throw off a foreign power.

703. Dan was to judge his people. And the comparison of this son to a serpent, indicates his prevailing disposition; and his success against his enemies is attributed to cunning rather than to bravery.

704. Gad means a "troop," as Dan means a "judge," and hence these terms are brought into the patriarch's benediction. And it is declared that, though a troop might overcome this son, he would overcome at the last. Though a sudden and unexpected attack might secure against him a temporary triumph, his perseverance would at last prevail. Hence the prominent trait in his character may be here inferred.

705. That Asher would be skilful in cultivating the earth, and make it yield "royal dainties," is all that is here asserted, and all we have a right to infer.

706. Naphtali was active and eloquent. This, and nothing more, is asserted of him.

707. The blessing of Joseph is enlarged upon; but no one can doubt what its meaning is in most of what is said of him. A few expressions only are of doubtful significance. "From thence is the shepherd, the stone of Israel." The nearest antecedent to this clause "from thence," is "Jacob;" and the meaning is, that from *him*, is the shepherd and the stone of Israel. Who more clearly sustained this relation, or filled this position than Joseph? He was emphatically the Shepherd of Israel; for he fed and nourished his brethren as a shepherd does his flock. He was the stone of Israel, or the rock, whose cool and refreshing shade was so grateful to the sheep as a protection from the scorching rays of the sun.

708. The blessings the patriarch was prepared to announce to Joseph, would *far* exceed any blessings that had been enjoyed by his progenitors. "Unto the utmost bound of the everlasting hills," is only an emphatic way of expressing the fullness of these blessings.

709. Benjamin is mentioned last as being the youngest; and the comparison of him to a wolf, may denote some prominent trait in his character; but his dividing the spoil, indicates a generosity with which the other trait must not be made to conflict.

710. All this is called a "blessing;" but the name is evidently taken from the general character of such announcements, and not from the specific character of what was said to each individual. For some of these announcements would more properly be designated as maledictions than as blessings; others simply describe the persons they relate to; and others contain an expression of the patriarch's wishes.

711. If those who regard this passage as a veritable prediction of coming events, shall insist on the expression that what is related was to take place *in the last days*, we reply that much of what is stated has no direct reference to the future; and what has such reference, is as applicable to the wishes of the patriarch that such things *might* occur, as to his prediction that they *would* occur. If there is an appearance of the contrary, that appearance may be referred to the importance that was attached to one's wishes, uttered under such circumstances, by which those who were in a condition to execute them, were held bound, by the most solemn obligations, to do so. Hence I remark, that if we find some of the things here announced, actually carried out, this circumstance is more naturally referable to this sense of obligation to execute the dying request of the patriarch, than to any inspiration that revealed to him the realities of the future.

712. We venture to affirm, that, aside from some particulars of fulfilment of the kind here alluded to, there is no just reason for regarding the passage as a divine prediction; for though some circumstances may be found in connection with the history of each tribe, that correspond in some measure with what is contained in the passage, yet a similar correspondence could have been searched out, if the announcement had, in each case, been quite different, or even opposite, from what it now is.

SECTION XXXIII. — DEATH OF JACOB.

CHAP. XLIX.

29. And he charged them, and said unto them, I am to be gathered unto my people: bury me with my fathers in the cave that *is* in the field of Ephron the Hittite,

30. In the cave that *is* in the field of Machpelah, which *is* before Mamre, in the land of Canaan, which Abraham bought with the field of Ephron the Hittite for a possession of a burying-place.

31. There they buried Abraham and Sarah his wife; there they buried Isaac and Rebekah his wife, and there I buried Leah.

32. The purchase of the field and of the cave that *is* therein *was* from the children of Heth.

33. And when Jacob had made an end of commanding his sons, he gathered up his feet into the bed, and yielded up the ghost, and was gathered unto his people.

CHAP. L.

1. And Joseph fell upon his father's face, and wept upon him, and kissed him.

2. And Joseph commanded his servants the physicians to embalm his father: and the physicians embalmed Israel.

3. And forty days were fulfilled for him; for so are fulfilled the days of those which are embalmed: and the Egyptians mourned for him threescore and ten days.

4. And when the days of his mourning were past, Joseph spake unto the house of Pharaoh, saying, If now I have found grace in your eyes, speak, I pray you, in the ears of Pharaoh, saying,

5. My father made me swear, saying, Lo, I die: in my grave which I have digged for me in the land of Canaan, there shalt thou bury me. Now therefore let me go up, I pray thee, and bury my father, and I will come again.

6. And Pharaoh said, Go up, and bury thy father, according as he made thee swear.

7. ¶ And Joseph went up to bury his father: and with him went up all the servants of Pharaoh, the elders of his house, and all the elders of the land of Egypt,

8. And all the house of Joseph, and his brethren, and his father's house: only their little ones, and their flocks, and their herds, they left in the land of Goshen.

9. And there went up with him both chariots and horsemen: and it was a very great company.

10. And they came to the threshing floor of Atad, which *is* beyond Jordan, and there they mourned with a great and very sore lamentation: and he made a mourning for his father seven days.

11. And when the inhabitants of the land, the Canaanites, saw the mourning in the floor of Atad, they said, This *is* a grievous mourning to the Egyptians: wherefore the name of it was called Abel-mizraim, which *is* beyond Jordan.

12. And his sons did unto him according as he commanded them:

13. For his sons carried him into the land of Canaan, and buried him in the cave of the field of Machpelah, which Abraham bought with the field for a possession of a burying-place of Ephron the Hittite, before Mamre.

713. In addition to the special obligation he had placed Joseph under, to carry him to Canaan, and bury him there, he here brings that matter before all his sons, and makes it his last and dying request. The place is described with the usual exactness and particularity. The burial of Abraham in that place, and of Sarah, and of Isaac, and Rebekah, had been mentioned before; but the death and burial of Leah is here, for the first time, referred to: and it becomes evident that she did not go down with Jacob to Egypt, but must have died and been buried before he left that country. The reason why his favorite Rachel, was not placed in the same sacred cave, has been elsewhere suggested. She died too far away from Hebron to admit of this; for in Canaan the art of embalming the dead was not known, as it was in Egypt.

714. There can be no doubt that, "being gathered to his people," has reference to a future state of existence, and that the ancients expected a re-union with their departed friends after leaving this world.

The phrase does not refer to the burial in the cave of Machpelah, with Abraham, Isaac, &c., as some suppose; for Jacob was gathered to his people as soon as he died, while his burial did not take place for several months, and is a separate and distinct event, as the account clearly shows.

715. The practice of embalming the dead was known in Egypt, in the most ancient times, but is now unknown; nor is it important that it be restored, as we know of no practical advantage it could yield. Still, what we now regard as unimportant, and indeed what *is* now so, may yet be found *to have been* one of the providential events of ancient times for bringing down to our day the knowledge of many important facts that had otherwise been lost. Forty days were required for this process: or the forty days may be the time allowed after the work of embalming was performed, to test its perfection.

716. The mourning ceremonies lasted seventy days; but whether this includes the forty of embalming, we cannot certainly determine.

Seventy days of mourning were probably the usual term with the Egyptians. The seven days of mourning, after arriving in Canaan, may have been the patriarchal custom. Abel-mizraim means the "mourning of the Egyptians."

A threshing floor was situated on elevated ground; and it was therefore a fit place for the funeral festivities, as the mourning here referred to, may, more appropriately be called.

SECTION XXXIV.— DEATH OF JOSEPH.

CHAP. L.

14. And Joseph returned into Egypt, he, and his brethren, and all that went up with him to bury his father, after he had buried his father.

15. And when Joseph's brethren saw that their father was dead, they said, Joseph will peradventure hate us, and will certainly requite us all the evil which we did unto him.

16. And they sent a messenger unto Joseph, saying, Thy father did command before he died saying,

17. So shall ye say unto Joseph, Forgive, I pray thee now, the trespass of thy brethren, and their sin; for they did unto thee evil; and now, we pray thee, forgive the trespass of the servants of the God of thy father. And Joseph wept when they spake unto him.

18. And his brethren also went and fell down before his face; and they said, Behold, we *be* thy servants.

19. And Joseph said unto them, Fear not, for *am* I in the place of God?

20. But as for you, ye thought evil against me; *but* God meant it unto good, to bring to pass, as *it is* this day, to save much people alive.

21. Now, therefore fear ye not; I will nourish you, and your little ones. And he comforted them, and spake kindly unto them.

22. ¶ And Joseph dwelt in Egypt, he and his father's house: and Joseph lived an hundred and ten years.

23. And Joseph saw Ephraim's children of the third *generation:* the children also of Machir, the son of Manasseh, were brought upon Joseph's knees.

24. And Joseph said unto his brethren, I die; and God will surely visit you, and bring you out of this land unto the land which he sware to Abraham, to Isaac, and to Jacob.

25. And Joseph took an oath of the children of Israel, saying, God will surely visit you, and ye shall carry up my bones from hence.

26. So Joseph died, *being* an hundred and ten years old: and they embalmed him, and he was put in a coffin in Egypt.

717. It was quite natural that the brethren of Joseph should entertain apprehensions for their safety, now that respect for the aged and venerable patriarch, would no longer restrain him from avenging their cruelty. "Thy father did command before he died," was the strongest appeal they could make; though the gracious disposition of Joseph, did not need any such appeal. That the father *did* so command we may presume, as it is reasonable to conclude that it would be a matter of conversation among

them; and nothing is said indicating that the story was fabricated. It is interesting to see the workings of human nature in the hearts of the brethren, who felt that they had justly incurred his displeasure, and to see the God-like temper and disposition of their brother, who was grieved that they should entertain any doubts of his gracious disposition, and who seeks at once to reassure them on this point.

718. We are not to suppose that the purpose of God to bring about a good result, from the sin of Joseph's brethren, does, in the least, exculpate the offenders. Though guilty of a base and unholy act, God had made that act the instrument of good; and now that the good was manifest, it was proper that they should reproach themselves no longer.

719. Joseph lived to see the children of Ephraim, and the grand-children of Manasseh. The generations here alluded to, commence with Joseph himself; hence the children of Machir were the fourth generation.

720. Joseph had been assured by his father, that his descendants would come again into Canaan, according to the divine promise; and this assurance is now repeated by Joseph himself, and made the ground of an oath exacted of his brethren, to bring him thither again and bury him in the promised land — an oath that was fulfilled, when the children of Israel went up to that country, under the conduct of Moses.

721. That the brethren of Joseph here referred to were his own brethren, or their children, we may not certainly determine, as the language may refer to either. It is not unreasonable to conclude that some, if not all his brethren, were yet alive. The obligation, however, would be felt to be binding on the children, as well as on the original parties in the contract.

INDEX OF PASSAGES.

Chapter.	Page.	Chapter.	Page.
I. 1	123	X: 1–5	238
2	137	6–20	235
3–5	138	21–32	233
6–8	140	XI. 1–9	236
9–13	141	10–26	233
14–19	146	27–30	240
20–23	148	31–32	241
24–27	150	XII. 1–9	242
26–31	212	10–20	243
II. 1–3	157	XIII. 1–4	243
4–7	150	5–13	245
8–17	201	14–18	246
18–25	214	XIV. 1–24	247
III. 1–24	202	XV. 1–21	250
IV. 1–16	217	XVI. 1–16	252
17–24	220	XVII. 1–27	254
25–26	223	XVIII. 1–33	258
V. 1–32	221	XIX. 1–29	260
VI. 1–4	225	30–38	264
5–8	174	XX. 1–18	265
8–10	227	XXI. 1–8	267
11–13	174	9–21	268
14–16	184	22–34	269
17–18	188	XXII. 1–19	270
19–20	185	20–24	272
21–22	187	XXIII. 1–20	273
VII. 1	188	XXIV. 1–67	275
2–3	185	XXV. 1–6	278
4–7	188	7–11	279
8–10	185	12–18	280
11–13	188	19–26	281
14–16	185	27–34	282
17–24	188	XXVI. 1–22	283
VIII. 1–19	189	23–33	285
20–22	227	34–35	292
IX. 1–7	228	XXVII. 1–40	286
8–17	230	41–46	298
18–27	231	XXVIII. 1–22	299
28–29	232	9	292

Chapter.		Page.	Chapter.		Page.
XXIX.	1–14	300	XXXVIII.	1–30	335
	15–30	302	XXXIX.	1–23	337
	31–35	303	XL.	1–23	339
XXX.	1–8	305	XLI.	1–36	341
	9–13	305		37–57	344
	14–21	304	XLII.	1–38	346
	22–24	303	XLIII.	1–34	350
	25–43	309	XLIV.	1–34	352
XXXI.	1–21	311	XLV.	1–15	354
	22–24	313		16–28	356
	25–55	313	XLVI.	1–7	357
XXXII.	1–32	316		8–27	307
XXXIII.	1–16	319		28–30	358
	17–20	321		31–34	359
XXXIV.	1–31	321	XLVII.	1–6	359
XXXV.	1–15	324		7–10	360
	16–27	327		11–27	361
	28–29	329		28–31	363
XXXVI.	1–3	292	XLVIII.	1–22	364
	1–19	291	XLIX.	1–28	366
	20–39	295		29–33	372
	40–43	292	L.	1–13	372
XXXVII.	1–36	329		14–26	374

www.ingramcontent.com/pod-product-compliance
Lightning Source LLC
Chambersburg PA
CBHW030404230426
43664CB00007BB/737